# Queen Anne's War

Also by Michael G. Laramie

*King William's War:*
*The First Contest for North America, 1689–1697*

*Gunboats, Muskets, and Torpedoes:*
*Coastal North Carolina, 1861–1865*

*By Wind and Iron:*
*Naval Campaigns in the Champlain Valley, 1665–1815*

*Colonial Forts of the Champlain and Hudson Valleys:*
*Sentinels of Wood and Stone*

*The European Invasion of North America:*
*Colonial Conflict Along the Hudson-Champlain Corridor, 1609–1760*

*The Second Contest For North America, 1702–1713*

MICHAEL G. LARAMIE

WESTHOLME
Yardley

Westholme Publishing, LLC
904 Edgewood Road
Yardley, Pennsylvania 19067
Visit our Web site at www.westholmepublishing.com

ISBN: 978-1-59416-358-6
Also available as an eBook.

Printed in the United States of America.

To my sister, De Anna,
and my nephews, Jake and Jared.

# Contents

## PART FOUR
### *Days of Musket, Tomahawk, and Sword*



## PART FIVE
### *Victory and Retreat*

MAPS

# *Preface*

The promised sequel to *King William's War*, *Queen Anne's War* navigates the second half of a quarter-century of conflict between the French and English in North America. King William's War (1689-1697), and the years preceding it, set the groundwork for the basic disputes between New France and the English colonies, but the conflict had resolved little beyond making it clear that the smaller French colony was more than capable of defending itself. *Queen Anne's War*, although filled with similarities, would have a different character than the one that preceded it. In the north, a good share of this was due to the neutrality of the Five Nations, which proved a major loss to the English cause and the removal of a significant threat to New France. With the French reluctant to operate on the New York frontier for fear of pushing the Iroquois back into a military alliance with the English, the conflict shifted to the New England border where the French-allied Wabanaki Confederacy was enticed into a third war with the English. As another "mournful decade" descended upon the New England frontier, English attempts on Port Royal, Nova Scotia (Acadia), and Placentia, Newfoundland would follow, and in a painful reminder of the lessons not learned from the previous conflict, so too did French efforts from the latter location.

To the south a new theater appeared as Spain, now an ally of France, would become embroiled with English South Carolina in both Florida and modern-day Georgia. The result was a clash of two diametrically opposed systems, and a disaster akin to the destruction of the Huron nation. The newly founded French colony of Louisiana would soon find itself bolstering the weak Spanish position in Florida before having to pivot to deal with the threat posed to the colony by the English and their native allies. As the war in the south progressed France and Spain soon realized that Charleston, the epicenter of English southern expansion and the Indian slave trade, would have to be neutralized, and to accomplish this, they selected none other than the most dynamic leader of King William's War, Pierre Iberville, to see to the task.

In the west, along the Great Lakes, English intrigues threatened the fragile Peace of Montreal by focusing on the defection of French-allied tribes. The aim was to create a brush war that would force the Iroquois to abandon the peace agreement and ultimately lead to the introduction of English trading posts into the region. When supplemented by traditional animosities between a number of tribes in the region, such actions would not only test the diplomatic skills of New France and their old alliances but the neutrality of the Five Nations as well.

The true scope of Queen Anne's War, however, would be demonstrated toward the end of the conflict when the English colonies, lacking ability, leadership, and most importantly, unity, appealed directly to the Queen for help. The result was a commitment on the part of the Crown to send a fleet carrying five thousand regulars and an extensive siege train to Boston for an attack on Quebec—the largest force anyone had ever seen in North American waters. It is perhaps interesting to note that at the start of King William's War, the Iroquois sachems told the governors of New York and Massachusetts to "cut off the head of the snake, and the rest would die." At the time they listened, gathered together a colonial force, and, under Sir William Phipps, sailed for Quebec. The attack failed, but it did not change the validity of the plan, nor lessen the cries of those who called for it once again. Yet it would take twenty-one years to enact another attempt, and as such, for all practical purposes Queen Anne's War in the north would end as King William's War had started, with an attack on the French colonial capitol.

While a number of patterns in this quarter of a century of conflict can be readily discerned, another appears from the background. Even though the differences in the American colonies covered the gambit from puritan New England to profit-driven South Carolina, there was a distinct identity forming among these enclaves. In each, a sense of independence was emerging, in part because of a lack of involvement by the Crown and in part because of a desire to be governed by their own charters and their own hand. In fact, this sense of independence hampered the colonial effort to deal with

New France. Connecticut for instance, one of the more populace colonies on the continent, refused to participate in troop allotments because they feared it would jeopardize their charter and remove the liberties granted under this concord. While Connecticut was the extreme case in such matters, all the colonies jealously guarded their charters and elected assemblies. This attitude was noted by one senior British officer, Colonel Richard King, when he arrived in Boston in 1711. Unless something was done to alter this trajectory, King wrote London, "they will grow every day more stiff and disobedient, more burthensome than advantageous to Great Britain."

How true, from the earliest days to the present, Americans have valued their liberty, and one day when they would learn the lessons of unity, they would prove beyond "burthensome" to Great Britain. However, if it is some consolation Colonel King, it can be said that you saw it earlier than most.

HUDSON BAY
RUPERT'S LAND
James Bay
Lake Winnipeg
Albany R.
Moose R.
Rupart's Fort
Rupart R.
Big R.
Nottaway R.
Hamilton R.
LABRADOR
CANADA
NEWFOUNDLAND
St. Johns
Placentia
GULF OF ST. LAWRENCE
St. Lawrence R.
Saguenay R.
Cape Breton Is.
Lake of the Woods
UPPER COUNTRY
CHIPPEWA
Lake Superior
ALGONQUIN
OTTAWA
MENOMINEE
FOX
Mississippi R.
Wisconsin R.
Des Moines R.
Lake Michigan
Fort Michilimackinac
Lake Huron
POTAWATOMI
Lake St. Clair
Fort Detroit
Lake Erie
KICKAPOO
ILLINOIS
Fort Pimitcoui
MIAMI
ERIGAS
Lake Nipissing
Ottawa R.
Quebec
Three Rivers
Fort Richelieu
Montreal
Fort Chambly
St. Lawrence R.
Lake Champlain
Fort Frontenac
Lake Ontario
Fort Niagra
IROQUOIS
MOUNTAINS
Allegheny R.
SUSQUEHANNOCK
Albany
Delaware R.
Hudson R.
New York
LONG IS.
NEW ENGLAND
Connecticut R.
Merrimack R.
Boston
Portsmouth
Casco
Kennebec R.
Penobscot R.
St. Johns R.
NEW BRUNSWICK
WABANAKI
Fundy Bay
Port Royal
N
E
W

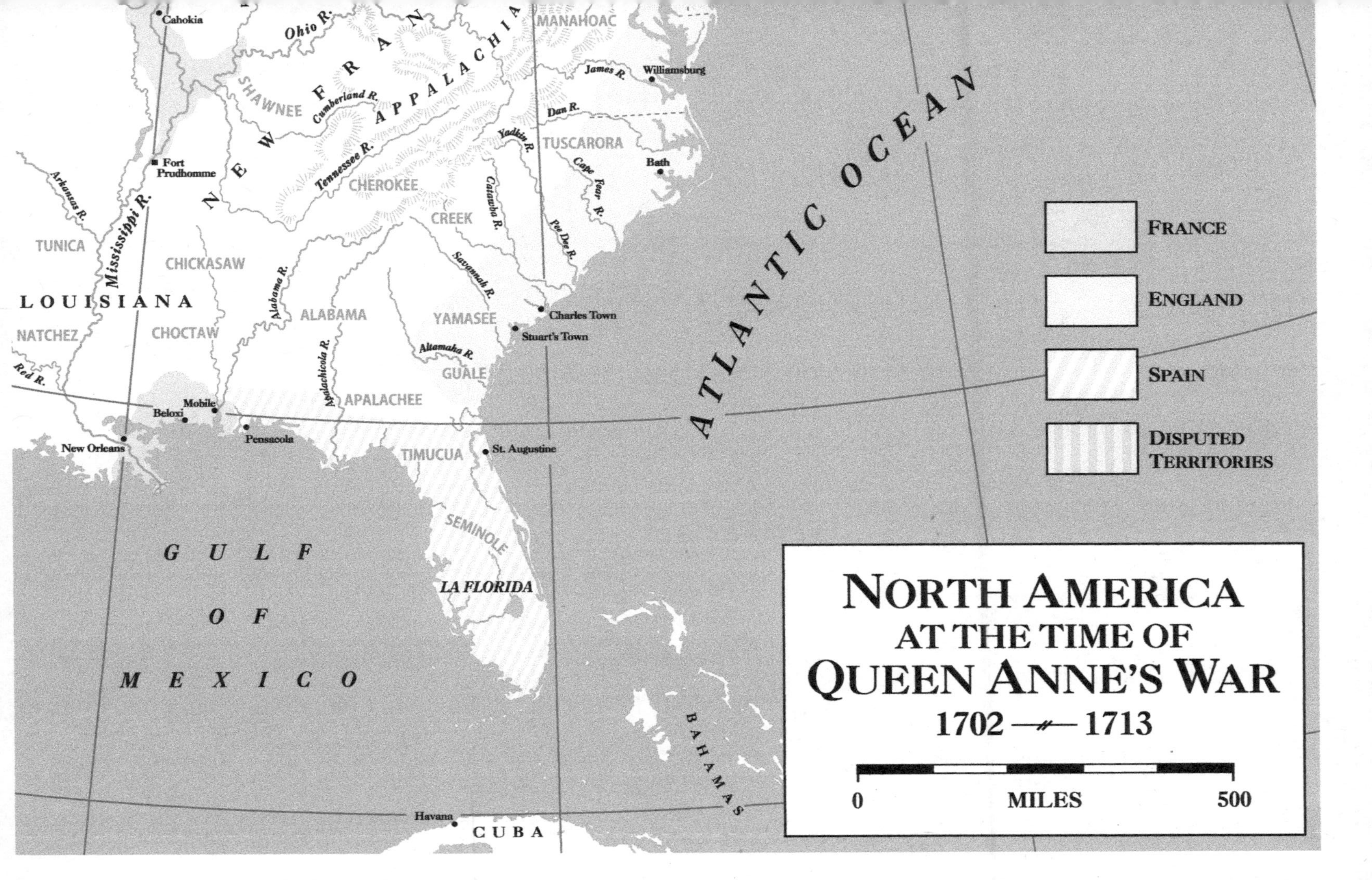
NORTH AMERICA
AT THE TIME OF
QUEEN ANNE'S WAR
1702 — 1713
0
MILES
500
FRANCE
ENGLAND
SPAIN
DISPUTED TERRITORIES
ATLANTIC OCEAN
GULF OF MEXICO
NEW FRANCE
LOUISIANA
APPALACHIA
LA FLORIDA
BAHAMAS
CUBA
Cahokia
Fort Prudhomme
New Orleans
Beloxi
Mobile
Pensacola
St. Augustine
Stuart's Town
Charles Town
Bath
Williamsburg
Havana
Ohio R.
Cumberland R.
Tennessee R.
Mississippi R.
Arkansas R.
Red R.
Alabama R.
Apalachicola R.
Altamaha R.
Savannah R.
Catawba R.
Yadkin R.
Pee Dee R.
Cape Fear R.
Dan R.
James R.
MANAHOAC
SHAWNEE
TUSCARORA
CHEROKEE
CREEK
CHICKASAW
TUNICA
CHOCTAW
NATCHEZ
ALABAMA
YAMASEE
GUALE
APALACHEE
TIMUCUA
SEMINOLE

# Part One

## *A Five-Year Interlude*

CHAPTER ONE

# A Servant of the Crown

THE EARL OF BELLOMONT, Richard Coote, smiled as the HMS *Deptford* dropped anchor in New York Harbor on the morning of April 2, 1698. It had been a long voyage for the newly appointed governor. It started early the previous year when a number of petitions from the American colonies reached the Board of Trade in London. At the time, King William's War (1688-1697) still had several months left before the Treaty of Ryswick would bring an end to the fighting. The war had gone poorly for the English colonies in North America, particularly for New York and New England. The difficulty lay not in the availability of manpower or resources within the colonies but from the political divisions that prevented their effective employment. New York and New England rightfully claimed that they bore the brunt of the war and that the other colonies, such as Maryland and Virginia, contributed little or nothing to the effort. These colonies in turn claimed an impoverished state and responded that they had no resources to spare. More importantly, they were not compelled to support the war effort and, as such, contributed as little as possible. Even between New England and New York, the two regions most heavily involved in the conflict, there was a lack of coordinated effort. Each pointed to their own needs and each jealously guarded its own authority. "Their Majesties' subjects here, tho' considerable in number," Governor Benjamin Fletcher of New York informed London, "are so scattered at a distance, and into so many distinct Governments, that they are divided in affection and interest, which renders them weak."[1]

Looking for a more effective defense against the French and their allies, as well as one free of the ill effects of intercolonial rivalries, colonial agents approached the Board of Trade in London with a plan for unification through the appointment of a single governor over New York and New England. While a return to the pre-Glorious Revolution Dominion of New York and New England was contemplated, it quickly found opposition. Instead, a position was contemplated that would unify the governments of New York, New Hampshire, and Massachusetts, against which the bulk of the French and Indian war effort had been directed. While this civil unification would provide for a more coherent defense, it was recognized that in time of war a single commander in chief was required for all of New York and New England, and as such, the post was embodied with these powers as well.

These agents nominated Bellomont for the position. The earl, an Irish peer, was known as a competent and dedicated official who was motivated by king and country rather than self-enrichment. In fact, Bellomont had already been nominated to become governor of Massachusetts after the death of Sir William Phips in late 1695, but arguments about pay, slow communications, and health issues stalled the process. With consent rising toward a unified command in the northern American colonies, Bellomont was approached again to gauge whether he would accept the expanded role. The earl agreed, and after more subdued arguments regarding pay, his orders, and the scope of his powers, he was officially appointed the governor of the three northern colonies, and his majesty's commander in chief of the forces of New York and New England.[2]

Like his appointment process, the earl's efforts to reach America proved frustrating. It was not until December 1697, three months after the Treaty of Ryswick was signed ending the War of the League of Augsburg and its colonial component King William's War, that the new governor, his family, and the new Lt. Governor John Nanfan set sail for New York. This time it was the weather that created the delay. A few weeks out of Portsmouth a gale scattered the governor's fleet of merchant and warships. Proceeding alone, the *Deptford* encountered a series of storms off the American coast, one of which severely damaged the ship's rigging and mainmast. Undermanned and running short on drinking water, after two weeks of trying to force his way through to New York, the ship's captain set a course for Barbados, arriving at the island on January 5, 1698. Repairing the vessel's damage and yet more bad weather delayed Bellomont such that it was not until

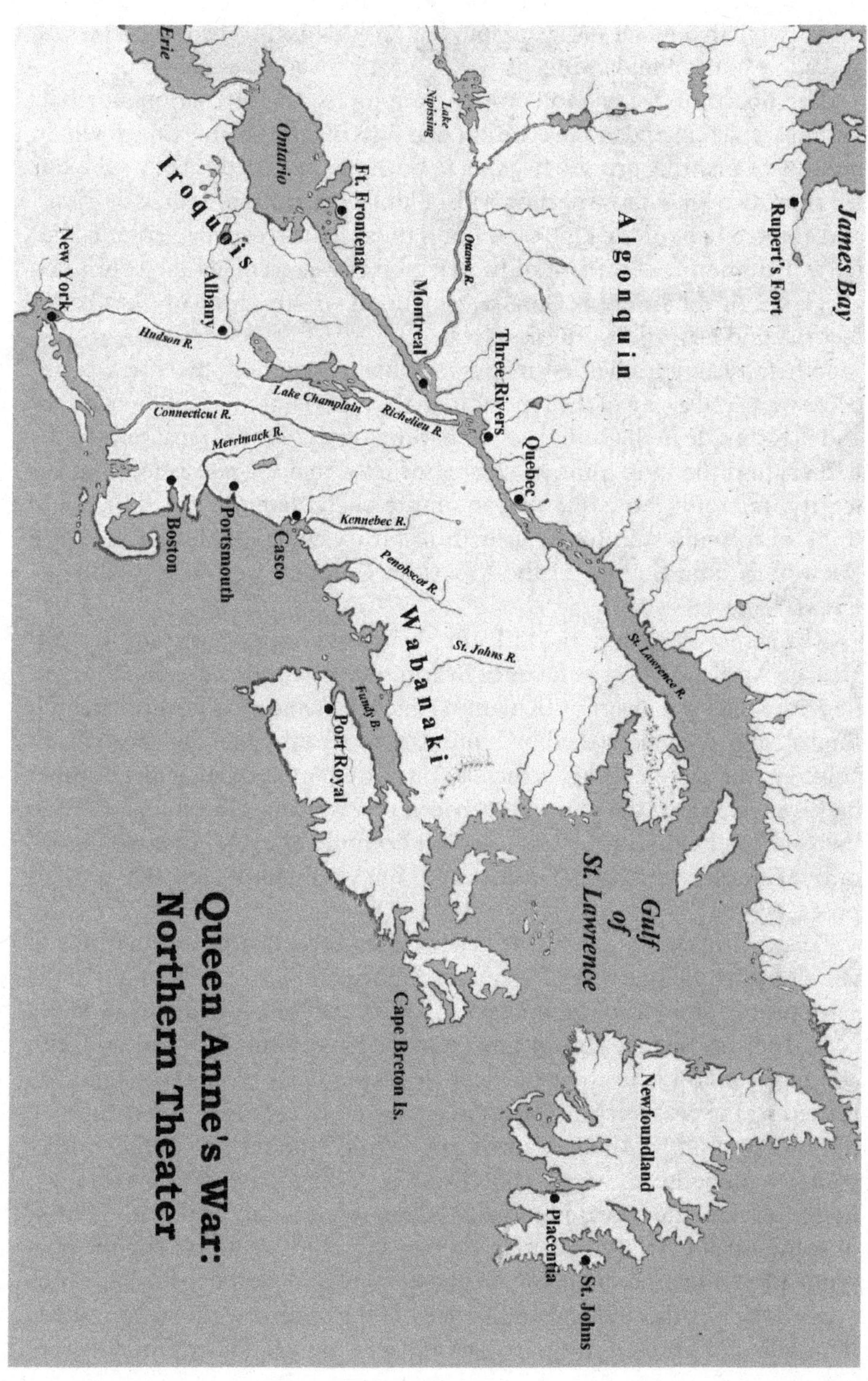
Queen Anne's War:
Northern Theater
James Bay
Rupert's Fort
Algonquin
Erie
Lake Nipissing
Ontario
Iroquois
Ft. Frontenac
Ottawa R.
Montreal
Three Rivers
Quebec
New York
Albany
Hudson R.
Lake Champlain
Richelieu R.
Connecticut R.
Merrimack R.
Kennebec R.
Boston
Portsmouth
Casco
Penobscot R.
Wabanaki
St. Johns R.
St. Lawrence R.
Fundy B.
Port Royal
Gulf
of
St. Lawrence
Cape Breton Is.
Newfoundland
Placentia
St. Johns

early March that he set sail again for New York. This time he was successful, and a few hours after landing he was officially installed as governor.

The Board of Trade had compiled a long list of instructions for Bellomont, which included the creation of a post office and cracking down on unlicensed printing presses. In general, however, the matters before the earl fell along two lines; those dealing with colonial corruption, to include piracy and enforcement of the king's laws, and those issues related to colonial defense. Paramount in pursuit of this last effort was securing the continued allegiance of the Iroquois Confederacy upon whom much of New York's security and territorial ambitions rested.[3]

When it came to the first matter, colonial corruption, the king's councilors were well aware of the type of man they had chosen to suppress piracy and illegal trade in the colonies. The earl was known for his zeal toward the Crown, and the king himself "thought him a man of resolution and integrity, and with those qualities the more likely than any other he could think of to put a stop to the growth of piracy, with which that province [New York] and the rest of the American Colonies were remarkably infested."[4]

The earl soon took to the task after being sworn in as governor of New York on April 2, 1698. The focus of Bellomont's attention fell upon the man he was replacing, Governor Benjamin Fletcher. While most governors, both English and French, backed by a number of wealthy merchants, were involved in the privateering business to one extent or another, and a number had even exploited the grey line between privateering and piracy to enrich themselves, the case of Fletcher was an example of excess that would not only create an international crime cartel but would ultimately cost him his post.

The approach was simple. Fletcher issued several letters of marquis to vessels under the pretense of attacking French and Spanish shipping in the Caribbean, or for patrolling and safeguarding the New York and New Jersey coast. Partially financed by the governor and his wealthy associates and with a letter of marquis in their pockets, the captains of these vessels quickly turned to the real purpose of their voyage and descended upon the rich hunting grounds of the Indian Ocean, taking little time to bother with a vessel's nationality in carrying out their task. With their part of the arrangement fulfilled, the captains carried their prizes back to New York Harbor or some small cove along the New Jersey shoreline. This is where the governor played his role by acting as the New York Admiralty Board, which verified the justification and authenticity of the captured vessel and released it for sale. The proceeds from the sale and any booty obtained from the cap-

Richard Coote, the 1st Earl of Bellomont. (*New York Public Library*)

tured prizes was then divided up before the raiders refitted their ships and started the cycle again.

In these efforts Fletcher was ably aided by New York resident Frederick Philpse. An original settler of New Amsterdam, Philpse had accumulated a huge fifty-two-thousand-acre manor that stretched north along the Hudson River from Yonkers to the Croton River. A member of the governor's executive council, and one of the richest and most influential men in the colony, Philpse was also a well-known financier of smugglers, pirates, and slave traders. In Fletcher this network found a perfect partner. Philpse introduced the governor to other powerful New Yorkers who, like Philpse, posed as upstanding members of society while at the same time engaging in the profits of the "Red Sea Trade," as piracy was referred to in polite circles.

The governor also found a receptive attitude in other members of his council and the denizens of New York City. At the time, the town was a struggling seaport of no more than 2,200 souls. For the inhabitants, commerce and money were in short supply in the best of times, and with war between France and England underway, these were not the best of times. Piracy, smuggling, and illegal trade brought money into the town, and for most people looking to survive in a frontier port there was no need to ask any questions that might upset their good fortune.[5]

With these elements in place, Fletcher issued letters of marquis to a string of known pirates, in particular men like Captain Thomas Tew, with an established reputation as a pirate in the Indian Ocean, and Captain Adam

Baldridge, an associate of Philpse who had trade connections with pirate enclaves in Madagascar. From this island pirates could strike out into the Indian Ocean with little fear of retribution. The Indian and East Indies trade and the riches of the Ottoman trade lay before them—ships loaded with spices, gold, and gems. It was a pirate's dream.

Soon Fletcher and his fellow conspirators were dispatching shipments of rum, powder, arms, and naval supplies to the pirate fleets of Madagascar with these vessels returning filled with the gains of the Red Sea Trade. It was a remarkable organization boasting impressive logistics not only to sustain the trade in terms of manpower and ships but to effectively circumvent customs and the king's taxes as well.

Another lucrative avenue was for notable buccaneers like Tew, Robert Culiford, and William May to pay a portion of their ill-gotten take in exchange for safe haven in New York. In fact, the atmosphere became such that very little was done to actually disguise a pirate's true purpose. In one case twenty-two merchants organized a charter and outfitted a vessel whose captain, John Hoar, made it publicly known that he was setting off to the Red Sea Trade. With the vessel's intent clear, the recruitment of a crew proved simple and Hoar's vessel cut a wide path through the Indian Ocean over the next year.

Fletcher's questionable practices, however, did not go unnoticed. Peter Delanoy, the former mayor of New York City, wrote London that "We have a parcel of pirates, called the Red Sea men, in these parts, who get great booty of Arabian gold. The Governor encourages them since they make due acknowledgment. One captain gave him a ship which he sold for £800, and every man of the crew a present of Arabian gold." In particular, Delanoy complained of Fletcher's conduct toward the colonial assembly. The sudden influx of pirates into the town had allowed the governor to squelch opposition in the New York Assembly and alter public votes by declaring his pirate crews' citizens and thereby using their numbers to either change the outcome of the election or intimidate the populace from voting.[6]

Delanoy was not alone, but with the War of the League of Augsburg still raging, there was little interest in openly addressing the matter of piracy. It would not be for six months after the signing of the Treaty of Ryswick that the Board of Trade even officially took up the subject. In the interim, more reports had arrived, many from the East India Company. They pointed to a pirate enclave in Madagascar and agreed that "most of them are English and come from New York," and one report from Bombay even went so far as to say, "It is certain that these villains frequently say that they carry their unjust gains to New York, where they are permitted egress and regress without control." The Board of Trade concurred with this assessment and informed King William on February 26 that,

> By further information that we have received it is evident to us that the pirates in the East Indies do resort to St. Mary near Madagascar, where they are supplied by one Baldridge (who has made himself the head of a disorderly rabble of Europeans and natives) with provisions and other necessaries sent thither by your Colonies in America.[7]

Enough time had passed that it was clear that too many privateers had refused to stop with the conclusion of hostilities. The corruption and destructive economic effects on British trade and the lost tax revenues caused by these pirates and those that supported their illegal activities was unacceptable. The Board of Trade called upon the king to act. First, to send a small squadron to Madagascar to deal directly with the pirate enclave. Since such an action greatly benefitted the East India Company, the latter had agreed to pay for half of the expedition. Second, as "the chief support of these pirates lies in your (American) Colonies," they called upon the king to demand his governors implement strict measures to halt these illegal activities. Otherwise, the Board of Trade informed the king, "If the said Proprieties and Chartered Governments do not speedily comply with what is required of them, as abovesaid, we see no means to prevent the continuance of this mischief without calling in the further assistance of Parliament." William responded by assigning the war ships as requested. He then wrote his colonial governors with copies of the Jamaica Act, a harsh set of anti-piracy laws, and directed them to convince the colonial assemblies to pass and enforce similar acts.

Although the king's directive would not arrive for several weeks after he had assumed office, it did not take long for Bellomont to see the nature of the illegal trade in New York and compile convincing evidence concerning Fletcher's role in it. At one point in his investigation a colonial revenue official informed the earl that "giving protection to pirates had not formerly been looked upon as so great a matter, and that all the neighboring Governments had done it commonly." Bellomont dismissed the comment and sternly informed the official that, regardless of what his thoughts were on the matter, "the King and his ministers regarded it as a high offence." News of Bellomont's intent quickly spread, setting off a flight of pirates and smugglers, and within a few months New York was no longer a haven for those who flew the Jolly Roger. It also created a strange encounter between Robert Livingston, an old friend and ally of the earl, and former governor Fletcher.

Livingston lodged a complaint against Fletcher, asserting that Fletcher had put "his hands to my face with these words, Sirrah, or villain, I am now out of Commission and a private man, and you are the occasion of all the mischief and I will be revenged on you and I wish I may find you with a sword by your side." When confronted by Bellomont, Fletcher admitted he believed Livingston was behind his recall but that he never said he would be revenged.[8]

As for Fletcher's associates, which consisted foremost of his council, they were dismissed one after another. Some for good reasons and some for simply "speaking most scandalous & reproachful words of his Majesty's person." There was also the matter of calling the colonial assembly into order and holding elections. Members of Fletcher's party along with a number of Jacobites "rode day and night about the country" drumming up support and clashing with Bellomont's supporters such that a good deal of "fighting and broken heads" resulted. While Fletcher's followers achieved their aim of dominating the assembly, Bellomont, in a speech before the politically hostile representatives, made clear his powers and position. "You need not be told to what a degree, faction and sedition have taken root in this Town; tis a thing so generally known. And there has been the utmost Industry used by some to spread the Infection all over the province," the governor started. "People must not be so deceived; this province is subject to the Crown of England," he warned the gathering. As such, the inhabitants "must be obedient to English laws, tis their duty and Interest to be so, and the angry men of New York must not Expect from me that Connivance at their ill practices that they were accustomed to some years before my coming to the Government."[9]

The matter, along with a step toward reconciliation from the governor, had the desired effect, and what was left of Fletcher's power quickly dissolved. By early May Bellomont had collected an overwhelming amount of evidence against Fletcher and his associates, enough so that the earl considered sending Fletcher back to England in chains. Although this did not occur, Fletcher did return to England and spent the next several years answering to corruption charges. He was eventually cleared on most of the serious accusations, but even so, he would never hold a public post again.[10]

With the matter of Fletcher settled, Bellomont turned to the second set of challenges before him and those that led to the creation of his current position—colonial defense. The governor had seen to elements of this before he departed for the colonies. The first issue to be addressed was the four independent companies of New York. These troops were recruited in England and commanded by regular commissioned English officers but

A view of New York City and the recently built Fort George c.1740. (*New York Public Library*)

were financially supported by the colony of New York and not the Crown. Reports reaching the earl spoke to the sorry state of these troops who typically garrisoned the fort at Albany and the other posts along the vulnerable New York frontier. Of the four hundred men required to carry the four companies at full strength, less than half this number was now listed on the rolls. Sickness, desertion, and warfare along the frontier had devastated their ranks. For those that remained their pay was in arears, their clothing in tatters, and their equipment worn out. Not that these were the only problems. The supply system had failed for lack of funds from the New York Assembly, and the bulk of the troops who were stationed at Albany found that the town was unable to support them.[11]

Bellomont asked that pay deductions applied to these troops be removed; that equipment, clothing, and munitions be sent; and in addition, that two hundred recruits be dispatched to bring the companies up to full strength. The earl also asked that £200 worth of warlike stores be purchased to be presented to the Iroquois. While the other recommendations were well received, beyond a handful of men, there would be no reinforcements for the independent companies. This lack of support led Bellomont and a few supporters to float the idea that the king should send soldiers from disbanded English infantry regiments to settle land along the New York frontier, but the costs involved both on the Crown and the colony's side quickly put the matter to rest.

While these actions were a good start, the earl was fortunate to be aided by a military expert and old friend, Colonel Wolfgang Romer. There was little question in terms of Romer's qualifications. The fifty-seven-year old military engineer had served in a dozen campaigns and sieges on the Continent before accompanying William of Orange to England in 1688. Romer's senior standing quickly translated into an engineering warrant, and he spent the next two years campaigning in Ireland as part of William's efforts to subdue the Emerald Isle. In 1692 he was appointed chief engineer for an expedition designed to operate against the coast of France, and the following year he was named chief engineer of the ordinance train destined to operate in the Mediterranean under the command of Bellomont. Romer occupied various positions over the intervening years, and by 1697 he was listed as extraordinary engineer, second only to the chief ordinance engineer, Sir Martin Beckman.[12]

Bellomont and Romer spent a good deal of time on the voyage to North America discussing the numerous reports the earl had received on the state of the New York and New England frontiers. Aware of Romer's talents, and in need of a professional assessment of the colonies' defenses, he dispatched the engineer to the New York frontier a few weeks after they arrived. Romer spent the next several months examining Albany and the surrounding posts. The scars of King William's War were readily apparent to the veteran. It was also clear to him the importance of the area, particularly Albany and Schenectady. "For I consider if these two places should one day fall into the hands of the enemy, the provinces of York, Jersey, Pensilvania and Connecticut, would be obliged, in a short time, to submit; and that Maryland, Virginia and New England would, consequently, greatly suffer."[13]

This might well happen, Romer pointed out, given that in his opinion the current defenses were a dismal assortment of makeshift measures, laid out without either guidance or thought to the actual security of the frontier. "It is a pity, and even a shame, to behold a frontier neglected as we now perceive this is," he informed Bellomont in one of his early reports. "Had the public interest been heretofore preferred to individual and private profit, which has been scattered among a handful of people with diabolical profusion, the enemy would had never committed pernicious forays on the honest inhabitants."[14]

The engineer identified five key locations, with Schenectady and Albany being at the top of the list. The former had been attacked and burned down at the opening of King William's War, and the latter, the keystone of the New York frontier, had been threatened on a dozen occasions. He recommended that poorly laid out wooden palisade structures at both of these locations be replaced with regular stone forts. In addition, he also pointed to the need to fortify two northern locations: Half Moon, located at the junction of the Mohawk and Hudson Rivers a dozen miles north of Albany; and Conestoga, about the same distance to the northwest along the south bank of the Mohawk River. These points protected by a "good guard house or stone redoubt" and garrisoned with thirty or forty men would act as barriers against French excursions and points of refuge for settlers in the region. Lastly, Romer gave some consideration to the hamlet of Saratoga located almost thirty miles north of Half Moon on the west bank of the Hudson River. The small settlement here had been all but abandoned during the last conflict. As the post secured English claims to the region he suggested that a palisade fort with a small stone tower at its center be constructed to encourage settlers to return and offer them some form of protection should French raiders appear.

Building these fortifications would not be easy, Romer warned the governor. Estimating the cost and extent of the proposed stone works was complicated by the general lack of masonry skills among the local populace. This at least, he was convinced he could overcome, but what worried him more was the attitude he had encountered among the local officials. "I find everything in a state of confusion through the management of some of your predecessors, and of those who prefer their own, to the public interest," he wrote Bellomont who was planning a visit to the area.[15]

Based on Romer's report and after personally viewing the decaying works at Albany in mid-July when he met with the Iroquois, Bellomont informed London that it was an act of providence that the French had not attacked Albany the previous winter. For had they done so,

> with half the number of men that they had provided at Montreal, they could not (humanly speaking) have failed to take it, though I do not think they would have thought it worth keeping. The plunder they would have had, but it was not that but the Five Nations that were their object, and it is more than probable that those would have revolted to them upon such a loss and disgrace. God be thanked for the province's escape.[16]

While the governor was deeply concerned about the weak state of the frontier defenses, at the moment the Iroquois worried him far more. Rumors had reached him that the Iroquois were considering a separate peace treaty with the French. It was a dangerous proposition for New York. Loss of the Five Nations as military allies would prove devastating to a frontier already ravaged by war, and just as importantly, politically it would stymie efforts to claim lands through the Iroquois either by purchase or arguments that they were English subjects. Behind these reasons, however, lurked a much larger threat. Should the Iroquois fall under the influence of the French, the entire colonial frontier from New England to Virginia would be at risk.

Fearing that the Iroquois would carry through with their plans to negotiate with the French, Bellomont traveled to Albany in July to meet with representatives of the Five Nations. The governor stressed that they were to make no peace without his approval, but the approach did not go over as well as he might have hoped. The sachems complained that even though a peace treaty had been signed between the French and the English, they were still being targeted by French and Indian war parties. If they were English subjects, how could this be? And where were the English while this happened? The Five Nations had done what their English brothers had asked of them and carried the war to the French, but now that the English had established peace with their enemies, they found themselves being urged to carry on alone. Bellomont's response was that he would settle the matter with the governor of Canada and that in the meantime he would order English troops to assist the tribes in defending themselves from these French and Indian excursions. The governor's comments were met with murmurs and skepticism but were generally accepted.[17]

For his part Bellomont attempted to carry through with his promise, penning a string of letters to Governor Louis de Buade, the Count Frontenac, in Quebec, warning the latter that he risked undermining the peace treaty and reopening the conflict should he not alter his present course, but Frontenac replied that these matters were internal to the government of New France and completely separate from the treaty signed between the two crowns. Frontenac had a reasonable case for making such claims. Although the governor would be hard pressed to demonstrate that the Five Nations were French subjects, viewing them as a separate entity, subjects of neither the French nor the English was not difficult to argue. First, the Iroquois themselves had repeatedly viewed themselves as subjects of neither government. English claims to the contrary meant nothing so long as there was no agreement in place between France and England on such matters. Were simple statements such as this all that was required, the French could just as easily claim that the Mohicans were French subjects and, by that logic, lay claim to vast tracts of New England and New York. Secondly, New France had signed several treaties with the Five Nations in the past, none of which required the participation or sanctioning by either the Dutch or the English. Thirdly, the conflict between New France and the Five Nations

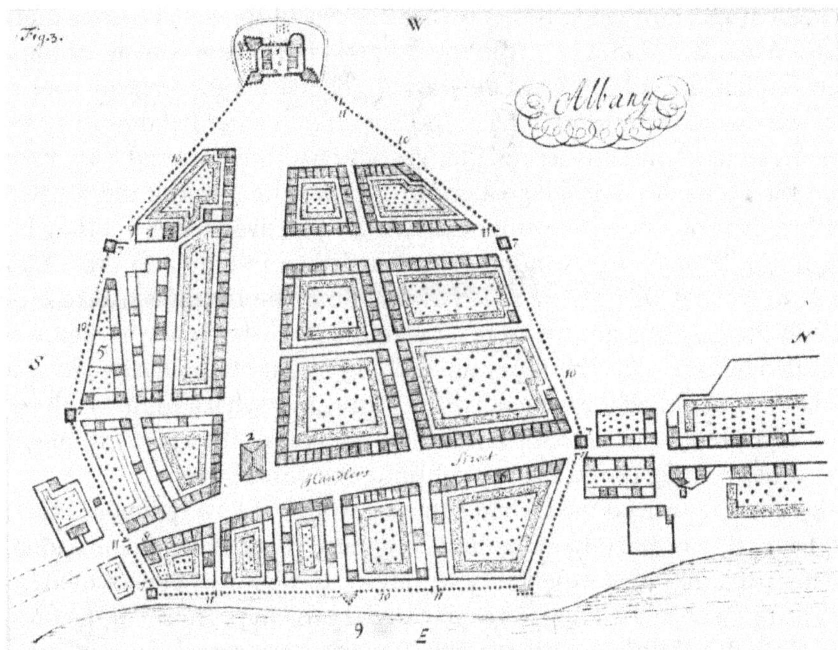


The John Miller map of Albany, 1695. Fort Albany can be seen to the west (top). (*New York Public Library*)

preceded King William's War and, as such, was to be viewed as a separate and distinct matter, which was further spelled out by the Five Nations (minus the Mohawks) dispatching representatives to Quebec to discuss a peace between the two parties.[18]

Bellomont's position was not as strong. Essentially his claims were based on a transfer of treaties and an extension of claims from the Dutch when England seized New York. The Dutch, however, never claimed sovereignty over the Iroquois, and, given the sorry state of the New Netherlands, never would have even considered doing so. It was certainly true that the English had signed several treaties of friendship with the Iroquois since their conquest of the Dutch colony, and the two had even acted as allies in the late conflict with New France, but none of these actions had ever specifically called the political autonomy of the Five Nations into question. For the moment, the bonds of friendship, Anglo-Iroquois trade at Albany, and a mutual distrust of the French attached the Iroquois to the English camp, but just as New France feared an Iroquois Confederacy in the hands of the English, the English feared a mass defection of the Iroquois to the French.[19]

More important were the actions and views of the Five Nations themselves. When Bellomont met with the Iroquois sachems at Albany, he found them "sullen and cold" toward the English. There was good reason for this. Part was due to the mishandling of Indians affairs under Bellomont's predecessor, Fletcher, and his representatives who had orchestrated a land grab from the Mohawks, but the greater portion was the result of the situation the Five Nations now found themselves in. For over ten years they had fought the French at the urging of the English, and although France and England were at war during much of this time, the Iroquois had received little in the way of actual assistance from the English. Now with peace established between the two, the entire military might of Canada and its allies could be brought against them, which is precisely what Frontenac threatened if representatives from the Five Nations did not arrive in Quebec within the next forty-five days to continue the peace talks.

Bellomont assured the sachems that he would use every Englishman at his disposal to protect them, but not convinced that this would be enough, he suggested that the Confederacy withdraw to Albany where he could better assure their safety. This, coupled with the broken promises of the previous conflict, did little to alter the Five Nations' dark mood. They of course told the governor what he wanted to hear—that they were committed to the bond between the two nations and that none of their leaders would speak with the French, much less travel to Canada—but they were too shrewd of politicians to do otherwise. When the council fires dimmed and the English moved out of earshot, other ideas were being expressed.[20]

CHAPTER TWO

# Pirates and Privateers

By the spring of 1699 Bellomont had purged enough of Fletcher's associates, or at least his zeal for the task had diminished enough, to plan a trip to Boston. The French and their Wabanaki allies had attacked a number of settlements in Massachusetts during King William's War, but they had been particularly hard on the Maine and New Hampshire frontier. The governor used the opportunity to have Colonel Romer view the fortifications on Castle Island in Boston Harbor and from there travel to Piscataqua in New Hampshire and Pemaquid on the coast of Maine to assess what would be required to fortify these points.[1]

Bellomont had good reasons to send Romer to these locations. First, Boston, the capital of the most populace of the American colonies, was particularly vulnerable to a seaborne raid. An actual occupation of the town was unlikely, as the Bay Colony could call close to ten thousand men to arms to repel any invaders, but a daring raid led by a French captain such as Pierre Iberville would be able to reduce the town to ashes before a sufficient force could be assembled to drive him off. The inhabitants of Boston faced several scares along these lines during the last conflict and were fortunate that a French plan to put the town to the torch was abandoned due to logistic reasons and a lack of resolve on the part of the French admiral in charge of the task.

The defenses of this prominent New England seaport relied on a small fort on Castle Island near the entrance to the harbor and a pair of gun batteries on the north and south seafront of the town. This later position was also backed by a crumbling fort, and if the defenders were fortunate, an English frigate or two might be in the port to add their guns to the defense. Manpower, in the form of local militia, was the strength of the town's defense. Close to a thousand men could be quickly called to arms and reinforced shortly thereafter by the militias of the surrounding towns. These resources, however, would be disorganized and slow to respond to a quick descent by a fleet of French warships, leaving much of the burden on the defenders of Castle Island and the North and South Batteries of Boston.

In June, after completing his initial survey, Romer submitted a brief report on Castle Island to the governor. The fort built there was clearly in need of a major overhaul. To this end the engineer had already begun drawing out a new fortification to strengthen the location, but in his opinion,

> Although the whole Castle Island were made one entire fortification and in condition to defend itself against a year's siege, as according to the new design it might, yet this could only serve the inhabitants of Boston and neighbourhood to secure their riches, but could not hinder but that an enemy might blockade and commit all manner of outrages even to bombarding, except the coming in at the passages from the sea be secured, and by that means an enemy be forced to stand off to sea.[2]

What was ultimately required was to prevent an enemy fleet from establishing itself in Nantasket Harbor from which they could assert control over the surrounding islands, land troops at their leisure, and block access to any fleet looking to relieve the town. To prevent this Romer submitted a plan which not only called for the reconstruction of the fort on Castle Island but for the establishment of a pair of fifty-gun batteries positioned on points of land "regulated so that they may make good defence in front, flank and rear."[3]

With this first task accomplished Romer traveled to Fort William and Mary at the mouth of the Piscataqua River on the coast of New Hampshire. Here he spent the better part of July examining the fort and a number of islands that dotted the mouth of the river. The location was of importance to the fledgling colony of New Hampshire as farther up the river lay Portsmouth, the colony's primary seaport. It was also of strategic importance to England, as the Royal Navy obtained most of its masts from the forests of southern New Hampshire through Portsmouth. The engineer found the fort, located on Newcastle Island, positioned correctly, but in its present condition "uncapeable of defending the entrance into that noble & important River not being sufficient to endure three or four days attack of an Enemy."[4]

By late August Romer was on his way to examine Pemaquid and Casco Bay to determine the layout of these harbors and what would be required to fortify these important locations along the Maine coast. At Pemaquid he found the abandoned stone Fort William Henry, captured by the French in August 1696. The fort had been reputed to be one of the strongest along the North Atlantic seaboard, but when Romer examined its remains he found that the stronghold had been constructed with clay and sand as opposed to traditional limestone. In his estimation the inherent structural weakness from such an approach played a part in the fort's demise. At Casco, as with the previous locations, the fort had been destroyed in the last conflict. It amazed the engineer that such a badly placed, poorly built, and ill-kept wooden structure could inspire the confidence to build the nearby town of Falmouth, which, like the fort, now lay in ruins. "'Tis great pity that so fine a country should be deserted," he wrote of the experience. From Casco Bay he stopped at Winter Harbor on the Saco River and then made a brief visit to the villages of Wells and York before returning to Boston in late October.[5]

Bellomont, who would spend over a year in Boston, was astonished when Romer reported to him that the fortifications from Boston to Pemaquid were either abandoned, destroyed, or in desperate need of repair. The governor had also been alarmed to hear news of Wabanaki and French encroachments on the Maine and New Hampshire frontier, as well as claims that the French had asserted exclusive fishing rights along the Acadian coast. However, he found his hands tied in both matters. First, the territorial issues were considered the domain of the French and English commissions formed under the terms of the peace treaty. As such, he was in no position to act on any of this information other than forwarding the news on to London. Second, although the New England frontier was a wreck and imperiled by another potential war with the Wabanaki, and even though most of the major ports in the region, including Boston, were vulnerable to a French or Spanish naval attack, he found the governments of Massachusetts and New Hampshire disinterested in the matter. Recommendations for repairing and rebuilding Fort William and Mary, and for improving the fort on Castle Island, which Bellomont referred to as "the poorest I ever saw," were quickly passed over without regard to their importance. Nor was there any interest in rebuilding the fortifications along the Maine coast, even though settlers were beginning to return. "There now being peace, they have no remembrance of the war," Bellomont informed the English court of the colony's attitude. "So long as they can sleep securely in this town of Boston they [think] nor look no farther."[6]

It proved a trying summer for Bellomont. He spent his days arguing with the various New England assemblies about measures to reduce piracy, the Navigation Acts, the collection of customs and duties, as well as the need for a naval officer at both Boston and New York whose job it was to monitor the local trade for contraband and illegal activities. In each case the governor found reluctant assemblies, not so much in terms of addressing the problems but more so in doing it with colonial funds. He forwarded plans to secure the woods in southern New Hampshire as a source of naval stores and masts for the British navy, and found his days consumed with a steady stream of petitions from local natives complaining that their lands had been unjustly seized. Bellomont met with several of these natives but found there was little he could do beyond forward their grievances on to the colonial assemblies, which he believed had sanctified the actions in the first place. "Tis a great scandal to our religion and nation that justice is not done," he informed the Board of Trade who ultimately possessed the power to address the problem.[7]

The bulk of these proceedings and many that would follow remained focused on stamping out piracy along the New York and New England coast. Bellomont employed a two-pronged approach to the problem. First and foremost was to deny the pirates safe haven, logistics, and markets for their illegal goods. This he accomplished in part by collecting evidence against Fletcher and dismissing the former governor's associates from the New York government. He then appointed a new naval officer and customs collector to New York and Boston, informing London that "I should prefer an honest able Judge, and Attorney General at New Yorke, before a Man of War and Soldiers, for the suppressing of Piracy and unlawfull Trade." While the New York merchants who had acquired a great deal of wealth in the Red Sea Trade put up a resistance, mainly through the assembly, Bellomont was insistent that any attempt to suppress piracy and unlawful trade had to start with honest government officials. Similar efforts were applied to questionable conduct in New England, and in regard to Rhode Island, where aiding and abetting pirates was so commonplace that the governor, Walter Clarke, had refused to swear observance to the Acts of Trade and Navigation, the Board of Trade recommended that Bellomont be given full powers to enquire into these matters. With the example of Governor Fletcher fresh in everyone's mind, the threat seemed to have had the intended effect, for Bellomont never conducted this investigation.

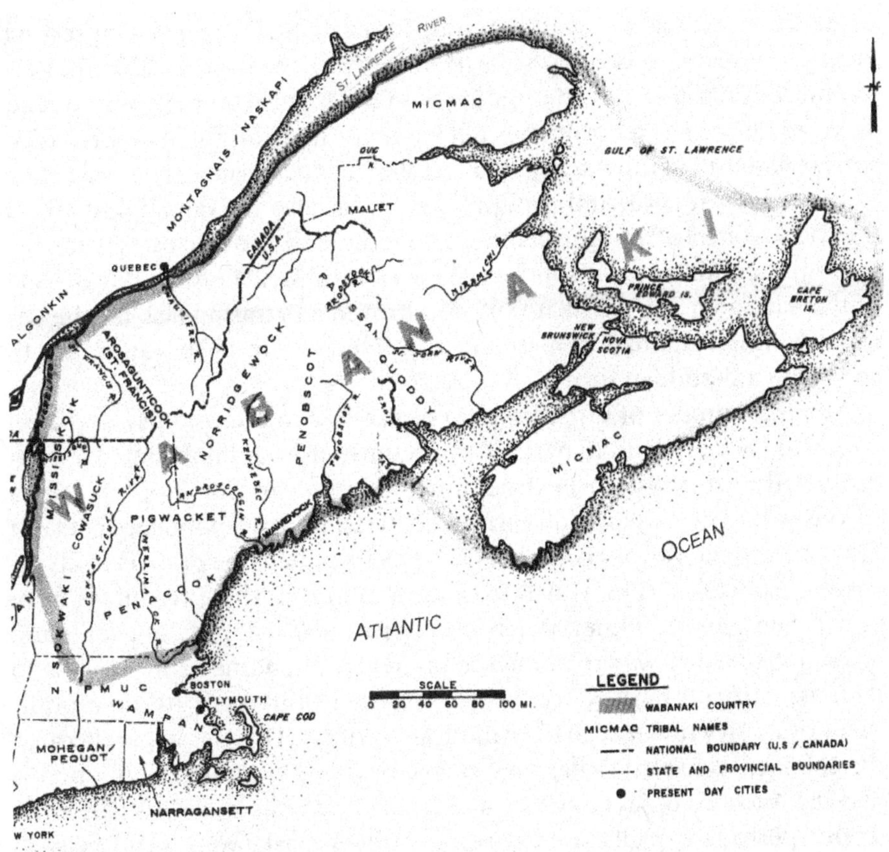


A map showing the extent and tribes of the Wabanaki Confederacy. The Wabanaki had a history of conflict with New England which had led to the First Wabanaki War during what was known as King Philip's War (1675-1678). With occasional aid from the French the five tribes that constituted the Confederacy (Abenaki, Micmac, Maliseet, Passamaquoddy, Penobscot) had later fought New England to a standstill during King William's War. (*Stacy Morin, cartographer, 1900*)

The second element of the earl's plan to squash piracy concerned military measures. Pay and recruits for the four New York independent companies was paramount, not only for the defense of the frontier but to guard New York Harbor and man the forts and fortifications in the area. Of even more importance was a number of warships to patrol the coast. "If I had a 4th-rate ship here (Boston) and a 5th-rate ship at New York," the governor informed London, "I would undertake to secure all the coasts from Piscataqua (Portsmouth, NH) to the southernmost point of Carolina from pirates, especially if the captains were honest fighting fellows."[8]

As frustrating as the political component proved to be in suppressing piracy, resources to combat it head on proved even more difficult. Bellomont was hardly alone in pleading with the English government to send more warships. The governments of the other American colonies forwarded similar requests, as did the governors of the various Caribbean Islands, such as Barbados, Jamaica, and Antigua. There was also the demand to escort the tobacco fleets from the southern colonies and provide escorts for the mast fleet coming out of southern New Hampshire. With the downsizing of the navy after King William's War, it proved a daunting task for the admiralty, which still had to maintain a sizable force in European waters to cope with any sudden turn of events.

While a number of warships were dispatched to the colonies, and New York and New England in particular, circumstances did not allow for a coordinated patrol system in these waters. Often the warship, typically a frigate, would be employed in carrying letters and correspondence between England and the various colonies. Each governor had one or two vessels involved in this function, which frequently removed these resources from anti-pirate patrols. Other warships stopped at Boston or Norfolk, and cruised the nearby waters briefly, before returning home or moving on to their assignments in the Caribbean or elsewhere, but there was no centralized Royal Navy presence in the American colonies. This was in part because the colonies were also to have provincial navies they could call upon. It is true that most colonies employed a provincial warship or two, usually a galley and perhaps a small cutter, to patrol shallow coastal waters and rivers in search of contraband activity, but to call them a navy would be a stretch. Undermanned, undergunned, and often not paid for long periods of time, these vessels proved of little help and often proved tempting targets for pirates. Just as importantly, the crews of these colonial vessels were a fertile recruiting ground if not closely monitored. "The vast riches of the Red Sea and Madagascar are such a lure to seamen that there's almost no withholding them from turning pirates."[9]

Often even if provincial or Royal Navy ships were available, they were too small to deal with the well-armed pirate vessels now being encountered. This was pointed to by a naval encounter on July 26, 1699, when a twenty-six-gun pirate ship named *Providence* sailed into Linhaven Bay, Virginia, and attacked the sixteen-gun Royal Navy gunboat *Essex Prize*. The battle raged for several hours before the *Essex Prize* limped away with over half of its crew casualties, leaving the nearby sloop *Maryland Merchant* in the attacker's hands. The news came as no surprise to Bellomont who on several occasions had been forced to watch large pirate vessels leisurely patrol the coastal waters of New York and New England because he did not have a large warship on hand to challenge them.[10]

In fact, Bellomont had foreseen such a problem and attempted to address it early on. Upon the earl's initial appointment to the governorship of Massachusetts in 1695 he had the opportunity to speak with Colonel Robert Livingston of New York while the latter was visiting London. When the topic of piracy was broached Bellomont found a sympathetic ear in Livingston, who had no love for Fletcher and his administration. Livingston warned the governor that it would be difficult if not impossible to halt this illegal trade, but as a first step toward suppressing these activities he suggested that a New York captain named William Kidd, who was currently in London, be given command of a warship to attack the pirates involved in the Red Sea Trade. Livingston characterized Kidd as "a bold, honest, and skillful mariner," who was "well acquainted with all the haunts of the pirates who prowled between the Cape of Good Hope and the Straits of Malacca." Such a man backed by the guns and crew of a Royal Navy warship could inflict serious damage on the Rea Sea pirates.

The idea appealed to Bellomont and he petitioned the king with the plan. At the time the admiralty was short on both men and ships, and as such, it rejected the idea. Not to be deterred, it was suggested that Kidd and his current crew be given a letter of marquis to proceed against both the French and pirates. The king initially liked the proposal and pledged to pay for one-third of outfitting the expedition, but under the advice of his councilors he later withdrew the money, although he encouraged the project to go forward. Sold on the idea, Bellomont approached several of his colleagues such as the Earl of Romney, who was master of the ordnance, the Earl of Oxford, who was Lord High Admiral of England, and Sir Edmund Harrison, a wealthy London merchant. These men, along with Bellomont and a few others, agreed to finance four-fifths of the expedition's cost, while Kidd and Livingston each agreed to split the remaining one-fifth of the estimated £6,000 to outfit the expedition. The logistics seen to, Bellomont met with Livingston and Kidd in London on October 10, 1695, to finalize the arrangement, issue Kidd's commission, and detail how any booty from the expedition would be distributed among the investors and crew.[11]

Kidd and Livingston purchased the thirty-gun vessel *Adventure Galley*, and after equipping the craft and recruiting a skeleton crew, Kidd departed Portsmouth, England, for New York in April 1696. When he arrived a few months later he presented his commission to Governor Fletcher, along with a small French ship he had taken on the way. Kidd would spend over half a year in New York during which time rumors as to his real purpose quickly spread and those looking for adventure and quick riches flocked to his crew. Finally satisfied with his preparations Kidd set sail for Madagascar in February 1697.

By the spring of 1698 the *Adventure Galley* had accomplished little in the Red Sea and Indian Ocean beyond the capture of a local sailing vessel loaded with cotton, an unintended action with the Dutch Mocha Fleet, and a brief skirmish with a Portuguese man-o-war that sent the privateer and its crew scrambling for their lives. At this point Kidd had stayed within the scope of his orders and the next vessel he met, the English *Royal Captain*, he traded traditional maritime courtesies with before letting it go its way. After a series of small local captures, which as with the earlier ones yielded little in the way of booty, Kidd found his crew on edge. All had signed on under the proviso that they would be paid with the profits from their captures, but almost a year and a half later they had little to show for their efforts. The temper of the crew coupled with the lack of success led to a number of incidents, and Kidd now routinely locked himself in his cabin at night surrounded by a bevy of loaded firearms. It was not just the mood of the crew that was changing but Kidd's as well, as pointed to by one instance where he killed a sailor with an iron-bound bucket after he found that he had broken into his chest.[12]

It was at this point where Kidd and his crew crossed the line. In early June 1698 the *Adventure Galley* encountered the English-owned transport *Quidah Merchant*. Kidd stopped the vessel near Madagascar and found that the captain was sailing under a purchased French pass. Given the attitude of his crew it's doubtful if Kidd could have let the heavily laden four-hundred-ton *Quidah Merchant* go without a full-scale mutiny. As it was Kidd did not pass on the opportunity, using the French pass as evidence that the vessel was cooperating with the king's enemies and, thus, was a legal prize.

Kidd set sail for St. Mary's Harbor, Madagascar, with his new prize, but during the return voyage the *Adventure Galley* sprang several major leaks that could not be stopped. The crew transferred the vessel's guns and supplies over to the captured merchantman before setting the *Adventure Galley* ablaze and continuing on their way. Upon reaching St. Mary's a number of Kidd's crew urged him to seize the nearby frigate *Moca*, a well-known pirate ship, and head to the Red Sea to seek their fortune. Kidd would later claim that he was for taking the frigate, as it was a lawful prize that rightfully belonged to the king, but he would not accompany his men to the Red Sea. Having seen enough, ninety of his crew deserted, seized the *Moca* in a brief skirmish, and departed the harbor leaving Kidd and twenty-five of the original crew watching from the deck of the *Quidah Merchant*.

Captain William Kidd, portrait by James Thornhill, c. 1695. Today regarded as a notorious pirate captain, the events behind his career paint a much different picture.

From here Kidd sold a portion of the prize ship's cargo, and after provisioning the vessel and recruiting a new crew he set sail for the West Indies. At this stage the legendary Captain Kidd appears a reluctant pirate, if one at all. While the seizure of the *Quidah Merchant* was questionable, sailing under a French pass was questionable as well, and many admiralty courts cut a wide path when it came to authenticating a privateer's prize and their conduct. This act aside, the fact that Kidd took so few prizes and that his crew mutinied because of this, points to either Kidd being intent on following his original orders or being one of the worse pirate captains of all time.

When Kidd touched port at Antigua in April 1699, he and his men were stunned to find that they had been branded pirates. With word having spread to several West Indies ports Kidd sought shelter in Mona, Hispaniola. Here he left the *Quidah Merchant* under a handful of the crew and an Antigua merchant who was contracted to sell the vessel's cargo. Using part of these proceedings Kidd purchased a sloop and set out for New York. Sailing north with forty of his men he stopped at Delaware Bay to take on supplies and then proceeded to New York. On his way, however, he heard news that Bellomont was in Boston and shifted his course for New England. Kidd put a messenger ashore in mid-June and then dropped anchor at Block Island, a dozen miles off the coast of Rhode Island.

Bellomont was surprised to receive a letter from Kidd asking for a meeting near Block Island, but he was delighted to comply. News of Kidd's exploits, and directives to arrest him and his crew, had reached the colonial governors in the spring. As one of the originators of Kidd's voyage, Bellomont was anxious to clear his reputation, and thus, the reputations of the powerful English lords and merchants that had invested in his scheme. Since receiving this news, he had been busy asking questions and reporting on Kidd and his possible whereabouts. Now Kidd had come to him and he was not going to pass on the opportunity.

The earl dispatched a small sloop carrying his envoys Duncan Campbell and James Emott. The pair met with Kidd a few leagues from Block Island on June 17, 1699. Kidd professed his innocence and claimed that he would have sailed directly into Boston, "but by reason of what his men heard in the West Indies of their being proclaimed pirates, they would not consent to him coming into any port without some assurances that they would not be imprisoned or molested." After a brief conversation Kidd gave Campbell a letter to deliver to Bellomont in which he claimed that "A sheet of paper will not contain what may be said of the care I took to preserve the owners' interest and to come home to clear my own innocence."[13]

Bellomont agreed to hear Kidd's case and on July 1, 1699, the privateer's sloop entered Boston Harbor. Kidd and his men told their story before the governor and his council. At first, the matter was handled in a cordial fashion with Kidd and his crew being released on their own parole, but after several examinations Bellomont had heard enough and began to fear that they were a flight risk. His council agreed, and the entire crew was jailed on the prison barge in Boston Harbor.

Not long after, fearing that Kidd, who was still rumored to have treasure buried along the coast, might bribe his way out of the prison barge, Bellomont decided to "try the power of iron against gold" and had the privateer placed in sixteen-pound chains. While the governor "found sufficient cause to suspect him very guilty, by the many lies and contradictions he told me," a few days later he would have proof of it. Kidd had repeatedly informed the governor and his council that the *Quidah Merchant* and her substantial cargo was safe and just waiting for his return, but after speaking with a pair of captains recently arrived from Curacao, Bellomont discovered that the *Quidah Merchant*'s cargo had been sold and the ship put to the torch. Several other captains arrived over the next few days confirming the story. The governor, who was careful throughout the proceedings to not be directly involved with Kidd for fear of an appearance of impropriety, sent a pair of councilmen to confront Kidd with the reports. Faced with the news, the privateer finally admitted that he had ordered the cargo sold, but he knew nothing of the ship being burnt, as he had left it in the care of an Antigua merchant named Henry Bolton and a few of his crew.[14]

"There was never a greater liar or thief in this world than this Kidd," Bellomont wrote the Board of Trade, while listing out the privateer's infractions. Were there any doubt as to where Bellomont stood on the matter it was made clear when he then asked the Board of Trade for their directions after the Bay Colony had refused to pass the stringent bill against pirates that the governor had presented. Bellomont was surprised by the assembly's response and reproved their conduct, but "Nothing would prevail: A pirate cannot suffer death in this province, and what to do with Kidd and his men, I know not, and therefore desire your orders."[15]

The decision to return Kidd to England to face trial was made early on, but it would not be until April 12, 1700, that the HMS *Advice* reached Portsmouth with Kidd and thirty-two other pirates in its hold. The opposition party in Parliament attempted to use Kidd to politically damage his powerful sponsors and allies of the king, but Kidd refused to speak to this subject. With neither his sponsors nor their political opponents interested in the proclaimed pirate, Kidd's trial for piracy and the murder of one of his crew was a forgone conclusion, and he was hanged in London on May 23, 1701, having proclaimed his innocence to the end.

Kidd's actions certainly bear scrutiny, particularly the several stops along the Atlantic coast burying treasure and visiting old pirate haunts and rendezvous points. There was also the hiding of the *Quidah Merchant* and the sale of her estimated £300,000 of East Indian goods, which Kidd initially lied about to the governor. There were also questions as to the 69 pounds of gold and 150 pounds of silver found onboard the sloop, and the later discovery of gems that were suspected to be used as a bribe on the governor's wife. These abuses aside, Kidd still had the *Quidah Merchant* and offered to return to Boston with the prize. He also produced the French passes that he had confiscated and used as reason to seize the handful of vessels he had encountered on his cruise. The gold and silver found on his vessel were explained by his need to sell off a part of the cargo to purchase the sloop and provision his men, and as for his alleged conduct toward his original crew, the fact that most had deserted to take up the Rea Sea Trade speaks volumes as to their volatile nature. Perhaps more importantly, Kidd had returned, and while his story was an untidy one, other privateers had been cleared of far worse conduct.[16]

Unfortunately for Kidd, his actions cast a shadow over the judgment of a handful of very powerful men, particularly the Earl of Bellomont, who was also in the unique position of doing something about this. While outfitting a privateer during the height of the War of the League of Augsburg was hardly illegal or unethical, Kidd's subsequent actions had cast a shadow on Bellomont's reputation, which would transform him from an enthusiastic investor to a man intent on apprehending one of history's most famous buccaneers. It is clear that much of the damage done by Kidd to Bellomont's reputation was self-perceived, given that none of the other investors, many who were close to the king, were ever questioned on the matter. From this perspective it seems clear that the issue was viewed by the court as a legitimate privateer that had gone rogue. It was hardly the first time such a thing had happened and likely not the last.

For Bellomont this was not enough. While the evidence against Kidd was sketchy, the governor never intended to grant the privateer clemency as spoken to in his letter to Kidd while the latter lay at anchor near Block Island. Instead, he was quick to make up his mind when it came to Kidd, no doubt impassioned by a need to restore his honor, but perhaps just as much by the need to make an example of a well-known pirate in order to deter others. In both cases Bellomont succeeded, but he would not see either. After a short illness the earl died at New York City on the morning of March 5, 1701, and was buried with full military honors at Fort William.[17]

CHAPTER THREE

# The Great Peace of Montreal

KING WILLIAM'S WAR HAD GONE POORLY for the Five Nations. Unlike the conflicts of the past where the Iroquois had dictated the terms and tempo of the engagements, in this most recent conflict the roles had reversed. The French and their allies were no longer content with simply repelling Iroquois raiders but were bringing the war to the Iroquois homelands. Governor Denonville destroyed the major Seneca villages in 1687, in 1693 several Mohawk villages were put to the torch, and in 1696 Frontenac, at the head of a large French force, demolished the villages of the Onondaga and Oneida. Although none of these expeditions resulted in major Iroquois losses, the combined effect on the Five Nations' agriculture and trade, and the displacement caused by the attacks, began undermining the military power of the Confederacy.

Combined with these major French-led attacks was the concerted effort on the part of New France's native allies to wreak havoc upon the Iroquois. The Abenaki, Algonquin, and French mission Indians had harassed the Mohawk to the point that one French observer noted "this nation of Aniés [Mohawk] has become the smallest of the Five Nations and is now the one that causes us the least concern." Matters were even worse for the Seneca, the largest and most powerful member of the Confederacy. The Ottawa, Chippewa, Potawatomi, Huron, and a host of other Great Lakes nations allied with the French began a systematic assault against this tribe, eventually causing them to abandon their traditional hunting grounds and shift their villages east in an attempt to place more distance between themselves and their adversaries. As if the attrition associated with the decade-long conflict was not bad enough, emigration of many elements of the Five Nations, particularly the Mohawk and Oneida, to the missions of New France or to safer harbors within nearby tribes, combined with the outbreak of multiple epidemics, continued to weaken the fighting strength of the Confederacy. Figures compiled by the government of New York clearly show the net effect. In 1689, at the start of King William's War, the combined fighting strength of the Five Nations was estimated at 2,800 men. In 1697 these numbers had fallen to 1,320, and even this count might be viewed as skewed if many of the war captives, integrated into the various tribes as per custom, were to be excluded from the tally.[1]

These losses aside, it would be far from accurate to imply that the Iroquois were defeated. They were not. The warriors of the Five Nations still had the ability to strike at the French and their allies. Charlevoix described their state at this point as more "stunned than subdued," while an Iroquois sachem portrayed their state to the English as "down upon one knee, but not quite down upon the ground." Whatever the verbiage, the Confederacy's plight had shifted to the point that elements within it were rethinking their stance toward the French and English.[2]

The Mohawk, who held a prominent place within the league because of their proximity to Albany and its source of English arms and goods, were for continuing a close relationship with the English and, if need be, for continuing the struggle against New France. Although some within the remaining elements of the Confederacy were of a similar mind, most of the leadership within the western tribes began thinking along different lines. The blows from New France's allies had predominantly fallen upon this portion of the Confederacy, and despite assurances from the English that the Five Nations were part of the peace agreement, they continued to do so. As a result, a number of factions began to take form within these western tribes on how to best deal with this problem. The first called for time to allow the English to enforce the Iroquois position within the treaty. Another pointed out that if their English allies were incapable of stopping the raids, they should make a separate peace with the French, one that did not include New France's allies, who could then be dealt with once the French were out of the picture. Yet another group argued that New France would not agree to any treaty that excluded its allies and that a more general peace should be agreed upon not only with the French but with their allies as well—one that would allow the Five Nations to assume a more neutral position between the colonial powers. And still others argued that since the French could not be trusted, it would be better to simply carry on the struggle with the hopes that the English would eventually have no choice but to become militarily involved again. Although there was no single agreed-upon policy, after some debate the centralized theme became that of exploring some form of a separate peace treaty with the French, regardless of what Bellomont or the English wanted.[3]

While Bellomont dispatched troops to Albany in fear of a major French strike against his allies, and the debates raged through the Iroquois longhouses, New France mourned the loss of their governor. On November 16 Count Frontenac complained to a fellow officer that he was not feeling well. The seventy-eight-year-old had suffered from asthma for some time, and now matters took a turn for the worse. On the 22nd, the bedridden count made out his will and a few days later died in the governor's mansion in Quebec. The funeral proceedings, the first ever held for a governor of New France, lasted three days, during which time the city's bells were echoed by cannon fire every half hour while blue-clad troops lined the streets from the Chateau St. Louis to the Recollects' cathedral where he was interred.

While the French mourned, the four western Iroquois nations, after much debate, agreed to send delegates to Montreal in the fall of 1698. Before making this journey, however, they met with New York's lieutenant governor, John Nanfan, in Albany to discuss "what proposals to make at Canada" and to request that a representative of that colony accompany them to act as a witness. Nanfan informed the sachems that such actions would only complicate matters. Then, seeing that the primary motive behind the venture was an exchange of prisoners, Nanfan completely thwarted the effort by informing the Five Nations representatives that the French had agreed to release all their Iroquois prisoners to Governor Bellomont and that, "there was no reason to doubt but when they arrived at their Castles would meet their prisoners they so much wished for." The statement served its intended purpose. Satisfied, the representatives of the western Five Nations handed six French prisoners over to Nanfan and called off their plans to travel to Montreal.[4]

Of course, Louis-Hector de Callières, the governor of Montreal and, upon Frontenac's death, now governor general of New France, had no intention of releasing his Iroquois prisoners to Bellomont, and when none returned over the course of the next few months, the Iroquois sent a pair of sachems to Montreal to inquire into the delay. The two met with Paul Le Moyne de Maricourt, a French officer who had been adopted by the Onondaga. They were surprised when Maricourt informed them that the

French had no intentions of releasing any Iroquois prisoners until the Five Nations came to Montreal to sign a separate peace treaty with the French. Clearly something was amiss, and against Bellomont's wishes, representatives from the Oneida and Onondaga traveled to Montreal in March 1699 in search of an explanation.

If there was celebration within the Iroquois and English camps over the passing of Frontenac or any thought that this would result in a change of French attitudes, it proved unfounded, as his replacement showed himself to be a more capable diplomat than his predecessor. The Oneida and Onondaga sachems petitioned Callières for the release of all Iroquois in French hands and for Maricourt and Father Bruyas to return with them to Albany, where the French prisoners in Iroquois hands would be exchanged and a general peace concluded. They also pressed the governor to have his western allies cease their raids as a sign of his true intentions toward peace with the Five Nations. Callières dismissed the requests. First, he made it clear that none of the conditions demanded by his predecessor had changed. Any peace to be made would be concluded at Montreal and would have to include all the nations allied to the French. Only then would a general exchange of prisoners take place. Second, the governor would halt the raids made by his eastern Abenaki and Algonquin allies for sixty days as a show of good faith, but not those of his western allies. Lastly, he agreed to exchange a like number of Iroquois captives for the four Frenchmen the sachems had brought along. The Iroquois, a little taken aback by the experience, left with their repatriated countrymen, promising to return to Montreal in June to continue the negotiations.[5]

Callières had little faith that the Iroquois representatives would hold to their promise to return in June. The English still had a great deal of influence over these tribes, and he found it unlikely that it would be so quickly undermined. Nor was he convinced of their sincerity toward peace in general, which is why he had refused to hold back the attacks of his western allies. This and the threat of expanded military action on the part of the French, along with Iroquois desires for the return of their prisoners, were the best incentives in his opinion for changing their minds.

As Callières had predicted, English political efforts prevented the promised June return of the Iroquois delegates. Once again, Bellomont's representatives seemed to satisfy the Iroquois with promises that their prisoners would soon be released by the French, but at the same time Callières was correct in his assessment as to the effect the raids of his western allies would have on the Iroquois desire to negotiate. Throughout the summer of 1699 New France's high-country allies struck at the western nations of the Con-

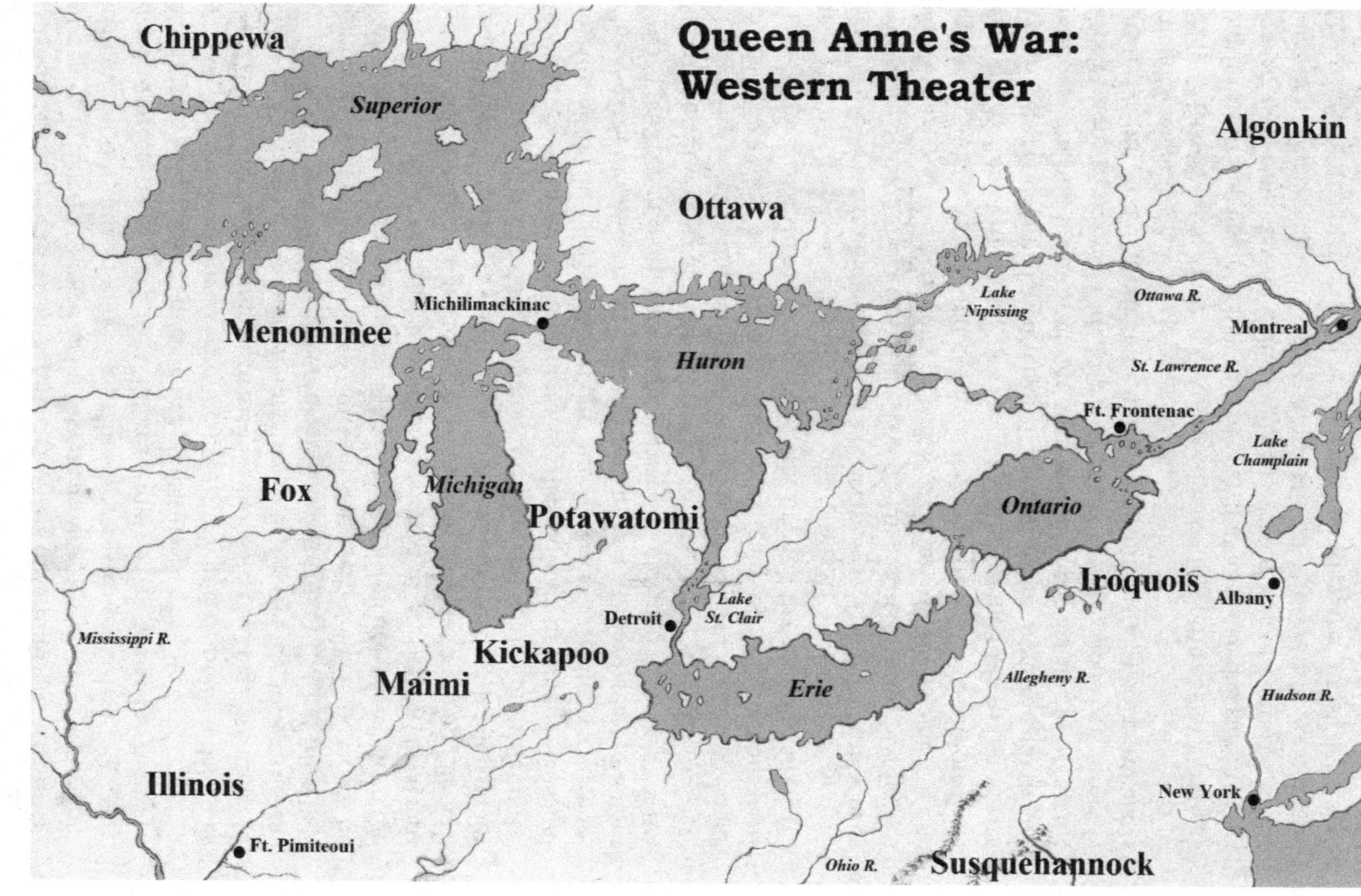
Queen Anne's War:
Western Theater
Chippewa
Superior
Algonkin
Ottawa
Michilimackinac
Menominee
Huron
Lake
Nipissing
Ottawa R.
Montreal
St. Lawrence R.
Ft. Frontenac
Lake
Champlain
Fox
Michigan
Potawatomi
Ontario
Iroquois
Albany
Lake
St. Clair
Detroit
Mississippi R.
Kickapoo
Maimi
Erie
Allegheny R.
Hudson R.
Illinois
New York
Ft. Pimiteoui
Ohio R.
Susquehannock

federacy to the point that in September a pair of Onondaga sachems returned to Montreal to once again ask the governor for a general prisoner exchange and to put an end to his allies "coming into our territory every day and breaking our heads." Callières simply shrugged at the requests. Nothing had changed as far as he was concerned.[6]

Nor had things changed with the English. While Onondaga delegates met with Callières, Iroquois sachems in Albany were asking, "we desire to know of Corlaer how to behave ourselves in this extremity, for we can endure it no longer." Like the governor of New France's reply, that from Bellomont's representatives was no different than before; the issue would be looked into, in the meantime stay on your guard, and don't speak with the French. It was not the course Bellomont wanted to pursue, but his hands were bound by the treaty and more importantly by the crippled financial state of New York. There was little he could do but plead with England for help in the way of "Orders, Soldiers, and Money": soldiers to defend the frontier and help secure the Iroquois castles, money to pay for arms and munitions for the Five Nations and to build a series of new forts to help secure the frontier, and orders directing him to take a more aggressive stance toward the French. Time was slipping away, he informed the ministry. "If a speedy and effectual course be not taken, we shall lose the Five Nations irrecoverably. I foresee it plainly; the French never applied themselves so industriously as they do now, to debauch them from us; and we on our parts have nothing, nor do nothing to keep 'em in good humour and steady to us."[7]

For the western elements of the Five Nations, particularly the Seneca who were bearing the brunt of the French-allied attacks, time was indeed slipping away. It was becoming clear that their English allies could do little to prevent the slow erosion of Iroquois fighting strength. In addition, there was the very real threat that the French themselves might tire of the peace proceedings and launch a powerful attack against the cantons with the intent of shattering Iroquois power once and for all. Were this to occur, the Five Nations would not only lose any negotiating position they currently possessed but would be left at the mercy of numerous, and not particularly friendly, neighbors.

In March of 1700, a pair of Iroquois ambassadors returned to Montreal, but it would not be until July of that year that a sizable delegation of six sachems appeared before Callières. The governor was discouraged by the fact that this delegation was comprised of pro-French Seneca and Onondaga representatives, and he was skeptical when they insisted that they spoke for all the western nations of the Confederacy. In the presence of a number of Algonquin, Huron, and Abenaki sachems, the Iroquois representatives asked for a cease-fire and promised to abide by a general prisoner exchange that, for the first time, included the French allies. To help prepare the way for this exchange, they asked for Maricourt, Father Bruyas, and Chabert de Joncaire, a Frenchman who had been adopted into the Seneca tribe, to return with them. After a few days' delay, Callières voiced his displeasure at the Oneida and Cayuga's representatives not being present at the meeting but agreed to send the Frenchmen holding six of the Iroquois delegates hostage to ensure his countrymen's safe return. Lastly, he scheduled another meeting for the end of August and demanded that representatives from all four western Iroquois nations attend.[8]

In mid-August representatives from all five Iroquois nations convened a league council at the Onondaga capital to speak with Maricourt, Father Bruyas, and Joncaire concerning Governor Callières's demands. Also present was an English representative, John Van Eps. Bellomont had learned of the French delegation's presence at the Iroquois capital and had sent Van Eps ahead in an attempt to break up the proceedings. Van Eps, however, was a novice when it came to diplomacy, and instead of attempting to woo the Five Nations away, he demanded that they send back the French delegation and report to Albany in two weeks. The tone of the message, which called their autonomy into question, irked the Iroquois sachems. "I do not understand, what my brother means," replied Teganissorens, the leader of the rising neutral faction within the Confederacy, "in desiring us not to hearken to our Father's voice, and to sing the war-song at a time when everything invites us to peace." They would first listen to what the French had to say, he informed Van Eps. Afterward they would go to Albany, in accordance with Governor Bellomont's wishes. The French ambassadors were quick to sense the Iroquois mood and capitalize on Van Eps's overbearing remarks. Father Bruyas stood before the Five Nations' council and pointed to how the English viewed the Iroquois as their subjects, ordering them to do as they please, while Joncaire pointed out that it seemed that the English wanted the Iroquois destroyed by war, so that once sufficiently weakened they could impose whatever rule upon them they pleased.

As it turned out, Bruyas and Joncaire's remarks were not required. The sachems had already agreed among themselves to go to Montreal. There was really little choice in the matter. Although the Iroquois nations were economically linked to the English, it had become clear that the military alliance that existed between the two had ultimately failed to protect and serve the interests of the Five Nations. Thus, Iroquois policy was shifting from the extremes, that of being pro-French or pro-English, to a more centralized policy, one that would maintain the economic ties to Albany but removed the threat posed to the Five Nations by negotiating a separate peace treaty with New France and its allies.[9]

The French ambassadors and nineteen Iroquois sachems from the Seneca, Onondaga, and Cayuga cantons entered Montreal on August 31 to the salute of the town's cannon. Before Callières and his councilors, and amidst representatives from the Huron, Ottawa, Abenaki, and the Iroquois of the Missions, the Iroquois orator apologized for the Oneida representative who was prevented from making the journey by illness. Nonetheless, the delegation now before the governor was empowered to speak for the four western nations of the Confederacy. "When we came here last," he began, "We planted the tree of Peace; now we give it roots to reach the Far Nations, in order that it may be strengthened; we add leaves also to it, so that good business may be transacted under its shade. Possibly the Far Nations will be able to cut some roots from this Great Tree, but we will not be responsible for that nor its consequences."[10]

As proof of this sincerity for peace, he then presented thirteen French captives held by the tribes and asked in return for the release of all Iroquois prisoners held by the French and their native allies. Lastly, to promote the peace, which the speaker made clear was against the wishes of Governor Bellomont, he asked that the Iroquois be allowed to trade at Fort Frontenac, because "Corlaer is becoming ill humored; he may, indeed, create disturbance; we would, therefore, wish to have recourse to that fort."[11]

"I am happy to open my arms to you in order to receive you as a good father," Callières informed the delegation, delighted at seeing the negotiations finally reach a turning point. He thanked the Iroquois for the return of their prisoners and informed them that he would immediately release those in French hands and those held by the nearby mission Indians. As of this point, all sides would bury their hatchets. He would see to it that the Far Nations, as the Iroquois referred to the French Great Lakes allies, and all the other nations allied to New France would abide by his wishes. To continue this peace, he placed himself in the role of grand arbitrator, guaranteeing to all the nations involved that he would seek justice for those that had been victims of any transgression, and if need be, he would bring all his military might to bear to punish those who would break this agreement. The governor would also see to arrangements at Fort Frontenac as the Iroquois requested, but there was still one important matter left to address, that of the native prisoners held by the Iroquois and his western allies. As it would take time for the message to reach the western nations and to collect the people involved, the governor set August 1 of the following year as the

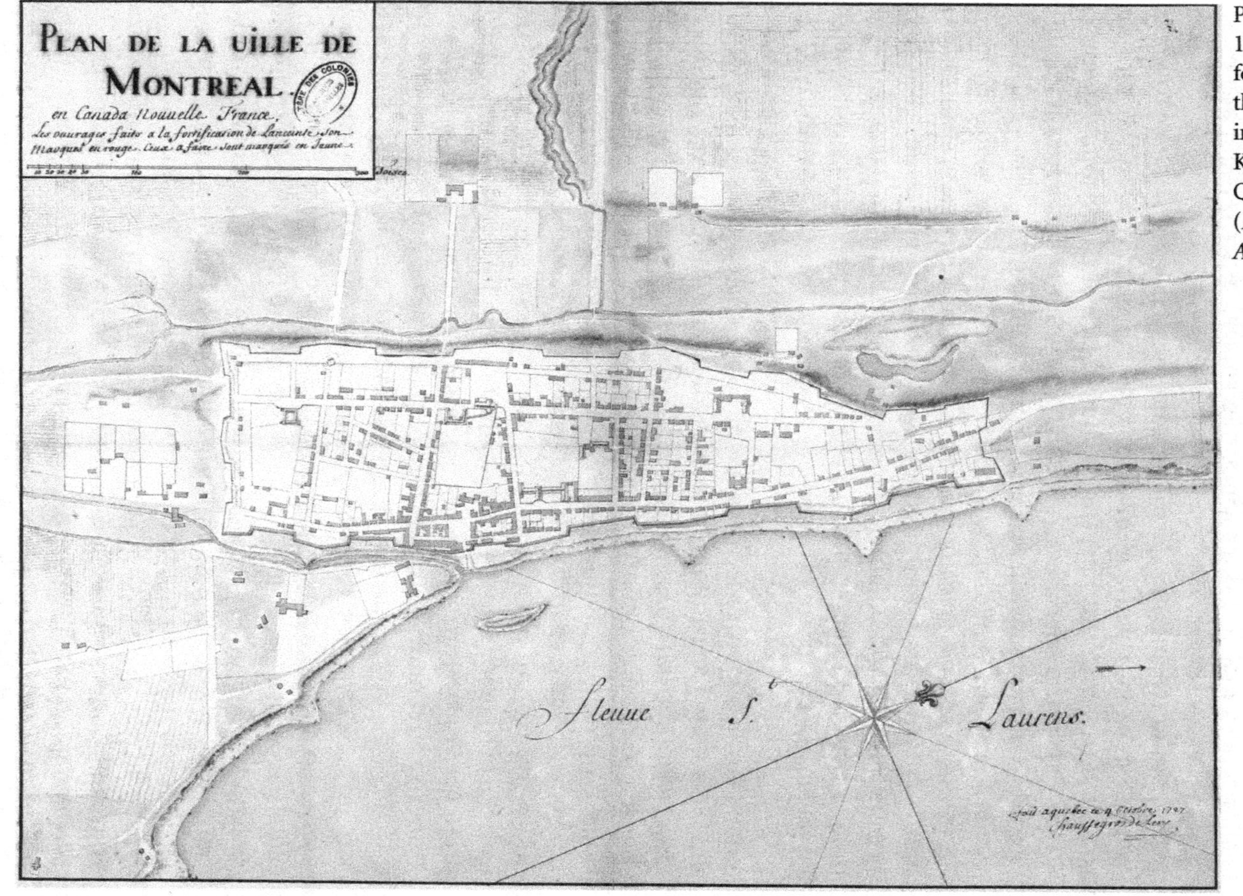


Plan of Montreal, 1727. Most of the fortifications about the town were put in place during King William's and Queen Anne's War. (*Library and Archives of Canada*)

date for the general exchange. All parties would bring their prisoners to Montreal at this time, where a final treaty would be signed by all involved.

Callières's words were followed by those of the ambassadors of the allied nations on hand. Each in turn submitted to the agreement and pledged to lay their hatchets at Onontio's feet, "never to take it up again except when it shall be his pleasure," and each in turn promised to carry the governor's word back to their own and any nearby nations. The Iroquois applauded both the governor's statements and the words of his allies and reiterated their own pledge. The ceremonies concluded with the signing of a provisional peace treaty, and by the end of the week, the delegates were on their way back to their homes with news of the agreement.[12]

For Callières, who seemed on the verge of accomplishing the extraordinary, it now became a waiting game. He dispatched couriers to each of the allied nations with word of the treaty and requests for them to bring their prisoners to Montreal next August. Although he did not express it outwardly, inwardly he was wracked by serious reservations. The current agreement was a fragile commodity. Any of a dozen things could undo it before it had a chance to take hold. An attack on the Iroquois by one of his allies who had not yet received word of the treaty, refusal of one or more of these tribes to release their prisoners, interference or nonparticipation by a tribe over which the French had little or no influence, or meddling by the English were but a few of the possibilities.

As it turned out, several of these incidents occurred, but in general his allies were as interested in peace as the Iroquois. One of the major points that threatened the process was reluctance on the part of Callières allies to return prisoners that had now been adopted into their tribes. The same issue, which taxed the efforts of the French emissaries, existed within the Iroquois ranks, but in the end, it was not enough to undermine the general effort. For the sake of the agreement all sides eventually concluded that they would only see a small number of their captives actually returned. Even the continued efforts on the part of the English fell short of swaying the Five Nations' resolve, except for the Mohawk, who, although they would sign the peace treaty after the fact, would remain firmly entrenched in the English camp.[13]

In late July 1701 the various native delegations began to assemble at Montreal. The Iroquois mission at Sault St. Louis was the first stop for many of these, as each came ashore here to announce their intentions and pay their respects. With these matters settled long strings of canoes made their way down river to the western French capital. The town's cannon announced each arrival and were quickly answered by jubilant shouts and

Governor Hector Callières. A skilled diplomat and negotiator, Callières would accomplish what was thought nearly impossible: a general peace treaty between the Iroquois and the French and their allies. (*Archives Nationales du Québec*)

salutes of scattered musket fire. Within a few days Montreal was transformed into a fair-like atmosphere. Festivals, feasting, and trading became the order of the day as over 1,300 native emissaries and their entourages swarmed about the shops and open markets, mingling and bartering with the inhabitants. Callières and his council were nearly overwhelmed. Each nation was greeted personally by the governor, and dozens of private audiences were held to see to last-minute issues or assure a delegate that his nation's concerns would be addressed.

The private and public preliminaries dispensed with on August 4 a general assembly was held to ratify the treaty. Ottawa, Abenaki, Potawatomi, Nipissing, Fox, Huron, Miami—thirty-eight nations in all comprising the allies of New France and the four western Iroquois cantons— assembled on an open field just outside of the town. Flanked by blue-clad soldiers, his principal officers, Jesuit missionaries, and the ranking citizenry of the colony, Callières stood upon a small wooden podium at the head of this congress and gave his opening remarks. It was a more formal restatement of the terms agreed to the previous September and only took a few minutes to deliver. There was a delay as the various interpreters translated the speech into a dozen native tongues, followed by a scattered applause, which slowly heightened to a stirring crescendo as the translators finished their renditions one by one. Wampum belts were distributed to the chiefs of each nation, and then one by one each took center stage to deliver their orations and to return the captives they had brought with them. When this was complete, the formal treaty was brought forward, to which each of the native representatives affixed their pictographs before Callières concluded the document with his signature.[14]

In a little over a few days, what was once thought to be impossible had become a reality. Peace now existed between the Five Nations, New France, and her multitude of allies. It was an incredible achievement, particularly in the way of commitment and patience on the part of Callières and his emissaries, both French and native, to reconcile the differences between the Iroquois and so many of his allies. This is not to say that the Treaty of Montreal solved every issue. It certainly did not. Individual warriors of the Iroquois Confederacy, particularly among the Mohawk, would take up arms again against New France and her allies, and in the following years the Confederacy would briefly suspend the treaty, but by and large the Five Nations as a whole would remain neutral until the closing years of the French colony. Beyond the obvious cessation of hostilities, the treaty was also a major success for New France in two other areas. First, it left the Iroquois Confederacy strong enough to act as a barrier to the trade ambitions of Albany. English efforts to establish a direct link to the Great Lakes nations were thwarted by the Five Nations, guaranteeing that the high-country fur trade would be channeled through Montreal. Secondly, and perhaps more important, the treaty had deprived the English colonies of their most active ally and exposed much of their frontier. For all involved this translated into one thing: New France had suddenly leveled the odds against its much larger adversary.

CHAPTER FOUR

# The Treaty of Casco

UPON THE DEATH OF THE EARL OF BELLOMONT in the spring of 1701 the various lieutenant governors assumed control of their respective colonies. For New York this presented a problem given that Lt. Governor Nanfan was in Barbados and not expected to return for several months. In the assembly the anti-Leislerian party and the Fletcherites were split on how to proceed, with one side claiming that the senior council member now acted as lieutenant governor, while the other side claimed that a simple majority of the council decided all matters. To complicate things Bellomont had called the assembly into session in April. Again, there was a divide as to whether or not the session would be legal without an executive. Another subset of representatives went even further, claiming that the assembly was dissolved upon Bellomont's death, but this group soon dispersed when their leader was expelled. Each side pleaded their case to England and little was accomplished. At least there was enough agreement among the vying political parties to pay for the troops garrisoned along the New York frontier. The House ordered the monies raised as well as a sum to reimburse a pair of council members who had paid for the garrison's subsistence out of their private accounts for several weeks. There was concern expressed for the fortifications of the colony, particularly on the Albany frontier, but given the deepening stalemate and uncertain legal ground upon which the representatives found themselves, the only other thing agreed upon was to suspend the session until Nanfan returned.[1]

Robert Livingston, who was embroiled in the current political disputes, penned a long letter to the Board of Trade about the current state of New York. Livingston's foremost concern was the safety of the colony. Part of this addressed the need for a more unified approach to defense. The current system was clearly deficient. The forts throughout the colony were in ruins and the troops that garrisoned them in an even worse state. Lack of clothing, supplies, and munitions had taken a toll. Certainly, illness played a part and the recent war claimed its share as well, but the bulk of the deficiency in the independent companies could be attributed to desertion. With large deductions taken from their pay, coupled with the high cost of goods in the colonies and a broken logistical system that left their pay months in arrears, many chose desertion over starvation.

To rectify these issues Livingston laid down a series of recommendations that ranged from raising troops in England every two years and awarding the soldiers large land grants, to manners in which to pay for these troops and new fortifications. To supplement these efforts, he laid out provisions for a more centralized command system that divided the current colonies into three large colonies all led by governors with military training. Perhaps the most important idea Livingston put forward called for the construction of several forts along the New York frontier closer to the Iroquois, so "that his Majesty's subjects be encouraged to extend their settlements into the Country, under cover of said forts, by the liberty of the Indian trade, without being imposed upon by the City of Albany or any other town or City." Trade with the Iroquois would help sustain these towns, which in turn would be in position to support the Five Nations in the event of a rupture with the French. The problem, however, was Albany. The prominent denizens involved in the lucrative Indian trade had no desire to see it taken away and, as such, had "always practis'd to hinder such settlements."[2]

In the end, Livingston correctly pointed out that the most important step that could be taken to protect the colony was to secure the allegiance of the Five Nations. This would not prove easy. The French had exerted a great deal of pressure on the Iroquois to seek a separate peace and seemed to be making serious inroads along these lines. Much of this stemmed from the belief that the English had not done enough to support the Five Nations in the recent conflict and had shown a lack of commitment toward pursuing victory. The Iroquois sachems complained that the English did not unite a large force to "drive that handfull of French in Canada into the sea," and when this did not occur, "for leaving them in the extremity to shift for themselves, with the little help given them from Albany, by which means they have been spent and wasted with a tedious long warr, which a united force

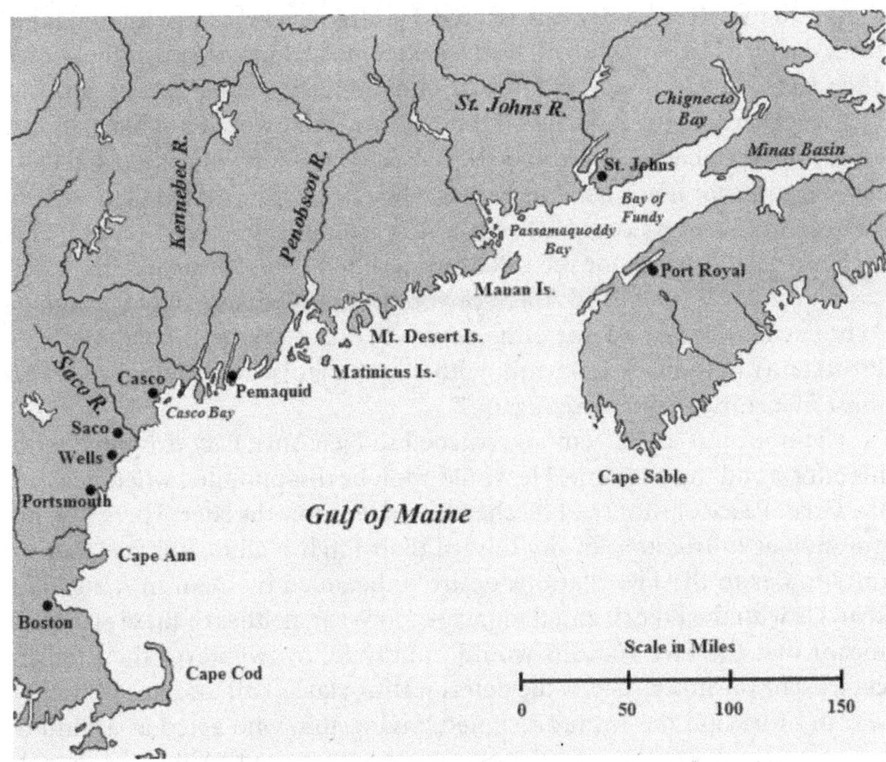


The coast of New England and Acadia (Nova Scotia) from Boston to Port Royal.

could have made an end of at one push." These resentments and the intrigues of the French would have to be neutralized or disaster awaited. If the Iroquois changed allegiance or even if they just let the French Indians pass freely through their country, then not only New York but sparsely populated Maryland and Virginia were at risk. Neither situation could be allowed to happen.[3]

It would not be until May 19 that the lieutenant governor arrived from Barbados. Nanfan agreed with Livingston about the dilapidated forts across the colony, the status of the independent companies, and foremost about the delicate state of the Anglo-Iroquois alliance. He quickly dissolved the current assembly and ordered a new session to convene on August 1. He then dispatched messengers to the Iroquois castles calling on the sachems to meet him in Albany in early July.

The new governor met with the Five Nations representatives on July 10, 1701. The two parties held talks over the next nine days. Nanfan reported that the Iroquois and the English had renewed the Covenant Chain between them and that their loyalty was assured. He also secured a large tract of land from the Five Nations who, in the deed, accepted King William as their lord and master. In addition to this, the Iroquois agreed to abide by Nanfan's directives regarding the French and their agents. They would not listen to the governor of Canada, nor would they allow any Jesuits into their villages. For the governor it was good news, but when he later suggested that English protestant ministers could be sent to the Iroquois, he met a rebuff. The sachems thanked him for the offer but declined. "As soon as wee have occasion for any wee shall ask them of you brother Corlaer," they explained. "The cause why wee ask for none now is because you both [Catholic and Protestant] have made us drunk with all your noise of praying, and wee must first come to our selves again."[4]

The ministers aside, Nanfan returned to New York City delighted with his efforts and the outcome. He would soon be disappointed when news of the Great Peace of Montreal reached him a few months later. There was no question as to Iroquois loyalty toward their English allies, nor was there a question as to the Five Nations desire to be aided by them in their long struggle with the French and their allies. However, neither of these attitudes meant that the Five Nations would blindly follow whatever the English claimed or promised. Given the deteriorating state of affairs, a peace treaty was in order and the Iroquois signed. Livingston, who acted as an interpreter and envoy to the Five Nations, was not surprised. "Altho' the French Governours are pleas'd to call their Indians, subjects of the French King, and our Governours in like manner call the Indians of the Five Nations Subjects of the Crown of England," he wrote the Board of Trade, "they do not so understand it, but look upon themselves in the state of freedom."[5]

To the north Lt. Governor William Stoughton took the reins of Massachusetts upon Bellomont's death. Stoughton had seen the colony through the final years of King William's War as acting governor after the death of Sir William Phipps in the fall of 1694. He was seventy years old and in poor health when the news arrived, but he assured London that all was quiet due to the prudence of his previous administration.

While little was accomplished by the reluctant lieutenant governor, one of the few issues the elderly statesman did address in his second term was the poor state of the colony's defenses. Not long after his appointment a letter arrived from the king. While addressed to Bellomont, the letter concerned Massachusetts. Many of the letters written by Bellomont concerning the colony had been supplemented by Romer's correspondence with the master of the ordnance, Lord Romney, who reported directly to the king. The result was a royal criticism of Massachusetts's part in King William's

War as well as its current attitude toward its own defense. Why had Fort Pemiquid, the anchor for several forts along the Maine coast, been "shamefully taken and demolished by an inconsiderable number of French and Indians," the king asked. And more importantly, why had it not been rebuilt? More was expected from the wealthiest and most populace colony in America. The king ordered Bellomont to go to Massachusetts and "signify unto our Council and the General Assembly of our said Province, that we are sensible of their neglect in not providing more effectually for their own security." The royal rebuke continued with orders to build and repair whatever forts were necessary for the safeguarding of the frontier. The Bay Colony was also directed to assist in the defense of the colony of New Hampshire as well as raise troops and money to come to the aid of New York as well.[6]

Stoughton and the assembly responded to these directives by raising money for the repair of the forts at Salem and Marblehead and for the building of a new fort on Castle Island. As to a new fort at Pemiquid, the governor informed London that the general consensus was that a fort at this location would do little to prevent the Wabanaki from attacking the frontier, and as such, no support could be found to raise funds for such an effort. As it stood the governor lamented that it would be difficult enough to convince the assembly to provide aid to New Hampshire, because of the extremely impoverished state of the colony after the ravages of King William's War.[7]

To address the defense of Boston Harbor Stoughton and the assembly turned to Colonel Romer who had previously surveyed the fort at Castle Island. Romer had concluded that the fort at this strategic location badly needed replacing with a more capable structure, and to this end he had started on a set of plans. With rumors of a rupture with France complementing the royal directive, the Massachusetts government quickly approved the project and set the Royal Engineer to work on what would become one of the strongest coastal fortifications in North America, Castle William.

One of the other defensive measures undertaken by Stoughton's government was a reaffirmation of the peace treaty with the Wabanaki Confederacy. In pursuit of this goal Massachusetts representatives met with Sagamores from the different Wabanaki tribes at Casco on June 3, 1701. While there was a consensus to maintain the peace, the Wabanaki rejected the English offer of protection and the idea that they must stop all travel to and from Canada in the event of a conflict. Addressing this last point, the Wabanaki spokesman noted that it was not practical given that "many amongst us care not to be deprived of the liberty of going whither they please." The chieftains agreed not to fly the French flag but showed no interest in giving up their Catholic faith or Jesuit missionaries. In the end, the Wabanaki Sagamores professed that if the English trading posts supplied their needs there would be little reason to join the French in the event of a rupture. "We desire to keep ourselves free, and not to be under the command of any party," they informed the Massachusetts representative. With the reaffirmation of the treaty a pair of stone cairns, known as the Two Brothers, was raised at Casco in honor of the agreement.[8]

Stoughton would barely live long enough to hear the good news and see Romer start work on Castle William. On July 7, 1701, the governor died, just a few months after his appointment. The event created a situation similar to that of Nanfan's absence in New York after Bellomont's death, in that the power of the government now fell upon the Massachusetts council. The senior councilor was to take the executive role under such circumstances, but the other twenty-seven councilors were not so quick to give up their powers to the eldest member and insisted on a majority vote for any major matter including military affairs. George Larkin, who had been sent by the Board of Trade to report on the state of the colonies, was astonished by the conduct of the Massachusetts government. It seemed little was getting done and what proceedings that were taking place appeared "very arbitrary and irregular." He then informed London that "As to the Laws of England,"

> They abhor the very thought of them, and Acts of Parliament they look upon to be only obligatory wherein the Province is particularly named, though they will make use of either of them to serve a friend, so that no one can tell what is Law and what is not, and there is little better to be expected until the Parliament shall think fit to take away this Charter, and H.M. shall be graciously pleased to send Judges of his own. There is not a gentleman that comes here upon any service for H.M., but what is really obnoxious to the people of the Country; they hate the very thought of a King or King by Government, and it is fear'd if some care be not taken for asserting H.M. power and right here and putting his orders in execution, they will in a short time set up a Government themselves.[9]

Matters regarding the leadership of both Massachusetts and New York were soon to change. When news of Bellomont's death reached England, it was decided not to appoint a successor but to instead separate the governments of New York and New England. Colonel Joseph Dudley, a former councilman in Governor Edmund Andros's deeply unpopular and short-lived Dominion of New England, was appointed governor of Massachusetts

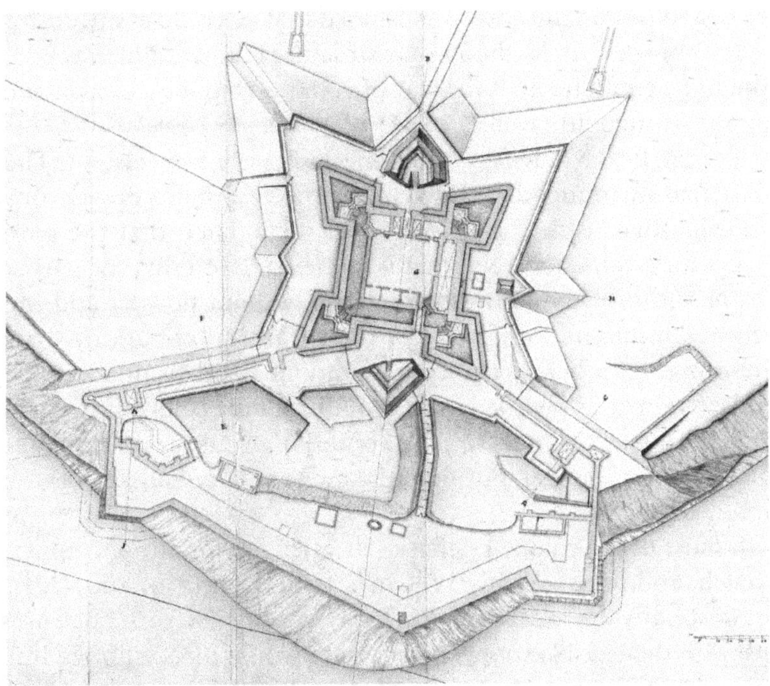

A plan of Castle William, 1705, by Wolfgang Romer. The fortress took Romer nearly five years to complete, but when finished it guarded the entrance to Boston until the departing British forces demolished the structure in 1776. (*Boston Public Library*)

and New Hampshire, while Edward Hyde, the Viscount Cornbury and a relative of the recently deceased queen, was appointed governor of New York and New Jersey.

While neither governor arrived at their post in 1701, Cornbury reached America first, dropping anchor in upper New York Harbor on May 3, 1702. For the first few months after his arrival the new governor spent a considerable amount of time surveying the defenses of the colony. What he found was depressing. When he reviewed the two independent companies at New York City, he found them nearly naked for want of clothing and with arms so bad that only twenty-seven were "fit to fire." Fort William Henry on the south tip of Manhattan was in ruins. The parapets were falling down and the artillery, what little that could actually be mounted for lack of carriages, was covered in rust. At Albany, where the other two independent companies were stationed, the situation was far worse. The troops there were also in a near-naked state, their arms unserviceable, and their pay eight weeks in arrears. Fort Albany, a stockade structure some 120 feet by 70 feet in size, was in such disrepair that the governor claimed that he could easily push down the walls by himself, and although the structure boasted some twenty-three cannon, none could be fired for fear of endangering the garrison and collapsing the stronghold's walls.

Farther north the defenses of Schenectady were nonexistent. The palisade that had surrounded the town had completely fallen down from neglect and the fort inside the town was so dilapidated that the governor mistook it for a cattle pen. Not that it mattered, given that the garrison of a sergeant and twelve men was completely without powder and shot for both their cannons and muskets. A fort at Half Moon built by Governor Fletcher some years before had been abandoned and eventually collapsed under the strain of its own weight. The militia of the colony proved no better. That of Albany was in reasonable condition primarily due to the efforts of Colonel Peter Schuyler, but that of New York City had not been called out in several years.[10]

With most of the colony's defenses ill-prepared for any encounter with the French, and news of King William's death having arrived, Cornbury sought to solidify the most important element of New York's defenses, the alliance with the Five Nations. The governor would meet with the Iroquois sachems and the River Indians in Albany on July 9. Here he heard that the Five Nations had been told by the governor of Canada that war between the French and English was imminent and that the Iroquois should abide by the Treaty of Montreal and remain neutral. From their words and actions, it was clear to Cornbury that this was the path the Iroquois would take, particularly the Seneca, Cayuga, and Onondaga upon whom much of the wrath of New France and its allies had fallen upon. Given the state of the colony's defenses and the attitude of the Iroquois, Cornbury asked the Five Nations not to disturb the peace but made it clear that if the French attacked either of them that both sides would unite to destroy the enemy. The sachems of the various tribes nodded in agreement. They agreed not to take up the hatchet first, but as to the unified front against a French incursion they were more reserved, pointing out that "we have had but little assistance from our Brethren during ye late war, we have been forced to wage war alone & lost many of our people but see none of our brethren either to assist us or to revenge the blood of those we had lost by ye French." The best Cornbury could obtain was that the Iroquois would consult with him under such circumstances before they decided upon the best course of action.

Combined with news that England was now at war with France and Spain, the sum toll was too much for New York. Until the Iroquois could

Governor Joseph Dudley. A member of a prominent Massachusetts family Dudley was viewed with skepticism due to his previous association with Governor Edmund Andros and the short-lived Dominion of New England and New York. While his tenure was not without difficulties, he surprised many of his critics by dismissing past greviences and successfully guided the colony through Queen Anne's War. (*Boston Public Library*)

be convinced to break their neutrality, the governor was resolved to do nothing to provoke the French. The frontier posts would be manned as best as could be, and new forts at New York City, Albany, and Schenectady would be built. Meanwhile, Cornbury would have to satisfy himself with penning letters to England calling for a combined land-sea attack on Canada. Little did he realize that the Iroquois had once again ensured the safety of the colony. The Five Nations were not interested in siding with anyone, and New France was not interested jeopardizing the Treaty of Montreal by upsetting Iroquois neutrality. Given this, there were no French plans to attack the New York frontier.[11]

The new governor of Massachusetts and New Hampshire, Colonel Dudley, would not reach Boston until June 11, 1702, almost a year after being appointed. The son of one of the Puritan founders of the colony, he was viewed by many as a double-edged sword. His association with Governor Andros during the establishment of the Dominion of New England, which stripped the colony of its original charter, would forever cast him as a totalitarian. On the other hand, he was a native, loved his homeland, and unlike many who sought such positions, possessed real talent. There was also the delicate matter of Andros's and Dudley's jailing during the Glorious Revolution. Many of the senior councilmen that he would have to work with were involved in this event and feared that the new governor would seek retribution. "As for the old Revolution pillars among us," one citizen wrote of the situation, "they begin to shake and tremble at the news of Col. Dudley's coming as Governor, and some of our little justices (I hear) with eyes lifted up cry Poor New England hath seen its best days."[12]

While rumors circulated that the new governor's landing would be opposed, nothing came of it. The Massachusetts native was delighted to be back home and was surprised by the cordial reception, expecting a more somber greeting given what had transpired in the past. The governor, however, then did something to diffuse any old grudges by speaking to a general amnesty without being solicited. Even Dudley's life-long critics commended the action, which was seen by all as a mark of leadership and a sincere desire to unify the colony.

Dudley had only been in Boston for a few weeks when news arrived in early July that war had broken out in Europe. Louis XIV's efforts to place his grandson on the vacant throne of Spain and his recognition of the deposed James II's son as rightful ruler of England had reignited the animosities of old, pitting France and Spain in a war against the Holy Roman Empire, the Dutch, and the English in what would become known as the War of Spanish Succession in Europe, or Queen Anne's War in North America.[13]

Much as it did in New York, news of war sent a shiver though the colony. Like New York the defenses of Massachusetts and New Hampshire were deeply suspect. A number of forts had been commissioned and built after William's letter to the colony, and more were on the way, but at the moment it was a work in progress. Munitions and funds were in short supply and key locations along the coast were still vulnerable. More importantly, unlike New York, there was no Iroquois buffer on the New England frontier to help protect the colony. Fortunately, relations between the Wabanaki Confederacy, who occupied much of Maine and Nova Scotia, had remained peaceful. Although war now existed between France and England, the peace treaty between New England and the Wabanaki Confederacy was still intact. Realizing the need to reinforce this treaty against French intrigue Dudley proposed a meeting with the Wabanaki chieftains in late July 1702. It would be an opportunity for both sides to pledge their commitment toward maintaining the agreement and to address any issues or grievances that might have appeared.

The governor's proposal found a receptive audience, and on July 27, 1702, after having toured the ruins of Fort Pemiquid and deciding that rebuilding the stronghold was not practical, he and his councilors met with Moxus and eight other Wabanaki chieftains at the outlet of the Kennebec

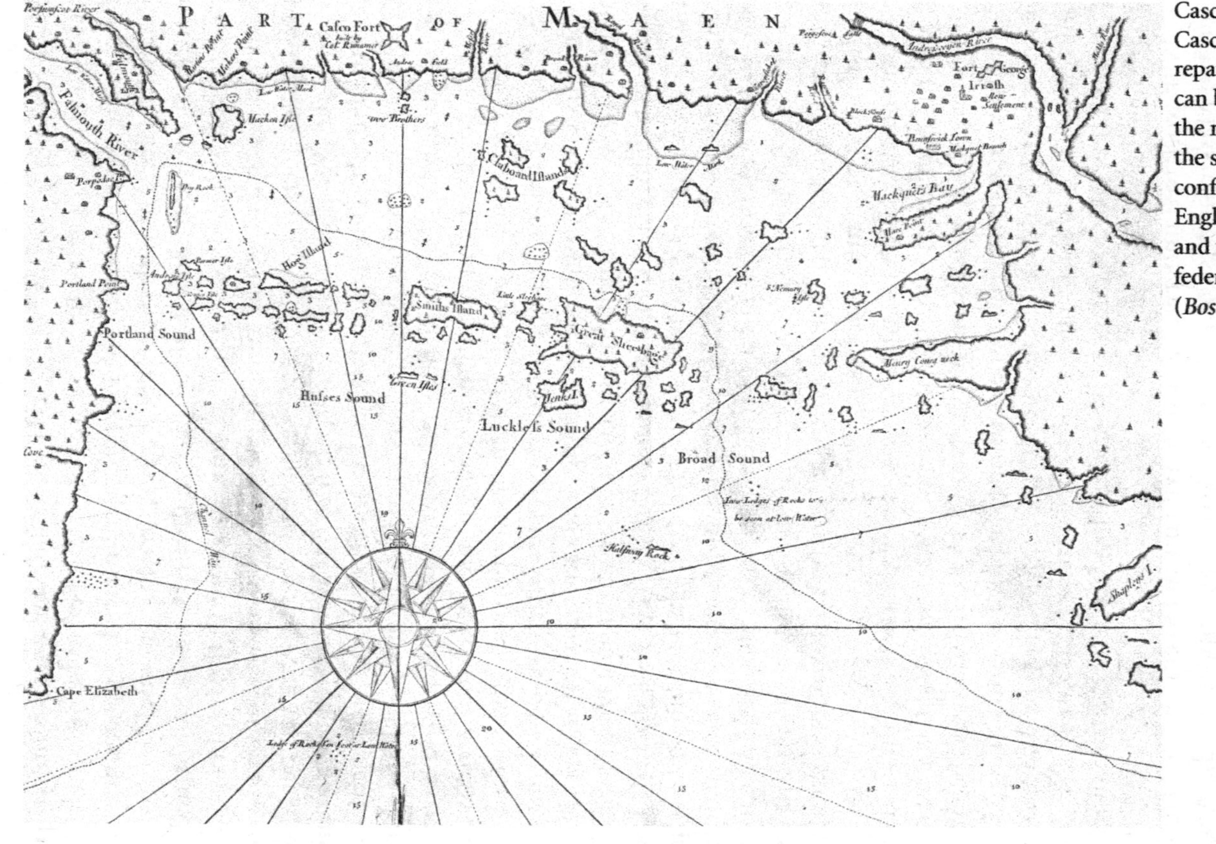


Casco Bay, Maine, c. 1720. Casco Fort, which Romer repaired and expanded, can be seen at the top of the map. The location was the site of a series of peace conferences between New England representatives and the Wabanaki Confederacy. (*Boston Public Library*)

River. Surrounded by his blue-coated guard and well over a hundred Wabanaki warriors in a dazzling array of colors, Dudley welcomed the chieftains in the name of peace. The governor pronounced to his counterparts that he was content with the treaty, and to show this, he would stop on his return at Casco and add a stone to the Two Brothers. He then informed the Wabanaki that he would continue to provide goods to the trading posts at Saco and Casco and would make sure that these goods were always in supply. Dudley then proposed a key element to maintaining the peace. He warned the Wabanaki sagamores that there was war between the English and the French. This meant that French and Indian war parties could be expected on the frontier. Most settlers would not be able to tell the differences between the Wabanaki and the French Indians, so to avoid any accidents the governor proposed that they stay to the east of the Saco River.

There was a chorus of nods and shouts of approval. Moxus stood and responded, thanking Dudley for his proposals, which were what the Wabanaki had sought. While their hunting lands stretched into New Hampshire in the west, the chieftains agreed to the wisdom of staying east of the river, particularly if the English trading houses were well stocked. There were some complaints regarding the price of English trade goods, which Dudley promised to look at, but in general, both sides agreed to maintain the treaty. "We will stand fast and true in our Covenants made," Moxus announced to the governor. Dudley was satisfied with the outcome as well, informing London that "Nothing but the French Priests amongst them will put them out of temper towards us."[14]

Thus far even Dudley's critics were pleased with how the colony had navigated the opening months of Queen Anne's War. Beyond a few privateers and some isolated incidents along the Nova Scotia coast there had been little in the way of activity. The same could be said for New York. The Albany frontier, which had been decimated during King William's War, remained quiet. It was an odd start to the conflict but one that both Dudley and Cornbury sought to take advantage of by accelerating their efforts to rebuild their crumbling defenses.

With work well underway on Castle William, in December 1702 Dudley and the Massachusetts council received continued support of the Anglo-Wabanaki treaty from a host of Wabanaki sagamores. Even so, the governor, along with many on the frontier, expected the Wabanaki to rise up in the spring. Elements of the militia were called out and the forts and garrison houses manned and supplied. Yet all appeared well, at least until April when an English privateer went ashore at Penobscot and a skirmish broke out leading to casualties on both sides. Dudley, expecting the Wabanaki to retaliate, sent a pair of militia companies to bolster the posts on the Maine frontier and passed word for the rest of the militia to stand in readiness, but surprisingly, nothing came of the event.

In June the governor sent word that he wished to meet with the Wabanaki at Casco to continue the dialogue between the two parties and affirm the ongoing treaty. The Wabanaki agreed, and on the morning of June 20, 1703, the area about the small wooden fort at Casco teemed with activity and fanfare. Beneath a series of tents, the meeting between the Massachusetts delegates and the Wabanaki sagamores convened, while 250 Wabanaki warriors tended to their nearby campfires or circled closer in hopes of gleaning something from the proceedings. The meeting went smoothly. Gifts were exchanged and small grievances addressed. The Wabanaki quickly made their intentions clear when they told Dudley that they would place another stone on the Two Brothers. They then announced to the governor that "they aimed at nothing more than peace." Dudley questioned the sagamores as to reports that French Jesuits had visited the tribes looking to undermine the treaty. The chieftains acknowledged that the Jesuits had indeed visited their villages but shrugged and said that they "had made no Impression on them, for that they were as firm as the Mountains and should continue so, as long as the Sun and Moon endured."[15]

Both sides appeared satisfied from what they heard, and after the traditional closing celebrations, the meeting broke up. Dudley was delighted with the results, writing the Board of Trade that the conference had concluded with "a better friendship with them than any other meeting." It appeared to all that the governor had once again secured the New England frontier, but some like Samuel Penhallow, were not so sure. Penhallow noted that when both sides fired an honorary salute at the end of negotiations, unlike the English, the Wabanaki guns were "charg'd with bullets."[16]

CHAPTER FIVE

# The Path to War

In the summer of 1702, a year after the Great Peace Treaty was signed, dozens of canoes pulled ashore at Montreal. Aboard were ambassadors from the Iroquois nations, including seven from the Mohawk who had refused to participate in previous years' negotiations. Governor Callières, who had been expecting the delegation, met the representatives with the fanfare and festivities that were customary under such occasions. The sachems speaking for the Seneca, Oneida, Onondaga, and Cayuga pledged their commitment to the treaty, and to Callières's satisfaction, the Mohawk representatives agreed to abide by the terms of the agreement as well. When the governor asked the representatives if they were going to side with the English now that news of war between France and England had arrived, he found they were not interested in siding with anyone. The Five Nations, in general, wished to preserve their neutrality so as to be able to hunt in peace and trade with both Albany and Montreal.

In pursuit of this policy of neutrality the sachems asked Callières "for some Jesuits as Missionaries to their Villages, and some Smiths to repair their arms, hatchets, and kettles." The governor had been hoping for just such an opportunity, and the fact that the Iroquois had broached the subject first delighted him even more. Wasting no time, he dispatched Father Jacques de Lamberville, one of his assistants, and a blacksmith to the Onondaga villages, while Fathers Julien Gamier and Francois Vaillant and a small party under Captain Maricourt departed for the Seneca homeland. Certainly, the prospect of Christian conversions motived the Jesuits; after all, the Iroquois missions at La Prairie, or Caughnawaga as it was known by the Iroquois, and that of the Lake of Two Mountains outside of Montreal demonstrated that such efforts could yield results. There was, however, far more to the appointment than this. Living among the Iroquois the Black Robes would become a respected voice for peace and maintaining Iroquois neutrality, while at the same time acting as a counterbalance to English intrigues. Of course, the missionaries would also provide Callières with a steady flow of information, which was perhaps the most important element as far as the governor was concerned.

As for the Iroquois, the Jesuits were simply another step in their shifting philosophy toward the French and English colonies. As Callières noted in his impressions of the meeting, they were indeed sincere in their quest for neutrality. The result of King William's War had been a realization that occupying a position between two warring colonies, both larger and more powerful than themselves, dictated such a path to ensure their survival. If this meant accepting Jesuit missionaries or Protestant ministers in their villages, so be it. As one Iroquois sachem noted, an adopted denomination was more a function of which side offered the best trade arrangements than anything else.[1]

While matters regarding the Iroquois had gone well, several other problems required the governor's attention. The first of these concerned the Great Lakes region, or the "high country," as it was called by the French. Several allied tribes in the area had become embroiled in a conflict with the powerful Sioux nation to the west. Callières feared that the war would expand and draw in other tribes, eventually destabilizing the frontier in the process. Were this not enough, there was the continuing struggle to reign in the *coureurs de bois*. Hundreds of these hardy and adventurous fur traders operated on the frontier, often living among the various tribes and in the process becoming *de facto* French ambassadors. While this was useful when it came to the defense of the colony, for years efforts had been put in place to discourage the practice, as it had the net effect of draining the colony of its manpower and resources. The goal had been to consolidate the French colony along the banks of the St. Lawrence, as well as to regulate the fur trade through a handful of posts for economic and logistical reasons, but with the lure of the profits to be made the *coureurs de bois* had continued to grow in both number and the extent of their activities. To counter this expansion previous policies had ranged from arrest and confiscation to issued licenses and specific trading locations, but it had achieved little.

Callières wrote the court that the current policy toward these adventurers was self-defeating. Whether branded outlaw or not, these men would always exist and would always choose this path for themselves, making the suppression of their activities not only incredibly difficult but likely to the detriment of French and Indian relations. More importantly, the connections to the French allied tribes of the region through these individuals simply could not be abandoned at this point, even if it were possible, for fear of creating a power vacuum that the English would quickly exploit. A balance was needed, not to eliminate these men but to better regulate their activities and prevent their trading with the English.[2]

It was a sound policy that Louis's ministers would take a step further. With another war before France considerations toward securing French claims in North America, which included the fledgling colony of Louisiana, and supporting Spanish titles in the region came to the forefront. The goal here was not the commercial profit or resources to be drawn from such lands but the nature of the claims and its byproduct. From the foundation of the colony French claims had followed a watershed principle, which made sense given the growth of the colony along these natural navigation routes. Thus, claiming the St. Lawrence, the Great Lakes, and the Mississippi Valley not only through discovery but occupation as well, would have the net effect of confining the English colonies to the east of the Appalachian Mountains and to the south by Spanish Florida and French Louisiana.

It was a policy that Louis naturally approved of, first because it hurt England and second because it mimicked his imperial efforts in Europe. The real question, however, was how to enforce these claims. To make such declarations and draw them on a map was one thing, but to secure them from the far more numerous English was another matter. It was here, in Callières's comments on the *coureurs de bois*, that an opportunity presented itself to accomplish this task. These men who had been viewed as renegades and outlaws for almost a half century were now to be bold agents of the king's ambitions. Their economic activities were now to be subordinate to their relations with the various tribes along with the lengths of these claims. The Jesuits would follow after this vanguard, and together the two groups would work to create a ring of native alliances—a force more than capable of impeding any English expansion efforts.[3]

It was an interesting solution that played upon many elements that Callières and others had previously mentioned. What better emissaries than those who spoke the local language and lived its tenants by choice? These individuals would often marry into the tribe, and in many cases, they and their offspring would even rise to leadership positions. While some of the

English, such as Peter Schuyler and Robert Livingston understood the effects of such an approach, many at the time underestimated its impact. Yet the answer seemed simple when viewed from almost any angle. As a member of a native tribe, were you going to listen to English claims or the words of a fellow tribesman that you have known for years and had fought by your side against your enemies? Such bonds are difficult to break in any culture and, if executed correctly on the part of the French, would imperil the entire English frontier.

This is not to say that the change in approach toward the role of the *coureurs de bois* and its application did not have risks; it had several. First, it was a vast amount of territory, and the few resources Canada and Louisiana possessed could not possibly be of much help. Second, it had the potential to embroil the French in regional conflicts and other entanglements, which would also sap their meager resources. Lastly, it still had the net effect of draining the strength of the core colony along the St. Lawrence, which was already vulnerable.

Callières's next problem was a disturbing report from Montreal. In June 1702 an Iroquois from Albany reported that an English fleet had departed Boston and was on its way to Quebec. A delegation of Wabanaki chieftains led by Jesuit Father Pierre de La Chasse arrived shortly thereafter and confirmed the news of a fleet fitting out in Boston, but he did not know where it was headed. The governor dispatched scouts down the St. Lawrence and readied the militia. He then ordered the troops in Montreal to Quebec and set to work improving the city's outer defenses.

As for the arriving Wabanaki delegation, Callières listened as the spokesman informed him of their meeting and the treaty with Governor Dudley. The New Englanders offered trade goods at low prices and did not seem to run out like the French sometimes did. Now that war had been declared against the English, the Wabanki spokesman asked if the governor wished for them to take up the hatchet and break off trade with New England? And if so, what means did he "possess to supply their wants at a reasonable price?" Callières nodded as La Chasse translated the last of the chieftain's question and promised the delegation that he would draw on the merchants of Quebec to furnish them. It did not prove as convincing an argument as Dudley's, and the Wabanaki mood shifted toward neutrality. The governor then asked the chieftains if they would come to the defense of Quebec if the English attacked. In response the Wabanki chieftains orated and spoke in circles for hours with the refined ambiguity that would have elicited a nod from any member of English parliament. Eventually, Callières wore them down and discovered that they would begrudgingly come to the defense of Quebec, not because of any great love for the French cause but more from "apprehension that should the English, whom they distrust, succeed in seizing that city, they might lose the aid they derived from us, and be destroyed in the end." When the conference ended it appeared to the governor that the Wabanaki might take the path of the Iroquois or, at the very least, were skeptical allies.[4]

The attack on Quebec never materialized, but one aimed at the French colonies in Newfoundland did move forward. Captain John Leake set sail from Plymouth, England, with a small fleet on July 23, 1702, and by late August arrived at St. John's. Leake would spend the next few months working on the defenses of St. John's and the nearby English holdings while harassing French shipping along the island's coast. He briefly bombarded the French defenses at Placentia but found the colony too well defended to risk an assault and contented himself with capturing close to thirty French vessels before returning to England in late October.[5]

For Callières, short on men and supplies, the fall of 1702 and coming winter were spent working on the fortifications of Quebec. Rumors of English overtures toward Port Royal and Placentia worried the governor, but there was little he could do to help. The Wabanaki appeared intent to continue the treaty they had signed with New England, and any thoughts of falling upon the weak New York frontier were put aside for fear of provoking the Iroquois to join the English cause. Given the circumstances Callières was reluctant to break the peace, believing that it would not benefit the colony, but even so, he formulated a plan to strike at the English, just in case the king wished "to attempt greater things by sea against Boston, or Manathe (Manhattan)."[6]

Callières would not live to see any English effort against the colony. In late May 1703 he suffered a stroke while attending mass and a few days later, on May 26, died at his home. His loss was a major blow for New France. He had proven an able administrator and a superb diplomat. He had completed Frontenac's early schemes by finding a path to peace with the Five Nations and had proven himself more than capable of navigating the colony down any difficult path. The bells that rang through Quebec and the long lines of mourners that filled the streets demonstrated that he would be sorely missed.[7]

Callières's replacement was Philippe Rigaud de Vaudreuil, the Marquis de Vaudreuil, and the current governor of Montreal. The appointment was temporary, but few doubted that it would be made permanent. Vaudreuil came from a long line of French nobility, and as with two of his brothers, he entered the army at a young age. In 1672 Philippe was given a position in the Musketeers, an elite regiment where the king held the title of colonel. He distinguished himself with this unit during the Dutch War and in the process caught the king's attention. While the Vaudreuil estate was worth a sizable sum, Philippe was the second son of five and in fact was quite poor. Without money to purchase a commission, and with few prospects of advancement, Philippe accepted a posting to Canada in 1687 as commander of the French marines being stationed there. He was acting governor of Montreal when the Iroquois fell upon Lachine in 1689, and his conduct left many to question his abilities to command in New France. Vaudreuil, however, soon proved these critics wrong. He led several wilderness expeditions during King William's War and in 1696 won Governor Frontenac's personal admiration for his "incredible diligence" and efforts against the Iroquois. When Callières replaced Frontenac in 1698, upon the latter's death, the vacant position of governor of Montreal was to be given to Vaudreuil. Now, just as Callières had, Vaudreuil had inherited the governor-generalship of New France.[8]

There was little to question in regard to Vaudreuil's abilities and experience, and even less regarding his valor, which had earned him the coveted Cross of St. Louis from the king. After the minister of the marine spoke in Vaudreuil's favor, Louis approved, and Philippe was made governor. While the choice was the correct one under the circumstances, Vaudreuil, bred a soldier, was more like Frontenac than Callières. The latter had pursued a purely defensive posture for the colony, choosing to work diplomatic circles based on his belief that the English colonies wished to avoid a conflict as well. While this did not necessarily further the glory of the king's arms, it was a prudent path given New France's weakened state.

Vaudreuil was of another mind. He agreed with Callières regarding the Iroquois and avoiding operations in New York, which might invite them to break the peace treaty, and he met with representatives of the Five Nations not long after his appointment, finding them committed to neutrality despite English efforts to seduce them and chase away the Black Robes. When it came to the Wabanaki and New England, however, the new governor's approach differed from his predecessor. Vaudreuil believed that it was vital that the peace treaty between the Wabanaki and New England be brought to an end, even if it meant rupturing the peace. His argument came straight from the Wabanaki's own words to Callières, and their lack of faith in the colony's ability to provide them the goods they needed to survive the conflict. King William's War had taught the confederacy to be leery of French promises. If nothing were done, the expanding trade arrangements between the Wabanaki and New England would leave the former dependent on these goods. Under such circumstance they would likely be seduced away from the French, removing a crucial barrier against English expansion into Maine and Nova Scotia. "I consider it highly necessary to embroil the [Indians] of those parts," Vaudreuil would inform the French court, "otherwise the Abenaquis, who were wavering, might enter into arrangements with the English, and be eventually opposed to us." There was also another important reason behind the approach. If the Wabanaki could not be convinced to attack the New England frontier, this would leave the resources of the most populous and powerful of the English colonies free to be employed in an expedition against Quebec as they had done in the previous conflict.[9]

The answer in Vaudreuil's mind was much along the lines of what Frontenac had proposed. The colony would fight the *petite guerre*, a campaign of raids, ambushes, and small war parties descending on the frontier—a war of terror designed to freeze their opponent and force him to disperse his superior forces in a vain attempt to defend an indefensible frontier. It was cheap and low risk, because it involved only a handful of men per expedition and took advantage of the resources and woodland skills of New France and its allies. However, Vaudreuil faced a problem. If there was to be no conflict along the New York frontier because of the Five Nations, then it was imperative that the Wabanaki be engaged to effectively employ this approach. "The service of the King and the good of the colony require," Vaudreuil wrote the minister of the marine, "that the Abenaki and the English be irreconcilable enemies."[10]

The governor had several tools at his disposal to set his plans into motion. He rightly surmised that many of the Wabanaki were still upset at the English, and letters reaching him from Jesuit Father Sebastien Rale, who presided over a mission in the area, informed him that his flock were "ready to take up the hatchet against the English whenever he [Vaudreuil] gave them the order." Men such as Rale held great sway over their converts and were not immune to the political aspects of their tasks. After all, the embers of the great religious wars pitting Catholic against Protestant had barely cooled, and the feeling on both sides that they were dealing with heretics simply made the task, and the justification for it, that much easier.

To push the Wabanaki into a decision Vaudreuil sent orders to Lt. Alexandre Leneuf de Beaubassin of the colonial marines to organize an expedition against the New England frontier. A veteran of King William's War, the lieutenant lived and traded in Acadia, making him an excellent choice. Beaubassin was able to recruit several hundred Micmac who had been less affected by the last war than their western brothers. He then proceeded to meet with the remaining Wabanaki sagamores to elicit their participation.

Governor Philippe Vaudreuil, the Marquis de Vaudreuil. Cut more in the mold of Frontenac than Callières, Vaudreuil would guide the French colony through Queen Anne's War and would remain governor until his death in 1725. His son Pierre would go on to become the last governor of New France. (*National Archives of Canada*)

In fact, Rale had already been pushing for an attack for weeks. He and those who supported the idea pointed out that the English, who the Wabanaki had expelled from the coast of Maine in the last conflict, were back—some in places where they had not been one before. This had not been agreed upon in the treaty. Their ancestral hunting grounds and their French father's lands were being intruded upon once again. English traders would now come to sell them rum and cheat them as they had before. The English simply could not be trusted. It was the English who had toppled the Two Brothers.

There were plenty who agreed with such arguments, and even the most reluctant among them had to admit that the words were true. When Beaubassin appeared with his force, and the Micmac chieftains with him echoed these sentiments, the more committed among the Wabanaki pledged themselves to the cause. Any hesitation soon dissolved, and within moments the rest followed, setting the stage for the Third Wabanaki War and a repeat along the New England frontier of King William's War's "most mournful decade."[11]

The planned assault would fall upon the recently repopulated Maine frontier from Wells in the south to Falmouth in the north. When his numbers were tallied Beaubassin found himself with close to five hundred Wabanaki and a score of French at his disposal, including Father Rale who happily added his efforts to the expedition. The numbers and element of surprise gave Beaubassin and the Wabanaki chieftains an opportunity to strike a coordinated blow against the English settlements by breaking into smaller parties and launching simultaneous attacks along the frontier. With the plan agreed upon, by the first week of August war parties began to trace their way through the dappled forests of Maine toward the coast.

The evening of August 9, 1703, was no different than those that had proceeded it. The humid summer month and long days meant hard work for the cluster of families in Wells, Maine. The town spread about the King's Road, as the main trek through the village was known, was a rough enclave of subsistence farmers and fishermen. The buildings that dotted the area were no more than three rooms and most were smaller. Barns and accommodations for the livestock held a higher priority than such comforts. It was a quiet frontier town like many others, and although the denizens of this village had successfully navigated King William's War, the diligence that came with this last conflict had long since vanished from their minds.

As August 10 dawned a hundred sets of eyes watched from the woods as the men of the town departed to tend to their fields. One of these men was Thomas Wells. He, however, was not headed for his fields but for a nurse, as his wife was in childbirth. He would not see her or his family again. A war whoop rang out, followed by another and a few shots as a French and Indian war party descended upon Wells's home and his neighbor's, Joseph Sayer. It was quick work as the attackers killed everyone in both homes including several toddlers, who would be too small to survive the grueling wilderness march back to the Wabanaki villages. Both homes were set to the torch and the war party slid back into the shadows searching out its next victim.

This scene was being repeated across the town as more columns of smoke appeared and sporadic shots rang out. Well-known woodsman and tavern keeper Stephen Harding managed to flee with his family to Joseph Storer's palisaded garrison house, but even here he found peril as Storer's eighteen-year-old daughter Mary had been carried off. Many men dashed back from their fields to find their homes engulfed in flames and their families buried in a shroud of ash and embers. Livestock was butchered and flame put to anything that would burn. Then, as quickly as they had appeared, the attackers filtered back into the forest. The raiders had either killed or carried away thirty-nine denizens of the town, mostly women and children. Reinforcements would arrive but far too late to be of any help.[12]

At Saco the morning had started with the crash of musketry and a chorus of war whoops as the French and Wabanaki swept through the settlement outside the old stone fort at the falls. The sudden assault left eleven slain

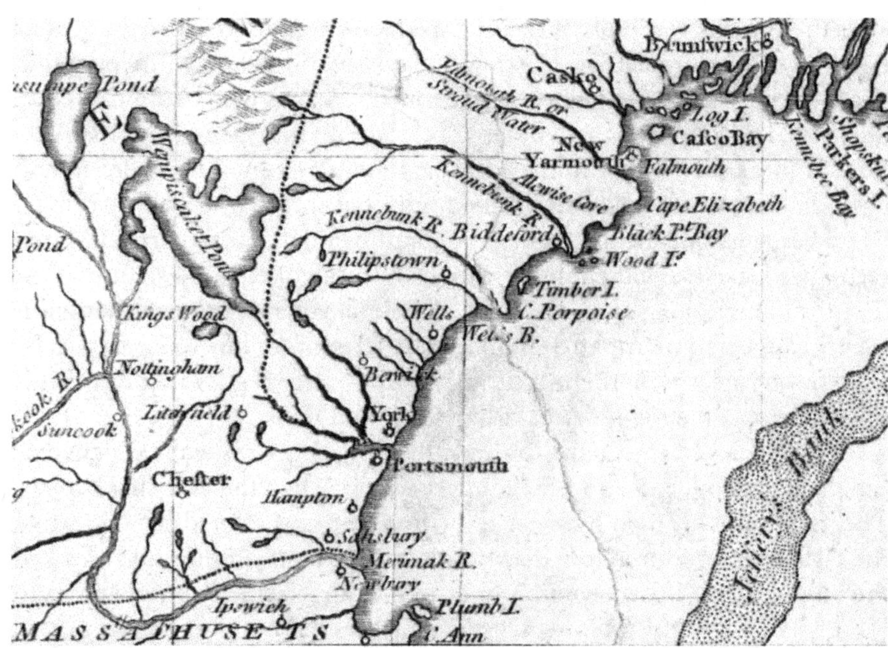


A portion of a 1781 map showing the coast of Maine, New Hampshire, and Massachusetts from Cape Ann to Casco Bay. (*Library of Congress*)

settlers in its wake and another twenty-four taken prisoner. It had also carried the war party to the walls of old Fort Saco where they sniped at the garrison, but making no impression, they soon tired and withdrew with their prizes.

At Spurwink on Cape Elizabeth the surprise was near total and twenty-two settlers, most of the same Jordan family, fell to hatchet and musket. Not far away at Purpooduck the attackers found the men away on their fishing boats. The score or so of inhabitants that could be found were dispatched without fanfare while eight others, all women and children, were led away. The fishing hamlet at Cape Porpoise was overrun as well and, for the second time in its brief existence, completely depopulated. Winter Harbor was attacked and the inhabitants forced to take refuge in Fort Mary from which they repelled the attacks made against them but not before three dozen had fallen before the onslaught. The nearby town of Scarborough proved better prepared and beat off the attacks until relief arrived.[13]

Thus far the French and Wabanaki plan had gone almost perfectly. The last and largest element in the plan was Falmouth on Casco Bay. The old fort at this location had been destroyed early in King William's War and after the conflict was replaced with a wooden palisade structure known as Fort New Casco or just Fort Casco. This four-bastioned structure operated as a trading post and a place of refuge for the citizens who had returned to the town. Here the Wabanaki opted for deception rather than ambush. The fort's commander, Major John March, and his garrison of three dozen had been on alert when a runner notified him that three chieftains carrying a white flag were outside the main gate. Standing on the fort's parapet March recognized the three chieftains as Moxus, Wanongonet, and Escumbuit. At first the commander considered sending an envoy out to meet them, but the trio appeared unarmed and there were no signs of any war party, so he went out to speak with them accompanied by a pair of guards and two elderly citizens of the town named Phippenny and Kent.

The sentries in the guard towers and along the fort's walls watched as the main gate opened and March's party approached the Wabanaki chiefs. The major and his men had just come to a stop and saluted the trio when the sagamores produced tomahawks from under their clothing and attacked the Englishmen. Unarmed and unprepared, both the elderly Phippenny and Kent fell to a few quick blows, but the attackers did not find March as easy a target. A large man noted for his great strength, the major disarmed one of the chieftains and kept the trio at bay with his newly acquired tomahawk. One of March's guards tried to come to his aid but a shot rang out from a nearby ambuscade striking him down.

The unequal contest soon broke up as the Wabanaki retreated at the sight of a squad of soldiers rushing through the main gate toward them. The garrison's quick actions had saved their commander, and now together they manned their posts and braced for the coming storm. However, the French and Indian war party showed little interest other than occasionally sniping at the fort. The nearby town was ransacked and burned, but no serious effort was made to challenge the stronghold. Over the next few days March understood why. Bands of French and Wabanaki began converging on the location. Finally, Beaubassin and his party appeared, bringing the besiegers' numbers to five hundred or so.[14]

The French lieutenant also brought energy and direction to the siege. The harassing fire on the fort was increased, and a captured sloop and a pair of shallops now fired on the water side of the fort. More importantly, a sandy bank along the water side approached close to one of the fort's walls. Using this embankment as shelter Beaubassin set crews to work digging trenches toward the wall. Progress was slow, but after two days the attackers were almost close enough to storm the fort.

For March there were few options. His men were exhausted after being under fire six days and nights, his supplies were failing, and there was nothing he could do to stop the French field works from advancing. If relief did not come in a day, or maybe two, he would be forced to surrender the fort or face annihilation. As it would turn out, March and his garrison would not have to wait long for an answer. The following morning a vessel could be seen entering Casco Bay. The sight caused all to pause and the firing slackened as eyes focused on the distant sail. Speculative whispers and occasional pointing continued until the fifty-foot ketch entered the Casco River and approached the fort. Any doubt was soon dispensed by a thunderous cheer from the fort's ramparts and a groan from Beaubassin.

With the flag of St. George flying from the main mast the commander of the Massachusetts warship *Province Galley*, Captain Cyprian Southack, ordered his gunners to their posts and shifted course to make a pass on the captured French sloop and shallops. The Wabanaki watched, contenting themselves with a few long-range shots at the warship, when suddenly five columns of blue smoke rippled down the side of the ship. A wave of grapeshot and ball quickly convinced those onboard the captured vessels to abandon ownership, but Southack was hardly finished. He next turned his attention to the hundreds of canoes lined upon the shore. Round after round of grapeshot ripped through the fragile craft and served as a deterrent to anyone foolish enough to risk saving their craft. Beaubassin watched, kicking at the ground and shaking his head as the cannon onboard the *Province Galley* slowly asserted control over the area. It was over. With the French works exposed to the warship's guns, and his supplies dwindling, Beaubassin called off the siege. The next day the French and Wabanaki departed, most on foot as some two hundred of their canoes had been destroyed.[15]

The timely relief of Fort Casco was one of the few things to go right for the denizens of the Maine frontier. Seven other towns had been attacked and close to 175 settlers had been taken or killed. Scores of homes had been burned and most of the livestock slain. Relief would come but too late in most cases. Columns of smoke and shattered refugees were all to be found. Apart from Fort Casco, the French and Indian attack had gone as planned. There had been little in the way of casualties among the raiders, and the results of their efforts were clear; the Maine frontier was in shambles and Governor Vaudreuil now had his war.[16]

# Part Two

## *New England and New France*

CHAPTER SIX

# The Frontier in Flames

For the remainder of 1703 matters did not improve for New England. Dudley called out the militia and dispatched four hundred troops to the Maine frontier to bolster the garrisons. A company of dragoons were employed on the King's Road along the coast, a company of infantry sent to Portsmouth, and another six hundred men assembled to strike back against the breach of the peace treaty. To supplement this force, which would place a huge financial burden on the colony, Dudley turned to his neighboring colonies for assistance. He asked Governor Fitz-John Winthrop of Connecticut for two companies and Governor Samuel Cranston of Rhode Island for another. Cranston informed Dudley that there were no men to be spared, while Winthrop, governor of the second-most-populace colony in America, also proved of little help although he did manage to forward a few dozen Mohegan scouts. The agreed upon defensive quota system and the primary purpose of Bellomont's position was already forgotten. "I have written in the most pressing manner to the Governors of Rhode Island and Conecticot for the advance of but 150 men between them," an angry Dudley informed London, "but can obtayn nothing, notwithstanding this Province do's wholly cover and secure them from danger."[1]

The governor of New York, Lord Cornbury, painted a similar picture. A lack of unity had led to disaster in King William's War, but the lessons seemed lost. "I wish they may be more obedient to H.M. than they were the last time," Cornbury informed the Board of Trade, "but I am afraid you will find they will not till they are compelled, either by some Act of the Parliament of England, or by such other method as the Queen will please to make use of, perticularly Connecticut and Rhode Island, from whence I am fully satisfyed we shall not have one farthing from them as long as they can help it." He then urged the queen to issue military quotas for the colonies and appoint a commander over their militias in time of war.[2]

Dudley ordered the women and children withdrawn from the garrisons in Maine and ordered all settlers on the frontier to spend evenings at their local garrison houses. Sporadic attacks continued along the frontier, typically conducted by a few raiders against isolated farmsteads. There was little Dudley could do about such actions, and at the moment, he was more focused on striking back. First, he equipped several sloops to augment the *Province Galley*. These vessels were to cruise the Maine coast and intercept any French aid being delivered to the Wabanaki. Second, he dispatched Colonel Romer to Casco with orders to improve the fort there. The idea was to enlarge the structure so it could be used as a staging point for expeditions into Wabanaki territory. Lastly, the governor assembled and equipped a force of 360 men. They were to be transferred to Fort Casco, and from there they would march for the chief village of the Pequawket, an Abenaki tribe along the upper Saco River.

While a politically expedient move, Dudley was skeptical of the effort. Even if the detachment reached the Indian village, he expressed doubt that they would capture anyone. They might burn down some huts, but the Wabanaki scouts would have seen their plodding column long before it posed a threat and evacuated anyone in its path. The governor would have preferred almost any other option than a war of a thousand cuts, but there seemed no choice. "The experience of the best men that have at any time been here," he reluctantly informed London, "can advise to no better method then by constant marches, especially in the winter to dislodge and starve them."[3]

As it turned out, the expedition under the command of now Lt. Colonel March did not even succeed in finding a village. The guides, who had not been to the area for over a decade, became bewildered by the changed landscape and were soon hopelessly lost. With his provisions nearly exhausted a frustrated March called off the attempt. The colonel would organize a second expedition a few weeks later which proved more successful, as six Indians were reported as slain and as many taken prisoner.

While a small victory, March's actions did little to stem the raids. On October 6 a large war party fell upon nineteen men from Black Point, Maine, as the latter were traveling to tend to their fields. A hail of shot and a sudden

A 1936 picture of the McIntire garrison house in York, Maine. Built in 1707 (and still standing) this stout design, and others like it, provided a point of refuge and defense against marauding French and Indian war parties. Many were also surrounded by a palisade to further discourage any attack on the structure. (*HABS/Library of Congress*)

charge overran the entire group save one, who dashed back to the palisade fort with the news. The fort's commander, Sgt. John Wyatt, listened to the rattled account and began to worry. He only had eight men with him in the stronghold, and the enemy numbers seemed far greater. A pair of sloops were in the port and their captains agreed to add their ships guns to the defense. It was enough to convince Wyatt to attempt to hold the fort, but when the French and Wabanaki began debouching from the woods the young sergeant began to question his decision. After a few volleys it became clear that the enemy's numbers were simply too great and the garrison abandoned the structure, retreating to the awaiting sloops.

Small war parties struck York, Hampton, and other isolated settlements along the coast, leaving in their wake ashes and a trail of dead and missing. At Berwick a pair of war parties sat in ambush until the routine supply ship pulled ashore. The two groups then launched themselves upon the vessel and the nearby homesteads. The attackers were chased away, but not before the captain of the vessel and three of his crew lay dead and five others from the town had been dispatched.[4]

Matters were desperate enough that the Massachusetts Assembly considered a bounty of forty pounds on Indian scalps. The resolution also provided the incentive of plunder and a portion of the sale of any captives taken. The matter sparked an instant debate. It appeared to be falling to the same level as the enemy, but few were interested in such arguments at this point. The measure did spur the formation of seven companies of rangers that scoured the woods during the fall of 1703 and into early 1704. Only one of these companies had any success. Led by Colonel William Tyng, the expedition struck at a reported Indian hamlet on Lake Winnipesaukee. In a reverse of the Wabanaki raids on the frontier, Tyng and his men struck without warning and slew the six inhabitants before they had time to resist.[5]

On January 28, 1704, the attackers returned. A small war party beset Berwick, Maine. The raiders first approached Neale's garrison house. The sentry, however, was alert and sounded the alarm. A young man and young woman caught outside the fort dashed for safety, but the attackers soon caught up with the woman and killed her with a well-aimed blow. It was now a race, and one that the Englishman would likely win, so one of the Wabanaki leveled his musket and felled him with a shot that echoed over the landscape. The war party continued their advance on the garrison house until they came within range and a shot from the sentry knocked down their leader. As the attackers dragged away their wounded comrade, the young man, who all thought was dead, sprang up and darted into the garrison house to the cheers of those manning its defenses. The raiders moved onto another garrison house, but by this time the entire town was alerted, and after a few shots the war party turned on the outlying abandoned houses. Hearing the firing Captain John Brown led a dozen men out of his garrison house to aid his neighbors. Brown stumbled across the war party as it was preparing to leave with its plunder and scattered them with a few volleys. The captain would have pursued his routed adversary, which abandoned its plunder and some of its own equipment, but unlike the Wabanaki none of his men were equipped with snowshoes.

A week and a half later a small war party struck farther south at Haverhill, Massachusetts. Watching for a period from the nearby woods, the attackers realized that Bradley's garrison house on the northern edge of the town was completely unaware of their presence. The gates to the palisades had been left open and no sentry was in sight. A few words were passed and the war party dashed for the opening and were inside before anyone realized what had happened. Bradley's wife, Hannah, who had been taken in a raid during King William's War, was boiling a pot full of soap when the raiders burst into the house. She doused the first attacker with the scalding liquid but was soon taken by those behind him. Several were slain and the rest, Hannah among them, were led off toward Canada.

The horrors of another grueling trek lay before Mrs. Bradley, but it was in fact worse than this, as she was pregnant. Worn down by a lack of food and long snowbound marches, she gave birth halfway through the journey. In reality the infant never stood a chance under the adverse circumstances. Hannah tried to care for the newborn, but when it slowed her down her captors dispatched the poor creature in a grisly fashion. She would reach Montreal where she was purchased by the French and in the spring of 1705 released back to her husband.[6]

There was little that could be done in response to such incursions. Vigilance was preached at every level, but long and brutal winter nights tested every watch. Thus far the attacks had been confined to the eastern seaboard. To the west, in Deerfield, Massachusetts, there had only been one small brush with French and Indian raiders during their initial August 1703 attacks when two men were surprised and carried off. Since then the war had shifted to the east, leaving the village on the Connecticut River to its own accord.

However, all was not well. In late May 1703 Governor Cornbury had received reports from Iroquois sources that the French had planned an attack on the town. The governor had passed the information on to Dudley, who notified Reverend John Williams, a longtime denizen of Deerfield. Williams, who had been present for several of the attacks on Deerfield in King William's War, took the warning to heart and preached vigilance to his congregation, but as the months passed and nothing happened the townsfolk became lax. By the time the snows set in such warnings were distant echoes as most became more focused on fending off the New England winter.

The various expeditions into the Wabanaki homelands had not amounted to much, but even so, the sagamores realized that it would only be a matter of time before they were more successful. To halt this trend the confederacy appealed to Governor Vaudreuil for assistance. The governor was happy to comply and assigned Lt. Jean Hertel de Rouville to lead an expedition against the Massachusetts frontier. Rouville's force amounted to fifty Canadians and marines and two hundred Wabanaki, Huron, and Caughnawaga, with the latter two being recruited from the Christian missions near Montreal and Quebec. In the past these mission Indians had proven reluctant to lift the hatchet against their Iroquois kin, but they had no such scruples when it came to attacking the New England frontier. The Wabanaki were from the recently erected St. Francois mission near the confluence of the St. Lawrence and St. Francois Rivers. Vaudreuil had been looking to attract a number of Wabanaki to this location, and Jesuit Father Bigot agreed to help by erecting a mission near a small Abenaki village.[7]

It was a large war party and a difficult one to lead for the thirty-six-year old Hertel. Fortunately, several of his younger brothers accompanied the expedition as well as a number of experienced partisans who Hertel knew well. The war party departed Fort Chambly in late January 1704 and marched south along the bank of the Richelieu River and then along the frozen skin of Lake Champlain. At the mouth of the Winooski River the detachment turned left and made its way into the primeval forests of Vermont. Near the headwaters of the Winooski the party shuffled east on their snowshoes until they intercepted the Wells River. Upon descending the river, Hertel was delighted to find waiting for him at the junction of the Wells and Connecticut Rivers a fifty-man detachment of eastern Wabanaki.

Hertel's weary force reached the outskirts of Deerfield on the afternoon of February 28. Scouts informed him that they could encamp in the woods at the edge of a meadow about a mile and a half from the northern side of the village. Here his men dropped their packs and prepared a cold meal among the scattered pine trees. They had marched over two hundred miles from Fort Chambly in the dead of winter. They crossed the Green Mountains through snow and slicing winds, sometimes only making a few miles a day, before turning south and tracing the western bank of the broad Connecticut River to arrive at their destination. At dusk Hertel moved forward with a number of scouts while his men stood ready for orders to advance. There were a dozen houses on the north side of the village, about an equal number to the south, and fifteen homes in the center of the village surrounded by a wooden palisade. It was here that many of the inhabitants had taken refuge for the evening, and it was here that Hertel looked to strike. For hours keen eyes watched the icy scene, the occasional trudging of a frozen sentry and the drifting smoke from chimneys the only perceivable motion.

Around 2 a.m. even the sentry no longer appeared, prompting Hertel to send word for his men to move forward. Being completely undetected it is perhaps surprising that Hertel did not attempt to surround the compound before storming the palisade, but it may be that the watch was better than the French commander had anticipated, or he feared being detected by an inhabitant in one of the houses outside of the fort, or perhaps it was simply a miscommunication among his diverse command. Whatever the case, around 4:30 a.m., Hertel's men were in position not far from the open north gate. The French partisan took one last look and then gave the signal to attack.

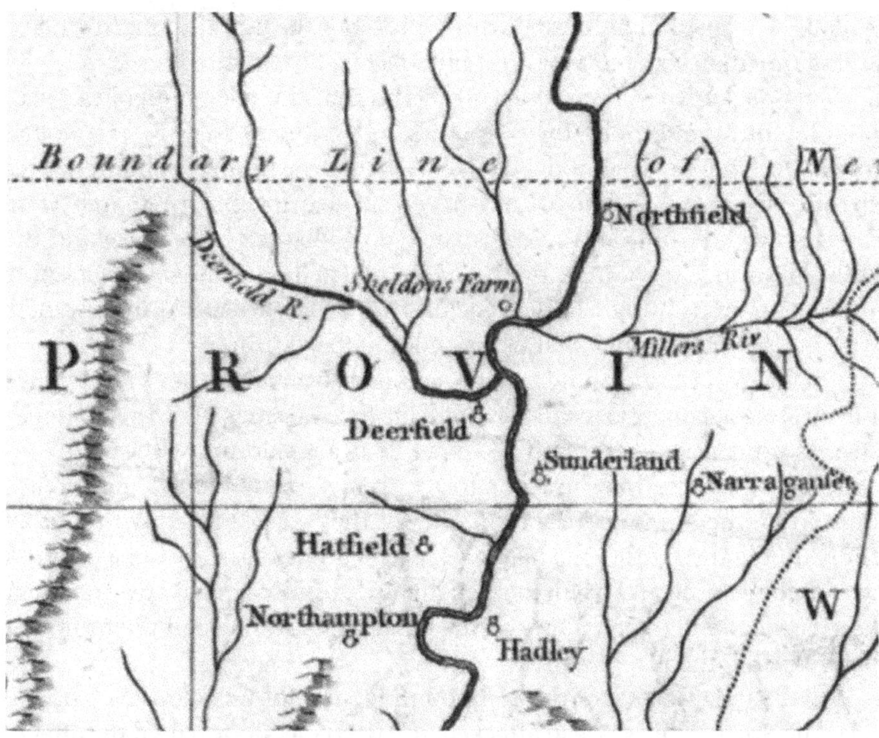


A portion of a colonial map from 1781 showing Deerfield and the surrounding Massachusetts towns along the Connecticut River. (*Library of Congress*)

Dudley had taken the warnings he had received from Cornbury seriously and dispatched twenty men to aid the town, but as 1703 passed into 1704 these troops, as well as the inhabitants, settled into a false sense of security brought on by the snowy winter months. Despite the urgings of Reverend Williams, they had forgotten how often French and Indian war parties had struck under similar circumstances during the last conflict and would now pay the price for not learning this lesson in diligence.

A sentry who was lax in his responsibilities was the first to pay the price, although he did perform one last duty by firing a shot and sounding the alarm. It was already too late for many. One of the first homes invested was that of Reverend Williams. Williams awoke to the sound of the raiders breaking through his windows and front door. After a quick glance he called the two soldiers living in the home to arms and returned to his room to retrieve his pistol. As a score of Caughnawaga entered the dwelling one broke through the bedroom door. Williams leveled his pistol at the intruder and pulled the trigger. The flint fell with a click, but the gun did not fire, likely saving the minister's life as several Indians quickly subdued him.[8]

The attackers quickly ransacked the house. The two soldiers escaped, jumping out the second-story windows, but Williams's family was not so fortunate. They were all quickly taken. Two of the younger children, ages six and six months, who would never survive the return march were dragged to the front door and dispatched. Williams's black slave and the children's nurse, a woman by the name of Parthena, showed incredible courage in attempting to intervene, but it mattered little to the invaders who quickly turned their war clubs and tomahawks on her.

On the eastern side of the fort, detachments overran Carter's house, capturing almost everyone inside, and outside the palisades they found similar success capturing several families in a few nearby homes without any resistance. Resistance was, however, forthcoming. As the French and Indians pressed on the homes a little farther away, they were greeted with musket shots. While these residents had been alarmed, they were not in a position to stop the assault, and when the Caughnawaga and Wabanaki overran their homes, they vented their anger on the inhabitants, killing half their number before taking the rest prisoner.

On the western side of the compound Ensign John Sheldon Sr.'s house, near the north gate, was also attacked. A barred oak door halted the attackers' advance and allowed Ensign Sheldon and another soldier time to seize their arms and fire at the war party, but given the enemy's numbers and the volume of return fire it was clear that any resistance would not last long. The ensign's newly married son and his wife, Hannah, jumped from a second-story window in an attempt to escape. Hannah twisted her ankle in the attempt, and could go no farther. She begged Sheldon Jr. to run to Hatfield for help, which he did with only pieces of cloth from a torn blanket wrapped around his feet. Sheldon's wife who was reloading muskets was killed by a shot, and Sheldon Sr. and the soldier with him made a narrow escape after one of the attackers found an open back door. Sheldon's two-year-old daughter, Mercy, was slain with a single stroke and his three other children taken hostage. Hannah was later discovered and taken captive as well.[9]

Hertel's men seized the meeting house in the center of town. Here and at Sheldon's home they collected their prisoners as detachments began to push on Sgt. Benoni Stebbin's house a little over a hundred feet away. By now, however, the occupants of this home were prepared to defend themselves. Besides Stebbin, there were six other men in the house, as well as four or five women, and over half a dozen children. The doors were barred and

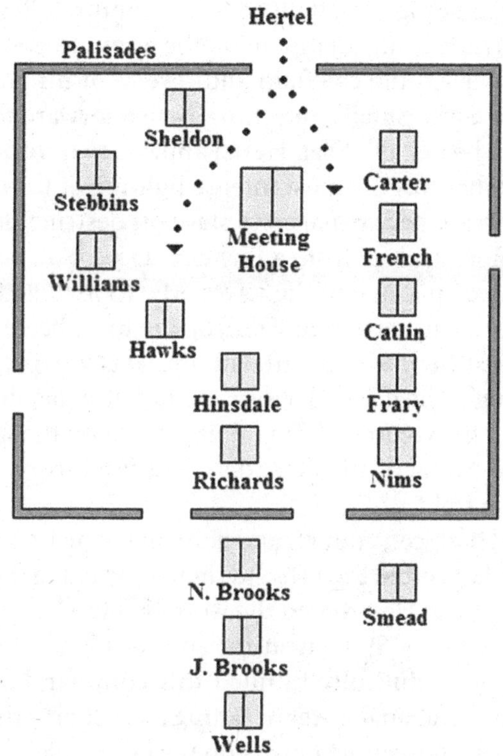


A diagram showing the location and ownership of homes inside the central palisades in Deerfield, Massachusetts. The opening moments of the French and Indian attack on the compound are depicted through the open north gate. (*Michael G. Laramie*)

the lower-level windows blocked. There were plenty of firearms and an ample supply of shot and powder. Just as importantly, the interior of the home's walls had been filled with unfired brick, which proved a sufficient barrier against the French and Indian musket fire that now began to splatter against the structure.

With the women frantically reloading, Stebbin and his makeshift garrison fired on the advancing enemy. The dozen or so French and Indians moving toward the home pressed forward, but the fire coming from the defenders forced them to break off their attack. A few more assailants joined the cause and returned half an hour later, but again the defender's fire chased them away. This time a much larger force was assembled, and led by Hertel, they surrounded the English home pelting it with musket balls. Stebbin and his men, however, were unmoved and a cheer could be heard coming from the besieged structure when a musket ball knocked down a French officer. The Caughnawaga chieftain who had captured Reverend Williams led a band of warriors in an attempt to set the homestead ablaze, but several well-aimed shots felled the chieftain and several of his party, sending the rest scurrying for cover. Small bands now dashed forward to finish the task, but they too were beaten off. Even Hertel appears to have been wounded in the arm during what was the most intense fighting of the morning.

While the garrison had managed to stave off destruction it had come at a price. Sgt. Stebbin lay dead from a French musket ball, one of his soldiers had been wounded, and one of the wives, Mary Hoyt, had been wounded as well taking her turn at a window during the most heated portion of the attack. The women stepped forward with muskets to replace the fallen soldiers, and although powder and shot were not at issue, the sheer number of the enemy and the volume of fire raining down on the structure painted a dismal picture. Some of the defenders had fired forty shots, and there seemed no end in sight.[10]

In fact, Hertel had seen enough and gave up trying to take the house. He left a few men to harass the English and then returned to the meeting house to organize his retreat. He ordered the wounded tended to and the nearby houses put to the torch. Starting at the southern end of the palisade the French officer's men dutifully fulfilled this command. Detachments of Caughnawaga and Wabanaki began leading away their prisoners, stopping to loot and burn the remaining houses on the north side of the town as they made their trek back toward their camp at the edge of the Great Meadow.

Many of the inhabitants, taking their chances, had fled out one of the fort's gates, disappearing into the snowy landscape without shoes or jackets. Others, like Sarah Kellogg, hid in their cellars. While this was a fairly successful strategy, its perils now became clear as smoke and flames wrapped their refuge. Kellogg, who had hidden under a washtub, was able to crawl through the blaze to make good her escape, but for many the flames accomplished what the tomahawk did not.

Hertel was anxious to leave. It was daylight and it had been several hours since the start of the attack. By now the nearby English towns would be organizing a relief force and the French commander wanted to be gone by the time they arrived. Keeping a small rearguard of thirty men in the town to finish the destructive work, he ordered the rest to withdraw.

At Sheldon's house, captured Mary Catlin waited with her family. Her husband and brother-in-law had been killed in the attack and now she and her children awaited their fate. Suddenly a badly wounded French officer, Ensign Francois-Marie Margane de Batilly, was carried into the house and laid on the floor. The wound was clearly fatal, and when Batilly groaned for water Mrs. Catlin quickly fulfilled his request, staying by his side to comfort him. When one of the other captives asked how she could help someone who had brought such misery down upon them, Catlin drew upon her Christian faith and responded, "If thine enemy hunger, feed him; if he thirst, give him water to drink."[11]

As Hertel's men began leaving several men carried away the French officer while others led away her son and daughter. When Mary stepped forward to leave with them a French officer held up his hand and shook his head. Even in the midst of chaos and among those who would slay someone for the slightest of reasons, mercy had its rewards. Her efforts had not gone unnoticed and as such Hertel ordered that she be left unharmed.

The French commander had been correct in his assumption that an English relief force would soon arrive. With his prisoners gone, a little after eight o'clock Hertel withdrew with his rear guard just as a troop of thirty horsemen entered the southern portion of the town. Here the relief force from the towns of Hadley and Hatfield met with Captain Jonathan Wells, whose garrison house had acted as a refuge for those who had escaped the perils to the north. Wells rallied a score of men and together with the reinforcements set off after the French.

This pell-mell pursuit chased off some of Hertel's stragglers who were still occupied in looting or firing at Stebbin's house and then raced forward to catch up with the enemy column. Without snowshoes the men plowed through the three-foot-deep snow, causing them to overheat and discard their jackets and shirts. With his forces strung out in a mad dash to catch the enemy, Wells began to worry. He ordered a halt to reorganize his men, but at this point no one was listening. Revenge was in command. The head of the relief column was over a mile from the town and rushing headlong toward the south bank of the Deerfield River when Captain Wells's fears came true. Hidden behind the riverbank Hertel had arranged his rear guard and a few dozen men from the main column. Peering over the bank the French partisan waited until a cluster of the enemy were within a few dozen yards, and then he and his men stood and delivered a devastating volley. This was followed by a chorus of war whoops as the French and Indian force dashed upon the dazed English, over a half a dozen of whom now lay motionless in the snow. The exhausted English broke and fell back upon Wells and his arriving troops, and together they conducted a fighting withdrawal back to Deerfield.[12]

Reinforcements would arrive at the town in the coming days, but no pursuit of Hertel was undertaken, in part due to a lack of snowshoes, and in part for fear that the French would slay their captives if pressed. As it turned out there were plenty of captives, 111 by count after the 49 dead had been found and identified, a difficult task in some cases. Over half the town had been killed or carried away in a matter of a few hours. Most of the homes in the palisade and many on the northern part of the town had been burned, and the resulting columns of smoke acted as a warning beacon for those settlements within sight. In all, it was simply another disaster in what was proving to be a woeful year.

Hertel's losses were far less, although difficult to gauge. In his official report to Vaudreuil he gave his losses as three killed and some twenty wounded. Later he confessed to the captured Reverend Williams that eleven had been killed, three French and the rest Caughnawaga and Wabanaki. In yet another account three were killed, among them a leading chieftain, and fifty wounded. The matter is further complicated by the fact that Hertel likely never really knew how many men he had with him. Such expeditions were not a formal military exercise by any means, and record keeping was not one of the organizational strongpoints.[13]

For Hertel and his men it became clear after a few days that the English were not following them. The French commander had made good time with his captives, in part because he had brought snowshoes with him for their use. The long caravan supplemented by a dozen dogsleds threaded its way through the woods. For those that could not keep up, which quickly included the Reverend Williams's wife who had given birth a few weeks before, the end was swift. At least in this instance the act was one of mercy and preferable to death by exposure or wolves.

Williams, who suffered through the trek, counted thirty-nine captives culled out of the line by the time they reached Chambly. Some, like the slaying of his black slave and Parthena's husband, Frank, in a drunken rage on the first evening or the callous use of the tomahawk for slight infractions such as being a bit too slow, were simply acts of brutality. But as the starving reverend shuffled forward against the northern winds, he saw acts that completely defied this mindset. Some of the smaller children were wearing out from the long march. Their captives, however, did not resort to the tomahawk but instead carried them on their backs until they had recovered. While Williams and others would simply see this as protecting an investment, it was more frequent than might be imagined and supplemented by other acts that could be characterized in the same vein. For instance, Mary Catlin's daughter Ruth was treated as a great lady and with enormous respect during the march back to Canada, while others were nearly or literally starved to death.[14]

While acts of humanity and cruelty can be found on all sides, and in all conflicts that have circled this globe, in this case the one explanation for the spectrum of behavior is the incredibly conflicting message coming from Christian teachings and the political actions of some of the missionaries who were preaching it. For the reader of today this is apparent, and as such it would be foolish to assume that some of the recipients of this communication didn't understand that one message was being overlaid with another. Perhaps in this struggle to live up to both messages we find part of the motivation behind such conduct. For others involved, the reason was much simpler, they just pointed to the French that accompanied them and shrugged.

Vaudreuil was delighted with the results of the expedition. A number of Wabanaki sagamores met with him in early June and thanked the governor for his swift response to their request for support. They then pledged themselves to the alliance. "We all come here to greet our Father," the Wabanaki spokesman made clear, "and to tell him that in this time of war, that we wish to risk with him, and strongly support the war that we undertook together." Within just a few months the Wabanaki confederacy had gone from wavering allies to staunch supporters of the French cause. It was precisely what the governor had hoped for. "Sieur de Rouville's party," he wrote the minister of the marine, "has accomplished everything expected of it, for independent of the capture of a fort, it showed the Abenakis that they could truly rely on our promises."[15]

CHAPTER SEVEN

# Church's Expedition

After six months of raids on the New England frontier Dudley had pressed Vaudreuil to consider a prisoner exchange, but he was met with a skeptical response from the French governor, who knew the English only had a handful of French captives. Suspecting what was behind Vaudreuil's response, Dudley saw an opening to not only promote a general prisoner exchange but at the same time strike back against New England's enemies. The previous year he had proposed an expedition against the French fort at Port Royal, Nova Scotia. The proximity of this port to the New England fishing fleets and trade lines warranted its capture before it became a safe haven for a pack of French privateers. The Massachusetts Assembly agreed and voted that an expedition be formed. Dudley would have liked to have carried through with this action but for two points. First, he had asked for England's assistance in the venture and had yet to hear anything. Second, he was skeptical of the colony's ability to capture the French stronghold with its own resources, and he could ill afford a disaster that would leave the frontier exposed to a counterattack.

With Port Royal off the table until he received a response from London, Dudley promoted using the resources allocated to the expedition to attack the Wabanaki. The proposal quickly found a receptive audience, in part because it also came with a commander, Major Benjamin Church. Before there was a Robert Rogers or the exploits of his famous rangers, there was Benjamin Church. In 1704 there were few Englishmen who understood woodland warfare as well as Church and certainly none with the same level of experience. Born in Plymouth County, Church was already in his midthirties when he participated in King Philip's War (1675-1678), and in King William's War, a generation later, he undertook four major expeditions against the Wabanaki. He employed the enemy's tactics, conducting long marches and traveling in canoes or small boats, and took the fight to their villages, often striking in the dead of winter when they were wrapped in a blanket of snow.[1]

The retired sixty-five-year old Major Church was so incensed by the news of Deerfield that he saddled up his horse and rode seventy miles to Boston to seek an audience with Dudley and offer his services to the queen. With the agreement of the Massachusetts Assembly, Church was made commander of the expedition and tasked with drawing up a plan of attack. After watching the old officer's gait during their meeting, Dudley confessed that he would have preferred a younger and more active commander for the expedition, but the nomination of Church brought a more important element into play. The major was something of a living legend, and as such, volunteers flocked to the cause.[2]

Dudley made Church colonel of the expedition on March 18, 1704, and ordered him to raise the necessary troops. Church recruited out of three Massachusetts counties: Bristol, Barnstable, and Plymouth. The colonel had all the militia companies called out, and after treating them to a few kegs of beer he "animated their hearts to do service." The work proved fruitful enough that he was able to enlist, "out of some companies, near twenty men, and others fifteen." With his quota soon met Church turned to recruiting his native contingent, which he believed would be instrumental in the campaign's success. The task put him through "a great fatigue and expense." In the end, however, the standard approach of gifts worked; it was just that several days of revelry were required before any level of commitment could be found.

Returning to Boston Church pressed Dudley to allow him to attack Port Royal, and after the governor invited him to watch a mortar demonstration on Boston Common, the colonel thought he had found his moment. Although Dudley agreed that it was the most logical target, he informed Church that without orders from the queen, "he must speak no more on the matter."[3]

As it was Dudley gave Church broad latitude to strike at anything else in Nova Scotia, or Acadia as it was referred to by the French. Church's force of 550 men had gathered at Nantasket where their transports were being assembled. Alongside these vessels were the three men-of-war that would act as the fleet's escort: the fourteen-gun *Province Galley*, and a pair of Royal

Navy frigates, the thirty-two-gun HMS *Gosport*, and the forty-eight-gun HMS *Jersey*. After loading the expedition's three dozen whale boats and supplies onto twenty transports, Church gave the order to set sail for Newcastle, New Hampshire, in early May.[4]

Dudley was delighted to hear that Church's force had arrived at Newcastle. Reports had reached him that a large French war party from Quebec was to rendezvous with a Wabanaki detachment with the aim of burning Newcastle and nearby Fort William and Mary, which controlled access into and out of the Piscataqua River. Given that the river was the primary transportation route for the King's Woods in southern New Hampshire, Dudley had every right to be concerned about the location.

Colonel Romer had previously surveyed Fort William and Mary and, finding it wanting, laid down a new set of plans. In late 1703 Dudley approved the project and ordered the Royal Engineers to rebuild the stronghold. Some foundational work was done that fall, and with the spring thaws work started once again on the structure. Romer pushed hard to complete the modifications on the fort, but as with his efforts at Castle William in Boston Harbor he soon found himself at odds with his colonial workforce. The lieutenant governor of New Hampshire and commandant of the fort, John Usher, attempted to remedy this problem by reminding the New Hampshire Council of the importance of the task and their obligation to support Colonel Romer who "has constantly been at the Fort from morning to night to put the same in a defensive posture." There was still a good deal of work to be done, but at the moment with a thirty-two-gun and a forty-eight-gun ship anchored at Newcastle, there was little to worry about in terms of French and Indian raiders.[5]

Farther southwest nothing could be further from the case. On the morning of May 19, the village of Pascommuck, located on a bend in the Connecticut River a few miles south of the town of Northampton, was beset by a French and Indian war party. As at Deerfield, the town was taken by complete surprise. The fifty-man war party under the command of Jacques Testard de Montigny, a veteran officer who had served throughout King William's War, swept through the unprepared village, quickly overrunning the town's fortified house and a number of nearby homes.

A few miles away a detachment of raiders surrounded an isolated homestead and called upon Captain Benjamin Wright to surrender. Wright responded with a musket shot that broke one of the attacker's arms. There were a few scattered shots, and when the war party realized that they could not take the home by surprise they "attempted to burn the house, by shooting spiked arrows dipped in brimstone upon the roof." The plan almost

A younger Benjamin Church when he was a militia captain. By Queen Anne's War the sixty-five-year old Ranger had lost a step, but was still active enough to conduct one last campaign against his old French and Wabanaki adversaries. (*New York Public Library*)

worked, but Wright's fifteen-year-old nephew, "wrapping himself in a feather bed, drew water from the well and put out the fire."[6]

The attackers soon gave up and looked for more fertile ground, leaving Wright and his family unharmed. The same could not be said for Pascommuck. Montigny's war party had carried off twenty-three prisoners. The French officer had sent one of the wounded prisoners back to the town to warn the remaining citizens that captives would be slain if the war party were pursued, but unbeknownst to the French officer the herald was mistakenly killed before delivering his message.

Before the return march to Canada had proceeded too far, a prisoner by the name of Benjamin Janes managed to escape. The French commander shrugged at the news and pressed on thinking that the English would not dare to follow after his warning. Janes reached Northampton with the news, and a troop of horse under Captain John Taylor was quickly assembled and raced off in pursuit. When scouts reported that the English were approaching, Montigny arrayed his men in an ambush and killed a number of his prisoners, as he didn't have the men to guard them. Taylor's rescue effort proved a disaster. The disorganized horsemen galloped into a French and Indian trap, which cost Taylor his life and scattered his men, ending any thoughts of further pursuit.[7]

It would be some time before Church and his men heard of the attack. On May 15 it was agreed that the warships would only remain at Newcastle for two weeks, as their presence would be quickly discovered and alert the enemy. To throw off any enemy scouts, Church and his men took the transports to the Maine coast. Halting at Matinicus Island some fifteen miles from the mainland, two longboats were sent ahead—one into West Penobscot Bay and the other into East Penobscot Bay. They met with instant success, surprising and taking a French merchant by the name of Thomas Lafebure, his two sons, and a Wabanaki.

Church questioned the senior Lafebure first but soon realized that it would lead nowhere. He then had his native troops put on their warpaint, gather together some brush and wood, and plant two stakes in the ground before each pile. With his props in place Church questioned the two brothers, giving them a choice: tell him the truth or face the flames. The two proved quite talkative. The eldest, Thomas, had a commission to raise a detachment of Wabanaki as part of a larger force that was destined for the area. They informed the colonel of the whereabouts of a sizable stash of supplies they had brought in preparation for this effort and the names of the two Frenchmen coming from Canada to organize the expedition.

The two captives along with a pilot name D'Young, who Church had released from jail because of his skills, took the expedition to the French supplies, which Church had loaded aboard his three dozen whaleboats. The trio then guided the English to the scattered homesteads in the area. There was little opposition to the overwhelming force, and within a few days Church captured most of the local inhabitants including St. Castin's (the younger) wife and children. The prisoners were in agreement that there were no Wabanaki in the area but that they were more likely to be found at Passamaquoddy Bay farther up the coast. Armed with this information Church put his longboats in the water and then ordered the transports to proceed to Mount Desert, where they were to rendezvous with the arriving warships and await further orders.[8]

Church and his flotilla of small boats descended on the Maine coast, spending several days waiting in ambush at a few known Wabanaki rendezvous points but to little avail. He returned to Mount Desert, and after taking on additional supplies, he informed the fleet to remain for six days and then set sail for Passamaquoddy Bay where they would find him.

Church and his flotilla of whaleboats returned to the Maine coast. Again, he found nothing at the normal stopping points between Penobscot and Passamaquoddy Bay. The sight of three dozen vessels under sail certainly did not help Church's chances of finding a large number of French and Wabanaki, but on the other hand no warning seems to have been passed to the Indian villages, implying that there simply was not a lot of activity along the coast at the time.

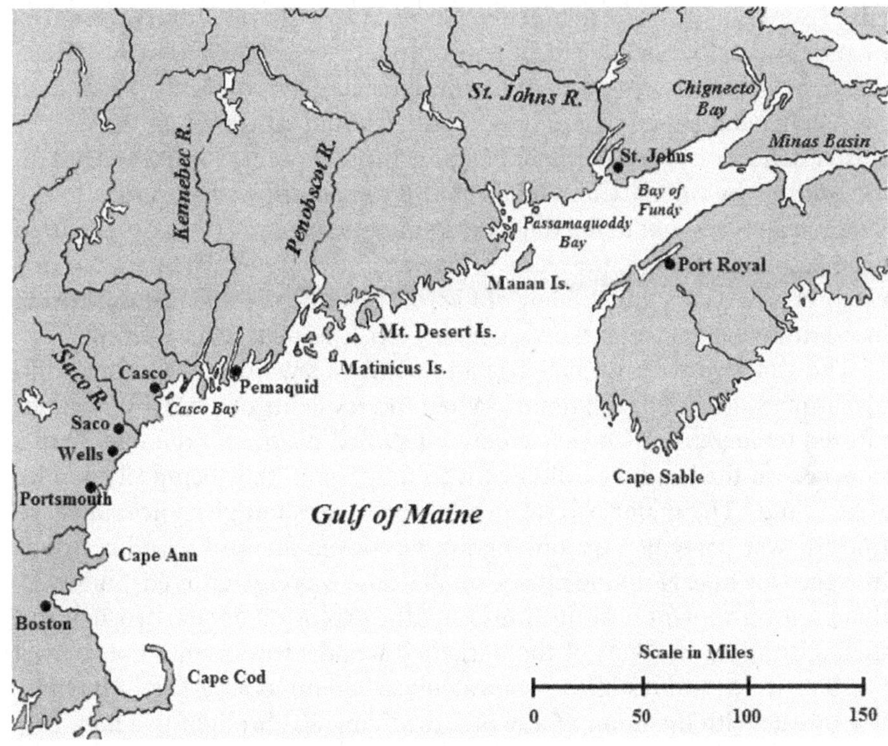


The coast of northern New England and French Acadia.

On June 7 Church entered the western portion of Passamaquoddy Bay and pulled his boats ashore on a nearby island. Here he captured several French settlers who informed him that there was a large French and Indian war party nearby, but they had fled upon the sight of Church's vessels. Church sent a small detachment to a nearby island with orders to destroy what homes were found and take as many prisoners as they could. The colonel then left a part of his force on the island to guard the prisoners and deal with the French and Indian war party should it return, and although it was dark, he pushed forward up the St. Croix River with 150 men. It proved a trying journey "by reason of the eddies and whirlpools, made with the fierceness of the current." One of the French prisoners warned Church that he had lost family to one of these whirlpools and, along with the three other French pilots, attempted to discourage the effort, but the old colonel would have none of it and pressed on.[9]

The detachment was rewarded a few hours later when they entered Oak Bay. Along the shore was a landing place that one of the pilots pointed out.

His prisoners had informed him that Gordeau and Charque, the two Frenchmen named earlier by the Lafebure brothers, lived not far away. Church ordered the boats ashore and, after leaving a detachment to secure the landing site, arranged his men in a long skirmish line and advanced on the nearby cluster of homes. When the elder Lafebure brother pointed to a wood hut on the edge of the woods, Church halted and passed orders for his men to use their hatchets and not to fire unless absolutely necessary. The colonel assured his men that this was to prevent warning any nearby enemy homes, but privately he was worried that many of his young soldiers would just start firing indiscriminately in the darkness, creating a risk as great as the enemy.

The attack proved no challenge and within a few minutes Gordeau and his family were in English hands. When the residents of a nearby bark hut refused to surrender, Church ordered it pulled down and the inhabitants knocked on the head regardless of who they were, "they being all enemies alike to me." The major had taken a few prisoners, but given he had yet to find the war party he was looking for, he moved forward with his troops into the tree line. Not long after a small home was encountered. Suddenly, there was movement near the house and the explosion of one, two, ten, and then a hundred muskets lit the darkened woods. It was what the colonel had feared. He and his officers repeatedly called for a cease-fire, and after a few threats with the point of a sword, the firing was brought to a halt. Perhaps two hundred shots were fired, resulting in the slight wounding of a Frenchman attempting to flee from the house and one of Church's men who was simply caught in the crossfire. Not looking to repeat the accident, the colonel returned to his boats around dawn.

Reports were that Charque's home was half a dozen miles upriver. Church advanced on the location with a detachment of troops, and while he captured Charque's home, his family, and several others, Charque himself escaped into the woods. The expedition would spend another day in the area, but by now the enemy had been warned of their presence. Church gathered up his plunder and prisoners, ordered the buildings and crops put to the torch, and returned downriver to await his rendezvous with the transports and British warships.[10]

Now nearing mid-June, Church set his eye on Acadia and Port Royal. The warships were to sail to Port Royal Harbor and await the colonel who, with his transports and longboats, was en route to the French settlements in Minas Basin. When Church reached the town of Grand Pre the tricky water levels and low tide forced him to delay an attack until morning. At sunrise Church's men landed and, after a few scattered volleys by both sides, the French retreated into the woods leaving the empty town in English

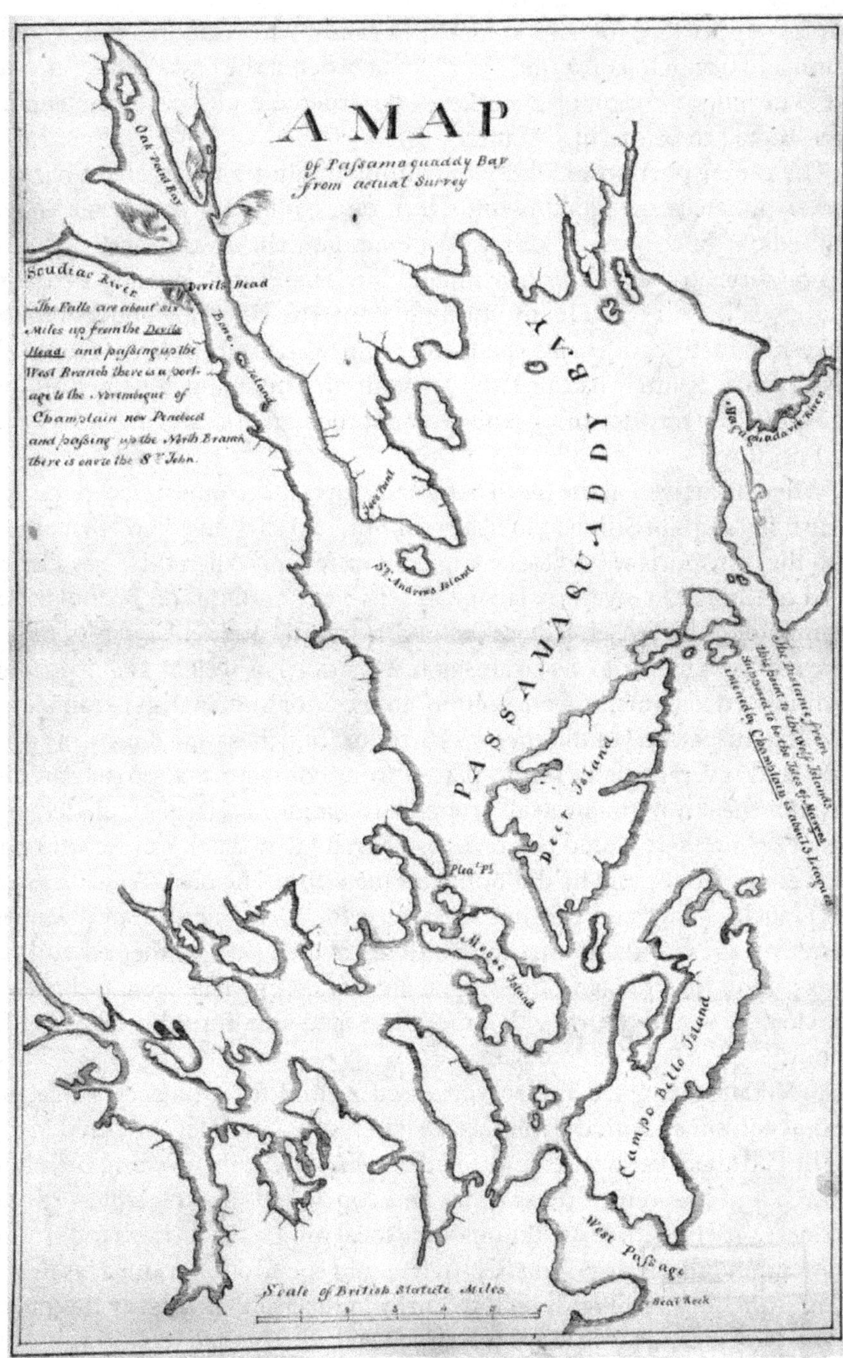


Passamaquoddy Bay and the outlet of the St. Croix River, c. 1800. (*Library of Congress*)

hands—empty save for several casks of brandy, which Church's men soon found and began to consume. The colonel ordered the casks staved in, and at the urging of several of his officers, he ordered a pursuit of the enemy who seemed to be driving off their cattle.

The center portion of Church's command, under a lieutenant named Barker, outpaced the flanking units and soon paid the price when a volley erupted out of the woods killing Barker and a man next to him, the only two fatalities the expedition would suffer. The French quickly fled and Church called off the pursuit not long after. The New Englanders built a makeshift fortification and spent the night watching the glow from the town, which Church had ordered to be fired. The major returned to the transports the next morning, and after another small-scale raid, he set sail for Port Royal.

When he arrived in the basin before the fort Church marveled at the tall British warships bristling with heavy cannon and carrying crews that along with the transports would easily triple his numbers. When these vessels arrived on June 22 Governor Jacques-Francois Monbeton de Brouillan, in command of the French fort, called out the militia and sent a pair of emissaries to the English to ascertain their intentions as well as stall for time. Additional detachments were sent out to monitor any English landing and warnings dispatched of the enemy's presence. Trenches were dug by the garrison and several small cannon placed to discourage an approach on the fort, but the stronghold was ill prepared to handle a siege. Fortunately for the governor, there would be no siege. Church knew that his orders did not allow for an attack and he did not press the point. The old colonel berated the French envoys and threatened to turn the fort's garrison and nearby town over to his Indians once he seized it. He then warned them that their raids on the New England frontier would not go unchallenged. If they did not stop, he would return with a thousand men and burn down the entire colony.[11]

Brouillan dismissed the rhetoric and waited for an attack while his troops, combined with the militia that had responded, a few hundred in all, continued their fieldworks and filled sandbags. On the evening of July 4 Church and his council of war met and concluded that, regardless of the colonel's orders, with the addition of the local militia the fort was too strong to attempt without siege guns. Church would spend a few more days in the basin launching small raids on the nearby French settlements. By this point in the siege Brouillan's troops were so weary that he had to stop work on the fortifications. "If in that time the enemy had pressed him closely," a French witness noted, "he would have been very embarrassed, it not being possible that people who are 15 days without sleep and working all day are well able to make war." Instead, on the morning of July 7 Brouillan and his officers watched in disbelief as the English fleet raised anchor and departed into the Bay of Fundy. Church would launch a few more raids on the Maine coast during the return voyage but with little results, and by mid-July the expedition was back in Boston.

Dudley was pleased with the effort, which seemed to have disrupted a planned French and Indian expedition against Newcastle. Church had taken nearly a hundred prisoners and wrought the same level of devastation upon the towns of Acadia that had been inflicted upon the towns of New England. Still, while Dudley viewed the expedition as a successful attempt to strike back and a way to secure more prisoners to force an exchange with the French, many did not see it in this light. Church had failed to engage a sizable part of the Wabanaki, who would simply return once the English were gone. More importantly, Port Royal had been left untouched. At first the public blamed the failure on Church, who with 1,900 men on twenty transports and three warships had not even bothered to make an attempt on the position. Soon, however, when reports of Church's orders circulated the finger pointing shifted to Dudley, who was accused in some circles of aiding the enemy. The well-known minister and writer Cotton Mather was one of Dudley's severest critics. "When Church went with his forces to Port-Royal he could easily have taken the fort or done anything in the world," Mather would later write the governor,

> but the reason which he has often given for his not doing it is, because you absolutely forbad him, you peremptorily for bad him. The cause you assigned was, because the matter had been laid before the queen, and the queen had sent over no orders for it, and though the queen had sent no orders we send with a pretence to take it—But the story grows now too black a story for me to meddle with it—The expedition baffled—The fort never so much as demanded—An eternal gravestone laid on our buried captives—A nest of hornets provoked to fly out against us—A shame cast upon us that will never be forgotten—I dare not, I cannot meddle with these mysteries.[12]

In fact, once Dudley understood how weak Port Royal really was after several of its supply ships were wrecked or captured, he wrote London that if another fourth-rate ship had arrived earlier that spring, Port Royal would now be in English hands.[13]

Church's expedition did little to slow down the attacks on the New England frontier. In late spring at the urgings of a number of chieftains among the mission Indians of Montreal, Governor Vaudreuil began to raise a large war party. The detachment was placed under the command of Captain Josue de Beaucours of the colonial marines. Beaucours, who had studied under the great military engineer Sébastien Vauban, had laid out much of the defenses of Quebec in the previous conflict. The captain had also distinguished himself in actions against the Iroquois, winning Frontenac's and the court's commendations. The troops under Beaucours consisted of 125 Frenchmen, many active young officers or cadets, and up to 600 mission Indians along with a pair of their Jesuit leaders. One of the largest war parties assembled to date, Vaudreuil noted that the force was sufficient to "attack whatever posts and villages they pleased."[14]

The target favored by the mission Indians was Northampton. With the selection it appeared that the Massachusetts town was doomed. The war party made the grueling two-hundred-mile trek and were but a day's march from their target when one of Beaucours's men deserted. The natives and many of the French were sure that the enemy village had been warned and balked at the attack. Beaucours tried to get them to shift targets, but many were no longer interested. The detachment quickly fractured as some returned home and others sought out opportunities in smaller groups.

A portion of this force would arrive before Lancaster, Massachusetts, on the evening of July 30, 1704. There were eleven garrison houses in the town, and after a quick survey it was agreed to assault six of them simultaneously. At dawn the raiders moved forward, but this time they found an alert town. The crackle of muskets and war whoops soon took hold, but although the war party was able to inflict a few casualties on the garrison houses, they had received too many in return and broke off the engagement after burning the town hall and several abandoned homes. Groton was struck next, and before the summer was out Almsbury, Haverhill, and York, Massachusetts, as well as Exeter, Dover, and Oyster River in New Hampshire had been attacked. For the remaining settlements along the Maine frontier it was a siege that consumed their towns one or two people at a time.[15]

While the French and their allies appeared to be unstoppable, such was not the case. By the end of the second year of Queen Anne's War English warships and colonial privateers had already captured a number of supply ships that the colony depended on for its survival. At Port Royal Governor Brouillan felt this painful reality. One of his supply vessels had been taken, and another loaded with supplies and trade items for the Wabanaki was wrecked in a storm along the New England coast. After Church's expedition the matter had become far more serious, as much of the local cattle and crops had been destroyed, forcing the garrison and the inhabitants to go on half-rations for three months. This in turn limited work on the stronghold, which fell into even more disrepair—not that it mattered given the small amount of powder and shot in the magazine, and the fact that many of his men's firearms had fallen into disrepair. It was clear that unless something changed, Port Royal would never survive a concerted attack.

For Governor Vaudreuil, supply issues were also causing problems. This was particularly true in delivering trade goods and supplies to his Wabanaki allies. The matter became serious enough that the governor had a number of Wabanaki moved to the St. Francois Mission where they could be better supplied and would act as a cover against enemy raiders using Lake Champlain and the Richelieu River. It was perhaps the only solution for the governor; otherwise several tribes in Acadia would have been forced to sue for peace, which would have put the entire alliance in jeopardy. Supply issues were also causing some concern to the west where the English continually looked to stir up controversy and create a situation that would force the Iroquois into the conflict. The lack of French trade goods did not help these matters, but Vaudreuil was fortunate in the leadership shown by his frontier diplomats and the Five Nations commitment to remain neutral.[16]

While his critics condemned him for his lack of initiative, for Dudley a new opportunity was presenting itself, one that would temper these voices. Although Vaudreuil's initial response to a prisoner exchange was less than promising, now that Dudley had secured a sizable number of prisoners himself, the French governor agreed to such negotiations. There was hope that if all went well these talks might lead to a cease-fire, and after that, even a peace treaty. For the Massachusetts governor and the average New Englander alike, anything that might bring an end to the French and Indian raids seemed worth pursuing.

CHAPTER EIGHT

# The Avalon Peninsula

King William's War had not been kind to the English settlements in Newfoundland. Iberville had destroyed almost every village along the coast, sent the inhabitants back to England, and sold their boats and catch. King William was quick to respond and significant resources were dedicated to securing Newfoundland from further attack. The forts at the key port of St. John's were reworked, as were the seaside defenses at this location. Naval assets were assigned to patrol the coast in search of French privateers as well as act as symbols of assurance to the annual fishing fleets. The king offered incentives to encourage colonists, but the profits of the fishing trade were incentive enough. The towns were rebuilt and the yearly fishing fleets continued their seasonal trek between the Canadian Island and the ports of England.

By 1700 some five thousand seasonal fishermen and their vessels were operating out of the reconstructed coastal towns, and almost another two thousand souls called these villages home. The fishing industry was thriving once again. So too was the illegal trade out of the colonies and the Caribbean, with the merchants of New England being the primary culprits. In particular, sugar and tobacco were shipped to Newfoundland and from there to foreign ports without the king's taxes and intervention. The Board of Trade and a string of naval commanders on station would address this issue but with little success. Nor was there stopping the flow of rum, which was also blamed on Yankee traders. "As these people are very prone to drink," one senior naval officer noted, "it causes unspeakable debaucherys, attended with thefts and idleness, and makes them ill servants and enslaved by always being kept in debt." As might be imagined a general disregard for rule of law followed. At least in this last instance there was some precedence, as the fleet admirals and captains that arrived at St. John's on an annual basis were often suspected beneficiaries of this illegal trade.[1]

By early 1702 concern over deteriorating relations in Europe spurred more English interest in the island's defenses. The centerpiece of these efforts was St. John's. While improvements to the harbor forts and the naval defenses, particularly the boom that restricted access to the harbor, had been considered and approved early on, actual work on these projects was carried out at a snail's pace. "The want of proper materials, and this a country that can't supply any defficiency, putts us often in difficultys," Captain Michael Richards of the Royal Engineers wrote of his plight at St. John's. Although the engineer wrote letter after letter spelling out his needs and requirements, little seemed to come of it. The town's commanders accused each other of misdoings and illegal activities, while the garrison of a hundred men, their clothes in tatters from years of neglect, most of their arms unfit for service, and their pay almost a year in arrears, began to desert in sizable numbers.

Arguments between the navy and the Board of Ordnance over payment further delayed matters, as did arranging for transport. The chain for the harbor boom almost fell prey to this interservice rivalry, and even as late as a few months before the start of the war, appeals for stone and materials to finish the forts were still being made by Captain Richards. With war approaching supply and personnel matters were addressed, which included placing the independent company at St. John's under Richards's command. Guns, building materials, clothing, tools, provision, ammunition, and money to pay the troops were forthcoming. So too was help in terms of manpower to finish the fortifications, as the king had directed the naval vessels arriving with the yearly convoy to assist in the work.[2]

While the English occupied the eastern and northern portions of the Avalon Peninsula, on the southwest shore lay the French colony of Placentia. Like the English settlements, Placentia was a seasonal fishing town. Anywhere from fifty to a hundred fishing vessels would arrive in the spring, ballooning the population of the coastal village to several thousand, and with their departure in the fall, reducing it to a few hundred. There were a few smaller posts nearby, but only Placentia occupied a defensible position. In fact, the formidable natural defenses of this harbor and town had thwarted several English naval expeditions against the port in the previous conflict.

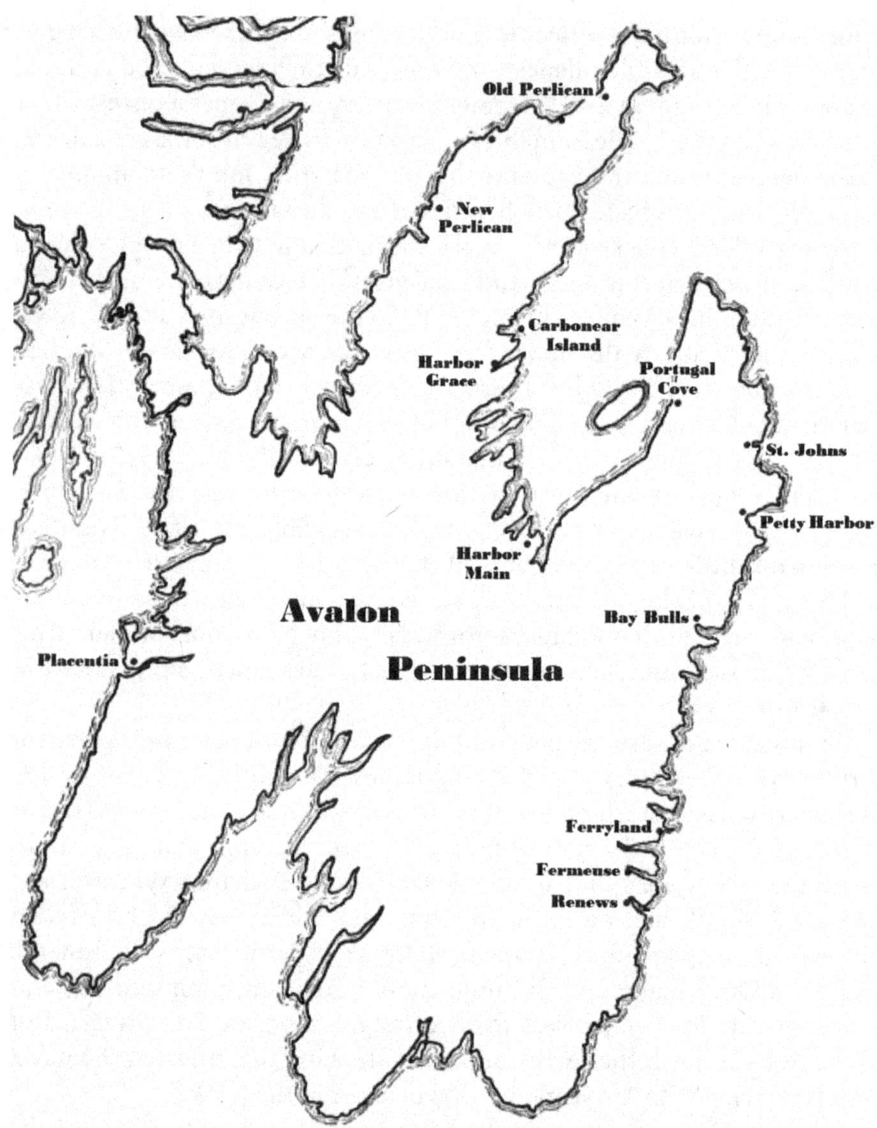


Primary French and English townships on Newfoundland's Avalon Peninsula.

It was easy to understand why. A battery of cannon was erected at Point Verde as well as on the opposite heights on the north side of the channel. Once past these guns an attacker would face several potential problems. On the heights to the north were several structures, one of which was a small fort armed with eight cannon and a pair of heavy mortars. These guns,

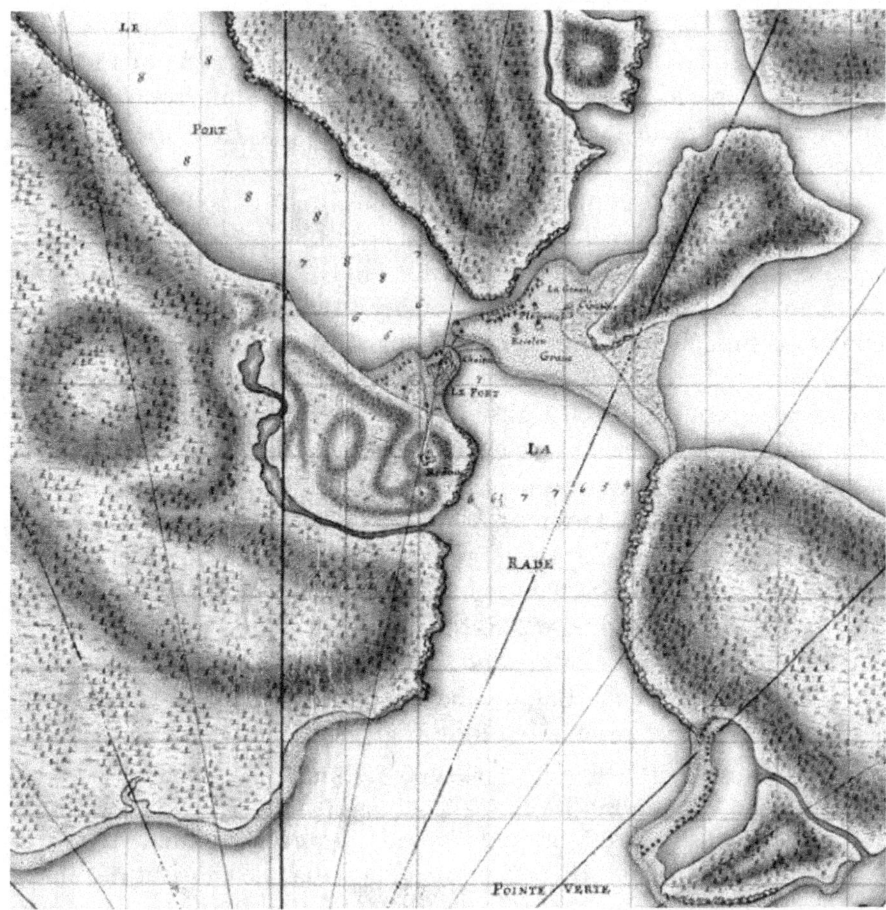


A portion of an earlier 1700s French map showing the defenses of Placentia Harbor. The fort sits at the narrow channel into the harbor, while a number of batteries are situated to immediately place any attacking vessel in a crossfire. Note that several small redoubts and posts were erected on the heights above the harbor entrance for additional defense, including Point Verde, at the bottom. (*Bibliothèque nationale de France*)

along with a few stationed on the heights across the channel, would have an unrestricted view of an enemy vessel as it sailed up the narrow roadstead toward Placentia Harbor. Upon reaching the headwaters of this channel the recently completed twenty-eight-gun Fort Royal would suddenly come into view. The stone and earth fort sat a few hundred yards away on the west side of the harbor entrance, which was barred by several cables and heavy chains. To supplement the fort's guns another battery was mounted on the heights to the east, which fired over a broad salt marsh, placing the entrance in a crossfire. These natural defenses aside, during fishing season several thousand men could be called upon to support the garrison of 150 or so soldiers and marines. Added to this would be a few French warships and privateers who frequented the port, making Placentia one of the better-defended posts in North America.

To make matters yet more difficult for the English, the French colony's governor, Captain Daniel d'Auger de Subercase, was a competent professional soldier who had served in Italy and France. In 1686 he joined the Free Companies of the Marine and the following year sailed to Canada as a captain of a company. He fought in King William's War, and after the massacre at La Chine, Subercase was prevented from launching what might have been a devastating counterattack against the celebrating Iroquois by none other than the current governor of New France, the Marquis de Vaudreuil. He would participate in several other campaigns during the conflict and would be promoted based on Frontenac's high opinion of his conduct. In April 1702, Subercase was made governor of Placentia, but it would not be until the following year that he reported to the post, having traveled to France first to settle some personal accounts.[3]

News of war between France and England in 1702 accelerated the work at St. John's, but for the English the opening moves in Newfoundland seemed promising. Commodore John Leake, who commanded the Newfoundland squadron sent out that spring, was directed to attack French interests on the island. Possessing clear naval superiority Leake did destroy several French fishing posts around Placentia, and even captured a few small cannon at St. Peter's, but after examining Placentia's defenses, he dismissed any thought of besieging the location.

Another matter to be addressed was the need for a fortified post in the northern harbors of the Avalon Peninsula to protect the English fishing fleet operating in this area. Trinity Harbor appeared the best answer and was proposed to London, but before the topic could even be discussed the French exploited this weakness. In early September a thirty-man French and Indian war party departed Placentia and paddled north. Upon reaching the head of Placentia Bay, they disembarked and carried their canoes over the Avalon Isthmus to Trinity Bay. Once in these waters the raiders fell upon several English homesteads, plundering and looting before eventually departing in a captured fishing vessel.

Leake departed with his squadron and the fishing fleet that fall. While a great deal of concern had been expressed regarding the defenses of St. John's, the commodore reported that the chain to block the entrance was still not installed as he found "no boomes to float it, nor does the country afford any." For the moment a pontoon ship was employed as a makeshift solution. The fort was still in need of materials, and as for the garrison of St. John's, Leake found them angry, with their primary point of contention being that they had been forced to serve in Newfoundland for so long with "no hopes, as they believe, of their returning." Richards was less diplomatic and stated that a pack of mutinous recruits had been sent the year before and infected the rest of the garrison. In his opinion it was to the point that nothing short of making an example of one or two was required.[4]

Even though there was disappointment that Commodore Leake had not been able to do more, the detailed information he provided inspired the inclusion of Placentia into a largescale naval operation for 1703. The plan called for Vice-Admiral John Benbow, in command in the West Indies, to be reinforced, and after operations against the French in the Windward Islands that summer, an effort would be made by his fleet against Placentia later in the year as they were returning to England. When news of Benbow's death reached England in January 1703 Vice-Admiral John Graydon was appointed to replace Benbow, and the basic plan was slightly modified. Graydon was to sail to Jamaica with four warships and seven troop transports. Once there he was to see to the defenses of the English island and, after supplementing his forces with elements of those already on station, set sail for Placentia.

Graydon left England March 13, 1703. For the most part, the journey would prove uneventful, but on the fifth day out Graydon's fleet encountered four French warships bound for Breast. One of Graydon's captains bore down on the French line, but the admiral quickly signaled him to disengage. Graydon interpreted his orders concerning Jamaica and Newfoundland to supersede anything but an engagement based on self-defense. The French squadron was not interested in a fight either and continued on to Breast.

On the morning of June 4, 1703, the seventy-gun HMS *Resolution* entered the roadstead at Port Royal, Jamaica, to the salute of cannon from the nearby fort. Accompanied by several other warships and transports, the broad pennant flying on the ship-of-the-line announced the arrival of Admiral Graydon. Graydon met with Governor Thomas Handasyd, where the admiral discussed his plans. While the sea and the enemy had proved accommodating during the crossing, sickness had devastated his soldiers and sailors. To make matters worse the squadron on station with Admiral Hovenden Walker had been devastated by a failed campaign against Guadalupe. Graydon informed the governor that only 120 of the 400-man regiment destined for the defense of the island were still present but that the vacancies had been filled with drafts from the other five regiments with him. After reviewing the unit Handasyd wrote the Board of Trade, "such poor, sorry, sick scrubs I never seen, most of them haveing neither shoe, stockin, shirt or cravat, and about 200 pieces of iron that had been firelocks, wch. can never be made so again." Graydon would only spend a few weeks in Jamaica. Supplies were difficult to come by given a recent drought, but Handasyd still managed to provide the fleet with some provisions. To solve his personnel problem Graydon sent press gangs out into Kingston and Port Royal the night before he left, and when he departed the next morning some forty to fifty involuntary sailors left with him.[5]

In late July a small schooner flying the fleur-de-lis passed by the guns of Fort Royal in Placentia. Onboard was Governor Daniel Subercase. Characterized in a 1695 list of officers serving in Canada as, "A good officer, a worthy man, but very violent and passionate," it would be this latter trait that the new governor applied to the defenses of Placentia. After inspecting the fort, as well as the outlying batteries and outposts, Subercase shook his head. Years of neglect and harsh weather had rotted almost anything made of wood. Everything from gun platforms to palisades were affected. The negligence also extended to the various earthworks erected, which had eroded to the point that a few were on the verge of collapse. Added to this the three companies of marines at his disposal were little different than the English garrison at St. John's; ill disciplined, poorly equipped, in arrears, and constantly on the verge of deserting.[6]

The governor put his garrison to work repairing the fortifications and had his officers drill their men to instill discipline. At the same time, he also organized an expedition to strike at the English. Lt. Francois Amariton would lead a party of fifty-one volunteers on a raid against Ferryland. Amariton's plan worked better than he could have imagined. After a long march across the peninsula, the war party burst out of the woods one morning and seized one of the town's blockhouses, several prisoners, and three small fishing vessels before the defenders realized what had happened. The rest of the inhabitants, close to three hundred, fled, including the crew of a brigantine which had sounded the alarm. Realizing that the enemy would likely organize a pursuit, Amariton burned the captured vessels and disappeared back into the woods with his captives. The French leader proved correct, and a large party of enemy were soon on his trail. The English caught up with the French war party near Fermouse, but Amariton, after being deserted by over half his men, ambushed the van of the enemy column, which facilitated his escape.[7]

Subercase was impressed with the expedition, but this soon turned to concern when one of the prisoners informed him that Admiral Graydon and thirty-three sail had left St. John's to attack Placentia. The governor sounded the alarm. While his garrison was too small to repel a landing, he was fortunate in that the English had decided to approach while the fishing fleet was still in port. This gave him perhaps 1,500 men to draw upon. Soon the sound of pick and shovel echoed through the hills day and night. A few weeks later a cheer rang out from the lookouts as the sixty-four-gun French man-of-war *Juste* and the fifty-gun *Hasardeux* approached the fort. Their arrival was well timed. Another three companies had been sent to aid Subercase, and combined with the guns and crews of the French warships, the governor now felt far more secure.

Graydon's fleet reached Newfoundland on August 2, 1703, but was then quickly scattered by heavy fogs. After rendezvousing at St. John's and combining with the warships on station, in late August Graydon dispatched a pair of frigates to cruise the waters near Placentia. The admiral followed a week later with a dozen warships and a score of transports. While it was one of the strongest fleets to ever arrive in Newfoundland, its size and strength was deceptive. Many of the vessels were in need of a major overhaul, and the rigging and sails on most vessels were a patchwork of repairs. Equipment issues aside, manpower was the real problem. The demanding Caribbean campaigns had weakened most and sickness carried away the rest. Many of Graydon's vessels were carrying half their crew compliment, with the difference being made up by soldiers from the five regiments aboard the transports. Even here, however, there was a problem. The troops should have mustered close to 2,500 men, but when a roll was taken, he found barely over half this number fit for duty. The admiral had hoped that the promised 500 men from New England would help offset his manpower problems, but this regiment turned out to be more like 140 men, and even this had been reduced by illness to less than half that number.

With his fleet positioned near the entrance to Placentia Bay, on September 3, Graydon held a council of war. Lines of small boats traced their way to the flagship HMS *Boyne* as the warships' captains and the regimental commanders gathered for the meeting. The council convened with status reports on the strength of the fleet's forces and the supplies on hand. It then shifted to intelligence on the enemy's strength. Reports from a handful of fishing boats taken reported that the enemy had close to three thousand men, and in addition, a pair of French men-of-war had recently entered the harbor, increasing these numbers. This fact alone was sufficient to question whether to proceed, but when coupled with the natural defenses of the harbor and the weakened state of the fleet, the venture appeared unlikely to succeed. The weather and season soon put the matter out of doubt. Heavy fogs, fall storms, and the prospect of a long siege with troops equipped for the Caribbean operations was enough for all to agree that the expedition, "under the present circumstances is altogether impracticable, and hath no probability of success."[8]

From here Graydon returned to England arriving in late October. The admiral was questioned as to his decision not to attack Placentia, but in the end, his arguments were sound and a number of professional officers under him concurred. Graydon, however, had political enemies, and when this route did not work, they accused Graydon of cowardice for failing to engage the French vessels he encountered on his outbound trek. It was, of course, a thin veil, and although Graydon was not court martialed, the House of Lords dismissed him from the service.[9]

Subercase smiled when news reached him that the English fleet had sailed off. The smile was not for the enemy's departure. Backed by sufficient manpower and a few warships, the natural defenses of the harbor made it impossible to take by sea without suffering massive casualties. He would not have attacked either. No, the smile was because the initiative had now shifted to him, and he planned to use it.

CHAPTER NINE

# The Siege of St. John's

One of the Newfoundland garrison that returned to England with Admiral Graydon was Captain Richards. The harsh winters had caused numbness in his arm, and as such, he had asked for a new posting. With several brothers holding senior positions in the military Richards soon found himself posted to the Duke of Marlborough's staff, but before he departed for Flanders, he penned a report on the defenses of St. John's and Newfoundland.

The scattered and isolated nature of the towns along the coast made them extremely vulnerable to a French attack, the engineer noted, particularly in the winter after the fleet had left. To make matters worse, any efforts to fortify these towns and harbors would come at great expense for little in the way of additional safety. Even St. John's was vulnerable, not to an attack from the sea but to a French attack from the landside "by reason that no one work can secure the whole, their dwellings being straggling and situation difficult." Fort William was also suspect, not because of the strength of its works but because of its unruly and undisciplined garrison, who the engineer recommended be relieved at once.

The best approach would be to order the inhabitants of the outlying settlements to rendezvous at St. John's for the winter. This concentrated manpower would reinforce the garrison and allow for additional fortifications to be built, including a wooden palisade around the town. At the moment, however, the commander of St. John's did not have the authority to give this order even if an attack was in progress. Richards was clear on this key lapse in the island's defenses. "I can't help giving my opinion, that if the inhabitants are not obliged to rendezvous at St. John's and put under direction of the officers, the enemy may improve the opportunity to dispossess us of those works."[1]

Given the exploits of Iberville a few years before, it was sound advice that brought a chorus of agreement but little in the way of change. The arrival of the annual fishing fleet and its escort squadron in the spring of 1704 quickly put aside such thoughts. With English warships now patrolling the coast and dropping anchor in several of the outlying harbors there was little to fear, and the focus soon shifted to securing the year's catch.

The season slid by with little in the way of French interference. A few privateers and vessels were taken at sea, while on the Avalon Peninsula French and English deserters wore a trail down between St. John's and Placentia over the course of the summer. The complaints of these men were the same—neglect, poor pay, and poor food—and once they arrived at what they thought were greener pastures, each quickly realized that nothing was different on the other side. At St. John's matters with the garrison were reaching near mutinous levels. In addition to the desertions, complaints from the troops regarding their plight and the overbearing actions of their commander, Captain Thomas Lloyd, were presented to the naval squadron's commander and senior officer on station, Commodore Timothy Bridge.

Bridge held a court of inquiry into Lloyd's conduct and soon found conflicting testimony. Lloyd seemed to have fulfilled his duties in equipping and paying the garrison, and the majority of the town's citizens including several who signed the original petition referred to Lloyd as "a man of honour and a good Governor." The commodore wrote in his report that he could not find evidence to support the charges against Lloyd and concluded that "The great desire the soldiers have to return to England, and not any ill-treatment they have received from Capt. Lloyd, is the sole occasion of their uneasiness and complaint against him, and that they threaten to desert, in hopes thereby to be the sooner relieved by other men from England." Even so, out of fear of a wholesale desertion once the fleet departed, Bridge consented to the garrison's request and suspended Lloyd, replacing him with his lieutenant, John Moody, who had also signed the petition.[2]

Subercase faced a disgruntled garrison at Placentia as well, although it never approached the state of that at St. John's. The veteran captain was not one to tolerate such things and kept his troops busy working on the fortifications. The arrival of the French fishing fleet, and the number of men it brought with it, all but secured the port for the season. This was well, because the French governor had been formulating plans for the fall and winter. After the departure of Graydon's fleet Subercase sent a letter to the French court outlining a plan for a winter attack on the Newfoundland settlements. Laid out along the same lines as Iberville's successful campaign in 1696, and even employing a number of officers and men who had participated in the previous raid, the plan quickly won approval from the French court. Orders were sent to Subercase to proceed and for Governor Vaudreuil to provide additional troops and supplies for the venture.

In the spring of 1704 Subercase dispatched the transport *Wesp* to Quebec. Vaudreuil organized the supplies and a troop of a hundred men, led by a dozen veteran officers such as Montigny, Rouville, and Captain Josue Beaucourt. The vessel departed for Placentia on All Saints Day and arrived before the French colony two weeks later. When the men went ashore and met with the garrison they were greeted by good news. A French officer by the name of La Grange, who had served under Iberville at Hudson Bay, had launched an attack on the English village at Bonavista. Departing Quebec with a hundred men in a pair of small barks, by August 18 he found himself at the north end of Bonavista Bay. To avoid detection, he anchored his vessels and proceeded at night in two small launches. Around 1 a.m. the two vessels glided undetected into the port on the west side of the Bonavista Peninsula. Here the raiding party found four large vessels at anchor unaware of their presence. La Grange sent one boat toward the 140-ton *Society of Pool* with orders to board the vessel, while he and the other launch targeted the 250-ton *Pembrook Galley*. Both vessels were armed with over a dozen cannon, and as the raiding party crept closer all held their breath and braced for a sudden broadside. However, none was forthcoming. Nor was the watch alerted until the French and Indian war party was upon the deck of the two ships. It was over quickly and quietly. La Grange sent a few men over to the unarmed *William*, which, carrying thirty tons of lamp oil, surrendered without any resistance.

Thus far La Grange's plan had proven wildly successful. He had captured three vessels armed with a total of thirty-four cannon and taken seventy-eight prisoners. There was only one English ship left, the fourteen-gun *Charleston*, anchored a few hundred yards away. Looking to secure this last prize La Grange sent his launches forward, but the English ship's captain, John Gill, proved far more alert than his companions. Seeing that the vessels were French he ordered his men to their stations and loosed a broadside at the attackers, sending them scurrying back to their prizes.

With his detachment back on board La Grange had his men man the captured vessels' guns. What had been a quiet morning now erupted into a close-range exchange of broadsides and musket fire that illuminated the harbor and thundered across the still waters. Alarmed by the gunfire the inhabitants of the town fled into the woods, but as the battle raged over the course of the morning they returned, lining the banks as spectators. For the outnumbered and outgunned Gill, the engagement had left his rigging in tatters and his ship hulled several times, but he had inflicted a good deal of damage as well. Enough it seemed that by 8 a.m. La Grange was willing to pursue other means to deal with the defiant New Englander. La Grange ordered the *Society of Pool* set ablaze and steered toward the enemy warship. The tactic almost worked, but the wind shifted and the fireship passed by the *Charleston* and ran ashore where it burned for hours. Undeterred, the French commander turned to the *William.* Filled with lamp oil the 115-ton vessel soon became an approaching inferno, its spilling contents creating pools of flame that drifted like bright islands on the water's surface.

It was a crucial moment for Gill and his crew who were still busy replying to the guns of the *Pembrook Galley.* With French aim and the wind holding true, Gill was forced to send men out in whaleboats to grapple with the flaming threat and steer it clear. With grape shot rippling the waters around them, after a few tense moments the task was accomplished and the *William* slid past, slowly disintegrating from the intensity of the fire. At this point La Grange threw up his arms in frustration. If he had been able to destroy or capture the *Charleston*, he would have turned on the town, but it was clear that the stubborn English captain refused to give in. Having seen enough, La Grange ordered the *Pembrook Galley* out to sea, and after releasing a number of the crew in small boats, he set course for Quebec with his two barks and new prize.[3]

Subercase and the officers gathering around him were pleased to hear of La Grange's success, but at the same time it raised a concern that the English might now be on the alert. This was indeed the case, but as it would turn out winter, or the late arrival thereof, would delay the expedition for two months which would prove more than enough time for English diligence to wane. Finally, near mid-January a deep freeze took hold. It was what Subercase had been waiting for, and on the morning of January 15, 1705, he ordered the 450-man expedition forward. There had been little in the way of snowfall so the sleds had to be left behind. Foolishly, this led to many of the expedition's snowshoes being left behind as well. Without the sleds each man had to carry twenty days' provisions, his arms, cooking utensils, and a tent—some forty to fifty pounds in all.

The French and Indian force pushed through half-frozen streams and rapids during their march, and then on the night of the twenty-second disaster struck. A violent Nor'easter had interrupted the mild winter, bringing days of white-out conditions, freezing winds, and drifting snow. The war party was forced to halt for three days. Not sure of their position and with their provisions being consumed faster than expected, Subercase sent scouts out into the blizzard to search for the coast. On the twenty-fifth these detachments returned with news that Bay Bulls was a little under ten miles away.

With the storm subsiding into a steady snowfall, Subercase set out the next morning. Now aware of his position, the French commander dismissed marching directly on St. John's given the state of the army's provisions. Instead, he would capture the English settlement at Bay Bulls, resupply, and then push onto the English colonial capital. That afternoon the first part of this plan was accomplished when the French detachment appeared out of the woods before the fishing village. Caught completely off guard the inhabitants immediately surrendered without a shot being fired.

After resting and replenishing his troops, Subercase departed for Petty Harbor at noon on the twenty-eighth. The rugged path from Bay Bulls to Petty Harbor, the lack of snowshoes, and a numbing wind made for a grueling march that fatigued even the most robust among them. At nightfall Subercase's men made camp where they stood, leaving the column and the prisoners that had been brought along strung out along the length of the trail for miles. At this point one of the French commander's officers suffered a near fatal accident. Pastour de Costebelle was near his tent when one of his men cut down a nearby pine tree that fell on the unsuspecting officer, covering him in an avalanche of snow and pinning him to the ground. It took an hour to free Costebelle, who when he woke up found that he could move neither his arms or legs. When Subercase found out he had a stretcher fashioned and ordered several men to carry the wounded officer.[4]

The next morning Subercase captured Petty Harbor in the same fashion as Bay Bulls, without a shot being fired. From here St. John's was but nine miles away, and more importantly, there was no indication from any of his prisoners that his target was aware of his presence. As much as the French commander would have liked to take advantage of this information and push on, it was impossible. The nature of his short march to Petty Harbor had left his men exhausted, leaving him with no choice but to rest his troops for several days before making any attempt.

On January 31, after leaving forty men behind to guard the prisoners, the detachment pushed forward. The war party reached the head of St. John's Bay around sunset and made camp. Fires were forbidden and it was a frigid evening. While the men gathered together fir branches for shelter,

Subercase and a number of his officers ascended a nearby hill that overlooked the town. The view was impressive and the town appeared unaware of his presence, but the waxing moonlight made it difficult to distinguish the outline of Fort William. Even so, it was agreed to attack before dawn. Three detachments were formed. The first, under Captain Beaucourt, was to proceed directly for Fort William and attempt to take the stronghold by surprise. The second, under Montigny, would focus on securing the town, while the third detachment, mostly troops without snowshoes under Lt. L'Hermitte, would follow and support the efforts of the first two.

A few hours before sunrise Beaucourt and Montigny's troops appeared out of the woods and dashed to their target. The latter had few issues. Completely surprised, most of the inhabitants were roused from their sleep and quickly surrendered, while a handful of those who resisted were quickly dispatched. Beaucourt also reached his objective and, according to one witness, "contented himself with taking a walk on the fort's glacis without anyone stirring." Indeed, there was no sign of the garrison, but for some reason Beaucourt did not attack. A little before eight o'clock one of Subercase's officers arrived before the fort to find L'Hermitte's detachment at the base of the glacis. The officer encouraged L'Hermitte to attack, pointing out that the fort's ditch was filled with snow, and as of yet, not a single Englishman had appeared on the ramparts. The lieutenant, however, was not interested and replied that he had no orders to attack.

Within a few minutes it no longer mattered. An English sentry appeared on the wall and sounded the alarm. Soon the garrison appeared, shoveling away the snow from their cannon and exchanging musket shots with the French. Any thoughts of storming the fort disappeared when the first cannon sent a cloud of grapeshot whistling through the French formation. The discharge of additional guns along the wall clarified the matter, and the French dashed back toward the town leaving two of their number on the glacis and a few now busy tending to their wounds. Whatever confusion that had led to the missed opportunity, one thing was clear: Subercase had captured the town and now had some three hundred prisoners.[5]

Lt. Moody in command of Fort William was fortunate that the French had not pressed their attack. The garrison consisting of forty soldiers and a handful of town militia was sound asleep, and the sentry who had taken to a bottle of rum to face the bitter evening was unaware of the French outside for over an hour. The fort had been lucky. Only confusion and delay on the part of the French had saved it. Even so, the garrison's response once the alarm was sounded was commendable, perhaps even more so given their rebellious nature. With the garrison now alerted and the fort's cannon oc-

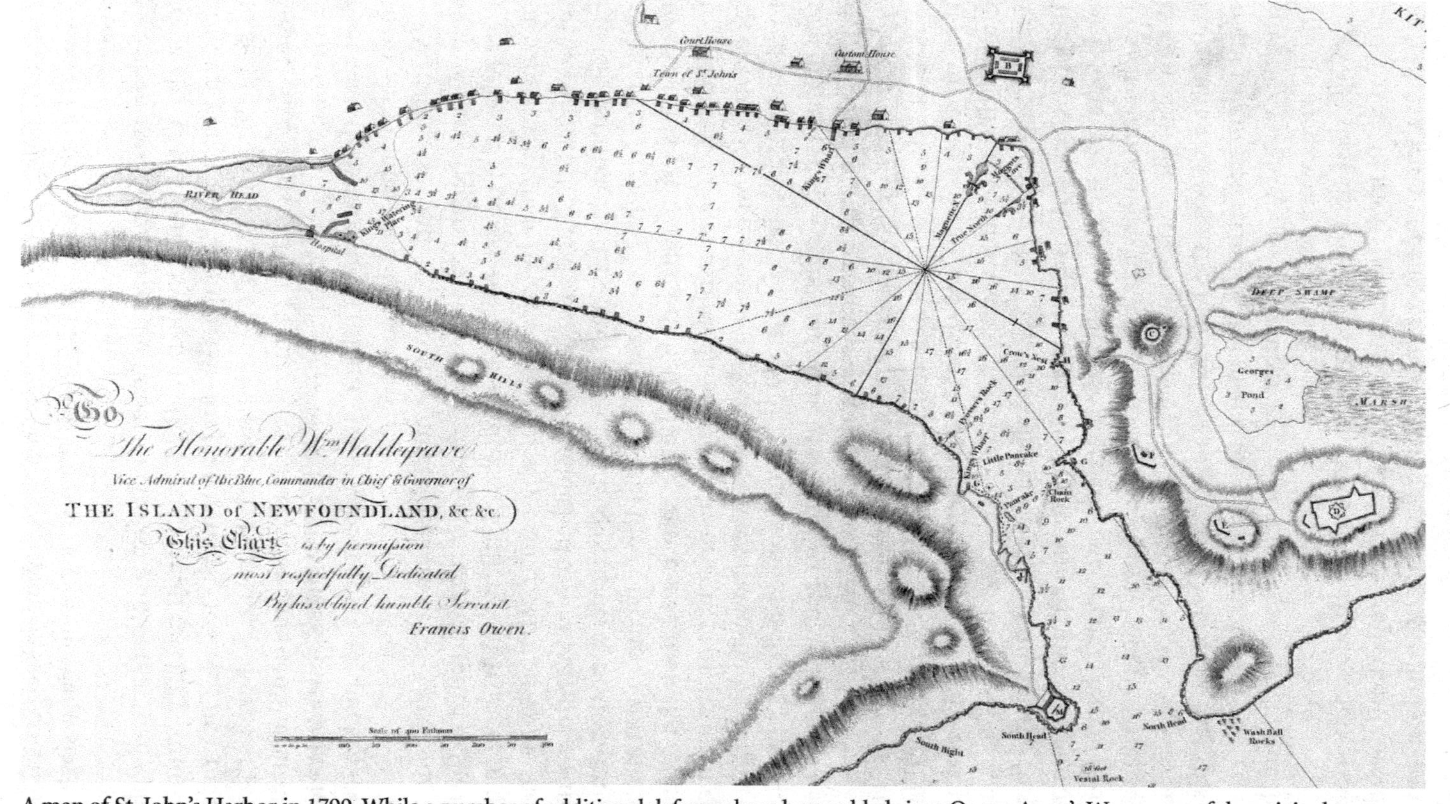


A map of St. John's Harbor in 1799. While a number of additional defenses have been added since Queen Anne's War, many of the original ones were simply upgraded over the intervening years. Key: B: Fort William C: Wallace's Battery D: Signal Hill E: South Battery F: Queen's Battery G: Chain Rock I: North Point Battery L: Frederick's Battery M: South Head Castle (*National Archives of Canada*)

casionally firing on the houses the French occupied, it seemed unlikely to Moody that the enemy would storm the fort, meaning that a siege was in order.

Subercase had reached the same conclusion and had actually planned for such a contingency by dispatching a small sloop carrying a mortar and ammunition from Placentia. For this plan to work, however, he would need to seize the stone "Castle" at South Head. Here Lt. Robert Latham and twenty-five men held the primary sea battery that guarded the entrance to the harbor. A large detachment of French and Indians appeared before the post that afternoon, but Latham's men were ready and quickly scattered them with cannonball and grapeshot.

With this second opportunity missed Subercase prepared for a long siege. A pair of abandoned batteries on the northern entrance to the harbor were seized and occasionally lobbed shots at Latham's men, more in the way of harassment than in expectation of any results. The buildings near the fort were occupied and guard posts established to monitor the enemy. The French commander then returned a hundred prisoners, mostly women and children, to Moody. The latter realized that the Frenchman was attempting to strain his provisions, but he had little choice and took the inhabitants into the fort. Subercase placed the rest of the prisoners in the town church, except for a few well-known traders and businessmen who he used as envoys to Moody. After a few days of planning and sporadic shots, Subercase sent one of these men, Colin Campbell, to the fort to demand Moody's surrender, but the English commander was not interested.[6]

After a few weeks of stalemate Subercase sent a pair of letters. The first was to Lt. Moody. The French commander offered Moody favorable terms if he surrendered and urged him to consider the fate of the English prisoners and the inhabitants within the fort's walls. If Moody refused, and the French were forced to attack, "I shall not be able to hinder the fury of ye Indians which with the rest of our troops do importune me vigorously to prosecute my design," Subercase warned. The second letter, which the French commander dictated to John Roope, a Royal Engineer who had been captured in the initial attack, warned Lt. Latham that Moody was about to come to terms with the French. The implication was clear that this agreement might not include Latham and his men, upon whom Subercase's entire fury would then fall. Neither English officer, however, fell for the bait, and the siege wore on.

While such circumstances typically favored the attacker, Subercase's men had no way to move the captured guns and, more importantly, would have to mount them in open terrain before the fort, as the ground was too frozen to dig siege trenches. Thus, the French and Indians entertained themselves with fleeting raids on the fort by a few dozen snowshoed troops. In return the fort's guns focused on the French troops bivouacked in the nearby homes. Each morning when the garrison spied smoke rising from one of the chimney's it was greeted by a twelve-pound cannonball or a hail of grapeshot. In most instances this morning ritual resulted in little, but through the sheer number of shots fired as the siege entered its second month, occasionally there were casualties and close calls. One morning a large-caliber round from a wall gun tore through the side of a house and shot the pillows out from under the heads of two sleeping French officers, leaving both unharmed. On other days wooden splinters claimed a few victims as cannonballs ripped through the wall. Because of the sloping terrain leading up to the fort the closer houses were partially masked, providing at least some measure of safety. Moody saw this problem as well and began using the fort's mortar to bring these homesteads under fire. The plunging explosive rounds did make the position more perilous, and in one case a brick chimney was struck sending forth a cloud of metal and stone projectiles that mortally wounded a prisoner and Subercase's nephew, the Chevalier De Leau.[7]

The hamlets near St. John's were raided and offered no resistance. After the towns were plundered the inhabitants were free to remain in their homes, "provided that if anyone deserted to go to the fort, all the rest would be put to the sword, to which they acquiesced, and remained free." At Torbay, the agreement quickly broke down when three settlers were caught heading for St. John's. True to their word, the French and Indians slew the rest of the town. At Quidi Vidi, less than a mile from Fort William, the town's inhabitants took matters into their own hands after this example and apprehended a villager attempting to desert. The man was dragged before the French by the angry mob and summarily executed, but the town was spared.

By early March it was clear to Subercase that the sloop carrying the artillery from Placentia was not coming, nor would it be able to pass the English guns at South Head even if it did. The fort also appeared better supplied and better defended than the French governor had hoped. His casualties had not been significant, less than a score, but sickness was a far more potent enemy. With the remaining Newfoundland villages still to be dealt with and the possibility of an early arrival of the seasonal English squadron, Subercase abandoned the siege. On March 5 the French commander ordered all but a handful of homes and vessels to be put to the torch. He then sent his sick and wounded to Quidi Vidi, where the inhabitants had agreed to transport them to Bay Bulls. The rest of the war party along with a train of prisoners marched off to Petty Harbor and from there to Bay Bulls.[8]

To deal with the smaller English villages Subercase divided his forces. Montigny and a detachment of his men were to attack the villages north of St. John's while Subercase and the rest of the forces would use captured vessels to raid the English ports to the south. Both tasks were performed with ruthless efficiency. Subercase burned Bay Bulls and every town south of this port before setting a course for Placentia. Montigny and his detachment fell upon the villages lining the shores of Conception Bay, plundering, burning, and taking the inhabitants hostage. The expedition met its only rebuff at the sheer cliffs of Carbonear Island. As with Iberville's expedition the villagers had fled to the natural fortifications of the island whose sole landing spot was dangerous even in the best of circumstances. Armed with cannon, stocked with supplies, and protected by several hundred men they refused Montigny's demand to surrender. Montigny wanted to attack, but it was not worth the effort so he satisfied himself with burning the town and sailing north in several captured vessels.

After destroying the remaining hamlets on the west side of Conception Bay the war party rounded Point Grates and fell upon Old Pelican and New Pelican on the east side of Trinity Bay. After working his way down the length of the bay, burning yet more homes and taking more captives, Montigny arrived at the head of Bulls Bay near the portage over to Placentia Bay in mid-April. Here he transferred his booty and a handful of prisoners over to an awaiting vessel and sent word to Subercase of his exploits. Montigny would then spend several days at Bulls Bay waiting for raiding detachments he had sent out to rendezvous with him.

With his forces consolidated once again word reached Montigny that Subercase wanted him to attack the settlements in Bonavista Bay. On May 8, after a brisk morning storm, Montigny set sail with sixty-one men to accomplish the task. After scouring the western side of Trinity Bay Montigny was forced to halt at Trinity Harbor. The icebergs and flows made it too dangerous to round the Bonavista Peninsula. Not to be deterred, Montigny's detachment set out by foot on May 13 and by evening were encamped on the Bonavista side of the peninsula. The next morning the detachment marched through brush and flowing water to within a few miles of Bonavista Harbor. Here Montigny rested his troops. A little before daybreak the detachment crept forward. Montigny had ordered the town invested before he gave the signal to attack. Within a few hours everything was ready and the partisan leader fired his gun to signal the attack. War whoops and hideous yells followed, accompanied by the sound of splintering doors, but in each

A portion of a 1770s map of Newfoundland showing Conception Bay, Trinity Bay, and Bonaviste Bay. (*Boston Public Library*)

case the attackers found no one. In fact, the entire town was deserted, having fled a few weeks before to a nearby island upon receiving a warning from St. John's. To make matters worse his men were short of provisions and the inhabitants had removed every trace of food before departing.[9]

Montigny sent out a score of hunters who quickly came across a dozen cows that the inhabitants either could not carry away or overlooked. The next day provided another fortunate capture when a few Wabanaki brought in a leading citizen of the town. As he had done for the last few weeks the man had come to see if anyone was in the harbor. The Englishman informed the French leader that there were 126 armed men on the island and a number of women and children. There was a battery of four cannon and entrenchments had been erected before all the landings. The rest of the citizens had fled across the bay.

The next morning, as his men were building a number of boats, the French commander was greeted by the sight of a small vessel in the harbor waving a white flag. Montigny ordered his men to let the ship pass and soon an English delegation was standing before him and his officers. "They asked if it was Sr. Montigny, who commanded this party, remembering that he had in the past destroyed the whole coast with d'Iberville," Montigny noted in his journal. "They were told yes," which seemed to have demolished whatever resolve they had found. The delegation asked if there was any way out of this situation. Montigny shrugged and said surrender. Otherwise, he planned to attack the island as soon as his ships were ready. It proved enough to convince the defenders, who surrendered after a brief negotiation.

Montigny and his detachment struck several more villages before finally sailing into Bulls Bay in early June. The next several days were spent dragging the plunder and small boats over the isthmus to Placentia Bay. After a brief weather delay the expedition set sail and by the afternoon of June 6 had reached Placentia.[10]

The French campaign of 1705 against English Newfoundland was every bit as devastating as Iberville's campaign in 1696. Between Subercase and Montigny, over a score of towns, hamlets, and villages had been destroyed, and a fleet of small vessels perished with them. Livestock was slaughtered, a few dozen settlers were killed, and hundreds were taken prisoner. In fact, the numbers were too large for the French to deal with, and most would be released to return to the ashes of their homes. While Fort William at St. John's had not fallen, everything around it was in ruins and by all appearances the English settlements on the Avalon Peninsula had once again been swept away.

For the English there were few positives. One was the defense of Fort William and the South Head Battery. While the troops had shown to be unruly at times, in the end they had proven to be good soldiers and were finally relieved later that year, some having served close to a decade on the island. Moody's and Latham's conduct was praised, as was that of the women re-

Jacques Testard de Montigny. Montigny had accompanied Pierre Iberville in his attack on the English fishing villages in Newfoundland during King William's War. He would go on to repeat this exploit during Queen Anne's War, as well as lead a number of French and Indian expeditions against the New England frontier. (National Archives of Canada)

leased back to Moody after the initial assault. They had helped repair the fort, often under fire, made cartridges for the garrison, and even acted as extra sets of eyes on watch, leaving one convinced that they would have grabbed a musket and manned the parapets if called upon to do so. When it came to the bulk of the citizenry, however, accusations were more frequent than accolades. Part of this was an extension of personal feuds. Engineer John Roope was accused of aiding and conspiring with the enemy, with speculation that his capture was arranged. The citizens of Quidi Vidi had their loyalty called into question, as did other towns. The matter was further complicated by the fact that the French had not burned a few homes at St. John's. This appeared to be enough evidence to accuse these owners of aiding the enemy, which further generated division among the colonists.[11]

The merchants of England complained of the losses and demanded that the queen take action. Once again, ships, men, and supplies were promised and plans formulated to prevent the devastation from happening again. When news reached Michael Richards, now a captain in the 1st Foot Guards in Flanders, he just shook his head. In the mind of the future chief engineer of Great Britain the answer was simple—unite the populace against the threat, until then the cycle would continue.

CHAPTER TEN

# The Fragile Peace in the West

THE GREAT PEACE OF MONTREAL had secured New France's hold on the west, but it was proving a delicate act to maintain. Unresolved, long-term animosities existed between many of the nations that had signed the accord, and matters were further complicated with the king's shift toward frontier diplomacy via the *coureur de bois*. The first problems appeared among Vaudreuil's allies. The governor met with an Ottawa delegation in late September 1703. Among other matters, the Ottawa representative pressed the governor on the war between the Chippewa, Sauk, and Fox. The Ottawa spokesman pointed out that something needed to be done or this war would spill over into Ottawa country and draw his nation into the conflict.

Vaudreuil realized that the chieftains were listening intently on his answer. After all, if the governor could not enforce the terms of the peace among his own allies, how long could the treaty last? He made it clear to the Ottawa chieftain that he would "put a stop to the War between their neighbors, and to oblige them to execute the general treaty of peace." In the meantime, he informed the delegation that he expected them to abide by the terms of the treaty.[1]

Fortunately for the French, the Iroquois were resolved to keep the peace intact. In October a delegation from the Five Nations arrived at Montreal. The Iroquois spokesman, Teganisorens, expressed condolences for the loss of Governor Callières. When they had last spoken with Callières he had pointed out that since the Iroquois were not English subjects, they could remain neutral in any conflict between the two colonies. Now, they came to confirm this pledge. They would preserve the peace and maintain it with all their might. If the treaty was to be broken, "it will not be by us," Teganisorens informed Vaudreuil, "but by the Europeans, who are bad men, who wage war for trifles, whilst with us, heads must be broken to force us into hostilities." The sachem then pointed out that it would be well if the English and the French followed the Five Nations' lead, but unfortunately he had heard news that the French-allied Wabanaki had already taken up the hatchet against the English. There was quiet among the representatives as the interpreter spoke his last phrases of French to the governor. Vaudreuil nodded at the words and then assured the Iroquois that the expedition in Acadia was a response to English aggressions—actions that required a stern response. He had no intention of disturbing the English of Albany, as they had not provoked him, but the English of Boston he wished to chastise. The governor then agreed to heed Teganisorens's advice and consented to forward their peace proposal on to the king for his consideration.[2]

Although facing difficulties with English attempts to convince his allies to attack the Iroquois, and discord between Antoine Le Motte de Cadillac and the Jesuits over the establishment of Detroit and the abandonment of the post at Michilimackinac, Vaudreuil had managed to maintain the fragile peace for almost a year. In the summer of 1704, however, the calm was broken. A group of Miami attacked a Seneca hunting party. A handful of Seneca were slain and the rest taken captive. Vaudreuil responded by sending an envoy to demand the release of the prisoners, hoping to diffuse the matter before it escalated. A larger break appeared not long after. An Ottawa chieftain from Michilimackinac named Companise, looking to reignite the conflict with the Five Nations, launched a brazen attack on an Iroquois trading party encamped near the walls of Fort Frontenac. There was a burst of gunfire and the call of war whoops, and within the span of a few minutes, it was over. Several Iroquois were killed and a half a dozen were led away into captivity. When Companise passed Fort Detroit he stopped to shout in defiance at the fort's garrison, which set off a chorus of war whoops among his caravan and a few jubilant musket shots. Alphonse Tonty, who was in command of the fort in Cadillac's absence, was stunned by the act. He ordered Ensign Jean-Baptiste Vincenne to take twenty soldiers and retrieve the prisoners. Vincenne took to the task with such energy that he and his men not only freed the prisoners and scattered the Ottawa war party but also routed another party of thirty Ottawa who had come to Companise's aid.[3]

Fortunately for Vaudreuil, the Iroquois did not retaliate against the Ottawa. Instead they sent an emissary to the governor to protest the breach of the treaty. The Iroquois waited almost a year, and when nothing had been done, in August 1705 a delegation from the Five Nations traveled to Montreal for an explanation. Vaudreuil returned several prisoners taken by the Miami and those liberated from the attack at Fort Frontenac. The actions pleased the representatives from the Five Nations, who informed the governor that although the Ottawa had claimed that the French were behind the attack, they did not believe this and in such matter would always speak directly with him to ascertain the truth. Thus far, the governor had acted in good faith and kept his word. They would keep theirs as well.

There was, however, still the matter of compensation for those Iroquois who had fallen, and it was not just on this occasion but a number of cases where the Ottawa had struck at the Five Nations. Yet, the Five Nations had not responded and violated the treaty. "Nevertheless," the Iroquois spokesman noted, "here have we been repeatedly struck without it appearing that our father has taken our part; had we acted as the Outtauois (Ottawa) has done, our father would have soon resented it." There was a chorus of agreement followed by a test. "Remember, Father, the promise which was given us at the Peace, that if any of your children struck another, we would form a union in order to exterminate the nation which might have struck the blow?"[4]

Vaudreuil was hardly interested in a war against the Ottawa with the Iroquois as allies. Such an event, although spelled out in the peace treaty, would play havoc with the French and Indian alliances in the region, opening the door to both the English and the Iroquois. The governor agreed that what the Five Nations orator had said was true but that it was also true that "a good father does not begin by killing his child when he is guilty of a fault; but when he persists in disobedience then he chastises him." He would demand satisfaction from the Ottawa, just as he would demand it of the Iroquois or any other tribe that violated the treaty. If this was not forthcoming then there could be talk of retaliation, but not before. The delegation agreed to allow the governor to pursue this course and broke up.

It turned out satisfaction was but a few hours away. As the Iroquois were preparing to leave Vincenne a delegation of Ottawa chieftains arrived. The Ottawa apologized to the Iroquois for the actions and promised compensation. The Iroquois accepted the Ottawa apology and proposals, and after a long celebration dedicated to the renewed peace, all parties departed in good spirits.[5]

In New York, Governor Cornbury watched the frontier and listened to reports of French and Iroquois meetings. There was little he could do at the moment to undermine French efforts and bring the Five Nations back into a military alliance with the English. In fact, there were good reasons not to upset the current situation. In the fall of 1703 news reached the governor that a thousand French and Indians had been seen marching toward Albany. When Cornbury arrived at the town a few days later he found confusion abounded. After restoring order, he sent out scouts. These returned within a few days with no news of an enemy expedition in the area, ending the brief panic that had seized the settlement. The event, however, had given Cornbury the opportunity to assess the defenses guarding the strategic town. The old Fort Albany was a crumbling mess, and the new fort was barely started. The town's palisades required significant repair, and a number of blockhouses along these palisades needed to be replaced. At least the governor was pleased with what he saw regarding the troops and militia. "I must say," he wrote London, "I could in eight and forty hours time have drawn together upwards of seven hundred men, reckoning the Garrison, the Militia of Albany, and that of Ulster Counties; and the Indians of the Five Nations were so ready that they all left their Castles and were coming towards Albany before I could send them any orders."[6]

A few days later the governor saw his southern defenses tested when word reached him that ten French warships were approaching New York Harbor. Again, Cornbury raced across the colony, this time to find out that ten French warships were really just a French privateer that had taken an English merchantman near Sandy Hook. While the militia of Long Island had responded, many of those within the city had fled into the woods. For those that did appear they proved to be ill-armed, ill-led, and confused, taking far too much time to organize their ranks. This was alarming given that the colony's forces were naturally divided between Albany and New York City, meaning that one could not quickly come to the aid of the other. To complicate matters, the fortifications of Manhattan were as suspect as those of Albany, and at both locations there was a universal shortage of small arms and powder. "Your Lordships will perceive," Cornbury informed London, "how necessary it is to have a standing Force in this Province, where we are exposed to the invasions of the Enemy by sea in the Southern parts of it, and to the attacks of the French and Indians by land in the Northern parts of it." Without this assistance from England the colony was in no position to attack, and without the aid of the Iroquois, it was questionable if it could even defend itself.[7]

As Vaudreuil suspected, Cornbury attempted to sway the Iroquois away from the peace treaty. One of the first and partially successful efforts the New York governor implemented was to place Protestant ministers among the Five Nations in hopes of counterbalancing the efforts of the Black Robes.

The Iroquois demonstrated their commitment to neutrality by allowing these pastors to sit alongside the Jesuits in council meetings. Both opinions would be heard, and both ignored or accepted if it suited the council.

Cornbury was more successful when it came to intelligence gathering. There were plenty of Iroquois who did not want the treaty and wished to fight with the English against their hereditary enemies. As such, these individuals freely traveled through the Iroquois cantons as well as the French-allied nations to the north and west. On several occasions Cornbury had passed on information regarding the target and timing of a French and Indian attack on the New England frontier, but although many were true, extenuating circumstances often delayed the French effort to the point that the warning had been forgotten and, perhaps more importantly, future ones treated with disregard.

In another attempt to influence the Five Nations Cornbury sent Colonel Peter Schuyler to the Iroquois villages to convince the sachems to send the Jesuits away but with no success. Schuyler then turned to making contact with the French-allied tribes. He sent presents to the Christian Iroquois at the Lake of the Two Mountains mission, and although some appeared receptive, Vaudreuil received word of this and had the gifts returned. In the end the sum total of these advances, overtures, and whispered advice amounted to nothing. For the moment at least, the Iroquois were committed to the treaty, and the French committed toward keeping it that way.

Vaudreuil spent the early part of 1706 dealing with the Ottawa. This nation's promises to the Iroquois the previous year regarding reparations had solidified the peace process, but their lack of effort in seeing these through brought the ire of the Iroquois down upon the governor. Vaudreuil dispatched Father Joseph Marest to Michilimackinac to convince the Ottawa chieftains to carry through with their pledge to the Five Nations. The mission proved a success, but there was hardly time to celebrate, as a far more serious crisis erupted between the Miami and the Ottawa.[8]

The matter in question occurred at Detroit. The recently erected post was the brainchild of Antoine Laumet de la Mothe Cadillac. Cadillac, a captain in the marines, had previously been the commandant of Fort de Baude at Michilimackinac. His responsibilities there included all of the fur trade in the northwest as well as acting as French representative to the native nations in the region. Cadillac held this post for two years. During this time, he explored the area and became convinced that Fort de Baude was not the best location from which to regulate the fur trade. A fort on the straits between Lake Huron and Lake Erie made far more sense. To deal with the *coureur de bois* and the ill effects of the illegal fur trade on the colony, Louis ordered the frontier trading posts closed in 1696. Frontenac had spoken with Cadillac as to his idea for a post at Detroit, and with his availability now open, he ordered the officer to France to present his project to the French court.

Cadillac was granted an audience and presented his case to the minister of the marine. The proposed location just south of Lake St. Clair would better handle the Indian trade and French interests in the area, Cadillac stated. Fort de Baude at Michilimackinac was not only considered too far and the weather too severe but was located amongst the French-allied nations. What was required was a post on the lakes in the neutral area between the Five Nations and the French allies. From here the French could exert influence over both sides as well as be in a position to thwart any English advances into the region. Cadillac pointed out not just the need for a fort and trading post at Detroit but, to secure the location, a small agricultural settlement as well. Part of this would be made up of members of nearby tribes and part by French settlers and soldiers. To reduce corruption the garrison would be forbidden to participate in the fur trade, and to strengthen French relations with the high-country nations, marriages would be encouraged, as would the establishment of missions and the construction of a hospital.

While the court expressed interest, many in the French colony opposed Cadillac's plan, claiming it would lead to the destruction of the fur trade. So too did the Jesuits who had a mission at Michilimackinac and had previously accused Cadillac of selling brandy and contraband to the natives. These critics delayed the matter, but in 1700 their objections were put aside by the king, who issued orders for Cadillac to erect his post at Detroit.

By 1706 Fort Pontchartrain, or Fort Detroit as it became known, and the nearby palisaded village had failed to live up to Cadillac's expectations. Cadillac and his second-in-command, Alphonse Tonty, the younger brother of Henri Tonty who had served with La Salle, had brought their wives in a show of commitment to the settlement, but this attracted few others. Opposition from the Jesuits, who had once again accused Cadillac of personally profiting by selling liquor and firearms, as well as interference from France, had slowed the settlement's growth such that it appeared no different than any other frontier post. Cadillac was at least successful in attracting nearby tribes to the area. Ottawa, Miami, and Huron villages dotted the landscape near the fort, and there was a constant flow of visitors from all the surrounding nations.[9]

While arguments, fights, and ill-conduct were not out of the norm for this rude frontier post, in the summer of 1706 this escalated to the state of near rebellion. The matter started with the Indian villages at Detroit. The Miami were reputed to have slain a number of Ottawa, a well-respected chieftain being counted among the fallen. The Ottawa sachems of the nearby village demanded reparations but were rebuffed by the Miami on several occasions. With little recourse the Ottawa turned to Cadillac for justice. The commandant assured them that he would attend to the matter, and after a few inquiries and conversations, Cadillac was convinced that the dispute was settled.

This, however, was not the case. Cadillac departed for Quebec a few days later, and not long after his second-in-command, Tonty, departed as well. With the matter still unresolved the Ottawa approached the new commandant, Ensign Etienne Bourgmont, with their grievance. The French officer dismissed their words with a tone that created suspicion among the sachems. Whether Bourgmont's response was a result of inexperience, callousness, or because he believed the matter had already been dealt with by Cadillac did not matter. Soon a rumor took hold among the Ottawa that the French wished to punish them for their breech of the peace treaty against the Iroquois and their slow response in carrying through with the agreed-upon retributions. This thought took on yet more credence when the commandant suggested that the Ottawa join a war party made up of the Miami, Huron, and Iroquois to strike at the Sioux. It appeared to the Ottawa that the venture was an excuse to either remove the men from their homes so the Miami could fall upon their village or that the other tribes would turn on them at some point during the expedition.

A few of the Ottawa sachems wished to approach the French for an explanation, but their suggestions were overwhelmed by those who wished to strike back at the Miami. Foremost among this latter group was a war chief known as Le Pesant. Le Pesant dismissed any idea of talking with the French, as the new commandant was untrustworthy. Instead, he suggested an alternative plan—that they act as if they were preparing to go on the Sioux expedition and then, when the moment was right, fall upon the nearby Miami village. While not all agreed, enough did so that the plan was adopted.[10]

A few days later on June 6, the Ottawa warriors departed to join the gathering war party. Up until this moment only the chieftains were aware of their plans. When the force reached the nearby woods, they were halted and the real intent of their mission explained. With his men whipped into a frenzy Le Pesant turned back toward the Miami village. He soon encountered half a dozen Miami, five of whom were dispatched before they realized what was happening. The sixth, however, escaped, sounding the alarm and entering Fort Detroit with cries that the Ottawa were attacking.

The warning set off a flight from the Miami village toward the stronghold. Caught in this rush was Recollect Father Nicholas Constantin. The father had been taken in the early moments of the Ottawa attack, but he was released and sent to the fort to tell Bourgmont that the Ottawa had no designs on the French and for the garrison not to fire on them. As Constantin converged with a cluster of fleeing Miami near the fort's main gate a volley from the pursuing Ottawa ripped through the formation, killing the father, several Miami, and a French soldier who was looking to reenter the fort. Believing the Ottawa were attacking the garrison, Bourgmont closed the gates and ordered his men to fire on the rebellious tribe. Muskets soon erupted down the length of the fort's walls, punctuated by the distinct thump of cannon which hurled grapeshot at the Ottawa ranks. At this stage there was no controlling either side, and for the next half hour the rattle of musketry and the bark of swivel guns echoed over the landscape. Suddenly cooler heads prevailed, and the fire ebbed away as the Ottawa withdrew, carrying over thirty dead and wounded with them.

There was now an uneasy peace as the Miami refugees remained in the fort under the protection of Bourgmont and his garrison. Le Pesant began to solicit aid of the Ottawa of Michilimackinac, and many were now being drawn into the conflict. Soon there was a plan afoot to form an alliance with the Fox and Sauk and attack the Miami villages on the St. Joseph River. News of this alarmed Father Marest and his colleagues, who realized such an action would likely ignite a large-scale war on the frontier. Marest spoke with the Ottawa and, after an impassioned effort, convinced them to set the idea aside. Even so, it was a dismal and volatile scene. "The greater part of the fields at Detroit had been ravaged," Marest wrote Vaudreuil in late August. "Only a few of the Miamis remained at Detroit, and the Loups had withdrawn." More importantly, "No news has yet been received from M. la Motte."[11]

In fact, Cadillac was on his way back to Detroit when an urgent letter from Vaudreuil reached him. News of the Ottawa uprising had reached the governor while he was preparing to meet with Iroquois representatives over the compensation promised to them by the Ottawa the year before. The information placed the governor in a difficult position. The Iroquois, who had also heard word of the disturbance, were quick to press the issue. "My father, your fire is a light from here even to Detroit," the Seneca spokesman stated.

> You know, as we do, that the Outaouas (Ottawa) a little while ago killed a Recollect, a soldier and some Miami and Oniatanous there. Remember, our father what you said to them last year. Abandon the Outaouas to us, and hold us back no longer; our warriors are all

> ready. Make us no further reply, for we have already made up our minds; and the words which we bring you here we are making known at the same time to our brothers the English. It is thus a settled matter; make us no further reply.[12]

Vaudreuil thanked the spokesman for his words, and admitted that the Ottawa had wronged him, but at the same time he chastised the Iroquois. "I am surprised that you should take up the axe against those who have attacked me without learning my will first," he said in a stern tone. He would take vengeance on the Ottawa but only after he had learned what had exactly transpired. The governor had sent a detachment to Detroit to collect this information, but in the meantime, he made it clear to the Five Nations that "I stay your axe until you and I are informed of everything." The forceful statement had the intended effect, and when several prisoners were presented to the Iroquois as part of the Ottawa's early commitment toward retribution, it became evident that the Five Nations would wait for the governor's decision before taking any action.[13]

Vaudreuil's response to the matter was further influenced by a meeting with an Ottawa chieftain a few days later. The sachem apologized for the incident. The Ottawa of Michilimackinac had nothing to do with these actions, he informed Vaudreuil, and if war was declared against them because of it, the governor would find more than the Ottawa arrayed against him. While Vaudreuil did not accept the apology, he did not doubt the sincerity of the threat that followed. Nor did he wish to escalate matters and create a whole-scale war among his allies, which would only embolden the Five Nations and their English friends. Instead, he looked to diffuse the situation by recalling the French priests and traders at Michilimackinac. His hope was that such a move would create division among the Ottawa and force the chieftains to turn in the guilty parties. The governor penned a letter to Cadillac and informed him of his approach. For the moment the commandant was to remain on his guard, but otherwise he was to wait for the Ottawa to make the next move.

Unfortunately, this letter did not reach Cadillac before he arrived at Detroit. Shocked at the Ottawa's behavior and left to his own devices, the situation almost took a turn that would have engulfed the west in war and collapsed the French fur trade. When he arrived at Fort Pontchartrain Cadillac found himself confronted with representatives from over half a dozen nations, a few allies of the Ottawa but most enemies. Councils were convened and those opposed to the Ottawa, led by the Miami, made it clear that they did not wish for peace. They urged the French commander to join their cause and then warned him that if he made peace with the Ottawa he could expect war from them.

Instead of diffusing the situation as Vaudreuil had hoped, Cadillac fed the flames. "We have been struck by the same hand," he responded.

> As for me, I declare to you all, Hurons, Miamis, Ouyatanons (Weas), Chavouanons (Shawnee), and Iroquois, to all who hear me speak, I wish to boil only one great kettle, and to put all the Outawas into it at once. Now, listen to me: if they discover us on our march and flee, they cannot sow; if they have sown, we will destroy their corn. The governor will give them no powder, and these people cannot live by the bow and arrow. They are dead men, without costing you the loss of a single man. If they shut themselves up in their villages and fortify themselves there, I promise to fire the palisade, and give you admittance. I will do it myself, at the head of the French soldiers and of your warriors, and I promise you not to leave a single Outawa on the earth.[14]

There was a chorus of approval and a few frowns from those not so anxious to start a war. Those in favor of the attack wished to proceed immediately to Michilimackinac with Cadillac and his men, but thinking better of the matter, the commandant convinced the nations involved to delay the attack until spring, when an army of eight hundred men could be raised for the task.[15]

In the end the delay had allowed Vaudreuil to find what he sought. During winter he sent orders for the Ottawa chieftains to come to Montreal and explain their side of the incident. Once the ice broke on the Ottawa River in the spring of 1707 a number of Ottawa chieftains, led by their spokesman, Jean La Blanc, set out for Montreal. Upon arriving at the isle on June 17 the delegation immediately called upon Vaudreuil to pay their respects as was custom, but the governor refused to see them and instead agreed to meet with them the next day.

The next morning La Blanc, one of the leading chieftains of the Ottawa nation, delivered a long speech. He blamed the cause of the event on the ill conduct of the Miami and the Huron, and rumors that the Miami would fall upon their village once they had left to join the expedition against the Sioux. It was at this point that it was decided to strike the Miami before they could execute their plan.

"What has happened to us at Detroit is very painful; I am vexed with myself when I think of it," La Blanc told the governor. He had attempted to meet with Bourgmont several times right after the affair to resolve the matter, but the French officer would not see him. La Blanc admitted to being involved in the melee, but he was not the guiltiest—that title belonged to Le Pesant, who would not listen to reason. It was he who had drawn the Ottawa into this dilemma, into this conflict with Onontio. They had come as asked. They had given their reasons and apologized. What else were they to do?

The governor waited two days and then gave his answer. He condemned the Ottawa for their actions and expressed anger over the death of Father Constantin and one of the garrison's soldiers. Still, he realized that not all were guilty, and those that were appeared deceived by Le Pesant. The governor wanted Le Pesant. "You have told me yourself that he caused all your misfortunes," he informed the delegation, "and so long as he lives it will only make quarrels for you with all the nations."[16]

La Blanc gave an honest reply. La Pesant was indeed guilty, and if it were just Le Pesant alone, he would seize him and bring him to the governor, but that was not the case. Le Pesant was "allied to all the lakes," and La Blanc sincerely doubted that he could be taken, as he was being protected by these allies. The chieftain then shrugged and pointed out that on the up side Le Pesant "was old, and cannot go far, and when he is dead, we shall have no more trouble." Then seeking a solution La Blanc added, "But while waiting, we promise you to listen to him no more."[17]

The governor did not dispute La Blanc's inability to capture Le Pesant, and he was willing to issue a general amnesty if they made retributions to the offended nations, but there were three conditions. First, they would shun and ignore Le Pesant. His word was to mean nothing to them. Second, he would leave the final say in all matters to Cadillac. Third, Le Pesant was not included in the amnesty. Not wishing to press the issue any further, the chieftains agreed and the delegation returned to Michilimackinac.[18]

Again, time proved an ally for Vaudreuil. Cadillac refused to trade with the Ottawa or grant any amnesty until Le Pesant was brought before him. The approach worked and Le Pesant soon arrived at Detroit. The renegade chieftain was thrown in irons. Fearing for what might happen the Ottawa chieftains begged for mercy, and to their surprise it was granted. In the end, even Cadillac saw the repercussions among Le Pesant's allies and the unrest it would cause if he put the chieftain to death. He had foolishly promised the Miami and a number of other tribes that he would put Le Pesant to the sword. His reversal would anger them, but he believed he could calm this with gifts and Ottawa reparations. Killing Le Pesant, on the other hand, risked sparking a new conflict. If Detroit was to be maintained as the primary French post of the upper Great Lakes, furs had to flow, and peace was the best way to make that happen.

While Vaudreuil was not aware of Cadillac's decision, it was in line with his thoughts on defusing the matter. More importantly, the Ottawa had turned in the renegade chieftain, and the fragile peace had been restored. "I agree with you, Reverend Father," Vaudreuil wrote to Father Marest of the events, "that the affair of Le Pesant is one of the most important that has ever occurred in the upper country. I have always regarded it as such."[19]

CHAPTER ELEVEN

# An Uneasy Truce

A LITTLE OVER A MONTH AFTER the attack on Deerfield Governor Dudley wrote a letter to Vaudreuil protesting the murderous conduct. "In this present war between my Sovereign Lady and the King of France," Dudley began his letter, "I look for every kind of hostility from your nation; but I have always justly expected that there would be no breach of the laws of the Christian religion which has always protected the poor peasant, the women and children from outrage or captivity, whom I find that the people of your government (who have joined the barbarous Indians) have pursued with the utmost cruelty, and you have held in a harsh captivity."[1]

Dudley followed this with a proposed prisoner exchange, informing the French governor that he now had over 150 French citizens in his hands, mostly from captured privateers. After not having received a reply to his initial correspondence, in December 1704 the Massachusetts governor dispatched several envoys to Quebec to ensure delivery of this proposal and two other letters relating to the same topic. Led by Phillip Livingston, the delegation, which included Livingston's uncle Samuel Vetch and the governor's son William Dudley, was delayed because of the harsh winter and would not reach the French colonial capital until spring of 1705.

Vaudreuil was hardly moved by the Massachusetts governor's accusations. What of the inhabitants of La Chine or a dozen other small French villages who were ravaged and burned by the Iroquois? The English had supplied and encouraged this behavior long before their alliance with the

Five Nations in the last war. What about this behavior which had left many empty homesteads along the banks of the St. Lawrence? In addition, did not the assembly of Massachusetts put out a bounty for scalps? Was this the Massachusetts governor's step toward preventing the outrage and cruelty that he accused Vaudreuil of pursuing?

As for a prisoner exchange, the French governor was not against such an idea, but he questioned Dudley's authority to carry through with any promise along these lines. "If you were the sole ruler in New England as I am here, I would not have hesitated to accept your word and it would also have been a pleasure to me to return all your prisoners," Vaudreuil informed the Massachusetts governor, "but as you have a council, which is often divided in opinion, and where you have nothing more than your vote, you ought not to take it ill that I must have assurances for the return of the prisoners coming to me, the more so because on my side, being the sole master, I am always in a position to keep my word."[2]

Although something of a slight toward Dudley, Vaudreuil was interested in an exchange. There were good reasons for this. The Wabanaki were becoming worn down by the frontier conflict. Although they had been successful so far, it had come at the cost of dozens of men—men they could ill afford to lose. There was also the question of supplies, not only for the Wabanaki and for the defense of Port Royal but for Canada as a whole. English privateers had captured several supply vessels from France, leaving the colony short on powder, arms, and goods to trade with the allied nations to the west. Weakened by these efforts the return of prisoners would have a much greater impact on the manpower-limited resources of Canada than it would on more populous New England.

To facilitate the exchange Vaudreuil tasked veteran marine Captain Augustin Le Gardeur de Courtemanche to return to Boston with the English envoys and negotiate the transaction. Courtemanche's orders were clear. He was to secure the release of all French and French-allied prisoners. He was to inquire into atrocities committed by Colonel Church during his expedition, and he was to demand unconditionally the return of Captain Jean Baptiste (Pierre Maisonnat) who was being held on charges of piracy. The governor made it clear that this latter demand was nonnegotiable. If Baptiste was not released, there would be no exchange.[3]

When Dudley heard Courtemarche's demands that Baptiste had to be released or there would be no deal, he viewed the negotiations as over. The people and merchants of Boston were not interested in letting a well-known pirate and murderer free to prey on their shipping once again, and Dudley was not interested in further testing his weak political footing. Fortunately, the Massachusetts Assembly was more interested in liberating New England prisoners and were willing to take the political fallout to accomplish this. After a short debate, the assembly empowered Dudley to negotiate for the return of English prisoners even if the arrangement included releasing Baptiste.

While Canada had reasons to pursue an exchange, so too did Massachusetts. During any ongoing negotiations it was less likely that the French and their native allies would strike against the frontier, as this would be viewed as an act of bad faith. Thus, anything that prolonged the talks was worth the effort to the beleaguered colony. More importantly, a successful agreement might also include provisions for a general truce, which would be even more desirable. Fortunately, these negotiations coincided with news of a general prisoner exchange that had been conducted between the governors of Martinique and the Leeward Islands. The positive news seemed to have had an effect on Courtemarche, who agreed, in defiance of his orders, to continue negotiations even though they did not include Baptiste.[4]

On the morning of July 6, 1705, the brigantine that had carried Courtemarche to Boston set out to sea. Onboard was the French envoy, Dudley's son William, and Samuel Vetch, an English merchant who had frequented Quebec in the past and would become a prominent actor in the final stages of Queen Anne's War in North America. The governor had entrusted the duo with a proposal for a general prisoner exchange and with a letter for Vaudreuil. They were to await the French governor's response and then return to Boston with Coutemarche.

On November 21, the New England envoys returned to Boston. Dudley's original proposals are not to be found, but certainly many were encompassed in Vaudreuil's counterproposal, which expanded the scope of the negotiations to include a general truce between both colonies and their allies. The outline for the treaty called for trade and fishing rights to be respected; the return of all prisoners held by the English, French, and their allies; and measures to punish those on either side that violated the treaty with hostile acts. In all, it was what both Callières and Dudley had sought at the start of the conflict. There was, however, a catch. Vaudreuil was ready to approve the treaty on the condition that Dudley "shall oblige the Governor of York, and all deputy governors to enter into the same Treaty, who shall be obliged to assent to, and sign the present Treaty before the end of February." If this was not met, "the Marquis de Vaudreuil declares that all these present propositions shall be null."[5]

Whatever hopes Dudley and the Massachusetts Assembly had in regard to the treaty were dashed by Vaudreuil's last condition and his insistence that certain fishing areas were to be exclusively French. Governor Corn-

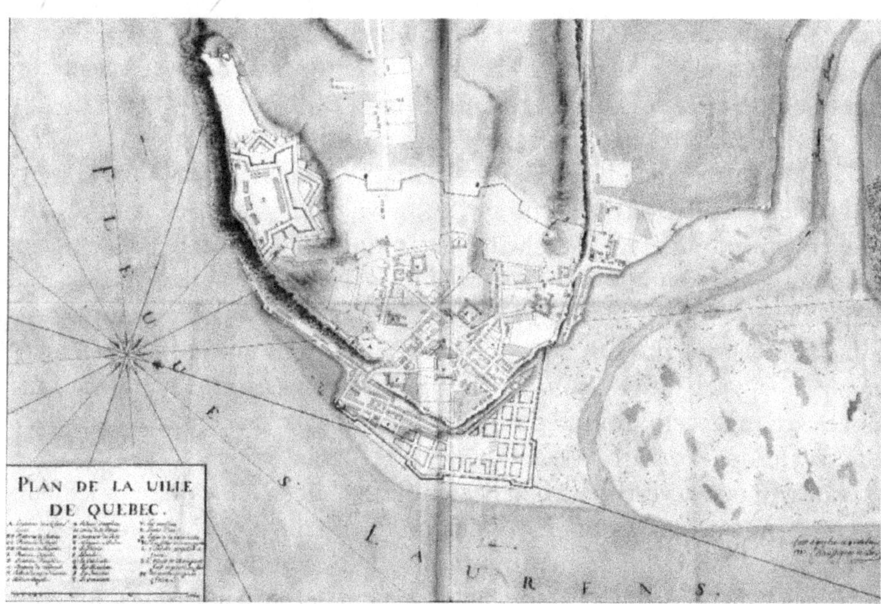


Plan of Quebec, 1727. The growth of the French colonial capital's defenses was never fast enough for the leaders of New France, but there is little doubt that the fortifications of the city had improved substantially from the beginning of King William's War. (*National Archives of Canada*)

bury's agreement was never forthcoming, and the assembly, after briefly arguing the matter, advised Dudley to reject the proposal. They did, however, support Dudley's efforts to at least arrange a prisoner exchange and left it to him how he wished to communicate the rejection to Vaudreuil.[6]

Believing a gesture of good will might facilitate an exchange Dudley had fifty-seven French prisoners returned to Port Royal. He then dispatched Ensign John Sheldon, who had accompanied the first delegation with Livingston, to Quebec to seek out a prisoner agreement with Vaudreuil. The latter was becoming suspicious of the entire negotiation. The February deadline had passed without a response from Dudley. To encourage an answer, Vaudreuil broke what had become a de facto cease-fire and sent a handful of small French and Indian raiding parties forward. He was convinced that this prodding would persuade the people of Massachusetts to agree to the terms of his treaty.

Sheldon's vessel did not reach Quebec until mid-March 1706. Many questioned the ability of the envoy to accomplish anything of note. Vetch referred to Sheldon as a simple country farmer who did not speak French that well and was hardly suitable for the title of diplomatic envoy. While perhaps true, what was more important was that Dudley's release of French prisoners and Sheldon's conduct before the French governor were successful in obtaining the release of forty-four English captives, which were met by their friends and relatives in Boston with great joy and fanfare.[7]

Sheldon also handed Dudley a letter from Vaudreuil. Dated June 2, 1706, it thanked Dudley for the gesture of good will and responded in kind. The French governor had no issues with continuing on with the exchange except that Baptiste had not been released. Dudley eventually agreed to this, and Baptiste was exchanged for Reverend Williams, who was taken during the attack on Deerfield. With no truce to be found, and no formal agreement in place between the two colonies, for the rest of the war the matter of prisoner exchanges fell into the domain of personal correspondence between the two leaders.[8]

For well over a year there had been nothing but small scattered incidents on the New England frontier. In April 1706 with the apparent failure of the peace treaty, a party of French and Indians fell upon the settlement of Oyster River, New Hampshire. Here they slew eight before being forced to retire. At first this was thought to be an isolated act, and as May and June progressed without incident, more became convinced that this was the case. With over a year of relative calm along the frontier many had become lax only to once again pay the price for this mistake.

In early July 1706 three war parties, comprising close to three hundred men, crossed the Merrimac River into northwestern Massachusetts. Their first target was Dunstable. Here the recent past was recalled in vivid detail. The nearby garrison house of twenty soldiers had not posted a watch, and when the French and Indian war party struck near sunset on July 8, they were inside the stronghold before the defenders realized what happened. Half the defenders were killed before the rest could get to their arms, but after a counterattack by the remaining soldiers, which led to an outburst of hand-to-hand fighting throughout the lower floor, the attackers were finally forced out of the house. A few minutes later an old man was brought forward. The prisoner informed the war party that a nearby garrison house only had two men and a boy inside. Liking these odds better, the attackers surged forward. One man and the boy escaped via a backdoor, while the other man frantically fired at the enemy with several preloaded muskets. Finally, he too made good his escape via the backdoor only to be apprehended after a short distance. Refusing to suffer the fate of the captured, he turned on his would-be captors and, after a brief struggle, escaped once again.

The next morning forty French and Indians fell upon nearby Amesbury and repeated their acts of pillaging and terror. Reading, Chelmsford, Sud-

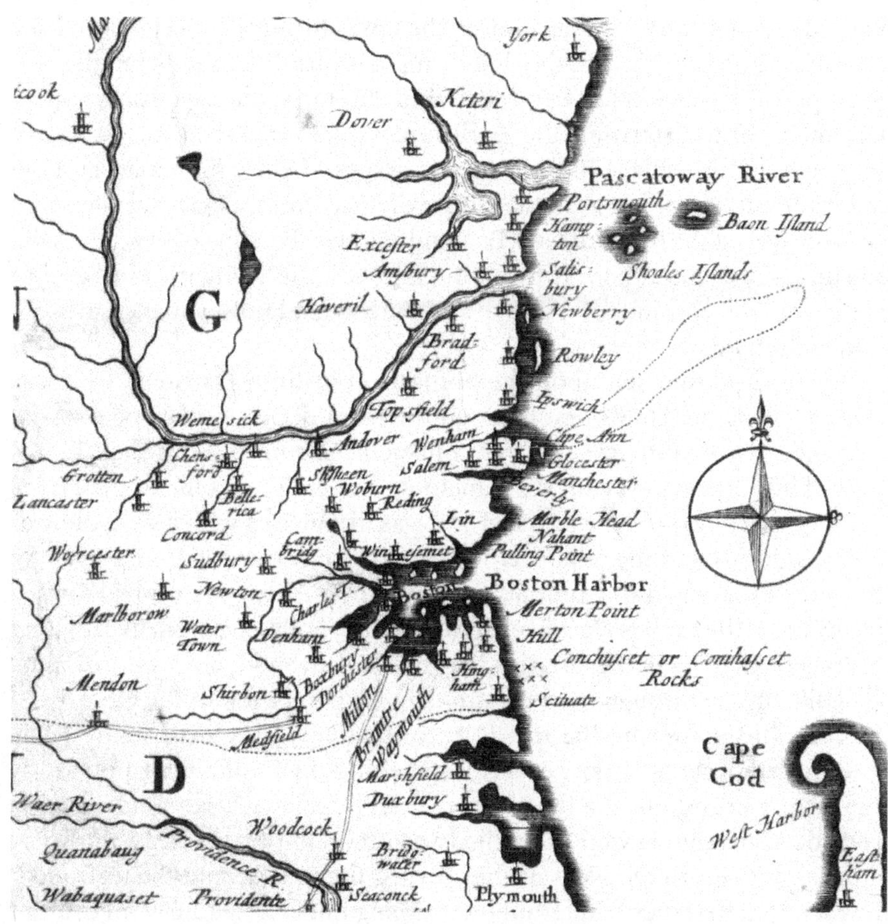


A portion of Cotton Mather's 1703 map of New England showing the Massachusetts and Maine coast from York, Maine, to Plymouth, Massachusetts. Only principal towns are marked. (*Boston Public Library*)

bury, Hatfield, Brookfield, and Groton, Massachusetts, were all struck within the next few days. Exeter, New Hampshire, was attacked, and the country roads that connected these points proved just as dangerous as packs of raiders set up ambushes along these thoroughfares.

While devastation reigned, the attackers did not always get their way. At Groton, Samuel Butterfield, a soldier assigned to the garrison, was helping in the fields when a large war party struck. While many fled, Butterfield fought back, killing one assailant and wounding another before he was overpowered and taken prisoner. Unfortunately for Butterfield, the attacker he had slain was a respected sagamore. The enraged captors debated on how to punish Butterfield, with death by whip and death by fire being the two most prevalent answers. It was then pointed out that the sagamore's widow had the right to determine the Englishman's demise. When the war party returned to their village Butterfield was dragged before the squaw and the question put before her as to the nature of his demise. There was silence as she considered the haggard New England soldier. "Fortune of war," she said, startling those about her. "If by killing him you can bring my Husband to life again," she continued, "I beg you to study what Death you please; but if not, let him be my Servant."[9]

At Reading they fell upon the homestead of John Harnden, who was away at the time. They burst through the front door, slew Harnden's wife and their three youngest children, pillaged their home, and then disappeared into the woods with the remaining five children. One of the Harndens' children was unable to travel and was dispatched with a swift blow to the head in front of the others. When the war party stopped for the evening the fate of the remaining four appeared gloomy. As the sun dipped toward the horizon the raiders ate and examined their spoils, occasionally laughing or bartering over a particular item they had stolen. Suddenly, a wave of musket balls zipped through the encampment, toppling a few of the French and Indians and scattering the rest. A second volley settled the matter. The raiders fled, leaving almost everything behind, including their previously captured victims and the four Harnden children. Their rescuers were the Harndens' neighbors who had rallied and set off in pursuit of the war party around mid-morning. Now, as they untied them, they told the distraught Harden clan that they had found their sibling under a tree a few miles away. The blow had not been fatal, and the child would recover.[10]

The same could be said for the Massachusetts frontier.

# Part Three

## *Three Crowns in the South*

CHAPTER TWELVE

# Fort Caroline

Although through the actions of Juan Ponce de Leon and Hernando de Soto Spain had claimed Florida and all points north along the North American shoreline, by 1561 not a single Spanish fort, settlement, or outpost had been erected to support these claims. The quest for gold had set aside such mundane matters. Besides, with a host of colonies in the Caribbean, Mexico, and South America there was little interest in the wind-swept Atlantic coast of Florida or the sandy pine shores of Georgia and South Carolina.

In France, however, there was interest. While Spain laid claim to these lands, so did France. More importantly, Charles IX of France was willing to back these assertions with a colony. Or perhaps it should be said that Admiral Gaspard de Coligny, an advisor and friend of the king, was willing to back these assertions. Coligny was a well-known Huguenot and corresponded with John Calvin on many occasions. Looking for a safe haven for the followers of his Protestant faith he approached the king with a plan to plant a Huguenot settlement in what is today South Carolina. With the issuance of the Edict of Fontainebleau, which allowed Catholic courts to banish Huguenots as heretics, a religious civil war had broken out in France making the king more than happy to agree to Coligny's proposal.

The man chosen for the task was Jean Ribault, a zealous Huguenot and an old naval officer who had a reputation as "a man expert in sea causes."

Ribault was given a pair of ships and the king's permission to found a colony in Florida. After seeing to the necessary preparations, on February 18, 1562, Ribault set course for North America carrying 150 troops and a cadre of young nobleman seeking adventure.[1]

Two months later the expedition was at the mouth of the May (St. John's) River near modern-day Jacksonville. After sailing a half a dozen miles up the river, the French commander put a party ashore. These men were immediately greeted by the natives, who proved friendly and eager to trade. Ribault erected a stone monument at this location bearing the arms of France and so impressed the local chieftain with the ceremony commemorating the structure that the latter presented him with a number of gifts.

Ribault moved north encountering a host of rivers on his way, which he named after the rivers of France. On what is today the southern part of coastal South Carolina, a storm separated the two vessels. When the weather cleared the French commander found the other vessel safely anchored in the mouth of a broad river. Given the size of the waterway Ribault named the river Port Royal, which it is still known by today.

Ribault spent his days charting the region until it was decided to build a fort and establish the colony. The French commander spoke to his men about their mission, looking for volunteers to man the fort while he returned to France for more men and supplies. He spoke to the acclaim that came with being "the first that ever inhabited this strange country" and how they now stood first citizens of a new colony in a new world. To the young noblemen who had braved the journey, Ribault noted that their exploits would be spoken of throughout the French court and to the king himself.

It worked. Twenty-five soldiers agreed to stay, and the earthworks of Charles Fort were soon raised on Paris Island. Ribault appointed Captain Albert de la Pierria to command the garrison in his absence, and with the structure nearing completion he departed for France in early June 1562. As the garrison watched the vessels disappear on the horizon few had any idea of what was in store.

The choice of the first colonists doomed the attempt to failure. All were soldiers who quickly put the fort in a strong state of defense but knew nothing about agriculture. Not that it mattered, given that it was too late in the season to break ground and plant. Instead, the garrison consumed its supplies and was forced to beg for help from the nearby tribes. Things did not get better. The fort accidentally burned down, destroying the provisions that the nearby tribes had donated. Isolated and short on provisions the garrison turned on Captain Pierria after the commander began ordering arbitrary and cruel punishments for minor infractions. He was arrested,

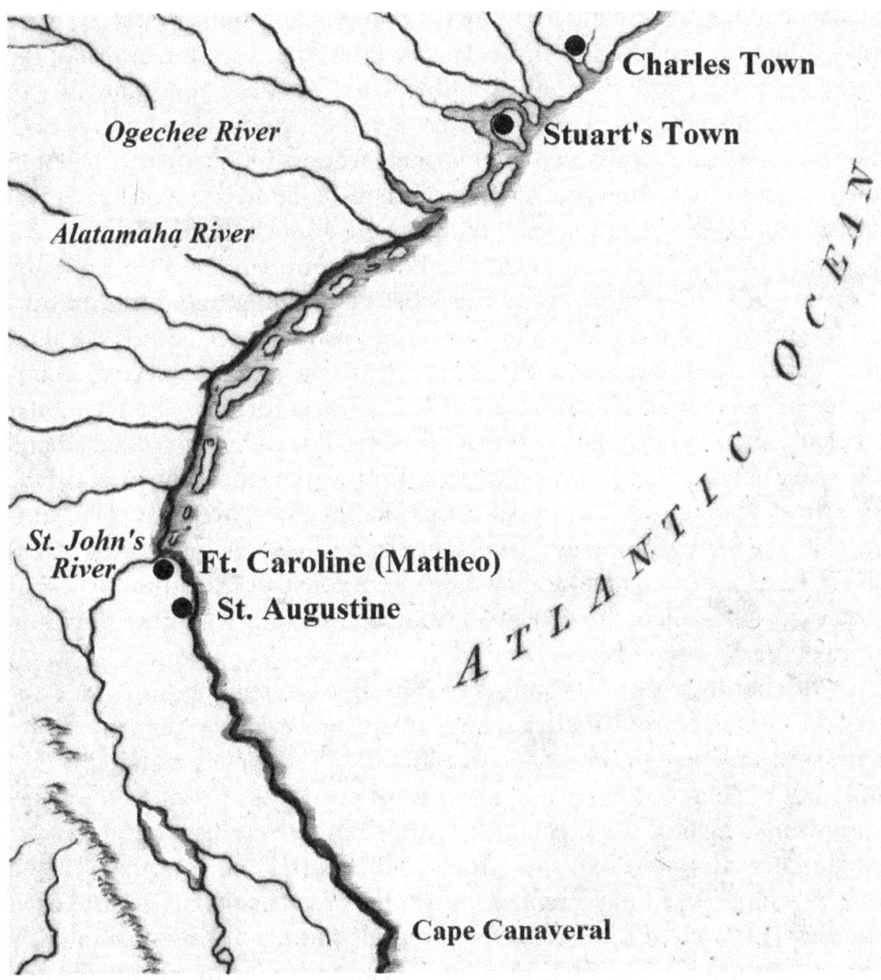


Early Spanish, French, and English settlements from Cape Canaveral, Florida, to Charles Town, South Carolina.

found guilty, and hanged. The troops, now under the command of Nicholas Barre, were resolved to return to France. By now it had become clear that something had delayed Ribault and no aid would be forthcoming in the near future. A small sloop was constructed, the fort was abandoned, and the garrison made its way out onto the Atlantic. A few survived, found adrift on a ship full of corpses.[2]

Ribault had indeed been delayed as a religious war raged through France. When peace was restored in 1564 a second expedition was sent under Ribault's second-in-command, Rene de Laudoniere. The king gave Laudoniere fifty thousand crowns and three small vessels, the sixty-ton *Isabella*, the eighty-ton *Le Petite Breton*, and the three-hundred-ton man-of-war *Faulcon*. Unlike the last expedition, this time the force included a large contingent of artisans, craftsmen, and farmers who would be instrumental in the colony's establishment. Departing Havre-de-Grace on April 22, 1564, three months later Laudoniere arrived at the May River, or the St. John's River as it would later be known. The French commander sent reconnaissance parties upriver for several miles before deciding on a location near the mouth of the river for a new fort. The position selected was a hill on the south bank about half a dozen miles from the river's outlet. An abundance of cedars and palms were put to good use forming the triangular stockade for the outer wall. A shorter inner wall was then constructed and the space between the two filled in with dirt from the moat dug around the structure. Planks and firing platforms were then laid over this to accommodate the fort's cannon and its defenders. A causeway was erected across the moat at the main gate, and bastions were constructed at the corners of the structure to allow the defenders to sweep the walls with grapeshot and musket fire.[3]

While hardly without its faults, Fort Caroline was still the strongest colonial position in North America. The problem, however, was the same as before. It was too late in the season to plant and the supplies on hand would only last a few months. As the provisions began to be rationed a mutiny was planned against the French commander, but it was discovered and the ringleaders ultimately banished from the fort. A second mutiny occurred not long after. Tired of searching in vain for precious metals a number of the garrison wanted to take one of the ships raiding against the Spanish. When they approached an ill, bed-ridden Laudoniere with the idea, he dismissed it out of hand and refused to sign the passage papers. The mutineers responded by informing him that "any opposition on your part is in vain." They then carried the sick officer to one of the vessels and placed him under lock and key. Shortly thereafter they drew up a commission and under the threat of death forced Laudoniere to sign the document.

The cruise proved to be a fateful mistake. At first, however, it appeared promising as the buccaneers seized a pair of vessels, one of which was carrying the Spanish governor of Jamaica and his two young sons. They demanded the Spaniard pay a steep ransom, to which he agreed. Thinking that a windfall lay ahead the French commander, d'Oranger, foolishly allowed the governor to dispatch the two boys to speak with his wife about arranging the payment. Instead the message was relayed to dispatch every

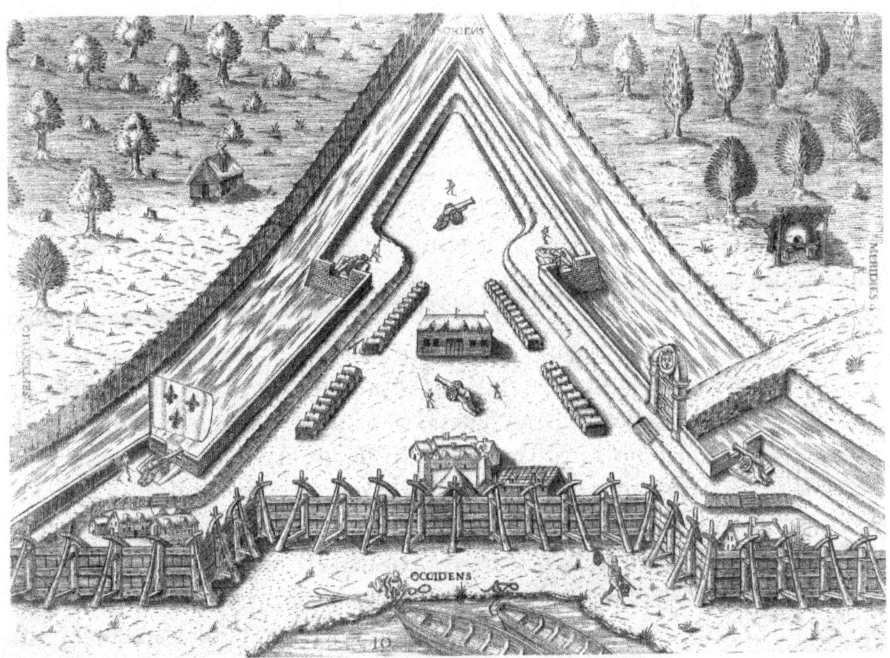


A period drawing of Fort Caroline on the south bank of the St. John's (May) River. (*Brevis narratio eorum quae in Florida Americae . . ., 1591, Plate X.*)

warship on hand that night and recapture him at daylight. The plan worked, as a squadron of Spanish ships appeared the next morning, quickly chasing off the French brigantine and recapturing the Spanish vessels as well as the governor.

Low on supplies and with a Spanish fleet actively searching for them, the mutineers thought better of their actions and returned to Fort Caroline. Laudoniere had received word of the brigantine's approach and prepared a reception. The vessel had no sooner dropped anchor in the harbor when it was boarded by thirty soldiers. The four ringleaders were carried ashore and, after a brief trial, were sentenced to hang. At the last moment the garrison pleaded for mercy, to which the French commander did offer a small compromise. He agreed to have the prisoners shot instead, but only if their bodies were hung on a pole as a warning to others. This seemed to satisfy the troops and the executions were swiftly carried out.[4]

As the months wore on several scouts returned with rumors of gold mines and other treasures. Most, however, brought news from other tribes and intrigues that threatened to consume the little colony. Although the native tribes were for the most part friendly toward the French, they were not toward each other. Laudoniere attempted to mediate several of their disputes, and when this failed, he foolishly attempted to force a peace upon the belligerents. The end effect was to alienate all of the tribes, making obtaining food a far more difficult task.

By late May 1565 famine had become the real threat. The natives had little and sold what they were willing to part with at high prices. Soon even this meager source had dried up, leaving the garrison to sustain themselves on roots and what little game they could catch. Efforts to obtain more food were rebuffed by the natives, and in one case the French envoy was robbed and killed. The starving garrison pleaded with Laudoniere to attack the nearby native villages and seize what foodstuffs were on hand, but the French leader, believing that such actions would only aggravate the situation, dismissed such notions. The orders would not last long. Matters finally became so desperate that Laudoniere feared an outright revolt, and as such, he consented to the plan.

The target was the Outina, a nearby Timucua tribe, who up to this point had been allies of the French colony. Laudoniere led his half-starved soldiers against the native village on the morning of July 27 and quickly overran the town, capturing the tribe's war chief and some sought-after provisions. Enraged by the betrayal the Outina struck back. Outnumbered and nearly surrounded Laudoniere requested a parley. Here he returned the war chief and a few captives in exchange for his unmolested withdrawal. The French had no sooner started their retreat when the Outina began showering his troops with arrows. This was followed throughout the day by darting attacks aimed at isolating small groups. The Outina warriors learned quickly where to strike the armored French and fell to the ground whenever the musketeers leveled their pieces at them. It was not until late afternoon that Laudoniere and his men arrived at Fort Caroline. The small amount of provisions they had carried away had cost the detachment two dead and over twenty wounded. More importantly, it had made new enemies at a time that the colony could least afford it.[5]

On August 3, shouts from the lookouts rang out. Four ships were approaching. A wave of excitement took hold as all concerned were convinced it was a French relief force, but when the vessels stood toward the harbor it became clear that they were English, not French. Laudoniere ordered his men to their posts, but it was not necessary. The English flotilla, commanded by Sir John Hawkins, was desperately in need of fresh water and sent a longboat ahead to request permission to come ashore.

The request was honored and soon Hawkins's men were taking on their precious cargo. The English commander met with Laudoniere, and finding his force Huguenots, he went out of his way to provide what provisions he could spare. He also sold Laudoniere powder, clothes, shoes, salt, and wax—all of which were in desperate need. The French commander then spoke with Hawkins about his plight and his decision to return to France. Even here Hawkins proved of service by selling Laudoniere one of his ships before he departed.

With another vessel on hand the French commander ordered the troops to load the heavy items in preparation for their departure. By mid-August all was ready, but it would not be until the twenty-eighth that the wind shifted in their favor. The order to make sail had just been given when a fleet of sails were spotted on the horizon. Laudoniere sent a bark forward to investigate, and when it failed to return, the French commander ordered his men to disembark and reoccupy the fort.

It was the worst of all possible situations for the defenders. For fear that the English or Spanish would use the abandoned fort, almost everything of defensive value was loaded onto the boats or demolished. Laudoniere's men work feverously through the night unloading the cannon and working on the ruined fort. It was something of a haphazard effort, but it would have to do, as the next morning seven ships approached the stronghold. After not responding to several hails, Laudoniere ordered the cannon to make ready to fire when the call rang out, "It is Mr. Ribault!" This was soon followed by a cheer that reached the oncoming fleet. Fort Caroline had been saved.[6]

CHAPTER THIRTEEN

# Huguenots and Conquistadors

DON PEDRO MENENDEZ DE AVILEZ, the intrepid and impatient captain general of the Spanish West Indies treasure fleet, listened intently as King Philip II of Spain outlined the task before him. Originally, Philip had detailed Menendez with charting the coast of Florida, in part to prevent wrecks along this coast, and in part as a preliminary to sending missionaries to the region. News of the French settlement at Fort Carolina, however, had altered these plans. Reports indicated that French privateers and pirates were using this post to raid the Spanish Caribbean. Should this colony grow or other French colonies follow, it would pose a serious threat to Spanish interests in the West Indies and the flow of treasure to Spain.

The king now ordered Menendez to remove this French challenge to Spanish territory "by whatever means you see fit," and when this was accomplished, he was to erect a fort along the Florida coast to prevent other interlopers. Originally Menendez only had a few ships at his disposal, in part because he was expected to pay for this in return for the lucrative arrangements that the position of military governor would bring, but now the king supplemented this force with another half-dozen vessels and an additional six hundred troops already on station in the West Indies.[1]

Menendez's fleet departed Spain in late June 1565. The eleven-ship convoy was soon driven back to port by severe weather. It turned out that the delay was beneficial. Several interested noblemen had raised detachments that now joined the expedition, placing Menendez's numbers close to two thousand. Setting sail once again, the captain general's new fleet became scattered in a storm near the Canary Islands. Several vessels were damaged and forced to return, leaving Menendez to press forward with only five vessels, uncertain as to the fate of the rest.

On August 9, the flotilla dropped anchor at San Juan, Puerto Rico. Here he received news that a French fleet under Ribault had passed bound for Florida. He also received some bad news as well. None of his other vessels had arrived, nor would any as Menendez waited in vain for nearly a month. Realizing that no reinforcements were coming, in late August he held a council of war. The captain general stated that it was his opinion that the force should immediately proceed to Fort Caroline and attack the heretics. True, it would be better if the original force were on hand, but this only meant more glory for those who accomplished the king's will. Most agreed with the captain general, but there were a few that questioned the wisdom of such a bold move. The French now appeared to be reinforced, and if estimates were correct, they likely outnumbered the Spanish force. Under these circumstances such a move seemed rash and had a very real possibility of turning into a disaster. While legitimate points, this badly outnumbered view was overwhelmed by calls to proceed, and soon even the dissenters were agreeing to attack.

By the end of August Menendez and his troops were off the coast of Florida, but after a few days of shuffling along the shore it was unclear not only where the French colony was but where they themselvs were. The Spanish commander eyed a number of natives on the shore and sent a detachment to obtain information from them about the French colony. At first the natives backed away, bows strung and ready. Menendez dared not follow for fear of an ambush, so he sent a condemned soldier with a bag full of trade goods to follow the tribesmen in an attempt to secure information. Most thought that they would never see the man again, but a few hours later he returned with several of the natives who informed the Spanish commander that the French fort was about twenty leagues to the north.[2]

After the celebrations that came with his arrival, Ribault's first order of business was to repair Fort Caroline. Both Laudoniere's and the newly arrived vessels were unloaded, and the supplies along with the new cannon that had been brought were carried into the fort. As for the stronghold itself, most of the issues could be repaired, and fortunately, the commander had a sizable supply of manpower at his disposal. This work had barely begun when reports arrived that five Spanish warships had scattered four of Ribault's vessels, which were anchored at the mouth of the river having drawn too much water to reach the fort. The drums beat out the alarm bringing all work to a halt as men snatched up their arms and raced to their posts.

Menendez had sighted the four French vessels the day before, but weather stopped him from reaching them before sundown. Still hoping to catch the ships by surprise he pressed on after sunset in hopes of being in a position to attack the enemy at daylight. The plan almost worked. At daybreak Menendez found himself anchored close to the French, and after some gestures that his arrival was peaceful, which seems to have fooled no one, the French ships cut their cables and fled.

Menendez gave chase but soon called off the pursuit and returned to the mouth of the St. John's River. About midmorning he ordered his vessels to proceed upriver toward the fort. The Spanish commander had every intention of pressing forward with his plan, but upon seeing five ships at anchor before the stronghold and two battalions of troops formed nearby, he thought better of the matter. With a strong French presence before him, and the possibility of the other four French vessels returning, Menendez called off the attack. The fleet was ordered south to St. Augustine, where the captain general planned to build a fort while reinforcements were sought from the Caribbean.[3]

Ribault's heavy vessels returned that evening with news of what had transpired and reports that the Spanish were ashore at St. Augustine. With this information in hand, the French commander summoned a council of war and announced his intentions to attack the Spanish before they had a chance to entrench or be reinforced. He would load almost the entire force at his disposal onto the four heavy vessels. These ships would deal with the Spanish shipping while he and the army landed and stormed their encampment. There was a unanimous chorus of disagreement. Laudoniere pointed out that the plan called for only eighty men to stay behind to guard Fort Caroline and that most of these were on the sick rolls. He then noted that violent storms could lash the coast for days, and if Ribault were caught in one of these with almost the entire French force, then all the Spanish had to do was march forty miles from St. Augustine to find an almost-undefended fort.

There were other calls of dissent as well, but in the end it made little difference. Ribault produced a letter from Admiral Coligny authorizing him to carry through with any operation he thought necessary in defense of His Majesty's territorial claims. The matter was settled, and by September 6 the expedition was ready, but because of contrary winds it would not be until the tenth that Ribault set out to sea. By late afternoon he was a league and a half off of St. Augustine.[4]

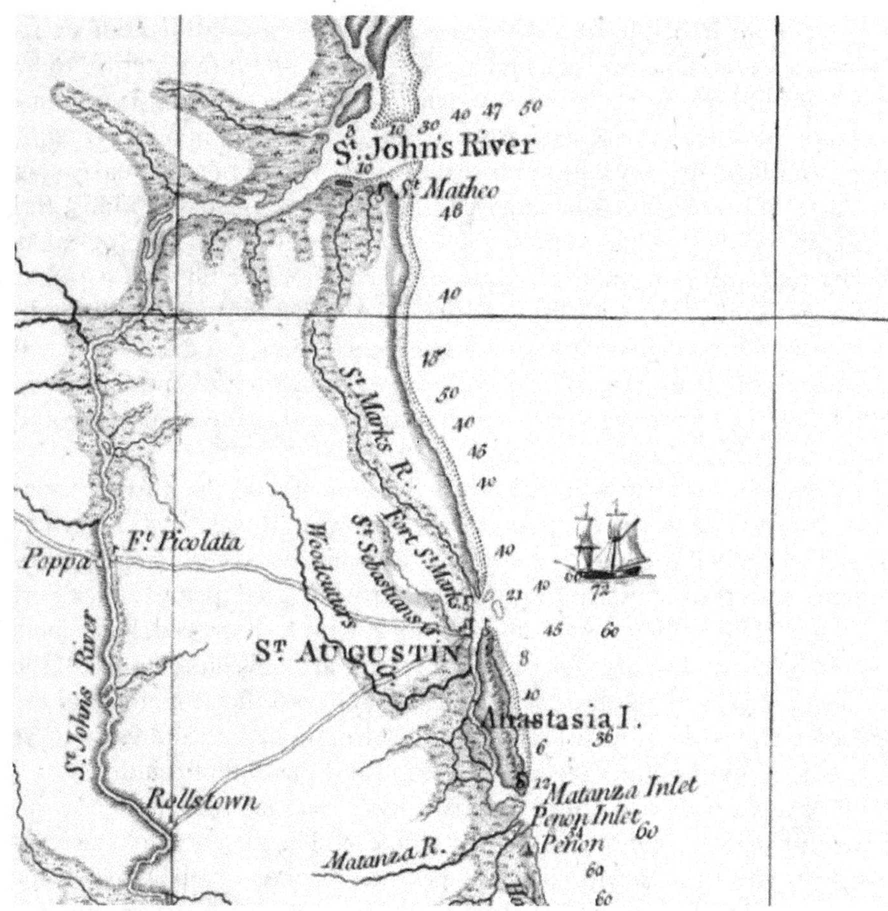

A portion of a 1775 map of Florida showing the location of Fort San Matheo (Ft. Caroline) on the south bank of the St. John's River, and the location of St. Augustine farther down the coast. (*Library of Congress*)

Menendez reached St. Augustine on September 7. He immediately dispatched a pair of officers and a fifty-man landing crew to select a site for an entrenched camp. The captain general went ashore the next day and, after receiving a native delegation, inspected the location chosen for the field works. Satisfied with the position, Menendez began disembarking his troops. When the French fleet came into sight on the afternoon of the tenth he accelerated the effort, fearing an attack the next morning.

The Spanish commander's fears proved well founded as Ribault, after chasing a pair of small Spanish ships back into St. Augustine, moved forward and entered the outer harbor a few hours after sunrise. Here, however, he was forced to halt for several hours in order to wait for high tide so his heavy vessels could clear the sandbar. For Ribault everything seemed to be working out perfectly. As he suspected the recently erected Spanish encampment on the west bank of the harbor was in disarray and in no position to repel an attack. In a few hours France, not Spain, would rule Florida. Pacing the deck of his flagship Ribault gave little thought to the rising winds, and when they did catch his attention, he was prepared to stand his ground. As dark clouds rolled in and the first gusts tugged at his warships one wonders if the words of some of the plan's critics did not pass through the admiral's mind. Rain soon pelted the decks of the French ships and the seas pitched the vessels in the narrow channel. When a whirling fury followed it melted Ribault's resolve, forcing the French commander to abandon his plans and order the fleet to stand out to sea.[5]

Menendez watched with delight as the French warships turned about and disappeared in the tempest of rain and wave. It was now his turn to strike. He called together a council of war and in a stirring speech announced his plan to march overland with five hundred men to attack Fort Caroline. The French fleet, if it were not outright destroyed, he argued, would be delayed for days by the weather, and in all likelihood most of the French forces were on these vessels. It would be a difficult march and the plan was not without its risks, he admitted, but Menendez addressed these by reminding all of their pledge to the king and the Catholic faith.

The captain general found the majority of his men ready to follow his lead and anxious to destroy the heretic colony. The plan was to take eight days' provisions and, with crews of axe men blazing a path, arrive in the woods outside the fort in a few days. If all went well, and they were not discovered, they would build makeshift ladders that evening and storm the fort from the nearby woods at sunrise. By the general's best estimates it would not cost him more than fifty casualties to secure the stronghold. If they should be discovered, however, Menendez would invest the fort and offer the garrison's commander terms.

Word of the attack spread through the Spanish encampment as did continued efforts by several officers to convince the general to abandon the effort. Menendez voiced his displeasure at such conduct and informed all involved that from henceforth such actions would be dealt with in a severe manner. The expedition departed the next day. It proved a grueling four-day march through waist-deep swamps, over rivers and creeks, and through dense forests filled with hanging moss. The entire time the wind lashed the column with slicing rain, leaving all exhausted and many wondering whether they would ever be dry again.

On the evening of the fourth day Menendez encamped in a downpour behind a belt of pine trees a few miles from the fort. With their supplies running low, their powder and match soaked, and most sapped of their strength it appeared that the expedition might end at this spot. In a council of war that evening many encouraged the general to retreat while the men still had enough strength to make the return march, but Menendez was of another mind. "It seems to me we ought to go and try our luck, the way we agreed," he informed those around him. "Even if we can't take the fort, we can send the trumpeter to demand surrender. For this we don't need dry powder. And what if the French learn you've gone without paying them a visit? They'll call us cowards!" Regardless of the difficulties, they had reached the walls of Fort Caroline unseen, and as far as the general was concerned, they could not come this far without making an attempt. The plea brought forth nods of agreement and calls for Menendez to lead them in the attack.[6]

The next morning amidst the fog and broken patches of rain Menendez led his army to the edge of the woods, about three hundred yards from the fort. The general dispatched two of his senior officers to survey the enemy works. These officers were returning from their task when they encountered a French sentry. The duo managed to subdue the Frenchman but not before he had let out a number of yelps. Standing at the tree line Menendez was convinced that these calls had come from his officers. Believing that their presence had been discovered and finding it impossible to wait any longer the general drew his sword and called upon the two companies beside him to advance.

A wave of Spanish troops ran toward the fort, not being discovered until they were within a few dozen yards of the structure. The alarm was sounded and a few scattered shots launched at the attackers, but it was already too late. There were several breeches in the fort's walls that had yet to be repaired and the attackers were quick to take advantage of this. Laudoniere attempted to rally the garrison, but by this point the enemy was already inside the fort firing upon anyone they encountered. To make matters worse the remaining part of Menendez's army had now launched themselves forward as well, sealing the fort's fate.

Laudoniere and a few others made good their escape. As for the rest, they were either slain or were now in Spanish hands. With word that the fort was secure Menendez turned his attention to the three French vessels in the harbor. He sent an envoy to demand their surrender. His terms were generous. Take the largest vessel along with the other crews and prisoners and leave. Captain James Ribault, the governor's son, replied to the request by demanding by what right Menendez had to attack the French when the two crowns were at peace. The conquistador leader was not interested in continuing the dialogue and ordered a pair of batteries to be set up near the shore. Not long after, while Captain Ribault was waiting for a reply, Menendez ordered a nearby cannon to fire. The round struck the vessel midship, tearing a hole out of the hull near the waterline. The ship's crew soon raised sail and Ribault's remaining vessels followed them downriver. Here they would later rendezvous with some of the French survivors, including Laudoniere, before setting sail for France.

Menendez's conquest of Fort Caroline had fulfilled part of his promise to the king. Now it was time to fulfill his promise to the church. The women and children under fifteen were spared. As for the rest they were executed and hung in nearby trees with a message that read, "These are not treated thus as Frenchmen, but as heretics and enemies of God."[7]

The general renamed the captured fort San Matheo and installed his sergeant-major, Gonzalo de Villarroel, as governor. Menendez had lost a fifth of his force, almost exclusively during the march north. He gave Villarroel three hundred of these men and planned to return immediately to St. Augustine with the remaining troops where he feared that Ribault's fleet might still appear. The men slotted to return with him were still too exhausted to make the march, so the general called on volunteers. Thirty-five came forward, and in a repeat of the earlier waterlogged experience, the conquer of the heretics arrived at St. Augustine in late September to a hero's welcome.

As Menendez set his men to work on fortifying St. Augustine, a pair of bad tidings arrived. First, Fort San Matheo had burned down in a suspicious fire. Second, the galleon *San Pelayo*, which had departed with a number of French prisoners bound for the inquisitors in Spain, had mutinied. The prisoners and a number of foreigners in the crew had killed the officers and taken control of the warship. If this vessel were to move against St. Augustine it could cause considerable problems. These events were soon forgotten when the general's greatest worry, the possible return of Ribault's fleet, was dispelled. Reports were that the fleet had wrecked along the coast 150 miles south of St. Augustine.

Ribault and his men had indeed been blown into the shoals along the western edge of the Bahama Channel. A few arms and a small supply of provisions had been salvaged but little else. The French commander organized the survivors and ordered a march north to Fort Caroline. Many doubted that such a journey would be successful, and it seemed more likely that they would surrender to the Spanish along the way. When the column arrived at a river a dozen miles from St. Augustine news of its existence reached Menendez, who pressed forward with a detachment to investigate.

Don Pedro Menendez de Aviles. The Conquistador Captain would expel the French from Spanish Florida and establish St. Augustine to dissuade any future interlopers. (*Library of Congress*)

When the tattered French forces encountered the Spanish, surrender seemed inevitable and preferred to starvation. With the promise of good terms, Ribault and his men quickly submitted. Menendez treated them as he had the garrison of Fort Caroline. The prisoners were led off in small groups and, along with Ribault, executed.[8]

Menendez, in a ruthless display, had rid Spanish Florida of the Huguenot colony. He now turned to fulfilling the second part of his promise to the king—erecting a fort and raising a small village to support this post. The matter of France and Spain in early Florida might have ended at this point but for one final blow struck by a French soldier of fortune and Catholic, the chevalier Dominic de Gourgues.

Gourgues was an officer in the French army who, after a bold stand against the Spanish in Italy, was captured and condemned to the galleys. The Frenchman's vessel was later taken by the Turks and carried to Constantinople. Fortunately, the galley was seized by a Maltese vessel on its maiden voyage, which granted Gourgues his freedom. From here the Frenchman returned back to the sea, and after a number of long voyages to Brazil and Africa, he had become known as one of the ablest navigators of the day. National pride, an element of vengeance, and ability were motivation enough for the chevalier to risk his entire fortune on a bold plan to strike back against the Spanish.

Gourgues purchased three small ships, selecting them for their light draft, which would allow him to enter the Florida rivers. Eighty sailors were recruited, and another 150 soldiers had volunteered, many of whom were French noblemen who agreed with Gourgues. To deal with the wet weather and keep costs down, a hundred of these men were armed with crossbows. Provisions for a year were purchased and stowed aboard the vessels, which departed Bordeaux on August 2, 1567.[9]

Although the officially stated purpose of the expedition was to secure slaves along the African coast, after a storm-swept voyage the flotilla at last reached the western end of Cuba. To better conceal his intentions Gourgues planned to double around the island and enter the Bahama Channel from the more commonly used western approach. Up until this point he had not informed the bulk of his men of the real intention of the expedition. In a heated speech he changed this, speaking to the cruelty of the Spanish in Florida and how he had risked his fortune to avenge the insult to the French nation. All had been kept quiet thus far, he pointed out. Which meant that the Spanish did not know of their purpose. No one would be expecting them. Now was time to strike back for the honor of France! Many were stunned, but most were quickly captured by his impassioned words and pledged to follow Gourgues wherever he chose to lead them.

So complete was Gourgues deception that when passing the mouth of the St. John's River, Fort Matheo, taking them for Spanish, fired a three-gun salute. Gourgues responded gun for gun before proceeding on to the St. Mary's River a little over a dozen miles from the fort. His light draft vessels easily ascended the river where he made camp. The expedition also had a fortunate encounter with a group of natives who were former French allies. Their leader, Saturiova, was not happy with the Spanish and pledged his support.[10]

While the renewed alliance would prove crucial in terms of numbers, what Gourgues really needed at this point was information. Saturiova had protected and cared for one of the French who had escaped from the fort. The young man's name was Pierre de Bray. The chieftain proposed that de Bray and a small party go to reconnoiter the fort. The group returned three days later with news that the Spanish had built two small forts, one on either side of the river, and that some four hundred men occupied these forts: two hundred in the main fort, San Matheo, and a hundred in each of the smaller ones. Undaunted, the French commander and his allies resolved to attack. The march from the encampment to Fort San Matheo was about twelve miles. Gourgues's men were fortunate to have covered half this distance the first day as a long downpour swelled the creek crossings and turned the makeshift trail into knee high mud. The troops covered the remaining distance the next day arriving a mile or so from the post on the northern bank that afternoon. Gourgues advanced with a handful of musketeers and examined the terrain about the fort. A small river swollen by the persistent rainfall proved a potential problem until one of Saturiova's men informed the French commander of a better place to cross.

The force set out the next morning, but when they arrived at the crossing, they found it too high and had to wait for low tide to continue. In the meantime, the weather cleared presenting Gourgues with an excellent view of the fort. What he saw did not please him. Instead of being quiet, the garrison seemed to be moving about the interior making him wonder if his column had been discovered.[11]

Around 10 a.m. the river levels had fallen enough that Gourgues led his men across along with a few of Saturiova's men, the remainder of which had crossed higher upriver in their canoes. The French gathered on the opposite bank behind a belt of pine trees that obscured their efforts. Thus far, secrecy had prevailed and not a soul at Fort Matheo had any idea that a French force was nearby. Gourgues motioned for his troops to form two detachments. The first would be led by his lieutenant, M. de Casenove, while he would lead the other. Once the army's ranks were formed, Gourgues walked down the length of the formations, passing words of encouragement, before at the head of his own detachment he gave the signal to advance.

The Spanish sentries in the small fort on the north bank of the St. John's River were startled when the French troops emerged out of the tree line. The alarm was sounded and a pair of old cannon fired over the heads of the attackers. With a shout, Gourgues's men threw themselves at the fort. There were a few shots from the sentries, but when one of Saturiova's men in the advanced guard by the name of Olocotora mounted the wall and killed one of the Spanish gunners reloading a cannon the rest took flight. Panic soon ensued and the garrison abandoned the fort. Unfortunately for the defenders, their flight led them directly into the path of Casenove's detachment. Caught between the two French forces, little mercy was shown and only a few were taken prisoner.

The small fort on the south side of the river began to fire its cannon at the invaders, but Gourgues was able to neutralize their efforts with a pair of cannon that he had brought with him and a pair taken out of the captured fort. Not wasting any time, Gourgues and eighty men crossed the St. John's in a bark that his allies had prepared, while Saturiova's men crossed in canoes and those too impatient to wait swam across. The garrison of the small Spanish fort had seen enough and attempted to flee into the woods but instead ran into an ambush by Saturiova's men where a handful were captured and the rest killed.

This left only Fort Matheo. Gourgues was well aware of the layout of the fort and its details from one of his men who had served there. After investing the stronghold and studying its strengths, the French commander decided to storm the walls. The next two days were spent building ladders and making preparations. The French commander had resolved to attack the following morning when eighty Spanish made a sally out of the fort. It was a foolish mistake. The detachment was quickly surrounded and annihilated. After witnessing the disaster, those left in the fort fled to the nearby woods only to find them occupied by Gourgues's allies, who made quick work of the panicked mob.

Gourgues let his troops pillage the fort before destroying it. The prisoners were led to the same spot where the French garrison was massacred to suffer the same fate. They were then hung in the trees with the message "I did not do this as to Spaniards, nor as to infidels, but as to traitors, thieves, and murderers."[12]

CHAPTER FOURTEEN

# Missionaries and Soldiers

True to his pledge to the king, Menendez would build Fort Augustine and the elements of a nearby town. Fire, hostile neighbors, lack of food, and mutiny stunted his project and at times even called the fort's viability into question. Menendez persisted, and the colony slowly took hold. In 1586 this was undone when Sir Francis Drake appeared off the harbor with a fleet of raiders. Drake encountered little in the way of resistance as the Spanish, now under Menendez's nephew, Don Pedro, evacuated the fort in the face of overwhelming numbers. A few shots were fired at Drake's men as they pushed forward into the nearby town, and this seems to have been enough for Drake to order the town to be burned. The abandoned palisade fort was relieved of its fourteen brass cannon and the garrison's payroll before being put to the torch on the Englishman's departure.[1]

The fort and town were rebuilt and in 1593 ten Franciscan missionaries and their superior, Fray Jean de Silva, arrived. One missionary described the new village as half a league wide, populated by clusters of wooden houses with palm roofs. "The Spanish," he noted, "make the walls of their houses with cypress wood because the part of it in the ground does not rot." A few years later the new governor, Gonzalo Mendez de Canzo, would institute more stringent controls over the growth, focusing on ordinances regarding the width and nature of the town's streets and marketplace. As it would turn out, whatever progress that had been accomplished after Drake's destructive raid was partially wiped by a fire out in the spring of 1599, and what the fire missed became the victim of a storm surge from a hurricane in September.

The recently arrived friars bemoaned the loss of their monastery in St. Augustine and the repercussions it had on their flock. "On account of its ruined and barren condition," Friar Blas de Montes wrote, "it is incapable of maintaining so many natives as are here." While the Franciscans were not the first religious order in Florida, they were certainly the most influential. The Jesuits had originally sought to undertake the colony's spiritual work and established a few short-lived missions under Governor Menendez, but they eventually abandoned their effort in 1572 after a native uprising and arguments with the governor about not wanting soldiers at their missions. The following year the Franciscans took over this task, and by 1583 the Chickasaw, Tocoposca, Apaca, Tamaicas, Apisca, and Alabama had all been visited by these missionaries. Several of Silva's friars established missions among the nearby Timucua tribes and revived the old missions among the Guale of southern Georgia, and still others traveled to the Apalachee and the tribes of western Florida and Alabama.

As in Canada, these missionary activities were capable of garnering large numbers of converts, and just like in the north, they were also capable of creating turmoil and conflict. In 1597 this last point came to the forefront when a young Guale war chief by the name of Juanillo took cause with a public rebuke by Franciscan Friar Pedro Corpa. Juanillo returned that evening with a band of followers, and after slaying Corpa in front of the mission's altar, he mounted the friar's head on a pole in front of the church. Appearing before his tribe not long after, Jaunillo listened to complaints and fears that the Spanish would make war on them. He answered these by saying that it had to be done. It was bad enough that the missionaries were destroying their skills and ancient way of life by banning their feasts, games, and celebrations, but what was worse was their oppression. "Although we are disposed to do all they require from us, they are not satisfied," the chieftain angrily told the crowd gathered about him. "But for everything they reprimand us, injuriously treat us, oppress us, lecture us, call us bad Christians, and deprive us of all the pleasures which our fathers enjoyed." He then asked all, "And what have we to hope except to be made slaves?"[2]

The impassioned speech, while likely more the product of vengeance than social justice, had nonetheless hit upon the latter. The crowd cried for vengeance and Juanillo pointed them to another mission, where they dispatched the friar and put his church to the torch. The rebellion soon grew and several other missions fell victim to attacks. The Spanish retaliated and

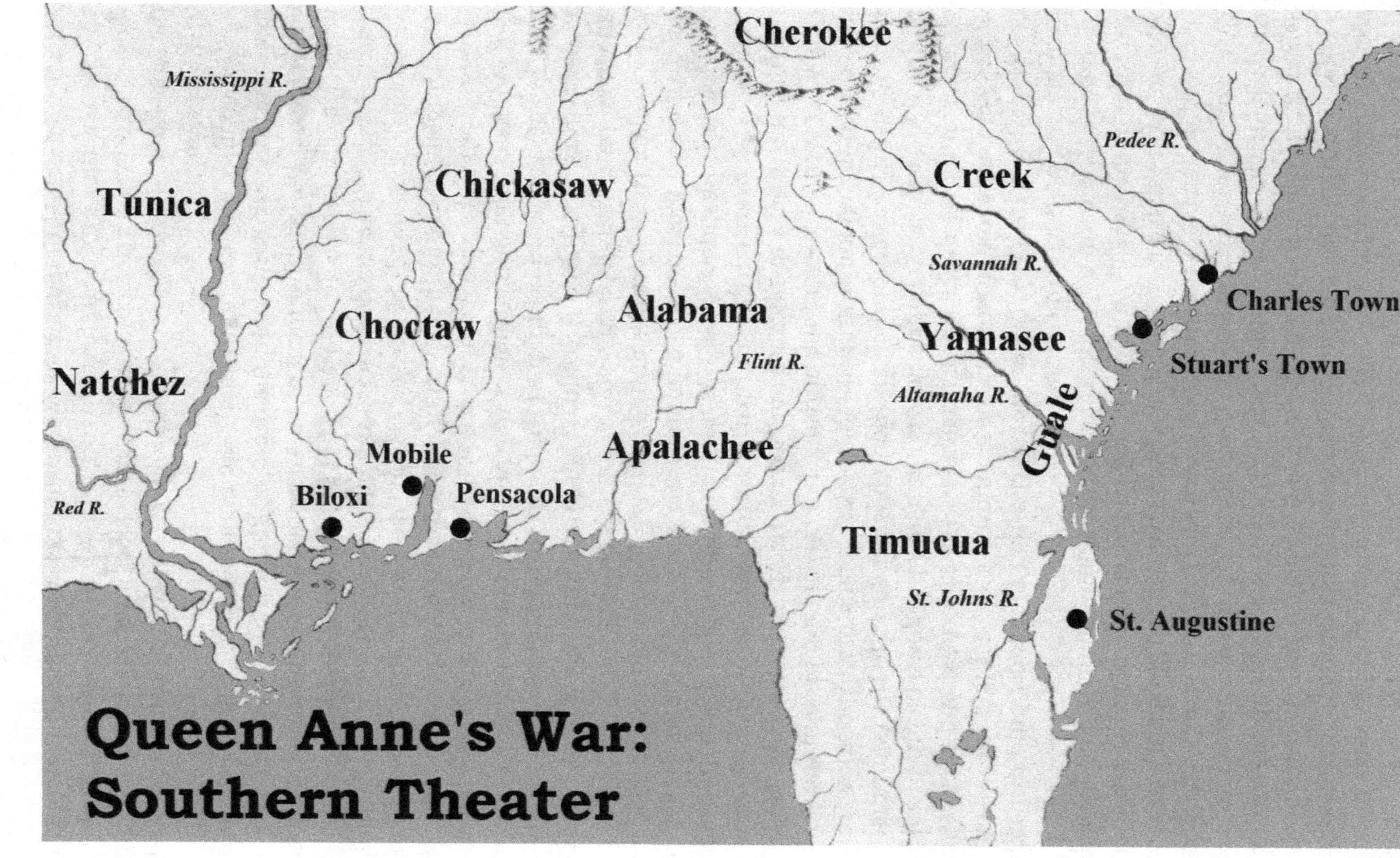
Queen Anne's War:
Southern Theater
Mississippi R.
Cherokee
Pedee R.
Tunica
Chickasaw
Creek
Savannah R.
Charles Town
Choctaw
Alabama
Yamasee
Stuart's Town
Natchez
Flint R.
Altamaha R.
Guale
Mobile
Apalachee
Biloxi
Pensacola
Red R.
Timucua
St. Johns R.
St. Augustine

launched an expedition against Juanillo and his supporters, but as might be expected, they proved difficult to catch. The short stalemate was broken the next year when a detachment of Spanish allies attacked Juanillo, killing the rebel leader and over a score of his followers, effectively bringing an end to the uprising.

The conflict did little to dissuade the Franciscans in their efforts, and more missions followed. With the death of Philip II, the new king took a closer look at the establishment of St. Augustine and the missionary effort in Florida. The Crown's outpost was not self-sufficient, and it came with a sizable expense. The missionaries also required support for their activities, which further strained the budget. There was also the fact that the friars had complained about the governor, the rampant corruption, the lack of support from Cuba and Spain, as well as the need for some agricultural activity in the colony. Some changes were made, but in the end, the cost was to be borne, as politically Philip III could not abandon the Franciscan missionary effort, nor militarily could he ignore the importance of St. Augustine in keeping foreign powers off the coast of Florida.

By the late 1640s missions dotted northern Florida and southern Georgia. To the west these posts had found fertile ground with the Apalachee of the Florida Panhandle. Yet all was not well in this region. Partly from the influences of nearby tribes and partly from a decline in Spanish goods reaching the tribe, a revolt was launched by the Apalachee in 1647. Not all Apalachee were in favor of the uprising, but this did not prevent the seven missions in the region from being burned. A retaliatory expedition from Fort Augustine was ambushed and soon bogged down to the point that it returned to the fort. The uprising was ultimately put down by pro-Spanish elements of the Apalachee. The ringleaders were executed and twenty-six others were sentenced to work on the fortifications of St. Augustine. All others were shown leniency, under the proviso that they too would dispatch men to work on the fortifications.[3]

Nine years later an uprising occurred among the Timucua. The Spanish governor at the time, Don Diego de Rebolledo, claimed that the rebellion was aimed at the friars, but the Franciscans blamed the governor's pattern of forced Indian labor practices and his demand for native troops. In either case, ten tribes participated in the effort, which even spread to the Apalachee, who showed little interest. The governor sent an expedition, seized the ringleaders, executed them, and displayed their corpses in the Timucua villages, bringing a swift end to the short conflict. The message seems to have taken hold, as there are no other instances of uprisings among these tribes, but the years that followed would be difficult. The great enemy,

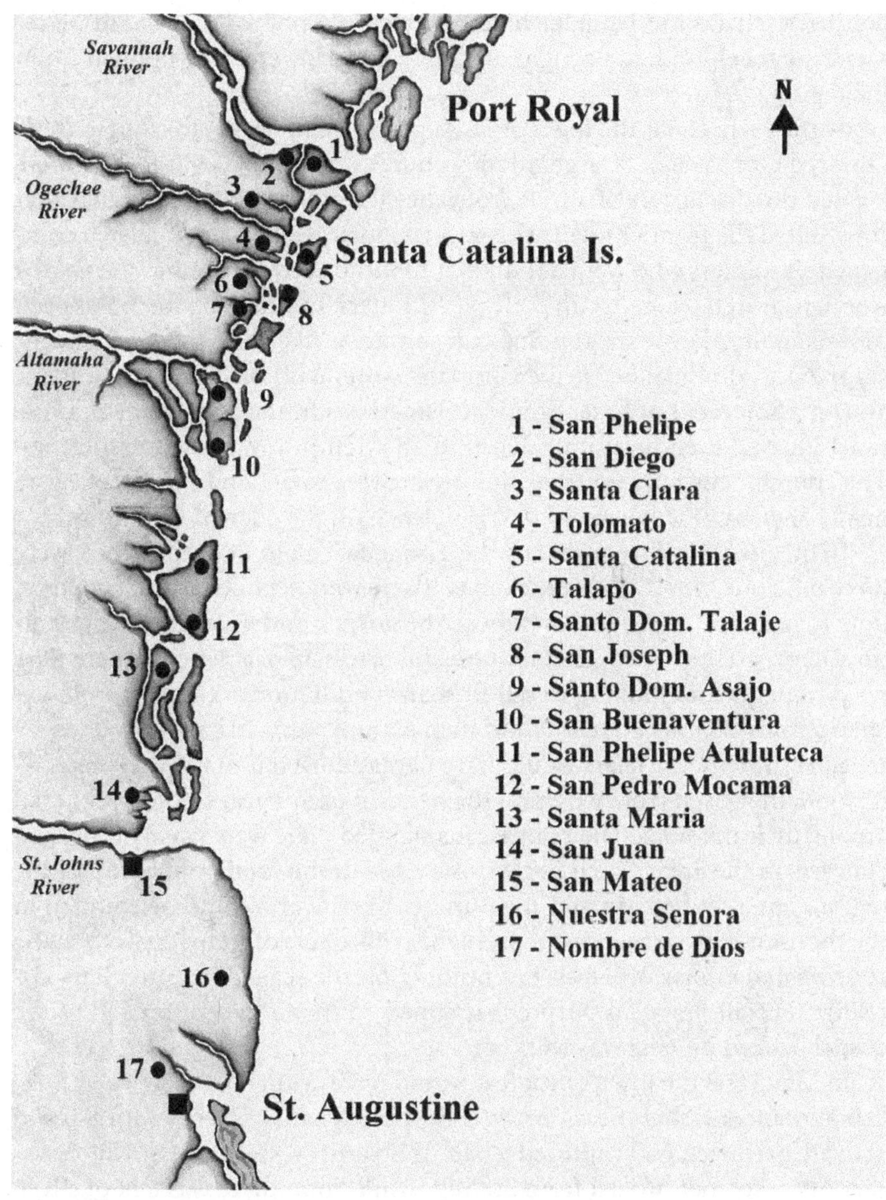


Spanish Guale missions along coastal Georgia. While the Franciscan friars were successful in bringing Christianity to the tribes of northern Florida and southern Georgia, they soon outran the ability of the Spanish authorities in St. Augustine to protect their network of missions. Native uprisings, suspicions of loyalty, arguments from the friars, and a shortage of firearms and powder further hampered Spanish efforts to use the denizens of these missions as militia to help secure the locations.

pestilence, struck the Timucua hard, and when combined with the displacement the rebellion had brought, it significantly lowered the population in the region.[4]

By the early 1660s the town of St. Augustine had grown to close to three hundred homesteads. A large wooden church and double palisade fort were located three-quarters of a mile from the cluster of wooden buildings that constituted the frontier town. The post was manned by a few depleted companies of soldiers who went about their monotonous motions as the nearby wooden church teemed with daily parishioners. In the town there was even more activity. Timucua and Spanish settlers walked the peaceful streets, stopping to do business at the company store, with blacksmiths, tanners, and an assortment of basic frontier businesses. On the edge of town, cattle ranching had even been introduced in an attempt toward self-sufficiency. The church bells rang on time, the streets were clean, and the homes were neatly aligned. It was a sleepy garrison town on the edge of an empire.

To the north and west, among the Timucua, Guale, and Apalachee, were forty missions, run by the Franciscans. There were schools to teach children how to read and write, instruction in the gospel, and coordinated agricultural efforts. These were generally peaceful places, in part because there were no trading parties looking to sell firearms and liquor to the natives in exchange for precious goods. While such actions were strictly forbidden by the government, the friars would have never allowed it in the first place. As it stood, they even frowned upon the handful of Spanish soldiers scattered among their missions. The Franciscans claimed there were twenty thousand converts in the area, which likely came close to the total population of the region, but by best estimates the number of converts could be counted in the thousands. There were still problems, more acts of individuals than the coordinated efforts of tribes, but nothing on the scale of the previous uprisings. For all practical purposes it appeared that a dual approach of the gospel backed by steel was working.[5]

In May 1668 the town's progress would once again be erased when English buccaneer Robert Searle arrived. Searle, a friend of Henry Morgan and activate privateer, had captured a pair of Spanish vessels, one of which was carrying a former official from St. Augustine. Soon there was talk of silver, which was more than enough for Searle and the other ship captains with him to set sail for St. Augustine. Upon reaching the town the English captain used his recent captures as part of a ploy. On the evening of May 28, the two Spanish prizes, with Searle's men tucked out of sight, slid past the fort toward the harbor. The harbor pilot came out in a longboat and demanded to know the vessels' business. He was told the pair had sailed from Mexico with provisions and supplies for the town. Satisfied, the harbor pilot signaled the fort that all was well.

Searle kept the pilot and held his position until nightfall without raising any suspicion. After sunset the two raiders sailed into the harbor and launched a dozen small boats. The cries of a Spanish corporal who was fishing at the time saved the fort from being captured, but the town was ill prepared for the onslaught. Leaping from their craft and splashing ashore Searle's men moved quickly into the town firing on those who resisted. Many fled, a handful of soldiers and citizens fought well but were forced to retreat, and the rest were captured. The fort was still in Spanish hands, but the town, the government buildings, the church, and seventy citizens were now in Searle's hands. Sixty Spanish and a score of buccaneers had been killed in the surprise attack which had only lasted an hour.

As he tended to his wounded Searle made a deal for the hostages, trading them for firewood and provisions. He did not return any of his Indian or black hostages, however, claiming that his commission allowed him to sell anyone who was not full-blooded Spanish. The town was put to the torch, and while the dejected sentries in the fort and the eyes of those who hid in the woods watched, flames devoured their homes over the course of the night. The next morning Searle and his men loaded anything of value onto their vessels and sailed off.[6]

Sadly, the town was accustomed to such occurrences, and once again, new buildings were raised to the rhythm of hammer and saw. Nor would they be the last raiders to visit the town. In 1682 a small group of buccaneers struck south of St. Augustine at Mosquito Inlet. A few homes were burned and a number of natives were carried away. The following year they returned in force. In March well-known English privateer Captain Thomas Paine enlisted four other privateers, one of whom was French, into a small flotilla and fell upon the Matanzas Inlet a few miles south of St. Augustine. The small watchtower at this location was taken by surprise in a night attack, and the nearby encampment looted. The next morning Paine organized his men into a ragged column and began to march north up the length of Anastasia Island.

A breathless sentry who had escaped the sudden attack informed Governor Juan Marquez Cabrera around dawn. The town was alerted and a detachment of thirty men under Captain Antonio de Arguelles was sent south to intercept the raiders. Although he was badly outnumbered the advance warning allowed Arguelles to prepare an ambuscade a few miles from the town. Paine's men, strung out and unprepared, walked straight into a pair of volleys that echoed across the island. A few of the privateers responded, but a third volley changed their minds, sending the disorganized column in a headlong retreat back to their boats. From here Paine and his vessels sailed into St. Augustine Harbor, but after eyeing a new fort that was being raised, they thought better of the matter and departed without a fight.[7]

While the safety of St. Augustine was in question by threats from the sea, another threat was brewing to the north. By 1675 the Franciscan mission system had grown to forty-four missions, but in doing so it had placed a considerable strain on the governor of Spanish Florida's ability to defend these locations. Part of this came from the friars themselves, who frowned on soldiers at their missions, pointing out that the soldiers tended to be disruptive, induced fear into the natives, and called the friars' authority into question. This approach finally manifested itself into a letter from the Franciscans to the king of Spain asking him to withdraw all Spanish troops from the Florida missions.

Although the Crown was an adherent supporter of the Franciscans' cause, it was also clear that the Florida mission system was overextended and vulnerable. As such, the king felt a responsibility to protect these missions and began to side with the governor on such matters. Even so, it was not as if the king rushed the resources to the area to address the threat. In 1675, near the height of the Spanish mission system in Florida, Governor Manuel de Cendoya only had seventy-five soldiers stationed among the forty-four missions in three different provinces. What was worse was that this left the Spanish commander with less than two hundred men to guard St. Augustine. The clear deficiency in troops, and because of St. Augustine's small population, an understrength colonial militia, led Cendoya to appeal to the king for a hundred more men, but with little in the way of results.

The weakness of this defensive system was clearly spelled out in the 1680s when English-supplied, and often English-led, Creek and Yamassee war parties descended on the Guale missions in search of slaves. A handful of Spanish troops and mission Indians attempted to stall the tide but were swept aside in a long-running campaign that would eventually end with the withdrawal of the Guale missions in southern Georgia.

At this stage there were only two answers: send more Spanish troops or arm the mission Indians. The governors that followed continually sought out more troops but to little avail as the Crown was not interested in the cost of maintaining a large force in Florida. The last element, using the mission Indians as militia, did gain some traction, but it also faced a number of hurdles. First were the Franciscans, although by now they too were starting to understand the need for a coherent defense against the Creek and Yamassee. Second was a long-running question of loyalty that came about

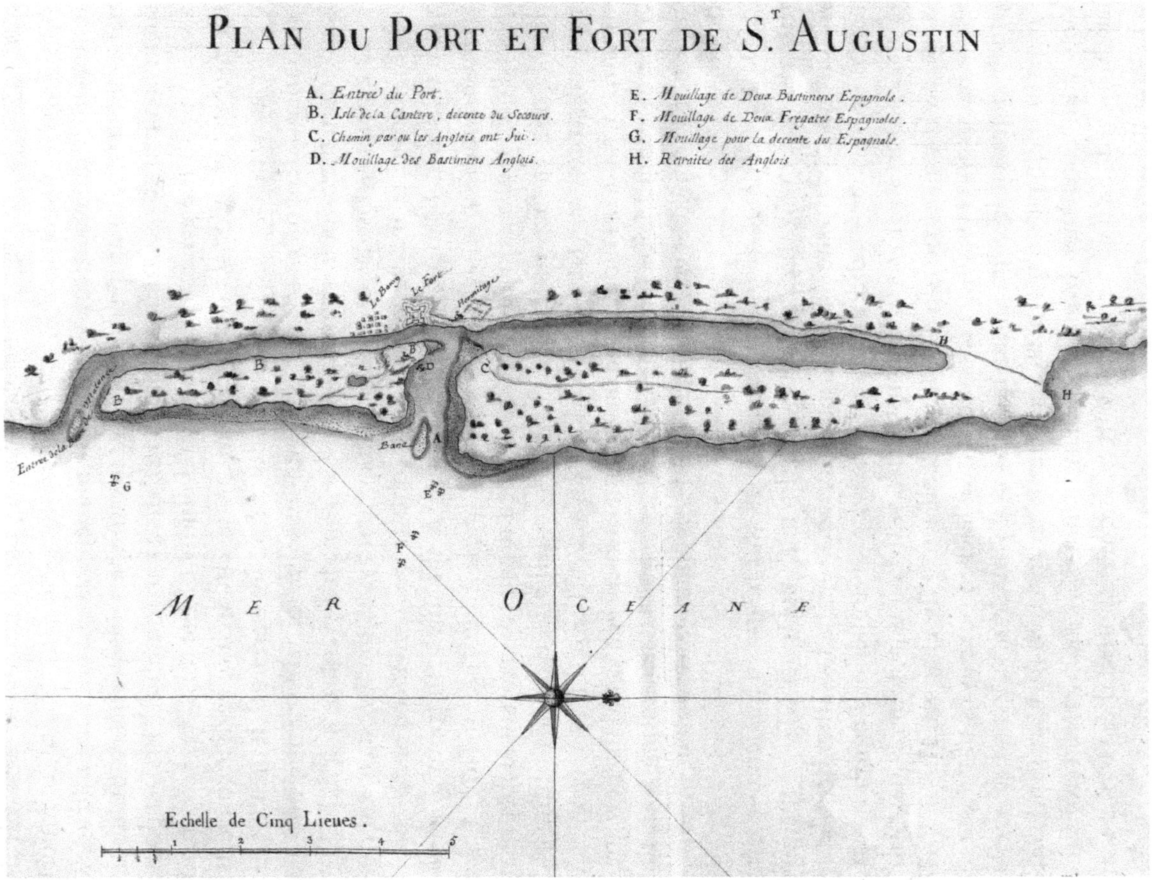

A 1745 plan of St. Augustine showing Castle San Marcos, the town, the site of the coquina quarry on Anastasia Island, and the narrow channel into the harbor through the outlying shoals. (*Library of Congress*)

after uprisings among the Guale, Apalachee, and Timucua. At least this element could be addressed by simply pointing to necessity. Third, and most important, were resources. While some money was put aside to build a few palisade forts, such as the one at San Luis in Apalachee territory, little was spent on firearms and training for the fledgling native militia. This last point also spoke to the general readiness and ability of the missions to defend themselves. The Christian converts, many the children of earlier converts, did not grow up engaged in the raiding and frontier warfare that their Creek and Yamassee counterparts did, and without some form of training and organization, they would prove to be at a serious disadvantage in a fight.[8]

The potential issues of the mission system aside, the threats to St. Augustine by Searle and his privateering cohorts had convinced Spain that a more substantial fort was required to protect the town. To see to this task Spanish engineer Ignacio Daza traveled to St. Augustine in 1671. Daza looked over the terrain and quickly decided to put the new stone fort near the old one. In fact, the new fort would actually overlap part of the old wooden structure. Daza also liked the layout of the old fort, a four-side structure with diamond-shaped bastions at each corner, as did the new governor, Sergeant Major Don Manuel de Cendoya. After meeting with the governor's council, it was agreed to build this enlarged version of the original fort.

Daza traced out the new fort and work was begun in September. The first task was to dig the forty-foot wide ditch. As the water edge of the fort was already close to the channel, high tide, rains, and bad weather frequently halted operations, as did the threat posed by a number of English buccaneers. The fort itself was to be constructed with coquina stone, a quarry for which had been opened on Anastasia Island across the channel. This in itself was a major undertaking. Pick and shovel hacked out pieces of the stone, which appeared like limestone but was really made of calcified seashells. Teams of men, typically Apalachee, Timucua, enslaved Africans, and convicts from Cuba, then wrestled the large chunks of the material from the earth, loaded them aboard small barges, and transported these to the masons near the fort.

Opposite: A 1756 plan of Castle San Marcos showing the layout of the fort and a cutaway of the arched bomb-proof shelters along the interior wall. A number of interior changes and a few exterior defensive arrangements were made to the fort over the years, but the basic character of the fortification remained unchanged from the time of Queen Anne's War. (*Florida State Library and Archives of Florida*)

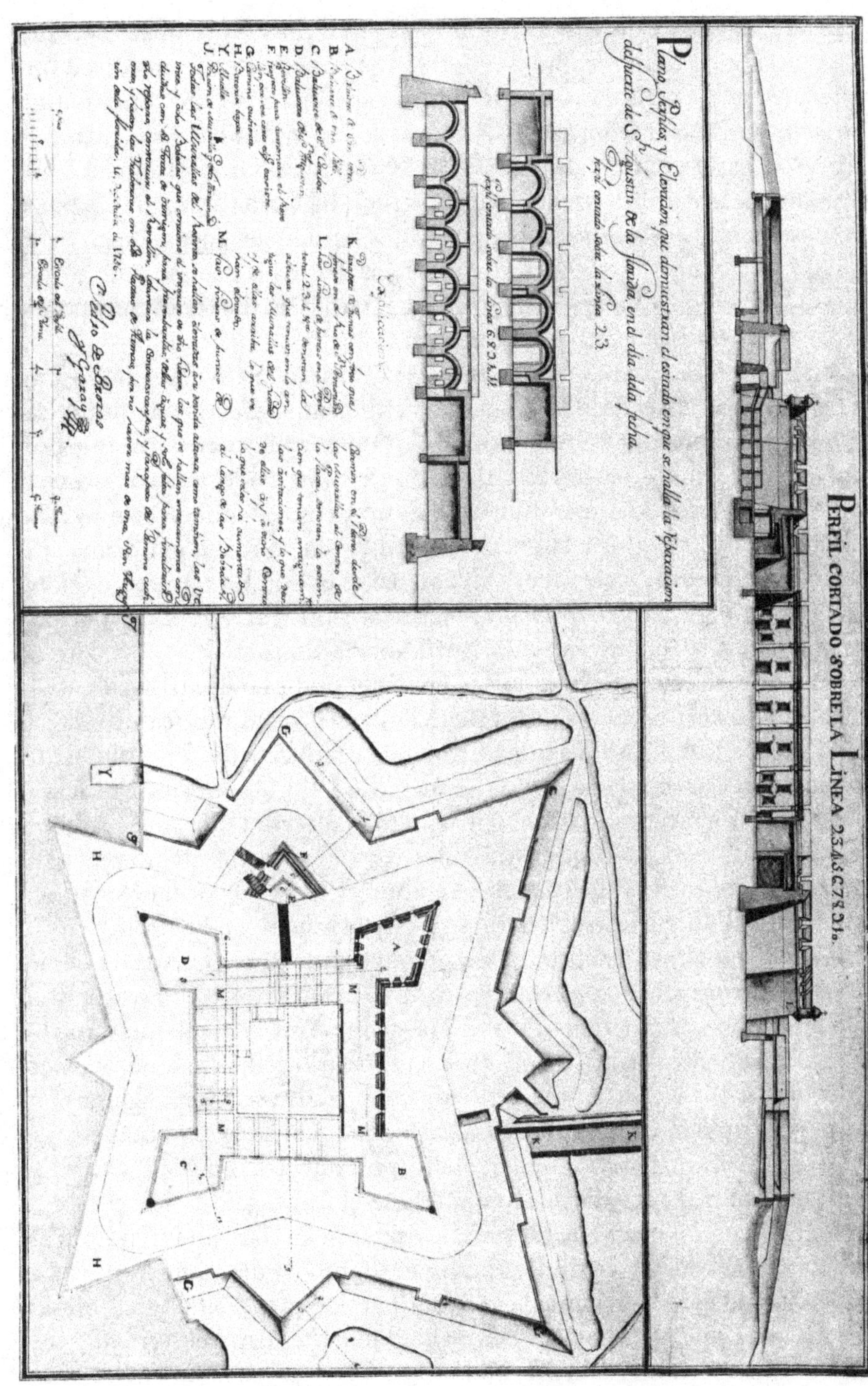
PERFIL CORTADO SOBRE LA LINEA

The first stone of the foundation was laid in early November 1672, but it would not be until the mid-1690s that the structure was considered finished. Money, corruption, apathy, and plague haunted the construction process, much as it would with Fort Port Royal in Acadia, Fort Albany in New York, and even the defenses of Quebec. A good deal of forced labor from the nearby tribes was used to construct the fortification, but even so, manpower was always in short supply. "It is hard to get anyone to go to St. Augustine because of the horror with which Florida is painted," the governor of Cuba wrote the year after work was started on the fort. "Only hoodlums and the mischievous go there from Cuba."[9]

Named Castle San Marcos, in the same vein as Castle William in Boston, the fort was a classic four-bastioned structure with a sizable one-hundred-by-one-hundred-foot parade ground. An outer wall, twelve feet thick on the land side and nineteen feet thick on the water side, was constructed along Daza's trace. An inner wall was then constructed thirty feet away. The space between the two walls was covered to act as firing platforms and braced by arches to create twenty-six casemates or bomb-proof rooms along the interior perimeter of the walls. A four-foot-thick and six-foot-tall parapet circled the structure and the protruding bastions.

The dirt from the ditch was placed in front of the landward-facing walls in a sloping fashion to create a glacis. The purpose of this feature was to mask the walls and bastions from direct fire by reducing the fort's silhouette. A causeway crossed the moat to the main gate, the landside of which was protected by a ravelin. To help cope with the ravages of tide and weather, a seawall was constructed along the water side of the fort. Watchtowers were later added to each of the bastions, and outworks in the form of small advanced posts were constructed for guard detachments and patrols.[10]

While well-constructed and thought out, Castle San Marcos did not differ greatly from other stone colonial forts of the day but for one exception. Technically, it was not built of stone. The coquina quarried on Anastasia Island was actually small seashells that had fused together in a porous network under the weight of the earth above them. It was much lighter than stone but could be easily worked and fashioned into blocks. Since there was no limestone to be found, oyster shells were burned and used with sand and water to make the mortar to bind these blocks together. The choice of building material must have seemed a risk to both Daza and Cendoya, although there were no options other than to import the stone from Cuba, which would have bankrupted the project at the start. Neither man would see the fort challenged and neither realized that they had inadvertently created a ballistic-resistant fortification.

By the time Castle San Marcos was completed the garrison for the fort and the troops assigned to protect all of the Florida missions was set at 355 men. This force was made up of three infantry companies, an artillery detachment, a small naval detachment, and a few dozen staff and logistical personnel. Actual numbers seldom reached the prescribed allotment of 355 men. Sickness and desertion, coupled with a sporadic and often unreliable trickle of recruits from Cuba and Mexico, typically left the tally ten to twenty percent below the directed threshold. In a time of crisis, the crews of any vessels in the harbor and the town's militia would double or even triple this number, but it also came with the cost of having to shelter the town's inhabitants, which would quickly tax the fort's food supplies. Almost three-dozen cannon lined the battlements, including a battery of sixteen-pounders that dominated the anchorage and water approaches. Although it had a number of issues that would be addressed over the years, at the turn of the eighteenth century, Castle San Marcos was one of the most heavily armed and defended forts along the North American coast. This was fortunate for the 1,500 or so inhabitants that called this port home; for to the north the English had established a colony at Charles Town and in doing so now posed a serious threat to Spanish Florida.[11]

CHAPTER FIFTEEN

# Carolina

THE NORTHERN PART OF THE CAROLINAS, which Charles II had granted under charter to eight powerful lords who had supported his return as king, had already seen a number of settlements, many originating from nearby Virginia and Pennsylvania. In 1669 these lord proprietors of Carolina financed a southern settlement as well. In August three vessels under the command of Captain Joseph West departed England for Barbados. On board were 150 settlers, supplies for the new colony, and their governor, William Sayle. The trio of vessels reached Barbados in October just in time for a hurricane to wreck one of the transports. Storms proved a problem again when they departed for the Carolina coast in February 1670, but by late spring they had dropped anchor in Charleston Harbor.

The original colony was erected at Albemarle Point across the Ashley River from modern-day Charleston, but by 1680 the latter location had proven so enticing that the town had moved to its present position at the end of Charleston Neck. Placed at the confluence of the Ashley and Cooper Rivers, and guarded by water on three sides, the new town occupied a naturally strong position. It needed to. Beyond threats from hostile tribes, the Spanish, who viewed the settlement as infringing on their Florida claim, had appeared on several occasions over the intervening years but backed away when they saw the precautions colonists had taken with their defenses.[1]

The colony and the region around it grew at an astounding rate. Much of this had to do with the abundance of food and the temperate growing environment. Apples, pears, and peaches abounded. There were vast forests of oak, cedar, and cypress—enough to build ships and dozens of towns. Soon, pitch, tar, and pine would be staple exports of the colony. Small seed populations of cattle, hogs, and sheep easily subsisted off the land even during winter and increased exponentially. Deer were found in "infinite herds," so much so that one witness described the area as one giant wildlife park. Indigo, rice, cotton, tobacco, and a host of other crops quickly took hold in the fertile land, and the nearby waters teemed with fish and whaling opportunities. Fireflies flittered above the land at night, and if anything was to be viewed in a questionable light, it would be the alligators that lurked along the banks, some the size of a horse "whose Scaly Back is impenitrible, refusing a Musquet Bullet to pierce it."[2]

The second element behind the population increase was the actions of the lord proprietors. A republican charter was prepared by none other than philosopher John Locke, and there was no religious test, other than not being an atheist, applied to anyone wishing to settle the area. Generous amounts of land were promised as well. Taken together with the bountiful land, the population of Charles Town, as it was known at the time, had by the early 1680s increased to close to 2,500 settlers and perhaps twice as many black slaves. The latter had been brought from the Caribbean to cope with the expanding agricultural efforts. In fact, availability of manpower seemed to be the only element limiting the growth of the colony.[3]

Conflicts with nearby native tribes like the Kussoes were quickly resolved by force of arms. The nearby Westro proved more problematic. The Iroquois-speaking Westro appear to be a late arrival to the area and one that did not get along well with their neighbors. A *de facto* alliance with the fledgling colony soon developed, which was of direct benefit to both parties. The colonists found a measure of security, while the Westro used the English to support their raiding activities. Falling upon the Guale and other nearby tribes the Westro seized an economic opportunity by selling their war captives off to English planters, often in exchange for firearms.

Problems soon arose, as many of these captives were from friendly tribes, thus their purchase was against the colony's charter, and as a result a number were later freed. The event also raised talk of bringing the practice of Indian slavery to an end. Even at this early stage, however, it would prove difficult. The supply and demand issues associated with the economics were in place, and vast wealth, power, and prestige were the potential rewards. This was true on the other side of the equation as well. The benefits an alliance with the English could bring, both in trade and military strength, were not lost on the Westro and those nations that would follow them in this practice. In addition, the Westro, much like other southern and northern tribes, took slaves as part of their mode of warfare. If the English wished to purchase these slaves for guns and other items of value that made the tribe stronger, so much the better. Thus, as long as there was a receptive market, it seemed likely that the trade would continue regardless of whether or not it was against the colonial charter.

With complaints about the Indian slave trade reaching them the lord proprietors weighed in on the matter by playing both sides of the fence. First, slavery was legal under the colonial charter. While the thought had been that the colony would change this in the future, at the moment the manpower was sorely needed. Second, they made it clear that friendly Indians were not to be subject to slavery. For the colonists this was all well and good, but who was to say who was friendly? Was it just tribes under treaty? What of the Spanish-allied tribes? Also, if slavers wanted to bring slaves in from the Caribbean or allied tribes wanted to sell them, what was the difference? One was fine but the other was not? To many in the colony it all smacked of posturing and waffling on the part of the proprietors. It was clear that the plan was to grow the colony by land purchases or by force of arms, yet Indian slaves sold by the colony's native allies were to be excluded from this even if it helped accomplish the primary goal? More importantly, many noticed that such directives, and their enforcement, were tied to revenue, with the size of the dividend check sent to England dictating the final policy in such matters.

Ruling a colony from across the Atlantic had many inherent problems, the foremost being a disconnect from the reality the settlers faced and how this reality meshed with greater economic directives being transmitted from England. The lack of clarity, and the slow and often vague responses from the lord proprietors clashed with daily colonial life, and because of this, the lord proprietors never held the power over the colony that they imagined, and the practice of Indian slavery not only continued but grew.[4]

A treaty was signed with the Westro in 1677 which forbade them from attacking tribes friendly to the English settlers. In exchange, the English traded arms and ammunition to the Westro, who would act as a screen for the colony against other hostile tribes. The Westro almost immediately broke the treaty, but it was not until a series of raids in 1680 against several friendly coastal tribes that the wrath of the colony fell upon them. There was really little choice. If the English did not enforce their treaties and honor their word to defend the tribes under their protection, they would have even

A portion of a 1711 map showing English South Carolina, Spanish Florida, and a portion of French Louisiana to the west. The map also shows native villages as they appeared near the end of Queen Anne's War. Note that South Carolina's southern border on this map includes St. Augustine, which was built over a century before Charles Town was established. (*Library of Congress*)

greater problems in the future. More importantly, the event encouraged the government to expand on its previous contacts with a group of Shawnee, or Savannah as they were called by the English, who had recently moved into South Carolina. This powerful western tribe offered lucrative prospects, and the Savannah for their part were interested as well. As a mark of friendship, the colony supplied firearms to the Savannah, who in turn responded by attacking and destroying the Westro's power in the region. The governor was then directed by the proprietors to "make peace with the Westroes, on such terms that they shall not despise us, and yet find it advantageous." If the Westro refused, the governor was to form a league of tribes that would compel them to do otherwise.[5]

Although the matter was dealt with, the lord proprietors questioned the motives behind the conflict. There were suspicions that the proponents of the Indian slave trade were behind the effort and concerns that it was not in the best interest of the colony. In either case they made a pair of suggestions. First, would it not be better to simply obtain slaves exclusively from the Savannah in order to maintain some level of control over the trade? Second, were the Savannah the allies that the colony sought strong enough to enforce peace through the area, and through the sale of firearms and munitions, could they be controlled?[6]

In fact, beyond their strength and their lucrative future trade connections, the Savannah fit perfectly into greater plans. Positioned on the colony's southern flank, the tribe now acted as a buffer against Spanish advances. This left the colonists free to turn to the nearby Creek tribes such as the Yuchi, Kawita, and Kashita to fill the economic void left by the destruction of the Westro. Provided with English firearms, the new target was the Guale. As Spanish allies no one in the English colony would care if they were attacked, and most would view weakening the Spanish as a public service.

Over the course of the 1680s several Spanish missions were attacked by large bands of Creek slave raiders, often led by several Englishmen according to one Spanish officer involved in the campaign. The matter became of such concern that the Spanish suspended their normal practice and began issuing firearms to the natives. It proved of little help as waves of raiders struck at the region over the next few years, scattering the populations and straining Spanish resources. By 1683 both the Guale and the Spanish had seen enough. Half of the tribe merged with the pro-English Yamassee, while the rest, along with their missions, were withdrawn to Florida.[7]

In 1683 another attempt at colonization would be made by the lord proprietors. This instance involved an agreement to sell land to Henry Erskine, the third Lord Cardross, and a number of Scottish gentlemen. The plan was to eventually send as many as ten thousand settlers to the region, but the effort began when Lord Cardross arrived at Port Royal with ten families and founded Stuart's Town. Unfortunately, jealousies and questions regarding the scope of Cardross's powers soon put Stuart's Town at odds with Charles Town.

By now the Indian slave trade had sunk its roots into the region. Like the fur trade to the north, the quick profits drew more settlers into the business. Guns were traded for slaves which drew more tribes into the practice, as each not only acted on past grievances and vied for standing among other tribes but consciously chose to be slavers rather than slaves. By 1685 the resulting power and money behind this practice had so influenced the colonial assembly that,

> The dealers in Indians boast that for a bowl of punch they could get whom they would chosen for Parliament and the Grand Council. By this means they have got Acts passed prohibiting the sale of arms

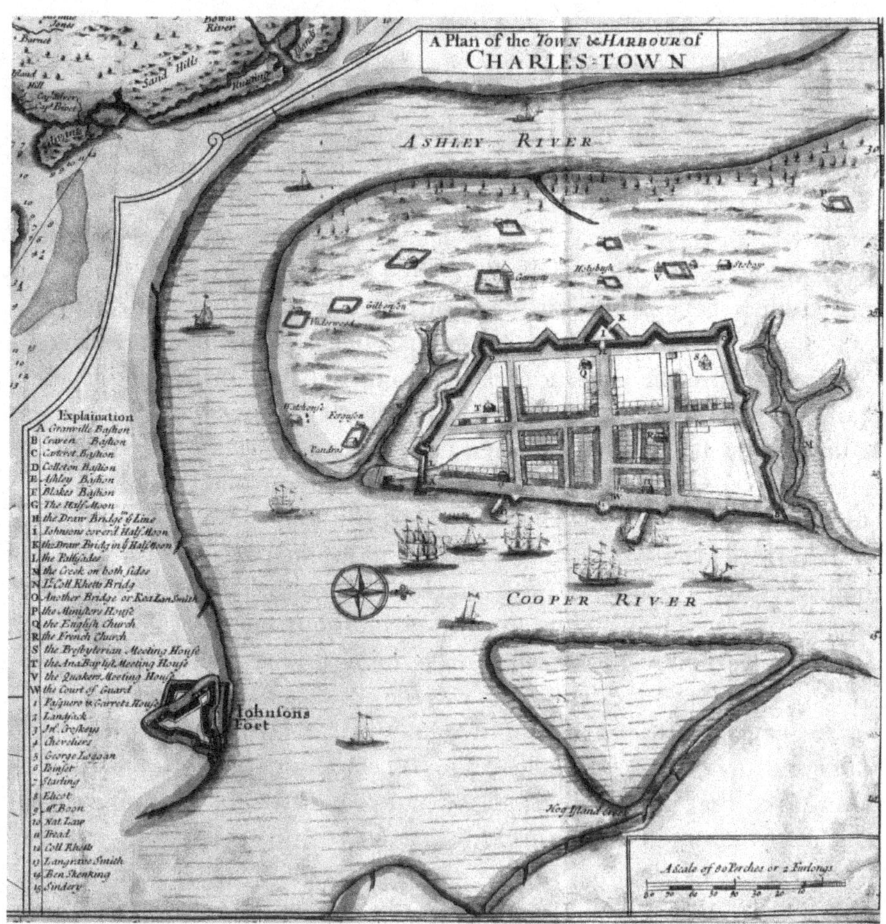


Charles Town and the surrounding area c.1711. Johnson's Fort, which was erected in response to a Spanish attack on the town in 1706, would play a prominent role in the defense of Charleston during the American Civil War a century and a half later. (*Library of Congress*)

> to Indians, on pain of forfeiture of all estate and of banishment, which they caused to be observed by others but themselves broke with impunity.[8]

The proprietors attempted to intervene and directed that no Indian was to be taken from Carolina unless there was a war between the English and that tribe. Even then the circumstances of the person's capture and their tribal affiliation was to be determined, "so that the barbarous practice of enslaving and transporting Indians by way of trade may be prevented." In the end it proved as effective as when Louis ordered the *coureur de bois* to stop participating in the fur trade.

There were other matters of concern as well. Illegal trade was on the rise, as was privateering and piracy. The citizens of Charleston were involved in all three at every level. Several high-profile figures and officials were charged with aiding privateers and pirates, and an act was passed to halt this behavior. The English customs official at Charles Town, however, was skeptical that it would accomplish anything, having found out firsthand that it was impossible to get a fair judgment in a Charles Town court.[9]

To the south news of an English colony at Charles Town had evoked limited replies from the governors of St. Augustine. Not long after the Albemarle Point colony had been erected, Governor Cendoya sent a detachment to investigate, but they abandoned the effort upon seeing the size of the English force. Again in 1672 a small force was dispatched to St. Helena Island to head off rumors of English advances, but nothing came of the matter. The real problem came not from the English but their allies. The English-armed Yuchi and Creek attacked the Spanish Apalachee in 1677, forcing an expedition to be sent out of St. Augustine to deal with them. They then turned to raiding the Guale missions, eventually causing their withdrawal in 1683. Added to this was the occasional incursion of English pirates, which seems to have haunted St. Augustine from its inception, and more pressing news about the new English colony at Stuart's Town. Reports had arrived that this English enclave had provided guns to the Yamassee. The latter then raided a Spanish mission and turned over twenty captives to the citizens of the town.

With this last piece of news Governor Juan Marquez Cabrera finally decided to act, and in the summer of 1686, he organized an expedition to deal with the English interlopers. One hundred and fifty troops were loaded onto three vessels, and under the command of Captain Tomas de Leon, they set sail for Stuart's Town. With only a handful of able-bodied men to defend the settlement, it quickly fell into Leon's hands. The English were taken prisoner and the village burned to the ground. From here Leon sailed north and raided the English governor's plantation on Edisto Island, killing his brother-in-law and carrying away thirteen of the governor's slaves as well as the tidy sum of three thousand pounds sterling. Pleased with their results, Leon set course for Charles Town, but a violent storm intervened and Leon went down with his vessel, the *Rosario*, while another vessel was run aground.[10]

It was perhaps bad enough that the expedition had ended in disaster, but what Cabrera had not expected was the English backlash from the raid.

The assembly was summoned in October and the sum of £500 raised to besiege St. Augustine. A pair of French privateers were chartered and a force of four hundred men was recruited. The supplies were being loaded onboard the ships and the men marshaled onto their vessels when the new governor of South Carolina, James Colleton, arrived from Barbados.

When Colleton discovered what was happening, he ordered the operation abandoned. Then, when he received a chorus of shouts at the unexpected turn of events, he threatened to hang any man who opposed his authority. The militia dispersed and the supplies were hauled back on shore to the grumbling of many. The lord proprietors thanked Colleton for stopping what might well have escalated into a war which would have engulfed the new colony. The proprietors scolded the colonial government. It appeared clear that the assistance they were providing to privateers and pirates, combined with the actions of the Scot's at Port Royal, had been the cause of the Spanish raid. The proprietors then noted that, although the colonial charter gave them power to pursue a defeated enemy that had attacked them, it did not allow them to proceed with an assault on the king of Spain's dominions. "No rational man can suppose," they argued, "that the subjects of any prince can be permitted to make war upon any of his allies for the reparation of their private injuries, or for any cause whatsoever, or that any such power was granted by our patent."[11]

In what further angered the citizenry, Governor Colleton befriended the Spanish envoy and worked out a trade agreement between the colonies. For the moment grievances were exchanged, and peace became the order of the day. Technically this was broken by news of England's entry into the War of the League of Augsburg, or King William's War as it was known in North America. However, when the lord proprietors declared for William, the populace agreed and went back to more pressing concerns. The lord proprietors then followed this with news of the conflict and orders for the militia to be mustered and powder to be stockpiled. The citizens shrugged and ignored the order. The conflict had made Charles Town's primary adversaries, the Spanish, new allies. There was the occasional threat of a French privateer or two, especially as they used to frequent the port before the war, and the remote threat of a French attack from the west with their native allies, but neither seemed to bother the citizenry.

Beyond aiding pirates and privateers, further fortifying Charles Town, and adding to its reputation as a center of illegal trade, King William's War had little impact on the new colony. There were no major military actions, and with peace established between Spain and South Carolina the colony was focused on commerce, not conflict. While suppressed, the attack on

Charles Town in 1686 and the threat posed to the colony by St. Augustine had not been forgotten. Nor had the Spanish resolved their basic issues with the South Carolina colony. English-armed tribes still raided Spanish territory in search of slaves, they still assisted pirates that probed St. Augustine's shores, and as the Spanish governors noted, the southern bounds of the English charter included St. Augustine. With Carolina traders pushing into the interior looking for new alliances and new opportunities to undermine the Spanish hold on Florida, it seemed clear to all that the peace would not last.

CHAPTER SIXTEEN

# Louisiana and the Brothers Le Moyne

IN 1700 A THIRD ELEMENT WAS ADDED to the Anglo-Spanish dynamic in the southeast. At the end of King William's War Pierre Iberville, who had drawn the French court's attention with a string of stunning victories in Newfoundland and Hudson Bay, proposed an expedition to claim the outlet of the Mississippi River for France. After the discoveries of La Salle and the reports of his able lieutenant, Henri Tonty, who had sailed down the river from the Illinois country in search of his former commander, there had been talk of this project. Suspect maps, questionable reports, rumors, and *ad-hoc* plans had followed, but nothing was carried to fruition. Now, with Iberville willing to undertake such an adventure an opportunity had presented itself. The success of such an operation coupled with French alliances farther upriver and along the backside of the Appalachian Mountains would go far in forming the barrier against English expansion that Louis had sought. With little in the way of risk and a huge potential reward, the project was approved and Iberville was given a pair of thirty-gun frigates to carry out the task.[1]

After departing Brest in October 1698, by January 26, 1699, Iberville in the *Badine* and Captain Comte de Surgeres in the *Marin* found themselves before Pensacola Harbor. Two Spanish warships lay at anchor on the other side of the sandbar and a palisade fort on shore covered the small town of perhaps 250 souls. Iberville's first thoughts were that the post had been established just a few months before in anticipation of the French expedition, but in this he was incorrect. While he was correct as to Spanish motives behind the settlement, the town had been established several years before in 1696 when General Andrew de Arriola erected Fort San Carlos de Austria and the nearby town of Santa Maria de Galve de Pensacola.

The Spanish governor was cordial and provided Iberville with wood and water, and while he was not to let a foreign vessel enter, a storm was approaching and for their own safety he would have a pilot guide the French vessels into the harbor. Iberville's initial thoughts were partially correct. The post itself was several years old, but word of French expansion along the Gulf Coast had reached New Spain, and in late 1698 a sizable reinforcement was sent from Vera Cruz to secure the position.

As it was, Iberville did not stay long. Sailing farther west a few days later, he came to Mobile Bay. Here, at the mouth of the bay, he found a good anchorage and shelter for his vessels. After exploring the bay in small vessels and making contact with a number of natives, Iberville decided to proceed with fifty men in small boats and canoes. Native guides would take him to the Mississippi, which was still several days away. On the night of March 2 Iberville and his men anchored at the mouth of the river. Mass was said the next day, and in a brief ceremony, the location was claimed for the king of France.[2]

There were still a host of questions, but for the French commander the path seemed clear. "It was necessary that I should ascend the river," he wrote the minister of the marine, "to become acquainted with its depth, observe the places proper for establishments, and visit the various Indian villages, which our Frenchmen said they had seen along its banks." In pursuit of this task Iberville was looking to find the Bayogoules, several of whom he had spoken with at Biloxi Bay a few days before. These representatives had informed him that the tribe's villages were several days upriver. In fact, it would not be until close to 200 miles later and the middle of March that the French expedition would reach the Bayogoules. Here Iberville met the Chief of the Monogoulachas, another nearby tribe, who was wearing a blue cloak that he claimed Henri Tonty had given him. Given that the natives had a number of steel axes and knives Iberville deduced that the story might well be true, but if so, then this must be the extent of French penetration down the Mississippi, as he had seen no signs of such activity on the lower portion of the waterway.[3]

When the chieftains began speaking about the tribes farther upriver Iberville began to question if he was actually on the Mississippi, given that

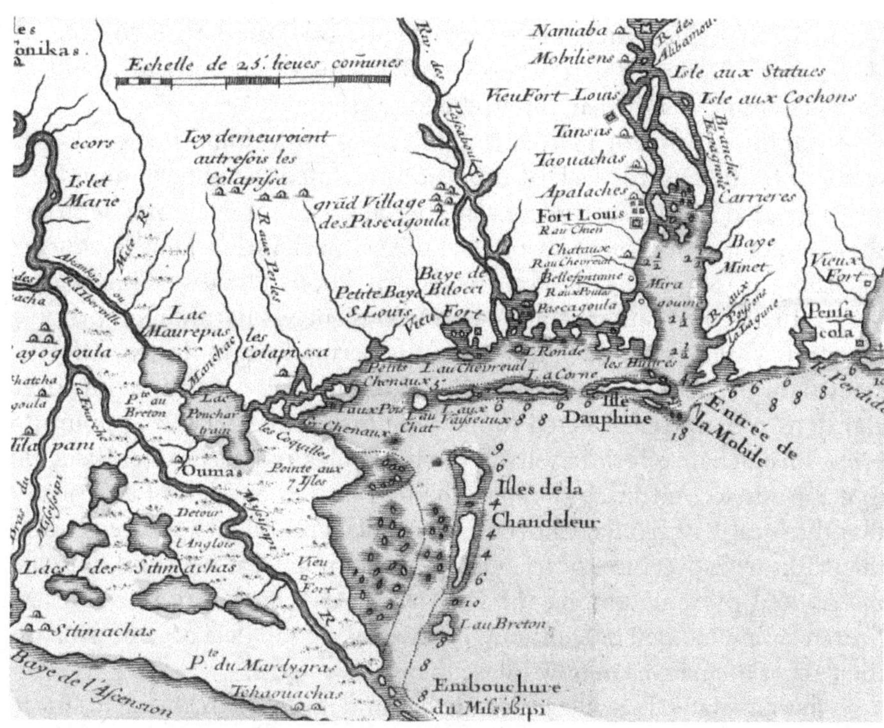


A portion of a 1718 map showing the lower Mississippi and Mobile Bay. The Spanish town of Pensacola can be seen on the right, or eastern, edge of the map. (*Library of Congress*)

none of these tribes appeared in the previously circulated Jesuit memoirs or Tonty's relations. Led by Bayogoule guides Iberville traveled farther upriver and met with the Houmas who were quite cordial and showed knowledge of having met with Tonty and other French traders. They too spoke of the tribes upriver, the Natchez in particular, and offered to take the French commander to their village.

Iberville, however, had seen enough. His men had traveled hundreds of miles, struggled against the river current for weeks, and were low on supplies. More importantly, there was still need to select a location for a settlement, and a fort to raise to defend it. On the advice of the Bayogoule chieftain, Iberville, now near modern-day Baton Rouge, took a shortcut and returned via Bayou Manchac (Iberville River) over Lake Maurepas, Lake Pontchartrain, and Lake Borgne, finally reaching his ships on March 31. The return voyage had also settled another matter. When speaking to the Houmas Iberville had learned that the Monogoulachas had a letter from Tonty. The French commander had his younger brother, Jean-Baptiste Le

Moyne de Bienville, purchase the letter for an axe. Dated April 20, 1685, it was indeed a letter from Tonty to La Salle, which removed any doubt in Iberville's mind that he had found the Mississippi.[4]

As for the location of a settlement, there was some doubt as several were scouted. In the end the lack of provisions dictated the choice more than anything, and Biloxi Bay was chosen. Iberville was not enamored with the choice, but for the moment it worked. Built on an elevation along the northeast shore of Biloxi Bay, the four-bastioned wooden fort was finished on May 1, 1699. Fort Maurepas, as it became known, was hardly an impressive structure with a crude ditch dug about its perimeter and firing platforms erected on the bastions for the garrison's dozen small cannon. A little over eighty men had been selected to man the fort, with Iberville appointing Naval Ensign Sauvolle de la Villantry commander and his brother Bienville to act as his second-in-command. The fort proved enough of a curiosity that the local Pascagoula, Choctaw, Pensacola, and Biloxi appeared before the works with overtures of friendship. A ceremony was held and Iberville distributed presents among the chieftains. Axes, picks, and even a few firearms were handed out, although there was a good deal of confusion on the part of the natives in how to use these latter items.[5]

A few days later, Iberville raised anchor and returned to France for more men and supplies. Those left behind began a more detailed survey of the area. While such actions provided valuable information and brought the French into contact with a number of the nearby tribes, it also led to a more threatening encounter. In mid-September Bienville and three others were busy charting a wide arc in the Mississippi River that would soon become known as English Turn. As the two French canoes threw out their sounding lines, a sixteen-gun English ship came into view. The vessel slowly ascended the river until it reached Bienville where it came to a halt.

Captain John Barr of the *Carolina Galley* was surprised to encounter Bienville. The latter then seems to have tricked the captain, who was sent along with another vessel to establish an English colony at the outlet of the Mississippi. Bienville informed him that the Mississippi was farther west and that he was currently in French territory. The ruse does not seem to have completely worked, as Barr and Bienville soon had words, with the former threatening to return in force next year and seize the area, but to Bienville's delight, no more came of the incident as Barr turned about and headed out to sea.[6]

Although he would not be informed of the event for several months Iberville and the new French colony had been fortunate. The failed English venture to occupy the outlet of the Mississippi had come within a few months of beating the French to the prize. For that matter, had Barr, who had another twenty-gun vessel waiting for him near the mouth of the river, pressed the issue he well could have made up for lost time by conquest and force of arms.

The thwarted expedition was the brainchild of Daniel Coxe. Coxe was a physician of some reputation serving as court physician for Charles II and later Queen Anne. The doctor also published early research into the effects of nicotine on animals and was a fellow of the Royal Society. In the 1680s Coxe purchased large tracts of land in western New Jersey. Although he never visited the American colonies his holdings were sufficient for him to be appointed governor of New Jersey for several years before the position was given to Sir Edmund Andros. Although Coxe sold his land in West Jersey in 1692 his interest in the trans-Appalachian region and its early explorers and maps flourished. The doctor's vision of the American colonies expanding into this region and capturing the vast fur trade propelled him to purchase an old land grant issued by Charles I. The "Carolana" grant had originally been issued to Sir Robert Heath in 1629. It covered the area west of New York, Pennsylvania, and Virginia, the colony of Carolina and parts of Florida, as well as the Mississippi Valley and lands beyond. While the purchase of the patent gave Coxe a level of legitimacy, his claims to English-held territory were not taken seriously, and those in French and Spanish territories were held in even less regard.[7]

Unfazed, in 1698 Coxe turned his attention to the lower Mississippi Valley and, in particular, the outlet of the Mississippi River. Part of the motivation behind this was brought about by the end of King William's War making such an expedition at least feasible, part was based on reports that the French were planning an expedition to follow up on La Salle's earlier claims, and a sizable portion was the product of Coxe's belief that the destiny of the American colonies lay beyond the Appalachian Mountains. Coxe proposed sending French Huguenots to settle the lower Mississippi Valley, and then, unlike most, he went to the effort of raising money and forming a company to undertake an expedition.

There were several prominent officials who agreed with Coxe's motives. Francis Nicholson, who was first governor of Maryland and later governor of Virginia, was one of the first to sound the alarm regarding La Salle's efforts to discover the mouth of the Mississippi in 1685. "I hope they will never be able to do it," he wrote London, "for if they should, and gain the Indians at the back of us, it may be of fatal consequence to most of these countries (colonies)." As Coxe outfitted an expedition to secure the outlet of the Mississippi, Nicholson wrote the Board of Trade with alarming reports that the French were planning great settlements in this area. Should they succeed in this task and win over the Indian nations along this waterway, combined with their current holdings along the Great Lakes and the St. Lawrence, they "will encompass all the English dominions here," he informed London.[8]

By October 1698 two small vessels had been outfitted to survey the Gulf Coast and make a recommendation as to the best site for a colony. The vessels departed London that month but first touched port at Charles Town where it was agreed they would wait until spring to resume their journey. In May 1699 the two vessels finally set sail for the Gulf Coast only to find, once they encountered Bienville, that they were too late. When Barr returned with news of his encounter, Coxe proposed an even greater plan, but while there was some interest in the scheme, it was not enough to convince either the king or Parliament to commit any resources to the venture, and as such, Coxe abandoned any plans to settle Carolina.[9]

On January 6, 1700, the signal cannons at Fort Maurepas and the nearby outworks boomed to life. Iberville had returned in the fifty-gun *Renommee* accompanied by Surgeres in the forty-six-gun *Gironde*. More cannon and muskets were set off in celebration. Supplies were offloaded and the fort's magazines filled with provisions, munitions, and trade goods. As it was Iberville would not tarry long at the stronghold. Before the week was out, he had departed with sixty men to once again ascend the Mississippi. The French commander met with the Bayogoule and Houmas again, securing their friendship and leaving Frenchmen behind to learn their language. Iberville also met with the Natchez, which one witness referred to as "the most civilized of all the nations," and their allies the Tenas. A peace treaty was concluded with this tribe before the expedition retraced its steps back to the mouth of the Mississippi.

There were a number of issues that alarmed Iberville. First was the English. While Captain Barr had departed peaceably, he might well make good on his threat and return in force this spring. Added to this were reports that the English traders of South Carolina had penetrated the backcountry and had begun to trade in slaves and furs with the fierce Chickasaw nation. In addition, there was news that the English had secured a number of smaller tribes in the area and had even begun making contact with the powerful Cherokee.

To deal with the possibility of Barr's return Iberville had sent his brother Bienville back to Biloxi to collect supplies and cannon for a post to be erected at Poverty Point, some thirty-eight miles below modern-day New Orleans. Upon descending the river, the French expedition found Bienville and a small gunboat waiting at the location. As the position was envisioned as temporary, a fort was ruled out. Instead earth mounds and firing platforms were raised for a six-gun battery. A cluster of half a dozen small log houses acted as the barracks and magazine for the outpost. Iberville assigned Bienville to command the post and then returned to Biloxi.[10]

While the fort at Poverty Point was being erected, Governor Don Andres de Arriola of Pensacola was marshaling together a force to expel the French from their new holdings. Arriola, who Iberville had met on his first voyage, was in a difficult position. When rumors of a French colony to the west reached him the previous year, he pleaded with his superiors for troops and supplies to expel the interlopers. None were forthcoming. In fact, even the routine supply vessels failed to arrive leaving the garrison on half rations. Sickness followed, further reducing the outpost. As vessels from Pensacola began to arrive at Vera Cruz carrying the sick and tales of desperation, Arriola, who was in Mexico at the time, was finally authorized to deal with the invaders, who were now thought to be English, not French. One hundred reinforcements were raised by emptying the prisons and sending press gangs into the city's slums. To carry these questionable troops to their destination the governor was given a twenty-six-gun frigate and one of the supply ships that had just arrived from Florida. Given the resources at his disposal Arriola held little regard for the mission and informed the king that the dilapidated presidio at Pensacola was not worth holding. It was too weak to defend itself, much less ward off intruders. If it were abandoned the monies saved could outfit a fleet of twelve warships, which was the only effective way to keep enemy vessels away from the coast.[11]

When the governor reached Pensacola, he began preparations for an attack on the rumored English settlement to the west. Even with his reinforcements, illness had reduced his overall numbers to around 150 men. By early March everything was ready. Arriola and his commanders gathered together one hundred men and loaded them onto four small vessels, and on March 4 they set sail for Mobile Bay. Having found little at this location the governor put a party of Spanish and Indians ashore about a dozen miles west of the bay. The scout returned a few hours later with news that there was a fort and several warships riding at anchor a few miles away in Biloxi Bay. Arriola had no sooner received the reports when a longboat flying an English flag was sighted and seized after a short chase. The ten men onboard were French, not English. The crew admitted to their deception and stated that they were returning to their fort at Biloxi. They then informed Arriola that another fort had been recently erected on the Mississippi and that a third fort four hundred leagues up the river was in direct contact with Canada.

Arriola released the prisoners and set a course for Biloxi. On the morning of March 23 he appeared before the bay. With a pair of fifty-gun French frigates at anchor and a garrison reported to be twice his number Arriola ruled out any attack. Instead he lodged a protest with Surgeres, who was in command in Iberville and Bienville's absence. The French fort was in clear violation of standing treaties between the two nations. By what authority had he occupied Spanish territory? The reply was that the fort was constructed to prevent the English from seizing the region. As for the fort's status, Surgeres shrugged and informed the Spanish governor that he was not empowered to make any decisions in such matters and would have to forward the protest on to France for a reply.

Outnumbered, Arriola satisfied himself with the warning and departed on March 27. Unfortunately, a tropical storm slammed into the coast on his return voyage, sinking three of his four vessels. Most of the crews were saved by French ships with many being taken back to Biloxi where they were treated until transportation could be arranged to return them to Pensacola. Thus, with the sole attempt by Spain to drive the French off the Gulf Coast a disaster, Arriola and the handful of effective troops under his command at Pensacola were relegated to the role of spectators.[12]

Iberville was informed of the affair when he reached Biloxi. With his time running short the French commander transferred what supplies he could spare from his ships to the stronghold's stores, tended to the structure's defenses, added sixty Canadians from his crews to the garrison, and met with a delegation of Natchez. The latter were amazed when Iberville took them aboard the fifty-gun *Renommee*. The tour had a positive effect on Franco-Natchez relations. The ambassadors and their entourage "could not but admire so great a canoe," and were stunned by the thunderous discharge of one of the vessel's guns. On May 28, Iberville departed after recommending that an expedition be sent to the Sioux country in search of a rumored copper mine. Whether a mine existed or not, the detachment would help promote communications between Louisiana and the Illinois country. An expedition to the Red River was organized as well, with the purpose of gaining information on Spanish posts and influence to the west. While the copper mine did not prove a success, it, like the Red River venture, proved invaluable to the French who began to map out a clearer picture of what lay before them.

Iberville would continue this pattern for the next several years, and as the colony slowly grew, a fortified post was established on Dauphin Island at the mouth of Mobile Bay. As a sandbar limited access to the bay, this location proved better suited to handle heavy vessels arriving from France.

A fort at Mobile would follow not long after as the primary French effort was shifted from Biloxi, not only to take advantage of the superior anchorage but to be in a better position to oppose English expansion into the region.[13]

It soon became clear that the major threat to French Louisiana was from the English not the Spanish. Carolina traders operating among the Chickasaw had led slave raids against the tribes along the Pearl, Pascagoula, and Tombigbee Rivers. While such events opened alliance opportunities for the French, thus far these tribes had been small and would not provide the safety the settlement required or the ability to address English expansion into the region. Better news would follow not long after when reports were that the Choctaw, a powerful nation of forty-five villages and over five thousand warriors, were at odds with the English and their traditional enemies the Chickasaw.

In September 1701 Choctaw emissaries arrived at Biloxi to ask for guns and French help in their war against the Chickasaw and the English. While this naturally led to an alliance between the French and the Choctaw, it was not the course Iberville desired. True, the Choctaw would prove a crucial shield against English attempts on the fledgling French colony, but it did little to break the influence of English traders over the Chickasaw and other tribes in the region. At first Iberville formulated a plan to capture these English traders and expel them, but reports reaching him indicated that there were simply too many to halt their efforts in this manner, and the plan was abandoned.

There were internal policy issues as well. Fur trade with Louisiana from Canada and the upper midwest was prohibited. This was done to protect Montreal and the other established trading centers, but it was having a negative effect on both colonies. Louisiana was in desperate need of such commerce, and the net effect of such an ordinance was to tempt French fur traders in the west to sell their goods to the advancing English, with whom they would get a better price than either of the French colonies. Iberville asked that these restrictions be removed but to little avail.[14]

With the death of Charles II and the rise of a Bourbon to the throne of Spain, Iberville sought to combine French and Spanish influence in the southeast to halt English expansion. Pensacola was well positioned to accomplish this task, but as the Spanish position there was too weak, he pressed the court to entice Spain into yielding Pensacola to the French as part of this plan. The effort roused national jealousies and fell on deaf ears, leaving Iberville to satisfy himself with constructing Fort St. Louis at Mobile to handle this role.

With a growing Franco-Indian alliance and an entrenched English position within the tribes to the north and east, Iberville sought the solution proposed by Frontenac and Callières in Canada—a general peace treaty between all the native nations mediated by the French. Such an arrangement would allow for trade among all parties and would bring an end to the slave raids, which in turn would blunt one of the major economic incentives behind Carolina traders' westward expansion. The problem was that such an agreement seemed impossible. The nations involved were relatively new to the French and their long quarrels with each other were part of how they defined themselves.

Although daunting, Iberville turned to the one man he thought could accomplish the task, Henri Tonty. Tonty, who spent much of his time with the Illinois had already made several trips to Louisiana, being one of the first to visit the area. His physical strength and organizational abilities, coupled with his noted skills as a frontier diplomat and his reputation among the Illinois and the nations of the Great Lakes, made him an excellent choice. The French commander ordered the royal stores of Fort Louis to provide Tonty with all the presents and supplies he required, and then in a sign of confidence in the diplomat's abilities, he noted that "if the supplies cannot be furnished from the Royal Magazine, let him get them from the Commissary and I will pay for them."[15]

With an escort of eight Frenchmen and two native guides Tonty departed on his 250-mile trek up the Mobile River. The party traveled through swamps and patches of sycamores draped with ghostly moss until they reached the Chickasawhay River. At this point they threaded their way through forests of hickory and oak that traced the riverbanks until they reached the first of the Choctaw villages. Here, among French allies, Tonty had few problems in convincing representatives to travel to Fort Louis for a peace conference. The difficulties occurred when he conducted the second phase of his mission and continued north to the Chickasaw homeland. The Chickasaw chieftains were cordial but initially at least suspect of French motives. Trade with the English and the strength that English firearms had brought to the nation was not easily dismissed for speculative talk about peace. This much Tonty expected. The frontier diplomat turned to a campaign of attrition with conferences and gifts handed out in a grand ceremonial setting. Speeches were exchanges, customs accorded to, and the slow erosion of Chickasaw apprehensions monitored for opportunities. When finished, it became even more clear how important Iberville's selection had proven, for the Chickasaw had agreed to attend the conference at Mobile.[16]

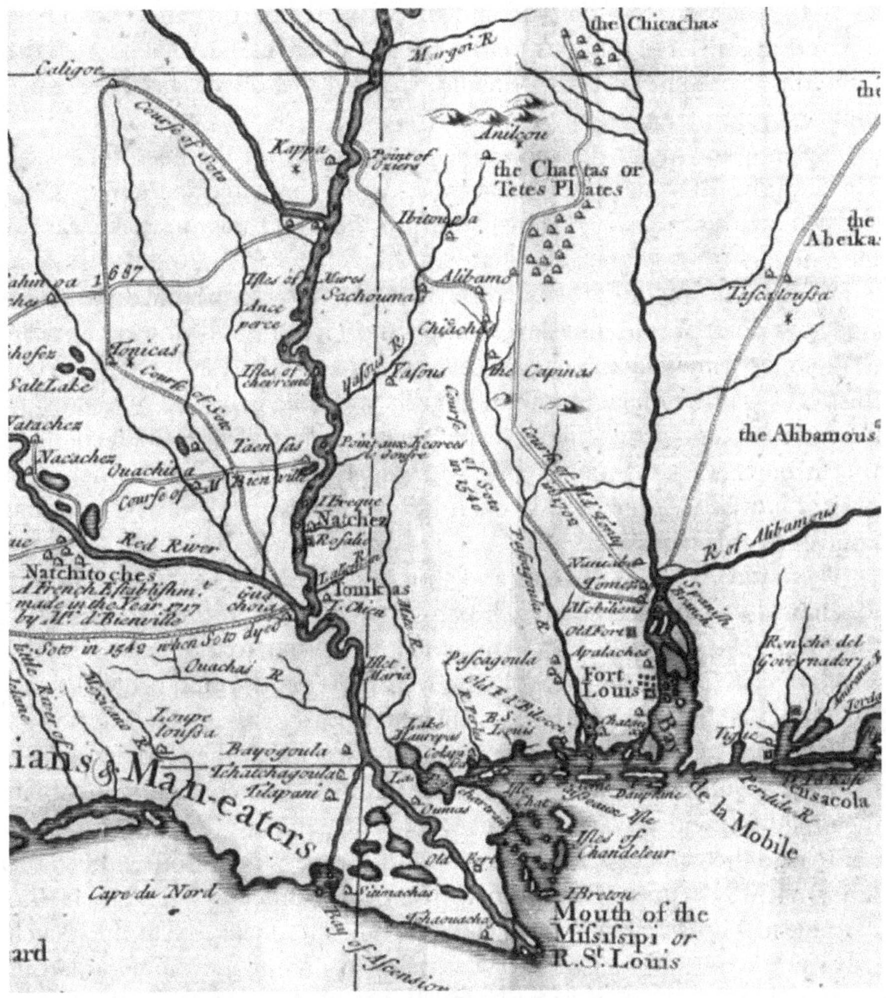


A c. 1718 map of the lower Mississippi Valley showing Henri Tonty's march from Mobile to the Choctaw and Chickasaw villages. (*Library of Congress*)

To the delight of all, the Choctaw and Chickasaw delegations arrived at Mobile in late March 1702. Iberville had also invited the Alabama, Tohome, and a number of smaller tribes to the talks. On March 26 the conference began in earnest with all the fanfare to be expected of such an occasion. It was in this forum that the French experience in frontier diplomacy came to the forefront. While the tribes were different than their Canadian counterparts their motives, methods, and reliance on ritual and custom were still the same. Working within the confines of these familiar patterns Iberville called the session into order and saluted each of the participants with a host of gifts ranging from muskets to iron cooking utensils. He then handed the ceremony over to his brother Bienville, who had already mastered the native tongue.

Speaking for his brother, Bienville informed all of the need for peace. The English had misled the Chickasaw and used them to raid their brothers and sell them into slavery. They had urged the Chickasaw to make war on the Choctaw and others, and what had this achieved? Yes, the English obtained their slaves, but at what cost? Ten years of war, over two thousand Choctaw killed or sold into slavery, and almost a thousand Chickasaw dead or prisoner. And who knows how many other tribes had suffered as part of this? This was the final aim of the English, Bienville bellowed out, pausing to scan the faces of the chieftains before him. They wish to weaken all of you through constant wars so that you will not be able to resist when they push you off your land. You know this, he emphasized. You have seen the English do this to others.

There was a chorus of nods and shouts as many showed their support for Bienville's words. The Frenchman spoke directly to the Chickasaw. If there was to be peace, then they could no longer listen to the English. If they wished to trade with the French, who were closer and would provide them what they needed at cheaper prices, then they must drive the English traders from the Chickasaw villages. Bienville then shrugged. If they did not do this then they could not be friends or trade with the French. The Frenchman then followed with a warning. This would leave the French with no choice but to arm the Choctaw, the Natchez, the Tohomes, the Mobile, and all the other friendly tribes. The Illinois, traditional Chickasaw enemies who Iberville had thus far restrained, would be called upon, as well as the French tribes to the north. The Chickasaw were brave, no one questioned this, but they would be swept away before so many French-armed nations. No doubt word of what had befallen the Iroquois had reached the Chickasaw chieftains, which only lent credence to Bienville's and Iberville's threats.[17]

It was enough to convince the Chickasaw to agree to a general peace treaty. Iberville sweetened the deal by promising to look into having the prisoners held by all the tribes released. In return he only asked that the tribes convince the Creek to trade at the French posts and that the Apalachee be left unmolested, as they were under his protection. The French commander then took a census of the tribes and handed out gifts of muskets to each of the chieftains to conclude the ceremonies.

The native ambassadors departed and French messengers were sent out to announce the treaty to all the tribes. "All the Indians seem to me very

Henri Tonty, left, c. 1680. (*Arkansas State Archives*) Pierre Iberville, right, c. 1695. (*National Archives of Canada*)

happy and willing to live in peace," Iberville noted at the end of the conference. In fact, the French diplomat's efforts were essentially a southern version of the Great Peace of Montreal. The effort, originally thought questionable if not impossible, had suddenly transformed the southeastern frontier. The English had been dealt a severe blow without a shot being fired, and perhaps even worse, the French had solidified an alliance that brought thousands of men to their cause.

Nicolas de La Salle, who had arrived at Biloxi in late 1701 as the king's first commissary of Louisiana, recorded his impressions of the event. "They promised each other peace in our presence. M. d'Iberville then made presents to each of these chiefs on behalf of the king. They testified to this with great gratitude and promised to remain attached to the French all their lives, and that henceforth they would have no trade with the English." La Salle, who was no fan of Iberville and his "band of brothers," nonetheless made it clear to the French court where the credit for this belonged. "I can say that the nascent colony is obliged to M. d'Iberville and M. de Tonty for this union, both who acted in this negotiation as well-intentioned men for the success of one of the King's most famous establishments."[18]

CHAPTER SEVENTEEN

# Moore's Folly

The Treaty of Mobile was a major victory for Iberville's fledgling French colony. The pact had not only secured the safety of the two hundred or so French settlers around Biloxi and Mobile but had temporarily erected a barrier to English expansion in the region. While a necessary step in Iberville's mind, it was not sufficient to guarantee the colony's future or even halt English influence over the Chickasaw, Creek, or a dozen other tribes. The reasons were simple. First, the population of Carolina, while not large, dwarfed that of Louisiana and Spanish Florida, and to make matters worse, it was growing at a rate that neither the French nor the Spanish colony could ever hope to match. Second, the quick profits of the Indian slave trade and the steady demand for slaves both in the American colonies and the Caribbean meant that there would always be an economic incentive for such activities regardless of the risks involved. Third was the problem that haunted all of New France; English goods were cheaper and more plentiful.

To further complicate the matter, the French commander also had to concern himself with his fickle Spanish allies. The commander of Pensacola found himself nearly abandoned by his superiors at Vera Cruz. Supplies were late in coming if they arrived at all, munitions were in short supply, and sickness ravaged his demoralized garrison. Iberville had been forced to send arms and supplies to help maintain this weak post. Really, he had little choice. Should the English seize this gulf port, a mere sixty miles from Mobile, they would not only be in a position to threaten the French colony via a military strike, but just as importantly, they would significantly shorten their trade lines with the Alabama, Chickasaw, and Choctaw. Given the low cost of English goods and the lure of the slave trade it would then only be a matter of time before they undermined the newly formed Franco-Indian alliance. Thus, whether by the sword or erosion, it appeared Louisiana would fall.[1]

One way to slow this effect was to stand against the Indian slave trade. Slaves were not allowed to be bought or sold at Mobile, and if possible, they were to be purchased by the colony and returned to their homes. By taking this stand the French would strengthen their alliance by gaining "the good will of the families and friends of those captured and all of the nations." Combined with ongoing diplomatic efforts, and a series of posts among the important Indian nations, a bond of friendship and respect would be formed that would act as a shield against English economic incentives.

While such a system was pursued, it was clear to Iberville that the real answer lay in seizing Charles Town. Regardless of French success, Spanish Florida, centered about Castile San Carlos at St. Augustine, was susceptible to an attack. Without French support it was likely to fall to the English in the next conflict, and the moment it did, "all the natives will at once be on their side." By moving against Charles Town, Spanish Florida would be saved and the Creek turned to the French, who then could be used to threaten the Virginia frontier. While concise in its goals, the proposal was somewhat optimistic in its considerations of the challenges involved, particularly when it came to the pro-English nations and their perceived reactions to such an event. Even with these imperfections the plan carried with it the elements of a powerful vision—that of pinning the English colonies along the Atlantic seaboard through a series of French and Indian alliances.

It would take time for the Peace of Mobile to take hold and for Iberville and his allies to convince the French court of the need to move against Charles Town. In the interim, more immediate steps were proposed to stabilize the Spanish Florida frontier. In January 1702 Iberville wrote the governor of Pensacola concerning the English slave raids against the Apalachee of western Florida. Thus far the Spanish and the Apalachee had assumed a primarily defense approach to these intrusions, a philosophy that had essentially stretched the limited resources of the Spanish and their allies and had done little to dissuade these activities. A more aggressive approach was required in the French commander's opinion, who then offered to help in any way he could with men, supplies, and weapons.[2]

Although the English and their Creek allies had struck the Apalachee the previous year it was not until a raid against the Timucuan mission of Santa Fe de Toloco in May 1702 that St. Augustine governor Jose de Zuniga y Cerda decided to organize a retaliatory expedition. Eight hundred Apalachee, armed mostly with bow and arrow, and a few dozen Spanish under the command of Captain Francisco Romo de Uriza marched north a few weeks later to settle the score. When news of Uriza's trek reached the Creek and a handful of Carolina traders, a counter force of five hundred men was quickly raised and sent south to intercept the invaders.

The two armies encountered each other late in the day near the Flint River. With only an hour or so before sundown both sides encamped for the evening. Just before daybreak the next morning Uriza's force crept forward. Seeing the Creek campfires still burning and their tents still in place, the order was given to charge. The Spanish and Apalachee burst out of the woods into the camp only to find it deserted. Realizing what had occurred Uriza frantically shouted for his men to fall back, but it was too late. A volley of musket balls tore through the attackers before the Creek came roaring out of their hiding places brandishing tomahawks and war clubs. It was over quickly. Close to six hundred Apalachee and Spanish lay either dead or in chains. The rest bolted south with bands of Creek warriors in close pursuit. It was a crushing defeat and an omen of what was to come.[3]

News had yet to reach Charles Town, but it made little difference. Rumors of war in Europe had set Governor James Moore into motion earlier in the year. Moore called for repairing defensive works, particularly along the waterfront, and increasing the number of men posted at key points around the town noting that "a good watch in Charles Town is convenient in time of peace and as necessary in time of warr as our batteries of great gunns which without a good watch will be of no use to us."[4]

In late August the South Carolina Assembly was having a heated discussion regarding the colony's constitution when a messenger entered the chambers. Upon hearing the herald's report Governor James Moore ordered the doors closed and informed the representatives that England had entered the war against Spain and France. Moore was quick to point out that the previous year there had been discussions concerning an expedition against St. Augustine upon the event of such news. He immediately called for this project to go forward before the French could strengthen the position, and then in a more telling statement he pointed out that the capture of this post would not only cripple the Spanish but "wee believe will open to us an easie and plaine way to Remove the French (a no less dangerous Enemy in time of peace then warr) from their settlement on the south side of the Bay of Appalatia."[5]

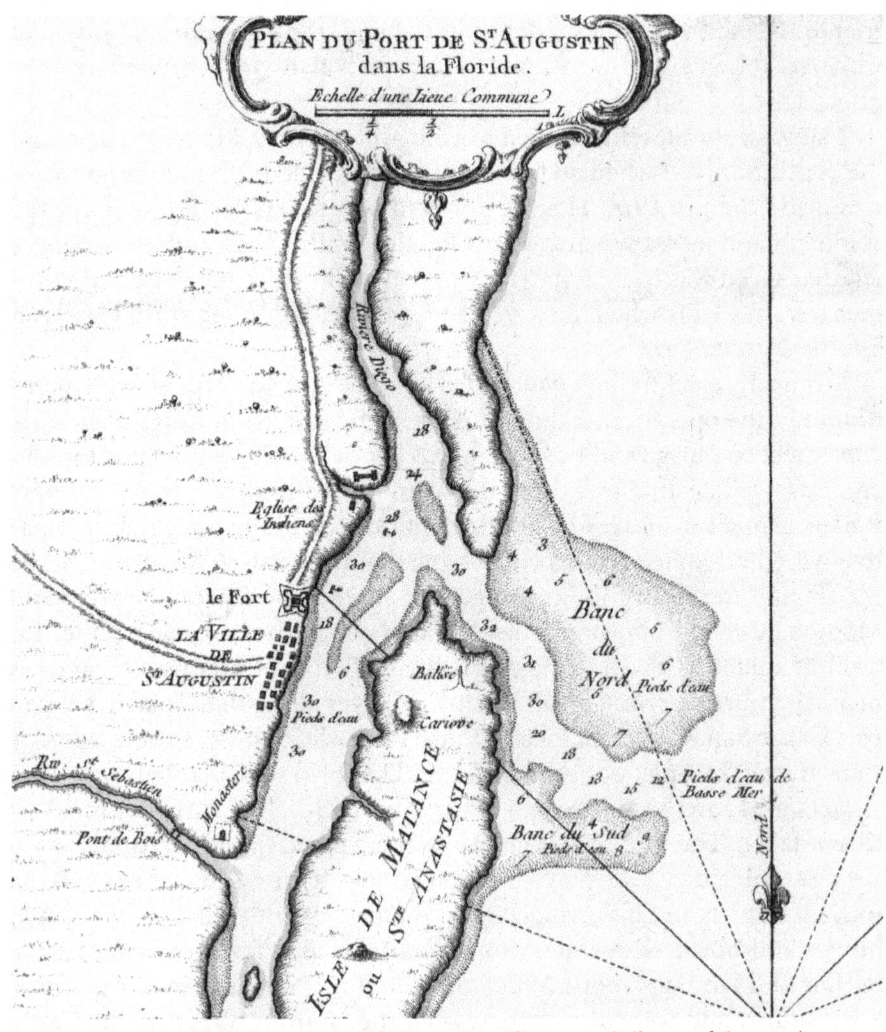


A 1764 map showing St. Augustine and the surrounding area. (*Library of Congress*)

While there was no love lost for the Spanish stronghold, and the memories of the aborted 1686 expedition were once again brought to the forefront, not all were so quick to launch an attack on one of the stronger fortifications in North America. Many were in favor of securing the colony's defenses before attempting any offensive operations, while others rightly cast doubts on the ability of the colony to conduct such an operation, questioned Moore's motives, and viewed the entire venture as nothing more than a slave raiding expedition by the governor and his "Goose Creek" friends. Heated words ensued, but in the end, the governor and his allies won over the assembly who voted to raise £2,000 to move forward with the project.

Many, for the aforementioned reasons, did not want Moore to command the expedition, but when no better individual could be found the governor was given the position. The hope was to secure ten vessels, six hundred colonists, and as many native allies for the venture, but given that Moore felt that speed was more important, only two-thirds of the projected numbers were available when the governor set sail with thirteen small vessels on a brisk October day.[6]

Strangely, even though Moore felt that speed and surprise were paramount in the operation, it did not prevent the fleet from stopping in early November to pillage and burn what was left of the Guale missions for several days. When this was done the army broke into two parts. Colonel Robert Daniels would lead a hundred colonists and the three hundred natives who had joined the expedition overland against St. Augustine, while Moore and the rest of the contingent proceeded by sea. On November 8 Moore's little fleet appeared outside the town's harbor, unable to enter for want of a pilot to navigate the outer shoals. Two days later Daniels and his men, after having seized a pair of small villages along their march, slipped past Castle San Marcos and dashed into the town. Shouts and war whoops were greeted by open doors and silence. The town was deserted.

While Moore had hoped to achieve some level of surprise, this had clearly failed. The town had long before received news and prepared for the siege by entering Castle San Marcos with all the provisions that could be moved. Daniels and his men occupied themselves with pillaging the empty homes and businesses while Moore spent the next few days entering the harbor and landing troops. When he met with Daniels they surveyed the Spanish fort and were dismayed at what they found. "Wee find the Castle much stronger than hath been represented to us by any person," he wrote the Carolina council. Heavy guns mounted along the shore side walls ruled out approaching the structure by water, and a wide moat covering the landside walls ruled out storming the stronghold with the ladders that had been brought. Not that it would have mattered, as the fort's normal garrison of 150 men had been more than doubled by the sheltered civilians, making any attempt to overwhelm its walls, which were studded with cannon, an extremely costly affair.

There were a few options before Moore at this point. First, he could conduct a formal siege. One of the fort's walls would be selected and a trench or sap dug toward the wall in a zig-zag fashion to minimize the impact of

Colonel Robert Daniels. Daniels was an old associate of Moore's and one of the "Goose Creek men," who participated in the slave trade and rejected most of the Lord Proprietors guidance regarding the colony. He would later become governor of South Carolina. (*South Carolina State Archives*)

Spanish cannon, which would certainly contest the effort. Firing parallels would be dug at regular intervals to cover the advancing trenchwork until a final parallel was erected at a distance close enough to breach the fort's wall.

The good news was that the fort had been invested, and tools had been brought to see to such a contingency. The bad news was that Moore lacked a crucial element to carry this plan through: artillery. He did not have any heavy mortars, which were commonly used to force the garrison off the gun platforms and into their bomb-proof shelters, nor did he have any heavy cannon to create a breach. In fact, only four light cannon had been brought, which were easily outranged by the castle's main guns, meaning that Moore's battery would be blasted out of existence before it ever got close enough to see if it could harm the structure.[7]

As the English army settled down around San Carlos the folly of the entire venture became apparent. Moore and his officers had greatly underestimated the strength of the fort and the operational surroundings, and while the governor understood a need for speed both to prevent the garrison from being reinforced and to prevent word of the Carolinian effort from reaching them, the operational security to assure this was nearly impossible. Nor was it helped by spending two days raiding the Guale missions. Even given these circumstances, it seems Moore failed to consider the scenario where the fort was not surprised. Castle San Marcos, a fort that the Spanish had spent twenty years constructing out of stone, had been built around a simple principal; it was too costly to take by storm. This meant that once the element of surprise was lost, the only way to proceed was via a formal siege, which in its most fundamental form was a duel of artillery—artillery that Moore did not possess.

Moore tried to put a positive light on the situation. The fort was isolated and contained in his estimation a thousand "eaters." Time was not on their side. "Wee can foresee nothing, but an overpowering and speedy assistance sent to the besieged, can hinder our taking the Castle," he informed the Carolina council. However, just in case it proved too difficult to starve the fort into submission he had dispatched a pair of sloops to Jamaica with an urgent request for artillery. In either case, the governor informed the council, he and his troops would not return until all hope had been exhausted.[8]

General Joseph de Zuniga had first heard reports of the English expedition on October 22, giving him several weeks warning. He dispatched a courier to Pensacola requesting reinforcements and ordered a sloop sent to Havana to communicate the threat. The decision was then made to house the town's citizens inside Castle San Marcos. There was really little choice. "Because of the lack of men, arms, and ammunition," he wrote Havana, "we are forced to close ourselves in the fort as soon as the enemy arrives." To deal with this contingency, supplies of corn were carried into the fort and a herd of cattle was driven into the area between the moat and the fort's walls to help sustain the 1,500 or so souls that sought refuge.

After examining the English flotilla that had appeared outside the sandbar on November 8, the next day the Spanish governor dispatched a small launch for Havana, sending it south around Anastasia Island via the Matanzas Inlet to avoid the enemy vessels. There was little Zuniga could do to prevent the English from seizing the town and investing the fort, and when it became apparent that the enemy was not interested in storming the stronghold, both sides settled down into a siege mentality.

Over the next few weeks, the Spanish commander probed the English lines and found several gaps that allowed him to bring in additional supplies from his Apalachee and Timucua allies. The fort's guns were trained on the siege trenches that snaked their way toward the moat, and the occasional sally by the garrison netted little more than a few prisoners and a handful of casualties. Zuniga slowed his rate of fire on the advancing enemy trenches, as it became clear that a long siege lay ahead. There was another reason for this. His artillery was old and too few, and the largest gun in his arsenal was a sixteen-pounder. More importantly his gunners had no experience to speak of and had "only a slight knowledge of the bronze and

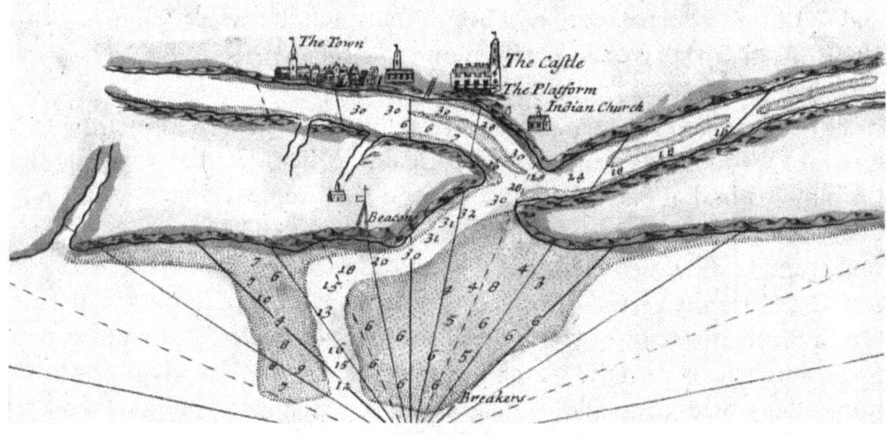


A 1711 map of St. Augustine. (*Library of Congress*)

iron guns which are mounted." Even so, over the next eight weeks over four hundred rounds of grapeshot and ball were launched at the English with mixed results. The good news was that it appeared that the enemy guns were smaller and much fewer in number than the fort could bring to bear. Although he had little confidence in their abilities, Zuniga nodded with approval when his gunners claimed to have disabled one of the English guns only to rush to the scene of an explosion a few days later when one of the fort's guns burst on firing, sweeping the firing platform with shrapnel that killed or wounded the entire gun crew.

Although he had suffered few casualties, after almost eight weeks of skirmishing, constant patrols, and digging, Moore had little to show for his efforts. The men, unsuited and unfamiliar with a siege, had grown restless and his four twelve-pound guns, one of which burst after repeated firings, had made no impression on the fort. His fleet was in control of the harbor and supplies had arrived, but with illness and dissention on the rise, if the artillery from Jamaica did not arrive soon the governor would be forced to abandon the siege. Around noon on December 26 the cries of English lookouts rang out, as four vessels could be seen approaching. Moore was delighted and barked orders to his troops on where to land the arriving cannon and how they should be deployed, but it proved a short-lived exercise as keen eyes soon made out the royal flag of Spain.[9]

This was confirmed not long after when a cheer rose from the castle's ramparts. For Zuniga and his beleaguered garrison, it was yet more good news. A few days before a small detachment from Pensacola had snuck into the fort with munitions and news that a relief force of a hundred Spanish and five hundred Apalachee had begun their march toward the fort. Now, as the line of sail led by two warships moved closer to the sandbar, it became clear that the siege was entering its last phase.

For Moore and his men, it was disaster. Reports indicated that the two warships were thirty- and forty-gun frigates, which dwarfed anything the Carolinians had afloat. Moreover, beyond the firepower resting on these two vessels, just the crews alone would add another 350 men to the enemy's ranks, and this did not even take into account whatever infantry had been sent to bolster the garrison. With his fleet trapped in the harbor by the arriving Spanish warships, facing fresh troops from Cuba, and rumors of a Spanish relief force on the march from Pensacola, Moore had only one option. After a brief council of war, it was agreed to spike the remaining cannon and put their small fleet and the town to the torch before retreating back to Charles Town on foot.

Zuniga ordered the arriving troops to cut off the English retreat, but they showed little interest beyond making an appearance of pursuit. As it was the Spanish commander did not press the point. He had managed the siege in a cool and professional manner. He had taken advantage of the ample warning to provision his fort and send for reinforcements. He husbanded his resources and challenged the enemy's siege works at every turn, while at the same time protecting the entire population of the town within his fortification. The general in turn commended the townsfolk's role in the successful defense of Castle San Marcos, and after watching them sift through the ashes of their homes after such courage, he asked the king of Spain "to grant considerable alms to aid these poor vassals who valiantly have defended this fortress and executed all orders exposing their lives with great bravery and zeal, but all are now in the street."[10]

Moore and his unhappy band made the successful trek home without incident. The governor drew criticisms from his troops, the citizens of Charles Town, and the English government abroad. Given his actions it is difficult not to agree. Although the number of casualties was low almost everything was lost, not all of which had been paid for, as part of the funds had been secured against the projected plunder. Riots ensued, and renewed accusations were made against Moore and his slave traders.[11]

For Moore it was a personal disaster both in terms of his reputation and the money he had sunk in the project, but it was not the end. As the calls for his replacement grew, he began to formulate another plan, not one to seize St. Augustine but one that would undermine all of Spanish Florida.

# Part Four

## *Days of Musket, Tomahawk, and Sword*

CHAPTER EIGHTEEN

# The Apalachee and the Siege of Charles Town

While the citizens of South Carolina viewed Moore's St. Augustine campaign as a dismal failure, this was not the case with many of the nearby tribes. The English had invaded and struck at the heart of Spanish Florida. So what if they had missed? It had been they who had carried the fight to the enemy. Did they not decimate the town and the missions in Guale and still walk away with booty and slaves? Who cared if Castle San Marcos stood a thousand years if everything around it was open to raiding? In fact, if the English foolishly expelled the Spanish from Florida and took the Spanish tribes under their protection, it would be a disaster for the slave-raiding nations. There would be a scramble as the various tribes sought new sources, which might even include each other. However, the best result had occurred. Spanish power in Florida had been weakened but not destroyed, and the English, certainly looking to avenge what they viewed as a defeat, would respond by falling upon the ill-defended tribes of Florida with their allies.

One of the first tribes to approach the English after the siege of St. Augustine was the politically important Alabama. Iberville had invited the nation to the peace talks at Mobile and was convinced of their desire to be part of the treaty. If so, this did not last long. Five French traders who returned with the Alabama after the talks were attacked. Four were killed in their sleep while the fifth, simply by circumstance, escaped with the news. Bienville organized a pair of expeditions to punish the Alabama, but neither came close to accomplishing anything of importance. A few months later, in April 1703, the Alabama petitioned the English for stands of flags to proclaim their alliance and for guns and ammunition to fight the French and Spanish.

The Alabama were not alone in this. A number of Creek tribes had put forth similar requests. A dozen of these tribes, led by the Cotewa, Coosa, Cuseeta, and Abihka, began to speak of a tighter alliance with the English. This political union would coalesce over the next few years to a treaty with the English where the participants acknowledged that their "Protection depends upon the English," and that the French and Spanish, being enemies of England, were now also their enemies. It would be the dawn of what the English would term the Creek Confederacy, although there are no mentions of Creek anywhere in the treaty.[1]

By late 1703 the growing English influence over these tribes offered a new opportunity for Moore's replacement Sir Nathaniel Johnson, a well-known figure in the colony and good friend of Moore. For defensive and political reasons these pledges of alliance among the Creek were of great concern to the assembly of South Carolina, who in September pressed the new governor "That all possible & Speedy care be taken to protect our Indians allies Living to ye south & westward of us, from such incursion of ye Indians that are allies of ye French & Spaniards which may so weaken us by ye Loss of them." The House was ready to assist in these matters of frontier defense by providing the governor with "powder and arms out of the public stores, by funds for presents, or any other means your Honors Shall think fit."[2]

Johnson and the assembly turned to Moore to oversee this task and directed him to make efforts to resolve the outstanding issues with the Spanish Apalachee by all peaceable means. There was little confusion as to what this entailed or what Moore and his allies had planned. The assembly, looking to distance itself from the nasty details of their directive, would not provide any funds for Moore's contingent, not that it mattered, as speculators were more than happy to provide money for what they believed would be a wealth of slaves and plunder.

Moore would not disappoint them. Gathering together some fifty Carolina traders and a thousand Creek he advanced on the Apalachee village of Ayubale in January 1704. When he approached the fortified mission waves of arrows forced his men to take cover. After a quick reconnaissance it was agreed to force the main gates and seize the fort by storm. Looking to set the example, Moore's Carolina traders dashed forward axes in hand to tend to the task. Scores of muskets flared in support of the effort, but the Apalachee were not to be so easily taken and drove Moore's men off with over a dozen casualties. For the next few hours, the engagement settled down into an exchange of arrows and shot as Moore's men prepared torches and bundles of wood. When all was ready several Carolinians and Creek dashed forward and set the mission on fire in multiple places. Moore waited for the fires to spread before he gave the signal to charge. There were pockets of stiff resistance, but numbers soon overwhelmed the defenders. Several hundred men, women, and children were taken captive, including the mission's friar.[3]

It was a restless night for all, especially after scouts returned informing Moore that a Spanish-Apalachee relief force had left San Luis and would be upon them at daylight. The information was correct. At first reports of the Anglo-Creek raiders Lt. Juan Ruiz began to organize a response. Within a few hours he deemed that he could wait no longer and pushed toward Ayubale with thirty mounted Spanish soldiers and four hundred Apalachee, many of the latter having been armed with muskets out of the stores. Ruiz arrived the next morning to find Moore and his detachment splayed before the town. The Spanish commander pressed forward and a hot engagement ensued, slowly dragging more and more men into the fray. While Ruiz had made some progress, it was clear that the English and Creek severely outnumbered and outgunned his troops. Low on ammunition and exhausted Ruiz's troops broke when a musket ball knocked the Spanish commander off his horse. Moore and his troops dashed forward and captured the wounded Ruiz as well as eight of his mounted detachment and a number of Apalachee. The rest fled, leaving some two hundred laying on the battlefield interspersed with a good number of Moore's forces. That evening, as the campfires burned and the wounded were tended to, Creek losses were avenged on a number of prisoners, both Spanish and Apalachee, in ghastly fashion. While Moore and his men were certainly aware of what was transpiring, they made no effort to intervene, nor would it have been wise to do so.

At this point there was little for Moore to do but march on the remaining missions. There would be no major resistance, and soon half a dozen towns had submitted, the only holdout being the palisade fort at San Luis. Because of his earlier losses, Moore elected not to attack San Luis, which was known to be garrisoned by the Spanish and armed with cannon. There was no need

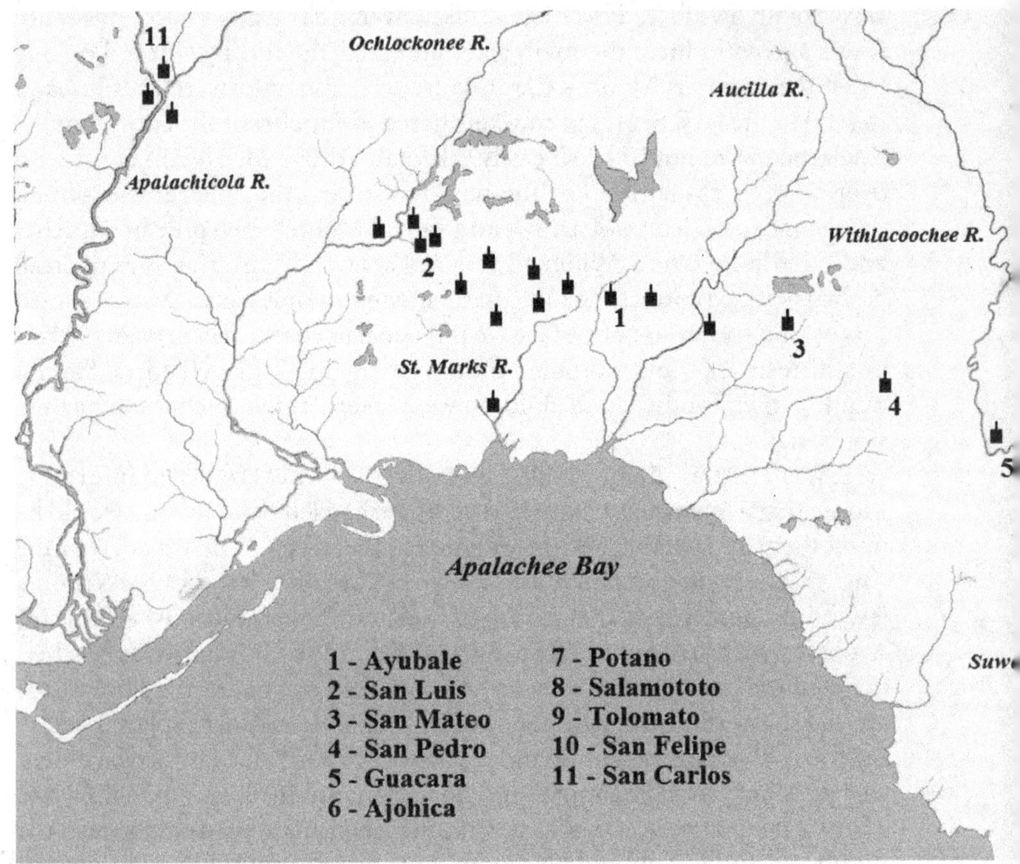


Spanish missions among the Apalachee and Timucua. The Aucilla (Oncilla) River was the traditional boundary between the Apalachee and Timucua provinces.

to. "Apalatchia is now reduced to so feeble and low a condition, that it can neither support St. Augustine with provisions, nor distrust, endamage or frighten us; (or) our Indians living between the Apalatchia and the French," Moore informed Governor Johnson. "In short, we have made Carolina as safe as the conquest of Apalatchia can make it."[4]

While no longer a threat this did not mean that the Creek and the English were finished with the Apalachee. A number of smaller raids culminated with a large-scale attack on the western Apalachee villages near Pensacola in July 1704. Overextended and short on arms the Spanish had still not supplied these villages with firearms. Once again, several thousand Creek descended on the ill-defended Apalachee homesteads, this time even surprising a Spanish shallop and killing or capturing twenty-eight of its

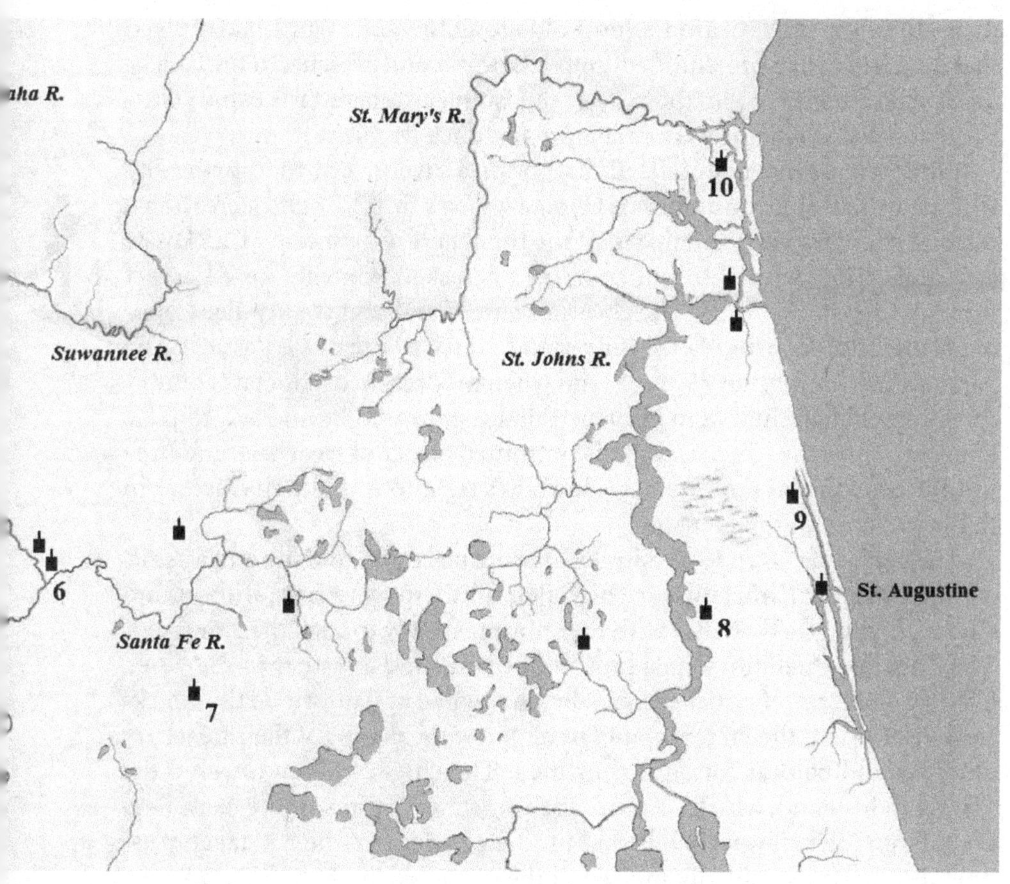


crew. The commander of Pensacola, Captain Don Guzman, wrote Bienville for arms and supplies, and while some were sent it made little difference. What was left of the Apalachee fled for St. Augustine or Mobile. The rest were either killed or carried away.

Spanish West Florida had been devastated. Thousands of Apalachee were moving north toward South Carolina, perhaps five hundred had been killed, and an untold number taken as slaves. The Spanish still held Pensacola, but even this would be fleeting as a fire broke out in October and consumed the fort as well as part of the town. With little choice, Guzman and his garrison abandoned the position and marched to St. Augustine.[5]

For the French colony at Mobile it was a perilous setback as well. The ongoing conflict with the Alabama would only worsen as the English and their allies had now secured a foothold along the gulf. Word had arrived that the English had presented a number of slaves and presents to the Chickasaw, in an attempt to win them over, and from Havana reports came warning that the Carolinians were preparing to attack Mobile.

While no attack materialized, bad news arrived from the north. The Chickasaw had sold a number of Choctaw slaves to the English, creating a rupture in the fragile peace treaty. At the time there were seventy Chickasaw at Mobile. They wished to return home and asked Bienville for an escort through Choctaw country. The governor agreed and sent twenty-five Canadians under his cousin, Pierre Boisbriand, to see to their safe passage. The party set out on February 9, 1705, and when they reached Choctaw country three weeks later, they were informed that they would be allowed to pass. However, since the Chickasaw had committed an act of treachery and broken the peace it was the Choctaw chieftain's right to verbally chastise them in the presence of the French.

The party was taken to a central gathering place and told to sit in a semicircle before the Choctaw war chief. Behind them were several thousand Choctaw who, like them, sat with their thumbs ready to cock their muskets. The Choctaw chieftain, with a pipe in one hand and a feather in the other, let loose a barrage of criticisms. Finally, he stopped and informed the Chickasaw visitors that the French would never know the depths of their treachery and it would be best for all if they died. The chieftain then lowered the feather in his hand, which set loose the Choctaw warriors in the back. Several of the Chickasaw were killed in the brief melee and the rest taken prisoner. Boisbriand, suddenly in the middle of the skirmish, was struck by a stray musket ball and was carried back to Mobile on a litter by the Choctaw. For all involved it was clear that the peace had now been shattered.[6]

For Iberville, convalescing in France, the continued threat of English expansion and the resulting cracks in Louisiana's defensive policy had one answer—the destruction of Charles Town. After falling ill for much of 1703, in February 1704 Iberville was called to Paris and given permission to launch an expedition against the English colonial coast. Such a plan had been proposed in the past and now with war between England and France it was adopted, but once again Iberville fell gravely ill. The expedition was at first postponed and then eventually cancelled.

It would not be until mid-1705 that Iberville felt well enough to approach the king with a plan to seize Barbados and prey upon English shipping along the North Atlantic coast. His plan was to raise a fleet of privateers in Martinique and St. Domingue (Haiti) and then quickly fall upon Barbados, which was too strong to be taken other than by surprise. From here he would

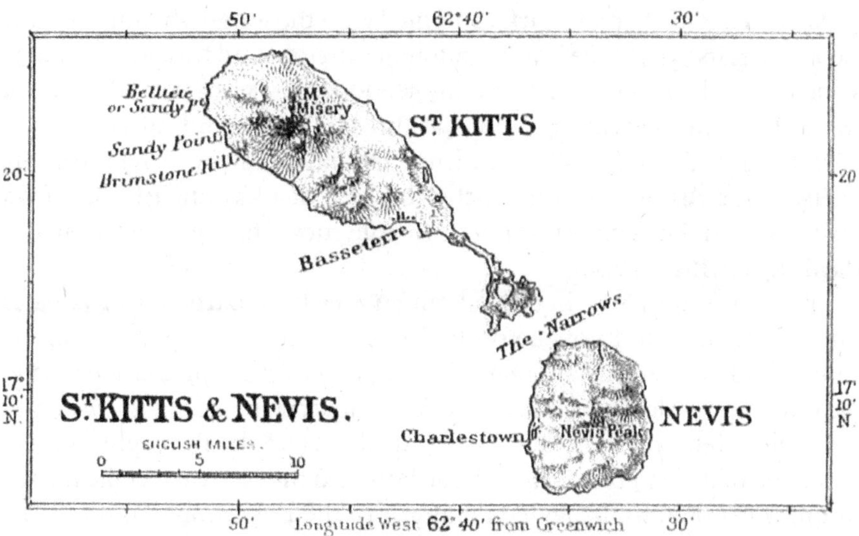


An 1888 map of St. Kitts and Nevis. Iberville would land at Green Bay on the southern tip of Nevis in April 1706. (Charles Lucas, *Historical Geography of the British Colonies*)

rendezvous with a pair of Spanish fleets at Havana, and after enlisting additional troops, he would implement his earlier plan to attack Charles Town.

As with his operations in Newfoundland and Hudson Bay Iberville planned to finance the expedition with plunder. After destroying Charles Town, he would send the Spanish back and proceed on to Chesapeake Bay. Here he would raid the Virginia and Maryland seaboard, capturing and holding several ports ransom while seizing any assets that could be sold in France. If all went well, he might even proceed farther north in search of more lucrative opportunities. It was without doubt a bold plan. Had someone other than Iberville been selected to lead it, it would have been a highly doubtful one as well, but Iberville had a reputation for accomplishing what most believed was improbable.[7]

Having secured a dozen French warships Iberville set sail for the Leeward Islands in early 1706. His fleet was scattered in a storm and it wasn't until March 9 that his flagship—the sixty-four-gun *Le Juste*—and six other vessels dropped anchor at Martinique. When he disembarked, he discovered that the commander of one of his two squadrons, the Comte de Chavagnac, having arrived several weeks earlier, had enlisted the help of the local militia and a number of privateers to launch an attack on the English island of Nevis. Although he had five large warships, a pair of small frigates, and twenty-four smaller privateers, Chavagnac could not find a good place to land his men. Weather and surf, combined with the island's handful of guns and active response, made him abandon the attempt and turn on the nearby island of St. Christopher, or as it is known today, St. Kitts. The admiral and over a thousand buccaneers landed at three locations and ravaged the ill-defended island for nearly a week while the inhabitants watched from the defenses atop Brimstone Hill. Finally, the sight of a few English ships from Barbados and Antigua was enough to convince Chavagnac to return to Martinique with his booty.[8]

The news undid any thought about an attack on Barbados or Jamaica, both of which would now be on their guard. After raising an additional eleven hundred men and another thirty-eight sail at Martinique and Guadeloupe to join his dozen warships, Iberville moved against Nevis. He arrived before the island on the afternoon of April 1. Here the fleet split into two parts. The first element continued north toward the Narrows, while the second part fell behind. Believing an attack to the north was imminent, the defenders forwarded what militia that was on hand to oppose a landing. During this time Iberville and the second division of ships steered for the southern portion of the island. Here, at a location known as Green Bay, several thousand men were put ashore in the early morning hours.

With most of the militia to the north, only about two hundred men were available to halt the French column marching inland. After pushing aside this English force in a brief skirmish, Iberville moved on the capital Charles Town and accepted its surrender as dawn took hold. Many chose not to surrender and retreated up into the mountains, where they dueled with patrols, but for the rest it was confinement in Charles Town. It was a stunning victory that had only taken a few hours to achieve and had cost the French leader less than fifty casualties. Five hundred militia, 330 sailors, over 1,000 women and children, and 6,000 black slaves were now in his hands. Twenty-five vessels in the harbor, several armed, were captured as well, as were all the armaments in the various fortifications. The French would spend several weeks on the island looting and plundering anything of value and burning the rest. When he departed on April 22 Iberville took over three thousand enslaved with him, three-quarters of whom he used to man his fleet while the rest were distributed among the various privateers who had joined the expedition.[9]

Nevis was in ruins, and word of Iberville's fleet soon set off a panic that would reach as far as Boston. For Iberville, it was a promising beginning to the campaign. Word of the success and the booty from it would draw yet more men to the cause. After returning to Martinique, Iberville set sail for Havana where he was to rendezvous with a Spanish force and implement the second part of his plan—an attack on Charles Town, South Carolina. The French commander had chosen a bad time to visit the Cuban port, as yellow fever had clutched the town for weeks. In early July 1706, a few weeks after his arrival, the great Canadian fell ill and died shortly thereafter.

While there were a number of questions concerning smuggling and illegal trade activities that would haunt the Le Moyne family and cost his widow a large part of his estate, there was no question as to what his death meant for all sides. Few French commanders in North America had shown such daring, the proficiency to strike unexpectedly from land or sea, or the ability to inflict such extensive damage with a handful of resources. Thus, the idea of Iberville with a fleet of fifty ships sweeping the Atlantic seaboard, had a ring of terror to it not seen since Drake, and when news arrived of his death, it brought a sigh of relief to the towns and ports along the colonial seaboard. For the French and Spanish, it was a blow that could not be rectified. Such leaders were rare and their loss felt at the highest and lowest levels. For the French court and the governor of New France, he had been a key resource in a limited arsenal by which the English colonies could be held at bay. For the soldiers and citizens of New France, he was more: a symbol of the individualistic strength of the colony, reinforcing a premise that one Canadian was worth twenty Englishmen.[10]

With Iberville gone, along with many other senior Spanish and French commanders who had also fallen prey to illness, the expedition gathering in Havana began losing steam. Many simply left, no longer having any faith in what they viewed as a speculative venture to begin with, while others fled to get away from the epidemic. At the urging of the Spanish governor what was left, five privateers and some eight hundred Spanish and French, set sail under the command of Captain Jacques Lefebvre in mid-August. The flotilla stopped first at St. Augustine. Here they took on supplies and were joined by a small galley manned by troops and Spanish mission Indians before departing for Charles Town.

News of Iberville's activities had spurred Governor Johnson to call out the militia, which he set to work on the defenses of Charles Town. Just as it had in Havana, an outbreak of yellow fever struck the colony, reducing the number of men available, which greatly slowed the work. On the afternoon of August 24, the English privateer *Flying Horse* dropped anchor before the town. The captain of the vessel, Peter Stool, immediately reported that he had seen five French warships at St. Augustine and had briefly exchanged fire with one before making good his escape.

Barely an hour later smoke signals could be seen from the lookouts at Sullivan's Island announcing the arrival of the enemy vessels. Lt. Colonel

Willian Rhett, who was in command of Charles Town at the time, sounded the alarm gun and sent riders out to notify the governor and the local militias. Had Lefebvre pushed forward at this moment he likely would have overwhelmed the small garrison and put the town to the torch, but instead Lefebvre and his pilots hovered off the south sandbar that stretched across the face of Charles Town Roads. Here they would spend the next several days sounding the waters in search of a safe passage.

The delay allowed the local militia companies time to gather at Charles Town. The defenders' spirits were buoyed when Governor Johnson arrived on the twenty-sixth. "His Presence gave great encouragement to the People, who had great Confidence in his Conduct," one participant noted, "he having been bred abroad a Souldier from his Youth." Johnson's first action was to order most of the militia to encamp outside the town to avoid exposing them to the yellow fever epidemic.[11]

The next morning there were shouts from the lookouts, which were echoed by the signal cannon on the town's ramparts. The Spanish fleet had cleared the South Bar, "to ye great surprize of our Pilots, who esteemed it almost impossible," and with the tide in their favor and a fair breeze at their back it appeared they would be upon the town within the hour. Instead the vessels continued north and dropped anchor below Sullivan's Island. That night martial law was declared, strong detachments were posted along the shoreside, and the entire town was illuminated "with lights from every window" from dusk until dawn.

Morning brought additional men to Johnson, who summoned a council of war. With a hesitant enemy before him and his numbers likely superior, Johnson pressed for an attack. It was agreed to fit out and arm a brigantine and a pair of sloops that were in the harbor as well as a fire ship. The little fleet would be placed under the command of Lt. Col. Rhett who Johnson appointed vice admiral. While work began on arming these vessels and raising their crews, a French envoy bearing a flag of truce arrived. The messenger was blindfolded and taken to Johnson, where in the name of the king of France he demanded the immediate surrender of the town and all the forces in it. In lieu of this, he continued, the governor could pay a ransom of fifty thousand pesos, and the invaders would spare the town. The envoy then looked to his watch and read off the time. The governor had one hour to decide. Johnson laughed at the idea and told the Frenchman that Charles Town was worth forty million pesos. He then informed the ambassador that he did not even need a minute to give his reply and promptly refused.[12]

Lefebvre was not surprised by the answer. He could see the small English fleet being outfitted in the harbor and estimated that by now the defenders

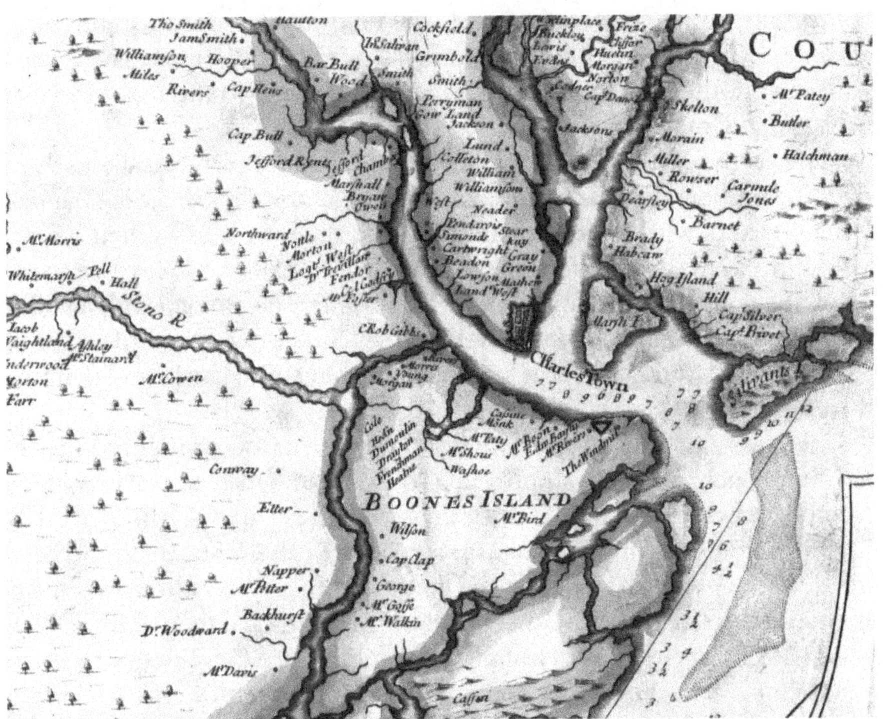


Detail from a 1711 map showing Charles Town, South Carolina, and the harbor. (*Library of Congress*)

likely outnumbered his forces, yellow fever or not. The real problem for the French captain was that the warship *La Brilliante* had yet to arrive. The vessel carried three hundred of the best troops, the cannon and siege equipment, as well as the army's commander General M. de Arbousset. Without these forces Lefebvre had no intention of attacking the town. Instead it was decided to put raiding parties ashore until Arbousset arrived.

On the morning of August 29 a pair of French and Spanish parties pulled their longboats ashore. The first landed on the neck of land between the Wando River and Sullivan's Island, and the second on James Island. The parties on James Island burned a few houses before they were chased away, while the one below the Wando River burned a pair of small boats and raided the nearby farms before encamping for the evening.

With reports arriving on the enemy's activities at Waldo Neck, the next morning Johnson dispatched 120 men under Captain William Cantey to deal with this force. Landing along the east bank of the Wando River a little before sunrise Cantey's scouts quickly located a small detachment of the enemy. These men scattered when Cantey's troops approached, but after rendezvousing with another small group a few miles away, they made a brief stand before the Carolinians before retreating back to the main force at Hartman's Plantation.

Here, in the open terrain, the French and Spanish arrayed themselves. With the numbers appearing roughly equal, Cantey deployed his men in a firing line and, with sword in hand, ordered them forward. When he was within fifty yards of the enemy flags, he ordered a halt and unleashed a volley on the French and Spanish ranks. The invaders responded with a volley of their own but were suddenly startled by a loud huzzah and the sight of Cantey's men dashing forward, many brandishing tomahawks and scalping knives.

There were pockets of resistance, but most fled. A creek behind the retreating French and Spanish proved as deadly as English guns when half a dozen men were swept away frantically trying to get across. Another thirty or so abandoned the thought and surrendered. In all twenty-three had been killed, wounded, or drowned in the creek. Another thirty-three were prisoners and the rest were sent on a headlong flight toward their ships. Of the latter, the English Indians in hot pursuit captured another thirty stragglers.

When news of the victory arrived with Cantey's return later in the day Johnson ordered the fleet, which had now grown to seven vessels, to prepare to sail out the next morning. In the early morning hours of August 31 Rhett ran his vice admiral pennant up the pole and ordered the fleet forward. With the English flotilla bearing down on him, Lefebvre had seen enough. With the wind in his favor he ordered his vessels back to the South Bar and out to sea. With bad weather approaching Rhett chose not to follow and returned to Charles Town with the news of the enemy's flight.[13]

The governor dispatched the *Seaflower* to scout the South Bar the next day, but it returned with no signs of the enemy. The battle appeared over and martial law was lifted in the town. That evening, however, reports arrived that a French vessel was landing troops at Sewee Bay, a dozen miles up the coast from Sullivan's Island. Rightly deducing that this was the missing French ship that the prisoners spoke about, the next morning Johnson sent Rhett with the *Seaflower* and Captain Stool's *Flying Horse* to harass the enemy vessel by sea, while Captain John Fenwicke with a pair of militia companies advanced upon their position by land. It proved a nearly perfect maneuver. Fenwick found the French and Spanish detachment the next morning and, after a brief skirmish, killed or wounded a dozen and took another sixty prisoners, among them the commander of the *La Brilliante*. The matter was no better for those who managed to make their way back to the French privateer. Rhett and his vessels arrived a few hours later and dashed forward with the intent of boarding the enemy vessel. Realizing that he was outgunned, outmanned, and caught between two forces, General Arbousett struck his colors and surrendered.

The action officially ended the only attempt made on Charles Town during Queen Anne's War. English casualties had been light, and the conduct of all, especially the old soldier Governor Johnson, who was seen on his horse at all hours of the day and night, was praised. The English colony had been challenged and rose to the occasion. "The malicious designs of our enemies are defeated," one witness wrote with relief, likening the attack to "a second Spanish Armado, who had they succeeded intended nothing more than the utter ruine of the flourishing Collony."[14]

For the French and Spanish, the attack had been ill conceived, poorly supported, and badly coordinated. With the resources committed the venture was questionable, but possible, if the element of surprise was maintained. Once Arbousett failed to appear, the plan collapsed, allowing the English to face two smaller opponents and defeat them one at a time. In the end the expedition had lost one of its vessels, its siege guns, a large amount of ammunition, and over a third of its force, with most being taken prisoner. Yet for all of the expedition's failings Charles Town had indeed been lucky, foremost because one is left with the feeling that had Iberville been present, things would have been much different.

CHAPTER NINETEEN

# The Port Royal Expeditions

FROM THE ONSET OF THE CONFLICT Dudley and most of New England had feared the descent of a French fleet along the coast. As it was French privateers, just as they had in the last conflict, operated out of the safe harbor of Port Royal, raiding the New England fishing fleets and transport lines. While this was bad enough, if a French fleet were to rendezvous with a privateer flotilla at Port Royal, it would spell disaster for maritime communities as far south as New Jersey. The sheer number of New England and New York militia would make any invasion attempt unlikely, but this did not mean that the invaders couldn't burn down a major coastal city and then depart before significant numbers could be gathered to oppose them.

To deal with this threat both Dudley and Cornbury were forced early on to address their crumbling coastal defenses. Much of this work had fallen on Colonel Romer of the Royal Engineers. He had improved the works around Salem and Marblehead, had built a new fort at Casco, Maine, laid down the foundations of a new fort at Albany, built Castle William which would guard the sea approach to Boston for seventy-five years, and from there began work on Fort William and Mary near Portsmouth, New Hampshire. Romer had also traveled to the Iroquois villages, laid out a potential fort at Oswego, New York, and built a brick magazine for Fort William Henry in New York City. Lacking skilled manpower, materials, money, and even basic tools, it had proven a grueling set of undertakings that wore on the engineer. Fortunately, the colonel's time in North America was coming to an end. The Board of Ordnance sent a letter dated August 8, 1704, informing Governors Cornbury and Dudley that the engineer's replacement, Captain John Redknap, would be dispatched as soon as arrangements could be made for his departure.

In March 1705 Captain Redknap arrived along with Romer's orders to return to England. This was perhaps for the best, as the old campaigner's patience, fractured by the lack of support from the colonial governments and his nagging ailments, was reaching a breaking point. "My pen is not able to express the calamityes and contempts I have suffered and do still suffer," a grateful Romer wrote the Ordnance Board upon receiving news of his recall, and in something of a summation of his relations with his colonial employers he added, "I wish Capt. Redknap may be happyer and meet with better treatment in advancing our Great Queen's service."[1]

There were still several months of work ahead on Fort William and Mary before Romer would depart, and during this time the engineer bickered with his replacement, his workforce, and just about everyone else who crossed his path. This is not to say that his arguments were not justified. The materials to finish the fort were on hand, but nothing moved forward. Ascertaining that the matter was one of money, or lack of it on the part of New Hampshire, Romer took the extraordinary step of offering to pay for the remaining work out of his own pocket. Having received no reply to two of these offers the colonel launched a tempest upon Governor Dudley in early June regarding the current arrangements, the work still to be performed on the fort, and Captain Redknap's apparent lack of concern over the state of the fortifications. Clearly wanting to finish what he had started, Romer again offered to pay for the remaining work, writing Dudley that,

> I thincke yor Excellecy could not have a better opportunity as now before you, to finishe; and yor Excellcy must be sensible of it, considering that in this joncture it is of the higest necessity, to secure that place by the chevaux de frise agt surprise: item, ye ravelin before the gate & couvering of ye same, & by that means to macke a good correspondency for a relieff, if occasion should offer; & lyckwyse the brustwork of ye whole poligon towards the neck, together with ye centry boxes & the settling of all that belongs to ye preservation of ye well, soe that a high flood mae not corrupt ye same in tyme to come, is at present all of the greatest necessity & my duty soe to lay before yor Excellcy.[2]

Had Romer left it with this sound argument he might have made a better impression on the governor, but instead he continued on, pointing out how he had endured numerous and unjust difficulties in the service of his task, how in doing so he had submitted to "slavish service in obeying & submitting to yor Excellcys orders & commands," and how he did not deserve "suche hard indurations as no notice taken of my proposals." In the end, he informed the governor, if his offer were rejected, "then I shall leave Capt Redknap in his good oppinion, & in a more weiser & better conduct to his quietnes, & shall be glad to see that hee (according to his oppinion) can & may do better service then I have donne."[3]

Dudley was taken aback by the tone of the letter, and after commenting on Romer's "huffing all mankind in these Provinces," made it clear that at the moment the monies required were not available and that per the directives of the Ordnance Board, and Romer's own wishes, Captain Redknap was now in charge. He then pointed to a long-standing problem with the engineer. "I will now tell you plainly that your angry & harsh treatment of every body these three years since my arrivall (the Lnt Governour, the Councellors & Comissioners of the Works, officers and soldiers) has been such that there is an universall displeasure taken against you."[4]

The matter was settled when Romer returned to England in October 1705, leaving Captain John Redknap to oversee his old duties. After dealing with the cantankerous colonel for three years Dudley found the tense relations between the New Englanders and the new engineer overseeing the defensive works along the coast "perfectly altered in Mr. Redknap's temper, and is thereby made very easy."[5]

Redknap's first order of business was to take over work on Fort William and Mary. In early June 1705, Governor Dudley ordered the engineer to repair the fort's barracks and a pair of angles that had been damaged by spring storms and rising floodwaters. Beyond this, there were still half a dozen pressing issues with regard to finishing the structure, the most important being the erection of a *chevaux de frise* about the structure to prevent the fort from being taken by surprise, the construction of a ravilen to protect the main gate, and finishing the breastwork along the land side of the fort. The tasks proved easy, as there were no funds available to do anything of significance to the fort. With work stopped, Redknap spent most of the year copying the plans of the existing fortifications along the New England coast, which were later transmitted to England. If anything, the work proved useful in acquainting the new engineer with the details of the fortifications recently erected and those proposed by Romer. This was especially true with the proposed fort at Winter Harbor, Maine, which the government of Mas-

A profile of one of the walls of Fort William and Mary by John Redknap, 1705. (*Boston Public Library*)

sachusetts was anxious to build in order to abandon the dilapidated structure at Saco. Redknap was ordered to lay out plans and construction costs for this new fort after having visited the area.[6]

In the spring of 1706 Redknap returned to work. The engineer's efforts became of more concern when reports arrived that a French fleet led by Iberville was planning an attack on either Boston or New York City. The reports were enough for the governor of New York, Lord Cornbury, to summon Redknap to New York City to oversee work on the defenses there. Redknap was prepared to leave, but with their own defenses in question the Massachusetts council refused to grant Redknap permission to depart until their coastal fortifications were put in order. Thus, the engineer spent the better part of the spring and summer seeing to this matter. He recommended that the city's north and south batteries be repaired and expanded, that efforts be made to repair the forts at Marblehead and Salem, and that a mobile battery of ten guns be placed on Noddle's Island while another battery of six guns erected at Cape Ann. He also recommended that a pair of fire ships be prepared to counter any naval attack and that Boston Neck be fortified.

The first order of business, however, concerned Castle William in Boston Harbor. In December 1705 the twenty heavy cannon that Queen Anne had pledged to the defense of the fort arrived. Given the season it would not be until mid-May that Redknap started work on mounting the guns. By the first week of August he was nearly finished with the task. He then turned his attention to finishing the outlying works of the castle and repairing the damage wrought by the spring and winter storms. By fall he was able to report to the Massachusetts council that most of this work was finished, but in pushing forward these efforts there had been little time to see to the other proposed works around Boston, and as such, nothing was accomplished in this area.[7]

In September 1706 Redknap finally secured permission from the Massachusetts council to travel to New York. When he arrived, he found the city transformed. A wooden stockade had been run from the East River to the Hudson River on the north side of the city supported by a number of redoubts, three batteries totaling thirty-seven guns had been placed on the East River, and three more batteries totaling seventeen guns had been placed along the Hudson River. Another battery of eleven guns was erected below Fort William Henry, and the fort itself had been put into the best possible state of repair.[8]

While no attack came on the eastern seaboard in 1706, it was clear with the increase in French and Indian raids along the frontier that the cease-fire was over. Although Dudley did not accomplish all of his goals during these negotiations, he had bought New England eighteen months of relative peace—time which was spent strengthening its defenses, raising men, and recovering from its losses. With Castle William and Fort William and Mary in a defensible state, Dudley set his sights on Quebec. His dealings with Vaudreuil during the peace and prisoner negotiations had pointed out to him how weak French Canada was. English privateers had intercepted their supply ships, and uncertainty among their native allies out west had further stretched their resources. Now seemed the time to strike. "If H.M. would be graciously pleased to give us but 4 ships of war and mortars," he informed London, we would remove "all the French from Canada and Port Royal."[9]

The response the governor received from London in the spring of 1707 made it clear that any proposal against Quebec needed to be vetted by several departments before there was any thought of committing resources to the idea. With a campaign against the French colonial capital unlikely, Dudley turned toward an old idea—the capture of Port Royal. In February 10, 1707, he penned a letter to Governor Fitz-John Winthrop of Connecticut, asking for his advice on the matter and if Connecticut would join the venture. Winthrop responded a few weeks later. He agreed with Dudley's assessment and pointed out that if Port Royal was not dealt with soon the French would turn it into an American Dunkirk. Yet, Winthrop doubted that the Connecticut General Assembly would agree. There would be concern that, if taken, it would just be returned to the French as it was at the end of King William's War, while others would question the wisdom of pulling troops away from the frontier, especially now that the French and their allies had stepped up their attacks.

Dudley would go on to write Cornbury and the New England governors with a plan to lay siege to Port Royal in Nova Scotia and officially solicit their aid. If the town could be taken, Dudley pointed out, it would deprive the French navy of one of their primary anchorages in the region and thus lessen the likelihood of an attack on either Boston, New York, or some other location along the eastern seaboard.

As Winthrop predicted, the Connecticut Assembly balked at the idea. Although the northern colonies were bearing the brunt of the effort and acted as a shield for Connecticut, the colony's legislature could not spare a man for the effort. It was a familiar theme, based in part on fear that participation would call the colony's charter into question. Dudley had better luck with Rhode Island, although the best that could be done was an armed schooner and a company of soldiers. New Hampshire also agreed to contribute a small number of troops to the force, and although Governor Cornbury of New York was not in a position to support the enterprise, he did honor Dudley's request to send Captain Redknap back to Boston so he might be employed in the expedition.

While he would have liked to have had more support from the other colonies, Dudley presented the idea to the Massachusetts Assembly on March 5. There is little doubt that the governor's feelings toward the conquest of Port Royal were genuine and were in the interest of New England as well as the Crown. On the other hand, there were also political reasons at work. A sizable portion of the Massachusetts Assembly never trusted Dudley, or at the very least found him suspect. The governor's frequent correspondence with French authorities and the accusations of trading with the enemy leveled against one of his envoys, Samuel Vetch, had further inflamed these suspicions. Thus, a successful attack on Port Royal would go a long way toward not only securing the New England coast but restoring the governor's reputation as well.

Fortunately, Dudley found a receptive audience in the Massachusetts Assembly. A few days later the assembly passed a stirring resolution stating

"That it is highly advisable & expedient That an Expedition be forthwith made to subdue the French Enemy in Nova Scotia, & particularly to take the Fort at Port Royal." Funds were appropriated, contracts signed, and the recruiters sent out to raise a thousand men for the expedition. Transports for the troops were procured from local merchants, an artillery train was assembled, and an escort arranged consisting of the *Province Galley* and the Royal Navy frigate HMS *Deptford*, which was on station.

Colonel John March, who had been busy on the Maine and Massachusetts frontiers, was chosen to command the land forces, which would consist of two regiments under the command of Colonel Winthrop Hilton and Colonel Francis Wainwright. Captain Charles Stucley of the *Deptford* would command the naval portion of the expedition, and when he arrived from New York, Redknap was commissioned Commander of the Ordnance with the duty of seeing to the actual details of the siege and the deployment of the expedition's artillery, which consisted of eight field pieces and two small mortars. "I also desire and direct you to advise and assist at the council of war," Dudley's warrant to the engineer spelled out, "taking the third place at the board."[10]

By mid-May the forces had been assembled and loaded onto the awaiting transports. The flotilla set sail on May 12 and after an uneventful voyage dropped anchor in the Port Royal Basin on May 26. Although the troops and their supplies were landed with little in the way of opposition, the expedition quickly began to flounder. Lt. Colonel Samuel Appleton with 320 men had landed on the north shore of the basin so late in the day that the detachment made little headway through the "hideous woods and fallen trees across our way, which sometimes we climbed over, at other times crept under."[11]

The expedition's commander, Colonel March, personally led the main detachment of 750 men who landed on the south shore a few miles below Goat Island (Isle aux Chevelures) the next morning. The broken, marsh-laden ground coupled with deep bands of dense forest slowed the colonial advance. By nightfall March was forced to make camp half a dozen miles from the fort, while to the north Appleton's men plowed through the forest until they too were forced to make camp still miles from their objective.

Earlier on the morning of the twenty-sixth a breathless runner found the new governor of Acadia, Daniel Subercase, in Fort Port Royal. He reported to him that fifteen enemy ships had been sighted near the entrance to the basin. The information sent the old soldier into motion. The drums beat the garrison to arms, while he sent orders for the militia from the nearby villages to report to the fort. He then sent the messenger back with

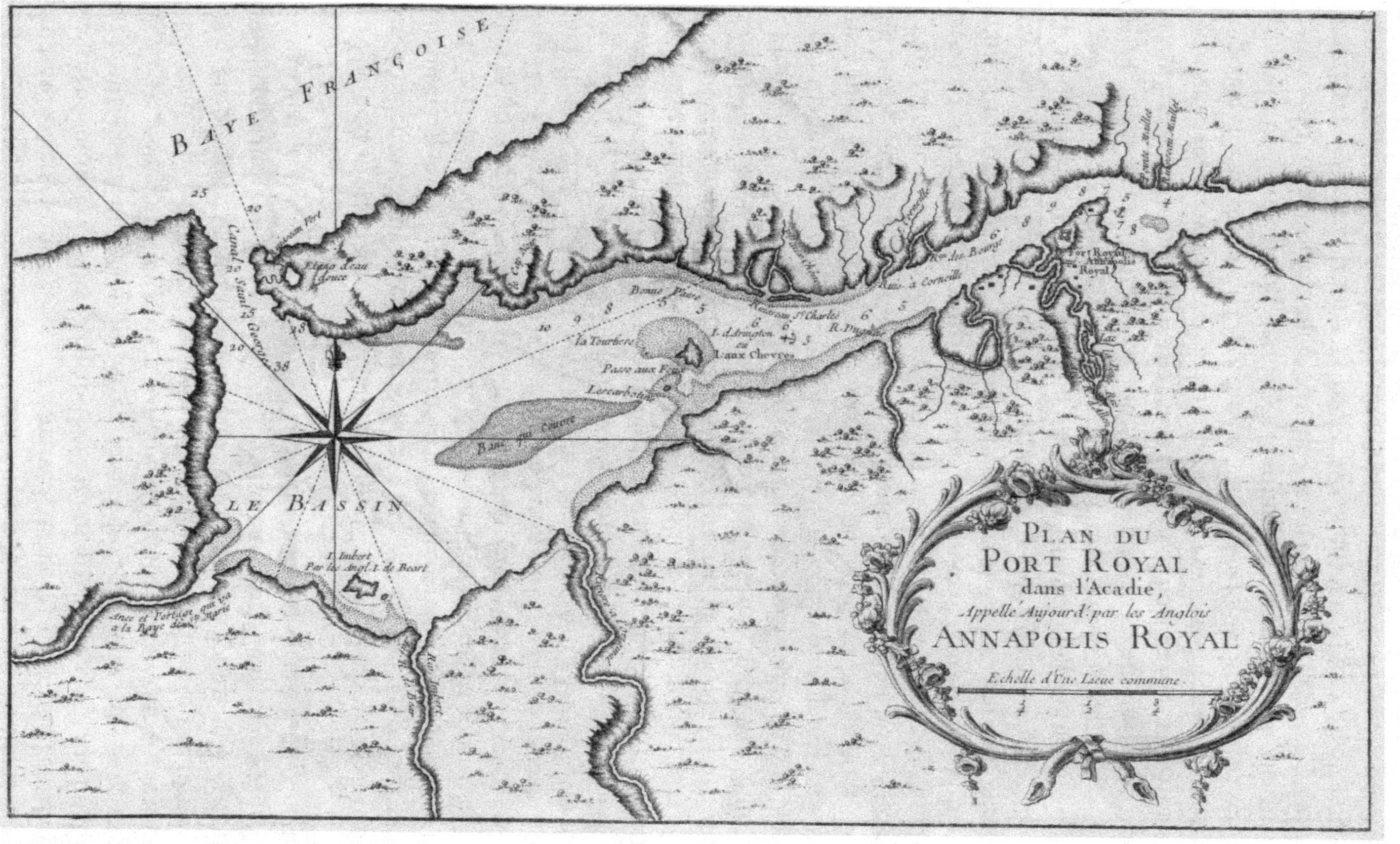


A 1744 French map of Port Royal, Nova Scotia, and the Port Royal Basin. (*Library of Congress*)

orders for the observation party to send regular updates on the flotilla's progress. When enough troops had arrived, the governor formed small detachments of forty to fifty men and sent them out in search of the English on both sides of the Dauphin River. The rest of his troops he set to work digging trenches, making gabions, and repairing the fort's weather-damaged walls. Once the militia was assembled Subercase had close to five hundred men. Fortunately, sixty Canadians had arrived the day before to bolster his numbers. Vaudreuil had sent them to help man a privateer that was being dispatched to the port, but at the moment Subercase had them digging trenches.

The next morning both Appleton's and March's detachments encountered Subercase's advanced guards. After a brief exchange of gunfire Appleton pushed aside a French detachment and marched to a point opposite the fort, "a little more than a musket shot over the North (Dauphin) River." March ran into a similar-sized enemy detachment at a small stream crossing. The French fired a few volleys and, upon hearing far too many fired back in response, retreated back to Allen Brook or the La Petite River as it was called by the French. Here they were met by another detachment of fifty men who lined the east bank of the tidal waterway. Shortly thereafter Subercase arrived with another 120 men to shore up this position.

March's men pushed forward and were greeted by a volley from Subercase's detachment. The fire halted the English advance, but it would not be for long. As the two sides exchanged fire it became clear to the French governor that he was badly outnumbered. Matters would only get worse along these lines as a good number of his militia bolted after the opening shots. Subercase had his horse shot out from under him, and after he was helped to his feet, he realized that it was only a matter of time before the English crossed the brook farther upstream and outflanked his position. With little choice the governor conducted an orderly retreat back to the fort, burning any buildings that might be of use to the enemy along the way, before taking up a position in front of the stronghold. The trailing English came to a halt a few hundred yards away, content with their accomplishment.[12]

At this point Captain Stucley took Redknap and Captain Ebenezer Wentworth in a small launch to within cannon shot of Fort Port Royal. After this reconnaissance it was agreed to land the artillery at Appleton's camp on the opposite side of the river. Over the next few days Redknap marked out the ground in advance of the artillery's landing. The engineer was clearly not happy with the arrangement. According to an account attributed to Arthur Jefferies, a former commissary under Colonel John March, "Coll Rednap being ashore mark'd out his ground & had begun to make some provision

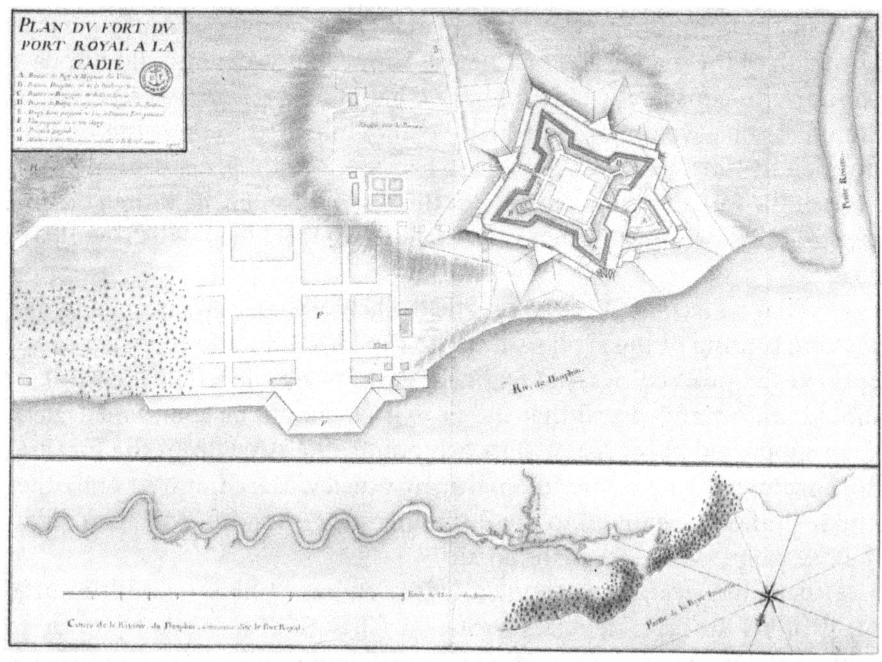


A 1702 plan showing the position of the French Vauban-style fort at Port Royal and elements of the nearby village. (*Archives Nationales de France*)

to raise his Batteries &c But placed as difficultly as possible might be, His Fretfull, spitefull Temper all ye time he was ashore sufficiently shewed his dislike to undertake wt he was sent about."[13]

Jefferies was correct in his assessment of the engineer. The ground Redknap had selected for the expedition's artillery was a poor choice. The majority of Fort Port Royal's cannon were directed to control water access to the Dauphin River and the fort itself was strongest along the shoreline. This meant that the location Redknap had selected was a position that would be subject to a severe bombardment while the trenches were dug and the firing platforms erected. This concentrated French firepower also seriously threatened the landing of the artillery and the vessels that would conduct the landing operations. If Redknap initially missed his error, the French gunners soon pointed it out, firing cannonballs and dropping mortar rounds into Appleton's camp over the next few days.[14]

During this time March proved content in sniping at the fort and burning down nearby homes. Subercase and his garrison watched as the English lit fire after fire, sending columns of black smoke high into the air and creating an eerie glow at night. The governor fired a few cannon at the enemy, more in an attempt to display his vigilance than a chance of causing harm. The truth of the matter was that he was short on powder and did not dare do more. To conserve what supplies he had, the garrison was told not to fire unless he gave the order, which he only intended to do if the English stormed the fort. As it was Subercase had to abandon his encampment in front of the fort, and now, along with the rest of his men, he waited behind the structure's weather-beaten stone walls to see what the English would do next.

On May 31 a council of war was held, likely at Redknap's urging, to discuss the landing of the artillery and the expedition's options. When called upon at the proceedings, the engineer gave his opinion that the artillery should not be landed and that the siege itself should be abandoned. Redknap supported his decision with two points: the strength of the fort and the unruly character of the colonial army. Stucley, March, and several other ranking officers defaulted to the Royal Engineer's opinion and agreed that the campaign should be abandoned.

Others, however, were stunned by the ruling. "I have heard him urge many of his Reasons," Jefferies wrote, "Ye Cheifest Yt it was not for him to venture all his Creditt & reputation wth such undisciplined & ungovernable men & unconstant officers. At the Fatall Councill of Warr he laid down ye Reasons & Improbability of ye enterprise & caused a Vote to pass not to break ground, & so be gone abt or buisness like Fools." Another journal of the siege, likely written by the lieutenant governor of New Hampshire, John Usher, painted a similar response to the decision to abandon the attack on the fort.

> The ground Col. Rednap marked out impossible for our artilery to be thither broughtt. Fr. never exspected us there, butt on other side the ground seizable. And now our greatt and fatall Councill satt to finish all. Col. Rednap opinion being asked declared nott to break ground (though our artilery there) by reason of disobedience and insufficiency of our men, nott being persons proper for him to venture his reputation on, and reply was made, our orders are otherwise then to send: this point gain'd, caused a consentt in all others. Adieu Rednap and Secritry, scared outt of there witts.[15]

Jefferies and several others claimed that such a decision was rash and that the artillery could easily be landed without danger at another location. For a moment this new opinion held sway over the council of war, but with Redknap still objecting, the determination of the expedition's leadership wavered and then finally defaulted to their original position. After spending several days slaying the local livestock, tearing up fences, destroying crops, and burning as many structures as could be found, the New England forces embarked for Casco Bay satisfied that they had crippled French efforts in the area.[16]

Subercase was stunned when he saw the English withdraw to their ships and sail out to sea. With every advantage before them the enemy had withdrawn without firing a single cannon at the fort, and in their haste, they had left a large number of tools and supplies behind. The governor and several around him speculated that one of the French deserters had spread the rumor the governor had started that five hundred Wabanaki and a hundred French were on their way to relieve the fort. Whatever the reason, it hardly mattered from Subercase's perspective. French casualties had been light, a few killed and a handful wounded or taken prisoner, and while the town had been plundered and burned, Fort Port Royal and Acadia still remained in French hands.[17]

The fleet returned to Caso Bay while Redknap and a delegation from the aborted expedition returned to Boston. When they arrived, they were greeted with jeers. A crowd of women brandishing wooden swords and mocking the party with chants of "Port Royal, Port Royal," met the delegates at Scarlet Wharf and followed them to the town hall chanting their insults to the beat of a small drum they had procured. Over the following days Governor Dudley listened to the reports and read the letters from those on the scene. The witnesses broke down into two camps—those in favor of Redknap's opinion and those who opposed it.[18]

In his own defense Redknap pointed to the strength of the enemy position. "The Fort of Port Royal," the engineer began his report to the governor,

> is a Fortification of Four Bastions a halfe moone, wth some other out workes, which have been newly made, there is eighteen pieces of Cannon, mounted upon the Ramparts, twelve and eighteen pounders, the Ditch is between twenty four and thirty foot broad, seven foot deep, the Ramparts about eight foot height from the surface of the earth. There is a Battery of twelve pieces of Cannon, six twenty four pounders and six thirty six pounders, wth one Morter, but these do not add much to the strength of the Fort, they being designed only to command all Vessels that pass up that River, it will be very difficult to bring them Guns upon the Ramparts, there are eight pieces four pounders, and eight Pateraroes belonging to the Galley wch may be mounted on any of the works, and there is no want of ammunition in the Garrison.[19]

According to a number of deserters, Redknap added, the garrison was close to six hundred men, and reports were that they were expecting reinforcements from the surrounding settlements any day. The expedition was outgunned and had less than the recommended three-to-one advantage in manpower. Coupled with a raw colonial army, it was a recipe for disaster. "I think it impossible to have done more," Redknap wrote to the Board of Trade of the incident, "unless we had had cannon and morters superiour to theires, to have thrown away the Country people in assaulting the place to no effect (would) had been much worse. . . . If we had sustain'd so great a loss upon any settlement of this province, then they would make a clamour of our being undone."[20]

Although there were dissenters who pointed to the intrepid work done by the New England soldiers in forcing the French back into their fort, Governor Dudley had already received a letter from his son alluding to the lack of discipline within the colonial ranks. As such, he accepted Redknap's assessment of the situation.[21]

Questions seemed to linger, however, as to Redknap's abilities, and such questions are understandable. Certainly, Redknap's selection of where to place the expedition's artillery was questionable and his approach to rectifying the error, via a council of war's opinion that the campaign be abandoned, is somewhat suspect given this error. In the end, however, Redknap's seemingly self-serving stance may have been the right decision. The expedition had badly underestimated the strength of Fort Port Royal, and the English artillery was too small and too few in number to challenge the guns of the fort. More importantly, it was clear to the Royal Engineer that any siege of the French citadel would be a long one, something that the inexperienced colonial army was ill prepared to deal with.

Dudley, however, was not interested in giving up so easily. Several of the more aggressive commanders urged the governor to order the fleet back for a second attempt on the French stronghold. Governor Samuel Cranston of Rhode Island agreed and even went further by suggesting that matters before the fort not be left to a council of war, which "may againe prove of Ill consequence." After reading the reports from the commanding officers and speaking with the members of the delegation, the governor ordered the troops back to Port Royal and promised to send them whatever reinforcements he could obtain. The thought was not to attack the fort but to cut off its supplies in hopes that it would be forced to surrender. Returning would also offer an opportunity to launch raids into the interior of Acadia with the aim of burning their villages and destroying their livestock. Lastly, returning offered a chance to undo the political damage that was now on display as clusters of women and boys paraded about waving their toy swords and mock flags to the music of an *ad hoc* marching band.

A large merchant ship, the *Ruth*, was converted into a frigate and loaded with provisions and munitions, as well as two newly raised militia companies, before being dispatched to the fleet riding at anchor in Casco Bay. With these reinforcements came orders to make a second attempt on Port Royal and a directive that frowned upon councils of war, instead placing all decisions in the hands of Colonel March.

March's force had only suffered around fifty casualties, hence the inclusion of the reinforcement increased his numbers. A twenty-four-gun warship had been added to the expedition, ample provisions had been distributed, and there was a sufficient supply of powder and shot. On paper at least, March's force was stronger and now armed with intelligence concerning the terrain around Fort Royal and a feel for the strength of the French garrison, so it appeared that an opportunity existed to correct any earlier mistakes. The naval force would block any aid coming to the fort by sea, while the army surrounded the stronghold, devastated the local countryside, and slowly starved the French garrison into submission.[22]

The only problem was that most of the army had little faith in their leaders, and most of their leaders had little faith in the decision to return. The men distrusted their officers and distrusted the Redcoats even more. In the same vein the colonial officers questioned their unruly men and resented Stucley and Redknap, who looked down on them and blamed the colonials for their own poor decisions and lack of commitment. Matters were also complicated by the term of the troop's enlistment, which was to be ten weeks. It was rapidly approaching eight and if the force was to return to Port Royal the expedition would certainly go well beyond the agreed-upon time, which might create other problems.

March ordered the fleet to set sail on July 17, but it was stopped by a wholesale desertion the night before. Well over a hundred men had disappeared from the camp along the shores of Casco Bay. When combined with a rash of earlier events, it left March in the position that the new companies did not even cover his losses from desertion. Not that the rest of the men were enthusiastic about returning. "The soldiers are utterly adverse and will at best be but passive in returning to Port Royal," one witness wrote his wife, "just as prisoners are transported." When the fleet set sail near the end of July Colonel Elisha Hutchinson reported March's strength at "743 officers and soldiers, sick and well." He then echoed the earlier statement. "They are so extremely dispirited, that we cannot look upon them equal to 300 effective men."[23]

The fleet did not sail directly for Port Royal but for Passamaquoddy where Dudley had ordered a series of attacks made on the French traders and settlers in the area. The army lingered at this location for over a week, which did nothing to improve its morale. March resigned claiming that both his spirit and health were broken. Command now passed to Colonel Wainwright, one of the officers who had urged Dudley to launch a second attack. The fleet finally set sail and on the morning of August 10 entered the Port Royal Basin. The following morning whaleboats and small launches carried the troops ashore. The landing spot was an orchard about two miles below the fort on the opposite side of the river.

Not long after the English retreated following their first attempt, a French privateer entered Port Royal Harbor. The sight of the vessel and its crew of 150 was a welcome one for the beleaguered garrison and the local citizens. The vessel carried provisions and powder. It also carried news that a sizable English force was preparing to return. Subercase believed the reports and used the increased manpower to further strengthen the fort and its outworks, including a redoubt built at the Le Petite River crossing.

The morning after the landing the French governor and his officers listened to scouting reports and watched the English column thread its way along the opposite shore toward a series of clearings across from the fort. The first clearing, a musket shot from the fort, proved too difficult to hold as the garrison poured musket fire onto the attackers and the fort's cannon swept their ranks with grapeshot. The attackers fell back to a second clearing a little below the first but still within musket range. It again proved too close, and on the twelfth, while Wainwright was landing his supplies, this position was abandoned as well.

The next morning a large French and Indian war party crept through the woods toward Wainwright's position. Around 8 a.m. this detachment began skirmishing with the English advanced guard. The firing would continue off and on until nightfall. Most of this accomplished little, but around 4 p.m. one detachment of nine English foolishly marched into the woods at the urgings of "a mad fellow" and were quickly surrounded and cut to pieces by the French and Wabanaki.

It proved a humid uneasy night broken by the occasional shot that alarmed all. The next morning Wainwright seemed to have grasped how dismal his situation had become. He was penned into an area about his landing spot. "Indeed," he wrote of his situation. "The French have reduced us to the same state which we reduced them, at our last being at Port Royal." What was much worse was the growing sick rolls. Violent fluxes, swelling throats, and those so filled with terror that they were unable to function were decimating his ranks such that "in a short time, there will not be men well enough to carry off the sick."[24]

It would get no better. While the colonel formed plans with his officers on what to do next, the French stepped up their attacks. Raiding parties sniped at the sentries while the fort's cannon and mortars rained shot and explosive rounds down on their position. On the sixteenth the English were forced to move their camp several miles downriver, out of the range of Fort Royal's guns, but it was a temporary stay. An attack by a French and Indian war party forced Wainwright to move once more, this time under the protection of the fleet's guns. Here the troops entrenched for three days.

Finally, on the twentieth, Wainwright left a small force to guard the landing zone, and under the protection of the fleet, he crossed the river to the south bank pulling his boats ashore on the edge of a large orchard. The men landed without difficulty, allowing Wainwright to quickly organize his ranks for the upcoming march. The columns had barely cleared the fencing at the inland edge of the orchard when a rolling volley erupted along the nearby tree line. The echo of the first shots had barely faded when another volley followed, this time punctuated with the sound of war whoops. In the woods before them was Baron St. Castin and a hundred French and Wabanaki furiously reloading their muskets as the English launched a scattered response. Castin called out and a third barrage was launched at the enemy ranks.

Thus far Wainwright's men had stood their ground and were ready to push forward on the enemy position, but orders came for them to fall back. News traveled quickly and Subercase, seeing an opportunity, sent Lt. Louis-Simon de la Boularderie forward with 150 men to support St. Castin, who was in pursuit, before following himself a few minutes later at the head of another 120 men. The three French detachments surged forward like waves behind the retreating colonials.

The tables quickly turned when a handful of English officers rallied their troops, turned them about, and set up in a firing line. This time it was St. Castin's turn to face an unexpected volley, which tore through his ranks and stalled his advance. Another volley cut through the French and Indian line sending them reeling backward toward the woods. Shouts came from the English officers followed by a "huzzah" as the New Englanders launched themselves forward in pursuit.

Castin soon encountered Boularderie's men pushing their way through the thickets and underbrush. The arriving French along with part of Castin's retreating force fired on the charging English, but it was not enough. The two lines collided and the matter briefly turned into a hand-to-hand melee before a wounded Boularderie sounded the retreat. The English followed and now collided with Subercase and a number of rallied French troops near the English column's earlier position. This time the English had seen enough. They exchanged fire with the French and then slowly withdrew in an organized fashion to their boats. By now Subercase had seen enough as well, and although he sent detachments to harass the enemy's withdrawal, for all practical purposes the battle was over.[25]

So too was the second siege of Port Royal. The English fleet sailed away the next day to the cheers and defiant shouts of the defenders. Perhaps not unexpectedly, the second attempt on Port Royal proved an even more dismal venture than the first affair. English losses, some sixteen killed and a score wounded, were not much different than the first attempt, and yet almost nothing was accomplished leaving one to ponder, given the severe morale and leadership issues that existed, why it was even attempted.

For the French it was a major victory. Their losses were small, with three killed and fifteen wounded, and little additional damage had been done to the surrounding countryside and communities. Subercase, who had proven his resolve in the first siege, had seized the initiative from the start of the second siege and did not let go until the English had departed. He had used his resources wisely and pressed the besiegers at every opportunity. The king was impressed with the governor's actions and awarded him a pension for his conduct and bravery.

For Dudley things were not so simple. The two expeditions were a blow to his reputation, and once again rumors began to circulate of a questionable relationship between the governor and the French. Renewed attacks on the frontier further complicated matters, leading to yet more objections regarding his conduct. Dudley, however, looked at the expedition's accomplishments and avoided pointing figures at several suspect officers, even though there were serious questions to be asked. In the end, while a failure, the governor had learned an important lesson from the undertaking; he would need help from England to subdue the French stronghold on Nova Scotia. The intercolonial rivalries, logistical entanglements, and a general lack of experience among colonial field officers convinced him to pursue this approach. In mid-October 1707 he sat down and wrote a letter to the Board of Trade. "I hope," he wrote on this idea, "to lay the whole matter before Her Majesty as to obtain the assistance and cover of some shipps and force from home, which may remove this troublesome neighbor."[26]

CHAPTER TWENTY

# The Destruction of Haverhill

As the year turned to 1708 New England found a reprieve in the form of a warm winter and a significant decrease in French and Indian activity. In fact, while a few smaller raids had been made on the Maine, New Hampshire, and Massachusetts frontiers the previous year, the number and size of these attacks had been far below the level of intensity encountered before the failed peace talks between Vaudreuil and Dudley. While it was true that the raids had resumed after these negotiations were abandoned, they appeared far more restrained compared to the first years of the conflict.

There were a number of reasons behind this decline. Part had to do with the turmoil concerning French interests in the west and the diversion of the colony's attention to maintain peace between its allies and the Iroquois. Another portion could be attributed to the failed peace talks, which had stopped all major raids for almost two years. After such a long interlude it would take time to gather together the resources needed to once again reach the pre-peace talk levels. In addition, some of the problem was due to losses sustained by the Wabanaki and, just as importantly, the inability of the French to consistently supply the confederation. Lastly, there was the economics. Vaudreuil simply did not have enough materials, supplies, or money to expand these raids, and as such, he limited both the frequency and size of the expeditions to husband his resources.[1]

There was yet another element to the problem, the English, and in particular the former mayor of Albany, Peter Schuyler. Schuyler, who had been active in King William's War leading an expedition against La Prairie in 1691, was well respected and admired among the Five Nations. The fact that the Iroquois had chosen not to listen to Schuyler's arguments before speaks to their desire for neutrality. Persistent efforts on the part of Schuyler and the English, however, were causing cracks in the Five Nations' resolve. Combined with this, Governor Cornbury frequently showered the Iroquois with presents in a blatant attempt to bribe the confederacy. In the summer of 1708, for example, he gave the Five Nations a large cache of provisions, "fifty pieces of cloth, half scarlet and half Iroquois, fifty guns, ten barrels of powder, some lead, three hundred shirts, one hundred and sixty kegs of rum, being two quarts per man, ten bundles of stockings, three hundred hatchets, and three hundred knives."[2]

While Cornbury's efforts did not achieve any tangible results, Schuyler was able to make inroads by taking advantage of the Iroquois neutrality to speak with a number of mission Iroquois who traveled from Montreal to visit their relatives in the Five Nations. Schuyler pressed on these individuals the need to remain neutral as well and avoid being used to strike at the English. One Christian Iroquois informed Vaudreuil that Schuyler had warned all of them that "The English whom you strike, are angry, and have resolved to go and devour your villages, and to establish themselves at La Prairie de la Magdalene, and next spring several vessels will go and take Quebec. This is settled. Your country is ruined; if you do not wish to perish, you Indians, profit by the counsel I give you. Take my advice, Brothers. Let the English and the French fight, and have nothing to do with either of them."[3]

While Vaudreuil was not impressed with the threatened invasion, the underlying message behind this neutrality movement soon gathered momentum within the Christian Iroquois missions, and when combined with the recent inactivity, it created a number of questions regarding their participation in the French war effort. In an attempt to rectify this problem, the governor called together a council of war chiefs from these missions in early June.

The grand council opened with the typical festivities. By now the citizens of Montreal had become accustomed to such events and went about their daily tasks as delegations of Huron, Iroquois, Abenaki, and Algonquin and their "Black Robes" met with Vaudreuil. The governor called for a large strike to be made against New England. After a series of deliberations that Vaudreuil noted "required the patience of an angel," a plan was agreed upon. It called for Lieutenant Hertel de Rouville, who had commanded the raid

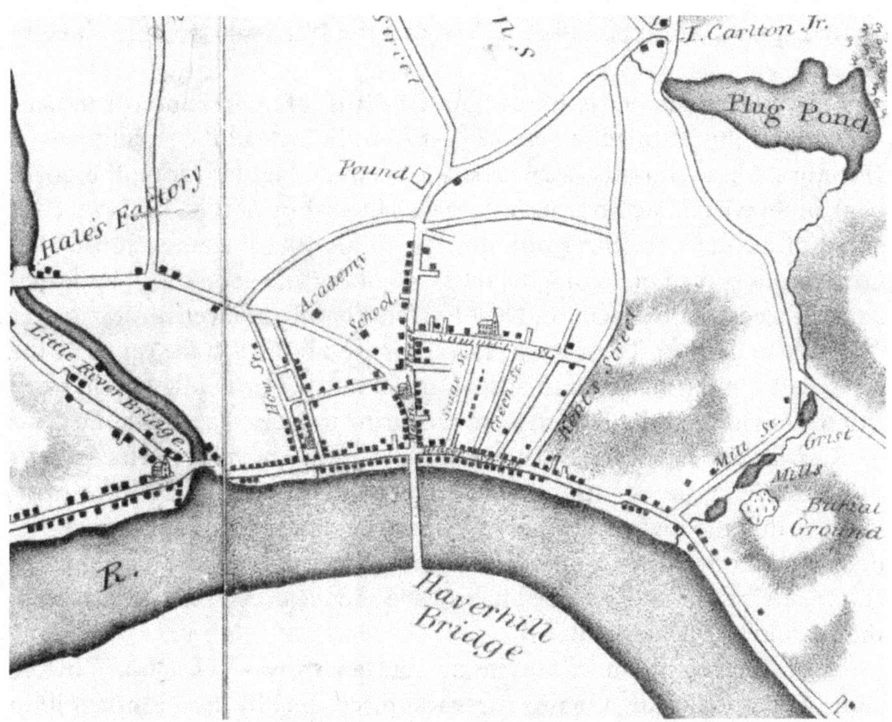


A portion of an 1832 map showing the town of Haverhill on the north bank of the Merrimack River and the surrounding area. (*Boston Public Library*)

on Deerfield, to lead a hundred Canadians and marines along with three hundred mission Indians on a raid against Portsmouth, New Hampshire. The force would depart from Montreal and rendezvous with a Wabanaki contingent at Lake Winnipesaukee and, from there, move against the important colonial seaport. There appeared to be a general consensus and the nations present agreed to furnish the requested numbers.

The war party left Montreal on July 26 and soon ran into difficulties. The force moved forward in two detachments, one by the St. Francois River and the other by Lake Champlain. The Huron in the former detachment soon departed after one of their number was killed in a hunting accident. Attempts were made to stop their flight, but the loss was considered a bad omen and none would continue. In the Lake Champlain party, the Iroquois began to defect. Some claimed sickness and the rest claimed they were leaving to avoid becoming sick. The losses cut Rouville's force in half, but it did not stop him and the remaining French, Abenaki, and Algonquin from pressing on with their task. After clearing the White Mountains, the party arrived at Lake Winnipesaukee to find that the Wabanaki were nowhere to be seen.[4]

After waiting a few days, it was agreed, because of their reduced numbers, to abandon the planned attack on Portsmouth. Instead the small town of Haverhill, Massachusetts, was chosen as a target. Nestled along the north bank of the Merrimac River near the New Hampshire border, the town consisted of a cluster of thirty buildings, with another dozen or so isolated homesteads spread out along the outskirts of the village. While it appeared another sleepy, unsuspecting New England hamlet, Haverhill was better prepared than most. There were several garrison houses in the center of the town that housed a company of soldiers forwarded by Dudley upon word from Schuyler that the French were preparing to launch a raid in the area.

Rouville arrived at the outskirts of Haverhill a few hours before sunset on August 28, 1708. Scouts returned at dusk and informed the French commander that the town appeared to be partially fortified and occupied by a detachment of soldiers. There were plenty of murmurs and a few doubtful comments, but Rouville pushed these aside and informed the war party that they would attack before dawn.

The French commander sent his detachment forward a few hours before sunrise. Around 4 a.m. the war party was discovered by local resident John Keezar, who was returning from nearby Amesbury. Keezar dashed into the village square ahead of the raiders firing his musket and shouting out the alarm, but it was too late. The town had not posted any guards, and like others which had committed such foolish mistakes, it would pay dearly.

Rouville's motioned for his men to break into small groups as a shot rang out, claiming the first victim who was streaking toward the safety of one of the garrison houses. The first house attacked was that of Reverend Benjamin Rolfe. The reverend heard the invaders coming and braced himself against the front door to bar their entry. It appeared a losing struggle for Rolfe, but fortunately, three of the recently dispatched soldiers were staying at his home. Unfortunately, they all fled upon hearing the war whoops and scattered shots. Unable to force their way inside several of the attackers fired through the door. One of these shots struck Rolfe in the elbow. Unable to hold the door any longer Rolfe dashed through the house and out the back door, but his pursuers caught up with him near the home's well and ended his flight with flashing tomahawks. The fleeing soldiers found no safety either. While they had a head start it was not enough, and one by one they were run down and suffered the same fate as the reverend.

Rolfe's wife and youngest child were found hiding in a closet and dealt with in a similar manner, but thanks to the heroic actions of the family's slave, Hagar, the rest of the family managed to conceal themselves in a chest under the stairs and beneath overturned baskets in the cellar. It was a terrifying experience as the raiders pillaged the cellar, overturning barrels and knocking down shelves just feet away. Finally, a word from the top of the stairs brought their search to an end, and they departed in search of another homestead.[5]

This scene was repeated among half a dozen homes, but the attackers did not always have their way. A pair of Abenaki attempted to force into the Swans' home while Mr. Swan and his wife mustered all their strength to brace the door. The attacker's efforts only seemed to magnify with frustration, and when they forced the door open a few inches it looked like the end for the couple. Mr. Swan pleaded with his wife to take their infant child and flee, but he had underestimated his wife's grit. Instead she seized the spit from over the fireplace and drove the three-foot-long iron shaft through the opening into one of the invaders. There was a shout and the pressure on the door immediately ceased. The Abenaki, having seen enough, shouted insults at the home and moved off in search of easier prey.

The town meeting hall and several buildings were now in flames, and as the sun began to filter through the smoke it exposed the sight of over a dozen motionless inhabitants scattered across the dew-covered grass. Shots and shouts still rang out as the disorganized raiders sought to finish their work. It would soon, however, be interrupted by the actions of one of the more intrepid citizens by the name of Davis. Grabbing a log Davis snuck behind Rolfe's barn and began to strike the structure, sending a hollow thump echoing through the village. He then shouted out fictitious commands and called for his imaginary forces to move forward as he continued to strike the building. "Come on! We have them!" rang out across the village square.

The bold effort had the intended effect, as Rouville's men halted their attack. Soon calls in French and Abenaki that the English were coming followed as the raiders attempted to reorganize their ranks. Davis's timing was nearly perfect as, in fact, the English were coming. At the other end of the town Major Samuel Turner had rallied his soldiers and was advancing on the enemy. Seeing the English column Rouville gave the order to withdraw and after a few parting shots between the two parties the attackers disappeared back into the tree line.[6]

Thus far Rouville's detachment had accomplished its task. He had burned down portions of the enemy town, slew several dozen, and taken another dozen prisoner. All that remained was to recover his packs and set a course deep into the woods to avoid any pursuit. Encumbered with prisoners and booty the war party was strung out for nearly half a mile as it threaded its way through the broadleaf forest toward its previous encampment. The column broke into a clearing, but before it could reach the other side a volley of muskets broke the silence. A few in the French advanced guard toppled over as another volley flashed down the length of the tree line.

Captain Samuel Ayer and his son had rallied nearly seventy men on the northern part of the town and marched to intercept the raiders. After discovering their encampment, and suspecting that they would return to recover their supplies, Ayer set up an ambush at the edge of a nearby clearing. The militia captain walked down his firing line, calling on his men to stand fast as return fire from the enemy ripped through the tree branches or embedded itself into nearby trees with a hollow knock. Although badly outnumbered Ayer did not have to stop the enemy war party but merely delay its progress. The militia of the nearby towns had been called out, and several mounted companies were already on their way.

Caught between two forces Rouville had little choice but to charge Ayer's position. A chorus of war whoops and hideous yells rang out as the war party surged forward led by the Abenaki war chief Asacumbuit brandishing the saber Louis XIV had given him. It is likely that Ayer and his detachment would have been annihilated were it not for the enemy's need to push through his position without delay. The engagement was akin to a wooden fence trying to stop a wave. A close-range skirmish broke out between clusters of men, while the rest of the war party swept past into the safety of the forest. After a brief melee which resulted in the recovery of a few of the prisoners, Ayer's son, his father now counted among the fallen, took command and retreated toward the arriving reinforcements.

Although the militia coming onto the field now numbered more than the invaders, no one was interested in following the enemy war party into the forest for fear of walking into an ambush, and the pursuit was called off. Many, along with Governor Dudley, would lament the decision. Over a score of French and Indians lay fallen across the landscape and more were seen being carried away by their comrades. Their supplies had been taken and they had spent the morning fighting and on the run. Had the fresh troops pushed on their retreat "more might have been done against them."[7]

What was certain was the devastation the marauders had wrought. The arriving troops helped put out the flames and bury the bodies. As it was a warm August day and there was no time to make coffins the sixteen fallen citizens were intered together in a mass grave. Just as many were carried away. Some like Joseph Bartlett, a soldier from Salem, would survive the harrowing march back to Montreal, the threats of being burned at the stake, the beatings and hard labor, to be eventually liberated at the end of the war. Many, however, were never heard from again.[8]

Smaller raids punctuated the rest of the year. Handfuls of raiders waylaid unsuspecting travelers or ambushed wood cutting parties, but no major raid on the scale of Haverhill would be forthcoming even though the minister of the marine pressed Vaudreuil to escalate such attacks. Even if he had wanted to the governor would have been hard pressed to step up his efforts. By the end of 1708 the fighting, with a brief pause during the peace negotiations, had been going on for over five years. While the larger English colonies could sustain such a prolonged conflict, French Canada could not.

It was not that the governor's actions or defensive policies had proven incorrect. The *petite guerre* philosophy as first employed by Frontenac had accomplished many of its goals. The English colonies had yet to organize an attack on the French colonial capital, and their recent effort against Port Royal had been a disaster. Regardless of English intrigues the Iroquois were still neutral, and the peace treaty in the west was still in place. There was no indication that the English would attempt to exploit the waters of the Champlain Valley as they had in the last conflict, nor that New York would play an active role in the conflict because of the Iroquois desire for peace. The remaining English colonies were divided and left to their own resources, with Massachusetts and New Hampshire bearing the bulk of the conflict, while the other colonies, farther removed, contributed little. This was the result Vaudreuil was looking for—to control the initiative, husband his resources, and face each colony one at a time.

From the governor's side the problem was not New France's war policy, which appeared to be working, it was simply a supply problem. English warships and privateers swarmed over the North American coast capturing French supply vessels at an alarming rate. New France was not self-sufficient and was far more reliant on its mother country than the English colonies, making such captures even more difficult. The resulting shortages of food, arms, and trade goods not only threatened famine among the populace and undermined the security of the colony but the network of alliances with the native nations as well.

The first of these issues lay in the colony's hands. Canada was more than capable of growing the produce required for self-sufficiency, but two underlying issues had prevented this. The first was the long conflict with the Five Nations. For security's sake, French settlers were forced into defensible villages and thus were only able to cultivate the lands near these towns, greatly restricting agricultural output. Second, the *coureurs de bois* and the lure of profits in the fur trade had diverted a sizable portion of the colony's activity, population, and resources that would have otherwise been focused on agriculture. The Great Peace of Montreal solved the first issue and opened up more land for use, but with the onset of Queen Anne's War it was of little help. "Increasingly, the people of Canada are cultivating the land," Intendent Raudot wrote the minister of the marine in early October 1708. "It is the only way for them to get out of the extreme poverty in which they are. This misery is caused by the high price of goods and of all the things generally which come from France. It is an evil which is caused by war and which will only end with peace."[9]

As to the matter of arms and trade goods from France, the problem could be attributed to the short-sighted view of a French king who had changed his naval directives midway through King William's War from control of the waves to commerce raiding. The effect of this change was not seen in that conflict, as the traditional naval elements to support New France were still in place, but by the midway point of Queen Anne's War it was having a pronounced effect on Canada. It is perhaps somewhat ironic that at the time Raudot was asking the minster of the marine to consider drawing masts and wood products out of Canada to help alleviate the misery in the colony, Louis was reducing his navy.[10]

Even with these logistical impediments, as long as the English colonies failed to act in concert New France could cope with the problems before it. Unfortunately for French Canada, the English would soon discover a way to unite—by appealing directly to the queen for help.

CHAPTER TWENTY-ONE

# Soldiers, Sailors, and Fishermen

The effects of Montigny's and Subercase's raid on the English settlements in Newfoundland in early 1705 rippled through the English fishing industry. For Major Lloyd in command at St. John's the answer was simple: seize Placentia. Lloyd considered an assault on the position in the spring of 1706, before the arrival of the annual fishing fleets. Both Placentia and St. John's were at their weakest at this point. The difference, however, was that 1,200 English had spent the winter in Newfoundland while only a quarter of the number could be found at Placentia. Although he met plenty of resistance, the major finally convinced the inhabitants to support him, but he was ultimately forced to abandon the effort for the lack of two hundred troops to lead them.[1]

While no attack would be forthcoming several measures were put in place to help prevent another French incursion. The naval presence was increased to six warships, a second infantry company was agreed upon for St. John's, and the commander of the annual fleet was given powers to establish militia officers and companies in all of the major harbors. Clothing for the garrison at Fort William, powder, materials for fortifications, and money were all pushed forward to rectify the problem. As before, the promises proved fleeting. Commodore John Underdown did organize the militia at St. John's and a few supplies and troops trickled into the town, but otherwise little else materialized.

While Lloyd could not strike at Placentia, another opportunity presented itself in early July 1707. Reports had reached St. John's that a number of French fishing vessels were operating out of the harbors and inlets to the north. The citizens of the town petitioned both Lloyd and Underdown to strike a blow against this fleet, which would not only disrupt the enemy efforts but prove a great encouragement to the beleaguered English fisheries in the region. With an opportunity to strike back at hand, the request was quickly granted. Lloyd and forty of Fort William's garrison were loaded onto the fifty-gun frigates HMS *Falkland* and HMS *Nonsuch*, and on the morning of July 26 they set sail.[2]

The next day Underdown encountered the HMS *Medway* near Cape Bonavista. The sixty-gun frigate had a French prize in tow but otherwise had seen little activity in the area. Underdown ordered the *Medway* to join the expedition, and the flotilla set a course for Bay Blanche. On the evening of August 2, the fleet halted near the mouth of Fleur de Lys Harbor on the northern end of Cape Partridge. The commodore sent Lloyd and some of his men in longboats to investigate. The major returned a few hours later with news that the site had been abandoned.

The next morning Underdown set a course north for Bay de Canada. Around 6 a.m. he encountered a vessel near Cape Canada. A brief exchange of signals ended with Underdown ordering his gunners to open fire on the vessel. The thirty-gun French privateer *Duke D'Orleans* returned fire, but when the *Nonsuch* and *Medway* added a few rounds to the *Falkland*'s ranging shots the captain of the French vessel reconsidered and lowered his flag. The commodore and his captains could see that there was a smaller French vessel at anchor not far away, but the treacherous shoals protecting it made it impossible for any of the English warships to approach. Underdown ordered the *Medway*'s prize into the harbor while Lloyd and his men landed in small boats. Caught in a crossfire from sea and land, the twenty-gun privateer struck its colors after a brief fight.

To Underdown's delight the captured captain informed him that a dozen miles to the north there was a privateer of thirty-two guns and another of twenty-six guns anchored at Conche Harbor. The commodore ordered Captain Thomas Hughs of the *Medway* to burn the captured vessels and then join him at Conche Harbor. Pressing on with the *Falkland* and the *Nonsuch* on the afternoon of August 5 Underdown surprised the two French vessels as they were getting ready to make sail. The privateers fired a few ragged broadsides at the English warships, but with a pair of fifty-gun frigates bearing down on them, the crews thought better of the matter and put their vessels to the torch before going ashore. The commodore realized

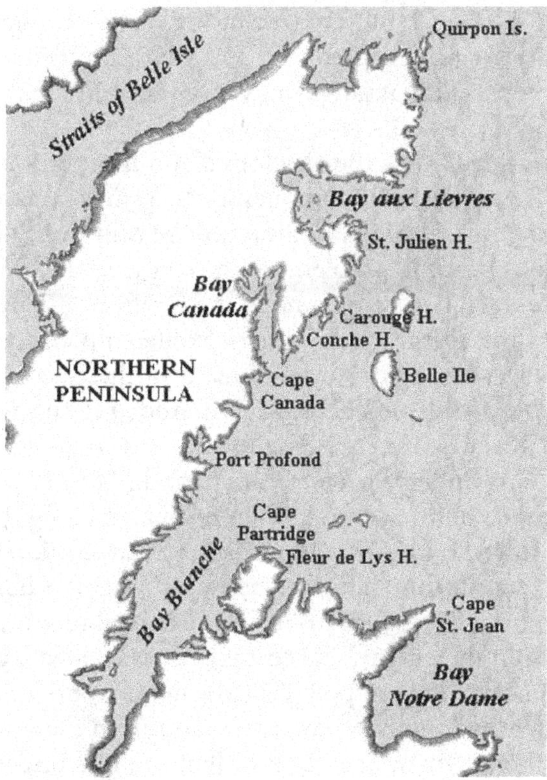


The area around Bay Blanche, Newfoundland.

that the Frenchmen were marching for Carouge Harbor about half a mile to the north. Now joined by the *Medway*, the English flotilla raced for the harbor, but the wind proved uncooperative and it was not until the following morning that they arrived. They were too late. Several privateers had departed just a few hours before. Underdown immediately turned north and sighted his quarry, but that was as close as he would get to them as the winds faded. Around 5 p.m. Underdown spotted a vessel in St. Julian Harbor. Once again, the vessel was positioned such that the commodore landed Lloyd and his men while the *Medway*'s prize approached by water, and once again the vessel fell into English hands.

While Underdown would have liked to have continued north his pilots only had a sketchy knowledge of the coast beyond. The commodore acquiesced and signaled the fleet to return to Carouge Harbor. After raiding a small fishing village and rendezvousing with the captured *Duke D'Orleans*, Underdown set a course for St. John's, arriving on August 17 with his prizes in tow. News of the successful venture quickly spread through the colonial capital and nearby towns. As predicted a surge of confidence followed and when the fleet departed that fall it was viewed in a different light than the previous year.[3]

Beyond a few small raids the Newfoundland frontier was quiet for the winter. Lloyd had requested that money, clothes, men, and an engineer to help improve the fortifications of St. John's be sent over with the spring fleet, but in the meantime problems with the garrison, and in particular with Lloyd's conduct, began to come to the forefront. Charges and countercharges from the citizens and soldiers painted a picture of corruption and abuse of power by Lloyd. However, many of these accounts vaporized once pushed upon, while others held merit. Added to this were the letters of praise from the citizenry regarding the major's conduct, including one from Commodore Underdown who, after speaking to Lloyd's "diligence, courage, and good conduct" during their campaign along the Newfoundland coast, informed London that "It is with great satisfaction I have likewise observed the friendship and decorum between him, his officers and the inhabitants, the most effectuall means in my judgement to secure this country in the winter from the enemy." Taken together it created a confusing and seemingly common pattern of political strife in the frontier town. The matter eventually reached the Board of Trade, and from there the queen personally wrote the major informing him that she had directed an official review into his conduct. "In the mean time," she continued, "we do hereby signify to you our utmost dislike of such undue practices."[4]

This letter was personally delivered by Commodore John Mitchell, who arrived at St. John's with the seasonal fleet in the summer of 1708. While the garrison received little in the way of funds and supplies, the engineer Lloyd had requested to replace the departing Robert Lantham did arrive. Captain George Vane was a descendant of the Vane's of Raby Castle. It seems likely he picked up his Jacobite sympathies from his family, for he served James II in exile until the latter's death in 1701. He then briefly worked as a military engineer for the state of Venice before entering the employment of the Electorate of Bavaria as a captain of engineers. When Bavaria withdrew from the War of Spanish Succession in 1703, Vane returned to England under the general amnesty offered to Jacobites by Queen Anne. In early 1706 Vane, pointing to his credentials and references, applied for a military appointment. The effort eventually bore fruit, and in the spring of 1708, he received orders to replace the current Royal Engineer at St. John's.

Given the history of the region and the importance of the Newfoundland fisheries, a second attack seemed likely to Vane, which only emphasized the urgency of the work before him. One of the first tasks he performed, with the help of Commodore Mitchell's fleet, was replacing the weather-damaged 660-foot boom across St. John's Harbor. Vane then turned to the outer works of Fort William where he oversaw replacing the rotting palisade that lined the stronghold's ditch. He then inspected and made minor interior repairs to the newly raised palisade fort, or the New Fort as it was called. Built adjacent to Fort William the New Fort held the recently organized militia companies of St. John's. After seeing to the cannon that lined the ramparts of Fort William and tending to the supply situation, there was little else to be accomplished before fall and the onset of winter put any major works out of the question.

As for Lloyd and the accusations laid upon him, Commodore Mitchell and several ship captains examined the witnesses and the evidence before departing for England. The council of fourteen officers concluded that Lloyd was innocent of the charges and that "All these complaints have been contrived by some few disaffected persons." The major was delighted with the ruling and in a sign of confidence informed London that the fort and the defenses of St. John's were in good order and that, when combined with the seven hundred men of the newly organized militia of St. John's, "I doe not apprehend any danger for this winter."[5]

In Placentia there were those of another mind. With Subercase's departure for Acadia a new governor was appointed, Phillip Pastour de Costebelle. It would have been difficult to have picked a better candidate. Costebelle had served in Newfoundland during King William's War as a colonial marine, rising to the rank of captain, and again during Queen Anne's War as the king's lieutenant at Placentia. Perhaps of more note was that both former governor Brouillan and the departing Subercase recommended Costebelle for the post.

The new governor concerned himself with improving the colony's agriculture and the arrival of new settlers. The defenses of Fort St. Louis were continually improved, and French and Indian patrols routinely scoured the nearby countryside. With Costebelle's promotion, in 1707 a new king's lieutenant arrived at Placentia. Joseph de St. Ovide was the nephew of Governor Brouillan and an old friend of Costebelle's. In fact, when Costebelle had first sailed to Newfoundland in 1692 his ship had wrecked on the rocky shores and it was St. Ovide who had arrived to rescue the crew and its passengers.

The two men worked well together securing the French colony, and while both looked for an opportunity to strike at the English the resources available put it out of the question. In late 1708 this changed. A pair of brigantines from Quebec had arrived as well as a ship bound for Hudson Bay. These were soon joined by the frigate *Venus*, which had recently captured a vessel carrying a few dozen French prisoners from Acadia. The sudden influx of manpower from the sailors onboard the four vessels and the liberated soldiers allowed Costebelle to move forward with a plan that St. Ovide had proposed to seize St. John's.

St. Ovide gathered together 125 Micmac, sailors, and colonists. He added the recently arrived soldiers to this, and Costebelle gave him another two dozen marines to augment his numbers. The plan had been to sail to the vicinity of St. John's and from there march against the town, but contrary winds and foul weather delayed the expedition until the middle of December, at which point the French commander abandoned the idea of proceeding by sea and set off by foot.

On the twentieth the party met a pair of small sloops Costebelle had sent to ferry them across St. Mary's Bay, saving them several days of hard marching. Crossing familiar frozen terrain and tolerating the grumbling among his troops, by New Years' Eve St. Ovide was encamped a little over a dozen miles from St. John's. Thus far the plan had been successful in that it appeared he was undetected. The expedition spent some time making scaling ladders in preparation to attack, and a few hours after midnight the column began shuffling forward. It was a still, clear evening, and the gibbous moon cast frozen shadows on the landscape. While not ideal conditions by which to surprise a fort, it did make for good conditions by which to scout the town. After spending some time gauging the terrain and seeing no signs of activity, the French commander ordered the column forward.[6]

A little after four o'clock on the morning on New Years' Day 1709 Lloyd, Vane, and their colleagues realized how unprepared the town really was when St. Ovide's men, some 160 strong, dashed out of the tree line toward Fort William. The sentry on duty in the southwest bastion of the New Fort could hardly believe his eyes when he saw the French column shuffling forward on snowshoes with ladders held over their heads. The startled soldier tried to fire a warning shot, but his gun misfired. By the time he reached a second sentry, who sounded the alarm, the French force was already at the ditch before Fort William.

The new palisade Vane had erected on the outer berm of the ditch forced St. Ovide's men to stop and use their ladders to navigate over the structure. A handful of muskets flashed along the ramparts of the New Fort and Fort William as the sentries at both locations became aware of the threat. Gunner William I'Anson was immediately woken by the gunfire and raced up to the ramparts. Here he met the gunner on duty who handed him a lit match and a powder horn to prime the already-loaded cannon. The man then informed I'Anson that he was leaving to warn the rest of the gunners. Left alone the undaunted, I'Anson darted to the first cannon and lowered the muzzle toward the attackers. Shouting "*Vive le Roy*!" St. Ovide led his men over the palisade and into the ditch. While the van of the attacking column was now below the cannons' maximum depression the main column was still climbing over the palisade a few dozen yards away. Having aligned the gun, I'Anson opened the powder horn to prime the piece only to find it was empty. With no other option before him, he raced off toward the powder magazine.[7]

It was now too late. Confusion reigned supreme. Almost no one responded to the alarm and many of the sentries abandoned their posts. Most of the musket fire was coming from the militia in the New Fort when St. Ovide and a few dozen of his men reached the fort's wall, which included the main gate and drawbridge. Hoarse commands followed as the makeshift scaling ladders were thrown against the structure, one after another, and then with a chorus of defiant shouts, St. Ovide's men went over the top.

Captain Vane arrived on the ramparts to find the French already over the wall and the drawbridge being lowered. The main gate was opened and soon a flood of attackers was inside the fort. Almost surrounded Vane ran to his quarters as shots flew past him. It proved a temporary refuge as the attackers peppered the house with musket balls as Vane tried to protect his wife. One of the French officers called on the Royal Engineer to surrender, and Vane quickly agreed.

St. Ovide's men surged through the fort, breaking down doors and collecting prisoners. Major Lloyd, who would be blamed for the disaster, was apprehended trying to open the sally port to let the town's militia into the fort. A few of the garrison went over the wall and ran to the New Fort, but most were captured. Within half an hour the task was complete. St. Ovide sent one of the captured officers over to the New Fort and demanded their surrender. If they refused, he would offer no quarter to his current prisoners or the garrison of the New Fort once he had taken it. The demand was agreed to and the flag lowered over the fort. The next morning St. Ovide advanced on the stone castle near the entrance to the harbor. Although there were sixty men, cannon, and supplies in this stronghold, it too surrendered without firing a shot, leaving all of St. John's and its inhabitants in French hands.

Questions abounded as to the conduct of Major Lloyd both prior to and during the attack. A number of witnesses pointed to the commanding officer's neglect, cowardice, and even possible treason, but Lloyd, aware of Vane's Jacobite sympathies, and the liberty granted to him by the French after his surrender, was quick to lay the blame at the engineer's feet. "That cowardly villian of an Enginier Capt. Vane," Lloyd wrote after the incident, "I am sure is a traytor, and will betray the Government whatever they trust him, had it not been for him I should not have been a prisoner here."[8]

For St. Ovide it was a spectacular victory. He had suffered three killed and eleven wounded in the attack which had left him with three forts, over fifty cannon, huge caches of supplies and ammunition, as well as the garrisons and all the inhabitants of the town. The *Venus* and several other vessels arrived from Placentia a few weeks later with a handful of reinforcements and returned laden with plunder and prisoners. Immediately after the surrender of the town St. Ovide dispatched a letter to the minister of the marine asking for several companies of marines to secure the new conquest. He then turned his attention toward Ferryland, sending a few vessels to capture the town, but well warned the inhabitants put up enough of a fight that the flotilla abandoned the effort.

By late March Costebelle had decided to abandon St. John's. There were rumors that the English were preparing a squadron to retake the colonial capital, and he needed St. Ovide's men to defend Placentia should an English blow fall there. St. Ovide had hoped that France would hold on to St. John's, but when Costebelle's orders arrived he carried them out with his typical efficiency. The New Fort and Fort William were put to the torch, as were the public buildings, a large number of vessels, and a number of settlers' homes. The stone castle was demolished but not before a premature explosion claimed one French officer's life and almost claimed St. Ovide's life as well. The garrisons, cannon, and supplies were carried to Placentia, while the citizens could either pay a ransom or be taken away as well.

By mid-April the task was completed and the expedition returned to Placentia to a hero's welcome. A few weeks later the fifty-four-gun French frigate *Fiddell* arrived at Placentia with two hundred soldiers. When the minister of the marine received St. Ovide's letter he ordered the troops to be dispatched, but later he thought better of the matter and ordered them to Placentia. Arriving with this vessel were a pair of letters for St. Ovide. The first sympathized with the French lieutenant's desire to hold St. John's in the king's name. The king had certainly been pleased by the young officer's spirit and conduct, but "Not being in a condition to take possession, it is better to raize the fortifications and transport the cannon to Plaisance." In the next letter St. Ovide found the king's approbation—an order granting him the Cross of St. Louis and the title of knight.[9]

# Part Five

## *Victory and Retreat*

CHAPTER TWENTY-TWO

# War and Profit

THE DESTRUCTION OF THE APALACHEE had shattered western Spanish Florida, but it would only prove to be the first phase of a greater tempest. Seeing that the Spanish were unable to protect their allies, Creek and Yamassee war parties descended on the Timucua mission north of St. Augustine. In late 1704 Creek raiders burned the San Pedro and San Mateo missions in Timucua province, carrying away scores of prisoners. The following year a large Creek raiding party laid siege to the town of Abosaya, recently erected by Timucua refugees. For close to three weeks the Creek invested the town and sniped at its defenders, finally moving on when a Spanish relief force was sighted. The remainder of the year and the opening months of the next would prove pivotal as Yamassee and Creek forces focused on the Spanish province. Abosaya was targeted again, and although the town was not captured, its inhabitants had seen enough and abandoned the location. Other nearby villages were not so fortunate, as demonstrated by the columns of smoke that dotted the countryside and the long lines of captives headed north. "We have these two . . . past years been intirely kniving all the Indian towns in Florida which were subject to the Spaniards," Carolina Indian agent Thomas Nairne wrote of the Creek and Yamassee raids, "and have even accomplished it."[1]

In early 1706 the main Timucua mission at San Francisco de Potano came under siege. Manned by the inhabitants and a small Spanish garrison the wooden palisades of the mission held, but even so many had seen enough and departed for safer venues near St. Augustine. The smaller villages that survived the onslaught followed suit, but many were too late and either lay motionless among the burning embers of their homes or found themselves now resigned to a life of slavery. As the frequency of the raids increased the authorities appealed to Governor Francisco de Corcoles y Martinez to be allowed to withdraw the surviving Timucua to St. Augustine. Unable to defend the remaining missions and villages, Martinez agreed, signaling the collapse of Spanish power in the region. The official withdrawal did little to stop the carnage and depredations. With the Timucua destroyed, central and southern Florida now became a hunting ground for the Creek and Yamassee as they traveled farther in search of slaves. One Spanish officer, Juan de Pueyo, wrote in late 1707 that there was little left of the Spanish missions in Florida. He calculated that thirty-two Indian villages had been destroyed and almost as many missions. Governor Martinez agreed, claiming the following year that "ten to twelve thousand" had been killed or taken and that the handful that had escaped now lived under the guns of Castle San Marcos. Matters were such that by the following year Nairne was able to inform London "that the garrison of St. Augustine is by this warr reduced to the bare walls, their Castle and Indian towns all consumed either by us in our invasion of that place or by our Indian subjects since, who in quest of booty are now oblidged to goe down as farr on the point of Florida as the firm land will permit."[2]

While St. Augustine was isolated along the eastern Florida coast, so too was the Spanish town of Pensacola along the Florida Panhandle. The town was rebuilt after a fire in November 1704 caused its abandonment, although the use of palm-thatched roofs, which helped propagate the former blaze, was still continued. Undermanned, isolated, and at the mercy of supply ships from Vera Cruz, the destruction of the Apalachee had further exposed the town to attack by the English and their native allies.

On August 12, 1707, a band of twenty to thirty Indians were spotted looting and burning the homes at the edge of Pensacola. Witnessing the display, the fort's commander, Sgt. Major Don Sebastian de Moscoso, ordered one of the cannon fired at the intruders. The idea worked and the raiders scattered, allowing several of their prisoners to escape. The alarm was sounded and for the next few days scouts returned empty handed having seen no signs of the enemy. Three days later there were no more questions regarding the enemy's presence, as three hundred Creek warriors attacked the fort at dawn. For three hours the garrison exchanged fire with the invaders, until the latter tired of the effort and retreated back into the woods. The next day the Creek returned, this time looting the abandoned

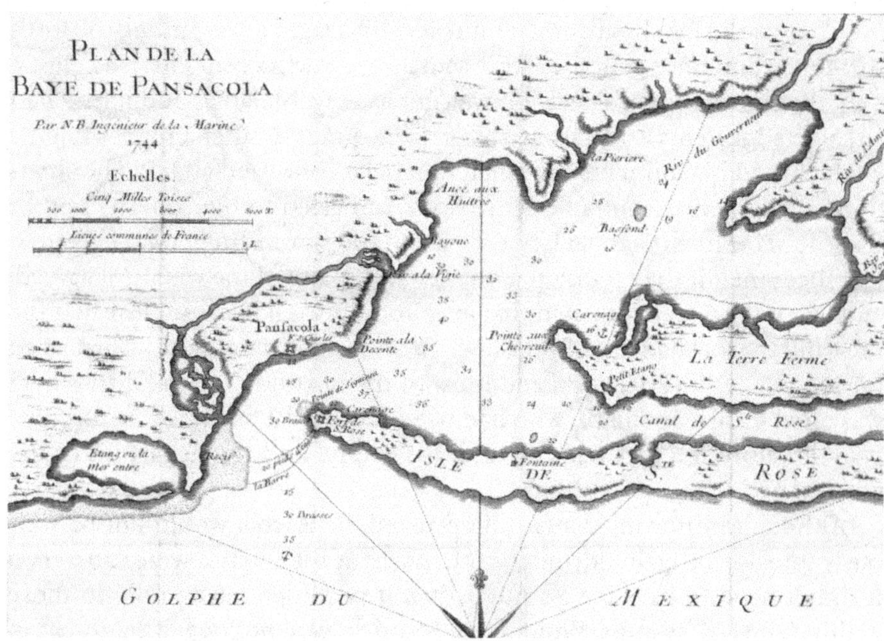


A 1744 map of Pensacola Bay. Note Fort de St. Rosa, opposite Pensacola Island, which was erected in 1723 and destroyed by a hurrican in 1752. (*Library of Congress*)

town and using the buildings for cover while they dueled with the fort. The following morning more Creek appeared, and during the daylong exchange in which Moscoso began firing on the town with his cannon, an English flag was raised over one of the homesteads. At nightfall the raiders put the town to the torch and departed.[3]

There were a number of small incidents over the next few months, but on November 27 a second assault against Pensacola began to take form. Early that morning a cry from a lookout directed the garrison's attention to a band of Creek, many mounted, and accompanied by several Englishmen. A pair of Englishmen approached bearing a white flag and were allowed into the fort. They delivered a surrender demand to Moscoso, who scoffed at the idea and sent them on their way. For the rest of the day the garrison stood at their posts, catching fleeting glimpses of the enemy as they invested the stronghold. At twilight the first shots rang out and as darkness descended the Creek, some two hundred strong, pushed on different parts of the fort, testing the defenders. Shouts, war whoops, and sporadic clusters of flashes filled the evening, but although the Creek had pressed them, the garrison held firm.

At dawn the two Englishmen returned, once again demanding the fort's surrender, and once gain they were sent away by Moscoso. This time, however, the commandant's decision was not as easy. Maladies and illness had already reduced his understrength garrison, and now after a night of fighting he found his numbers too small to repel a concerted attack. The situation was desperate enough that Moscoso appealed to the convicts sent to the fort to perform manual labor as part of their punishment. He agreed to free these men if they took up a musket and manned the walls. All agreed, and when the Creek returned that afternoon it soon became clear that the fire from the fort had not diminished. The two sides sporadically skirmished for the rest of the afternoon and most of the next day. On the thirtieth all was quiet until a Spaniard, who had been captured a few weeks before, appeared before the fort with news of his escape and the departure of the enemy.[4]

Although minor incidents still occurred, Pensacola would not be seriously threatened again during the war. As far as the English were concerned it didn't need to be. Like St. Augustine, it provided haven only to those within range of its guns. Besides, the Spanish were no longer the threat in their eyes but the French. One of the leading proponents of this last thought was Carolina Indian agent Thomas Nairne. An Indian trader and slave raider, Nairne was a Scottish immigrant who arrived in the colony in the mid-1690s. Having spent a great deal of time with the Creek, Yamassee, and a number of other tribes, Nairne began to perceive the part such allies filled in a greater vision of English expansion throughout southeastern North America. Shortly after his election to the South Carolina Assembly in 1707, Nairne was appointed the colony's first Indian agent—a position that required he spend most of the year among the different tribes.

In late 1707 Nairne, aided by well-known Chickasaw trader Thomas Welch, placed a plan to attack Mobile before the South Carolina Assembly. There were few in the assembly who did not understand the threat the French colony posed, especially when rumors of another Franco-Spanish attack on Charles Town began to arrive. In November the plan was approved. The troops were ordered to be raised and the operation would proceed under the proviso that the pro-French Choctaw and Yazoo could be convinced to join the expedition, or at least to remain neutral. The following spring both Welch and Nairne attempted to fulfill this last condition. They visited the Chickasaw and Tallapoosas, pushing the idea of trade with Carolina and an alliance with the English. Nairne even "ventured his life" and traveled to the Choctaw in an attempt to make peace with them, but they were not interested. The proposed expedition was abandoned, but not for this reason. Reports now seemed to confirm that a large Franco-Spanish force was being assembled in Cuba to strike at Charles Town. The threat was serious enough that not only was Nairne's expedition called off, but his native allies were now to be held in reserve in case of an attack on the colonial capital.[5]

No invasion force arrived, but fear of an attack would stretch through the spring and summer. On July 10, 1708, Nairne, looking to garner support for another effort against Mobile, wrote a letter to the secretary of state, the Earl of Sunderland, outlining his views on Carolina Indian affairs and the role this played in colonial expansion.

> I have had a personall view off most of these parts, either formerly when a Commander in the warrs, or this year by travelling, altho my inquiries and serches of this kind are not finished, yett considering the juncture, that peace must of necessity in some small time be concluded, I could not dispense with myself from laying before yr. Lordship a map of such travells and observations as I have already taken, to the end yr. noble Lordship may at one view perceive what part of the Continent we are now possest off, and what not, and procure the articles of peace to be formed in such a manner that the English American Empire may not be unreasonably crampt up.[6]

The Carolina Indian agent spoke to the threat posed by the French in Louisiana by pointing to that colony's alliances. If the French were able to win over the Choctaw, Chickasaw, Alabama, and even the Creek, combined with their alliances farther up the Mississippi, which could be called upon for support, the entire colony of Carolina and even Virginia would be at risk. Hence, the Indian nations of the southeast held the balance of power in the region between England, Spain, and France. Given that Spanish Florida, short of the forts at St. Augustine and Pensacola, was now under the control of England's Creek and Yamassee allies, the best way to shift this balance over to the side of England, or Great Britain now that the Union treaty had been signed, was to seize Mobile.

While Nairne had convinced the South Carolina Assembly that he could take the French stronghold with 1,500 allied Indians and 45 Carolina traders, short of this immediate remedy, a long-term approach was already in motion. "Our friends the Talopoosies (Tallapoosas) and Checasas (Chickasaw) imploy themselves in making slaves of such Indians about the lower parts of the Mississipi as are now subject to the French." Such actions, he noted, when combined with "The good prices the English traders give them for slaves" and cheaper English trade goods, would draw them away from

French influence. This would allow for trading posts and a colony in the area, with the goal of further negating French influence and eventually driving them out of the southeast.[7]

Not long after this letter, in an act of overt revenge, Nairne's political rival Governor Johnson had him arrested on a charge of treason. The matter concerned Nairne's enforcement of the Indian trade, in particular the habit of some English traders to turn one allied town on another in order to make a quick sale of the prisoners. Nairne attempted to intervene in such a case, which ran afoul of Governor Johnson's and his friends' business interests. While the charges were bogus, it forced Nairne to travel to England to exonerate himself, which not only collapsed the planned campaign against Mobile in 1708 but for years to come.[8]

With South Carolina's plan to attack Mobile set aside, Queen Anne's War in the southeast would settle down into a pattern not unlike what was seen in the north before and during King William's War—a struggle to meld together shifting alliances among the minefields of native rivalries and intercolonial intrigues. For Bienville and French Louisiana, this was tolerable as, short of a complete diplomatic collapse, it had a high probability of ensuring that the French colony would survive the conflict. A direct attack on Mobile, on the other hand, especially if timed such that no naval vessel was in port, had potentially devastating consequences. Fortunately for Bienville, no seaborne attack on Mobile would materialize, leaving the fate of the French colony in the hands of its talented twenty-five-year-old acting governor.

It would have been difficult to have found a better choice than Bienville. First overshadowed by his brother Iberville, with the latter's loss Bienville's talents came to the forefront and he rose to the challenges placed before him. After the open rupture between the Choctaw and the Chickasaw in early 1705, Bienville's skills were put to the test. Throughout 1705 and 1706 he attempted to reestablish the peace treaty between the Choctaw and Chickasaw, while dealing with a number of ruptures between smaller tribes, and an attack by several thousand English-led Alabama and Creek that carried off three hundred of his Choctaw allies.

In early 1707 he responded to reports that the Jesuit missionary to the Natchez, M. St. Cosme, had been killed by the Chitimacha for organizing and equipping a coalition to strike at the tribe. In March a force of Biloxi, Bayogoulas, and Natchez fell on several Chitimacha villages, burning them and carrying away scores of prisoners. As if his current problems were not enough, in late 1707 an urgent plea for help from the commander of Pensacola reached Mobile. Bienville, with a hundred French troops and supplies, rushed to the scene, dropping anchor in the Spanish port in early

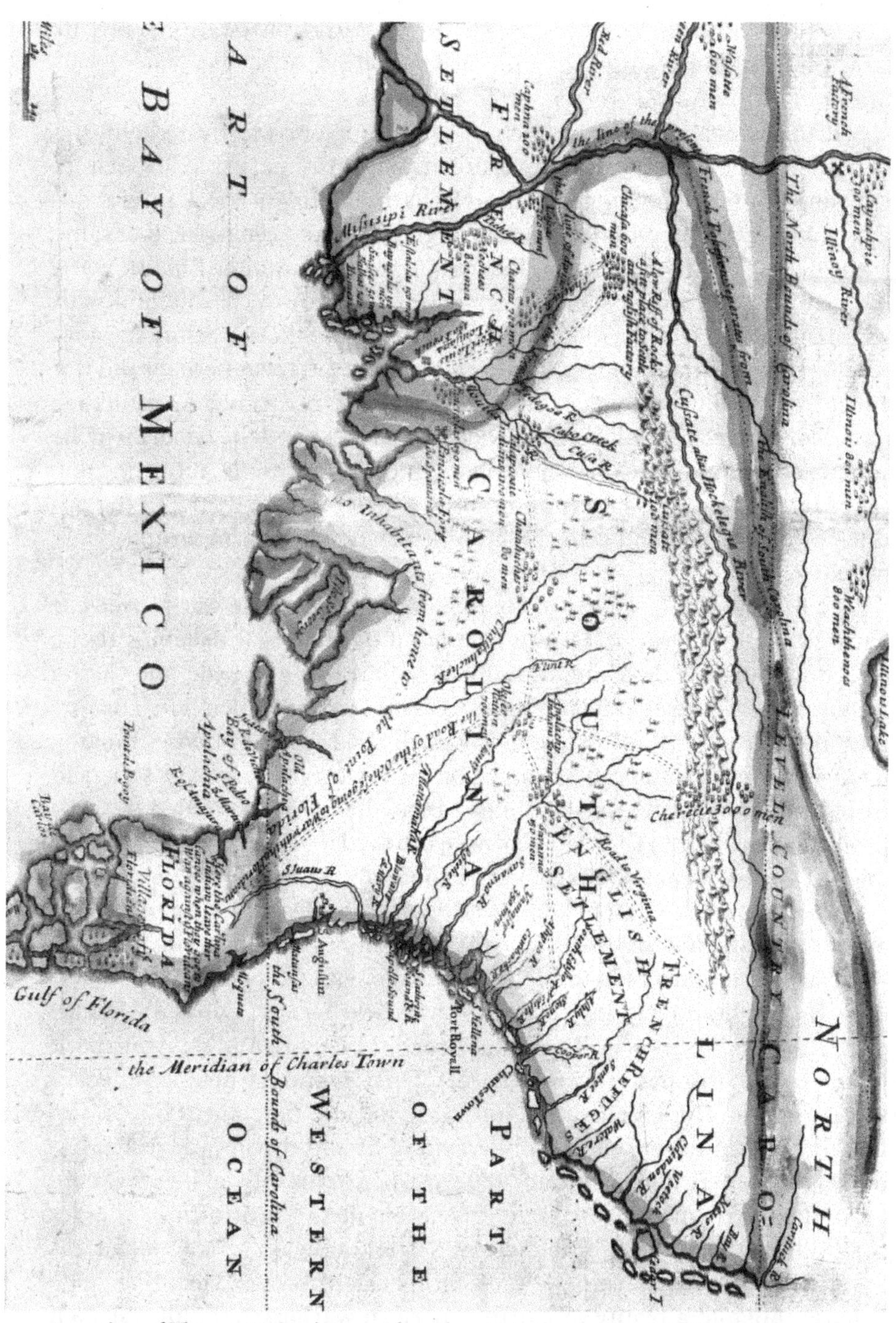


A portion of Thomas Nairne's map of southeast North America, c.1708. (*Library of Congress*)

December. While the siege was over his arrival was well-received, particularly in regard to the supply of gunpowder, as the Spanish garrison was almost out.[9]

Throughout these trials, which in total threatened to overwhelm the fledgling colony, the French governor displayed remarkable leadership. Drawing upon his Indian negotiation skills, his ability to speak several native languages, and his understanding of grandeur and ceremony that came with such negotiations, he was able to successfully counter English commercial interests with personal connection, making each chieftain with whom he visited feel like the most important ally or matter before the governor. He would then send each away with small gifts that perhaps did not equate to the value of English presents but were more valued because they represented a connection between the French leader and the tribe. Bienville supported this approach by rejecting the Indian slave trade, returning any slaves that fell into his hands, promoting a general peace between the nations of the region, and punishing French traders who had wronged any tribe.

For Bienville and Louisiana, the remaining years of the war proved exhausting. External foes aside, internal ones proved more threatening to the leader of Louisiana. The king's commissary, Nicolas de La Salle, and Curate Roulleaux de Vente would lay a series of charges against Bienville. The former sent a letter to Paris in late 1706 detailing a series of offenses ranging from illegal trade and graft to having burned two Chitimacha prisoners in front of the fort's gates. It was not just Bienville, La Salle pointed out. His brothers Iberville and Chateauguay were involved as well. "They are rogues," said he, "who pilfer away his Majesty's goods and effects."[10]

When this and a series of additional letters from De la Vente and La Salle appeared before the minister of the marine, Count Pontchartrain, the latter was alarmed and decided to replace Bienville with M. Nicolas Daneau de Muy. He also decided to send a new commissary, Bernard Diron d'Artaguiette, with him. The new governor was to arrest Bienville and send him back to France as a prisoner to answer charges. Then he and the new commissary were to conduct an investigation into Bienville and the state of the colony. De Muy would never reach Mobile, falling ill and dying in Havana, but d'Artaguiette arrived in February 1708 and began his official investigation.

While d'Artaguiette would not give Bienville a list of official charges against him, the minister of the marine's letter to Bienville had spoken to a few, particularly the burning of the Chitimacha prisoners. Here Bienville's defense spoke to a reality of North American warfare that didn't sit well with the sensibilities of Paris.

Jean-Baptiste Le Moyne de Bienville. Another of the famous Le Moyne brothers. Although never officially made governor of early Louisiana, Bienville acted as such and would successfully guide the infant colony through the perils of Queen Anne's War. After the conflict he would go on to found the city of New Orleans. (*British Library*)

> The Indians always kill as many of their enemies as they have had killed by them, without which it is considered disgraceful to speak of accommodation. To act otherwise would be to expose one's self to be considered a coward. In the beginning of the wars in Canada there was opposition to putting the Iroquois to death; on the contrary, they were sent away with handsome presents, and it was seen that they mocked us, treating the French like women who did not dare kill them for fear of their revenge. Monsieur the Count of Frontenac finally took the stand of burning them, men, women, and children, cruelly, which had so good an effect that afterwards they did not dare come in war against us without fear.[11]

As it was it did not take d'Artaguiette long to reach a conclusion. His report to the king was a complete exoneration of Bienville. The charges laid against him were slanderous, and given the miserable state of the colony, which consisted of less than three hundred French settlers who hadn't been supplied in years, it was impressive that Bienville had prevented a complete collapse of the king's colony.[12]

Bienville would remain at the helm of the French colony, which suffered through its share of hardships. In 1709 famine was first. Heavy rains had ruined the local crops, and until a supply ship arrived, the inhabitants were reduced to eating acorns. The recently built Fort Louis at Mobile flooded as well, and after concluding that this would be a reoccurring issue, it was moved a few miles south the following year. Beyond the occasional retaliatory military forays, particularly against the Alabama, that typically amounted to little, and skirmishes between French-allied tribes and English-allied tribes, Bienville struggled to maintain the peace. His primary target was the Chickasaw, but his best efforts were undermined by a lack of trade goods. The governor wrote that the Chickasaw with whom he had maintained a good relationship had turned to the English "not being able to obtain from us their needs." The shortages proved even more problematic among the colony's allies, as it weakened their resolve and made them more susceptible to English offers.

While an unsteady peace had reigned over the last few years, in May 1711 news came that Choctaw and Chickasaw were once again at war. Bienville and his officers suspected that the English were behind rupturing the peace, and in this they were correct. In early 1711 the South Carolina Assembly began preliminaries toward another attempt on Mobile, although it would not be until late in the year that Thomas Welch and two hundred Chickasaw fell upon several Choctaw villages carrying away over two hundred prisoners. Around the same time Theophilus Hastings led a 1,300-man Creek force into Choctaw territory. Cutting a wide swath, Hastings reported that he had burned over 400 homesteads in his march, killing at least 80 Choctaw, and taking another 130 prisoners, mostly old men and children.

The attack proved the last major incident in the area before word of a truce reached all parties. While this didn't stop smaller raids aimed at procuring slaves, it did stop the larger state-sponsored ones. For Bienville what mattered was the colony had survived. The French and Indian alliances had held regardless of English intrigues and Spanish failings. There was still much to do and much before Bienville, who would go on to establish New Orleans in a few years, but for the moment at least, it could be done in relative peace.

While most in South Carolina thought that targeting the French allies would lead to weakening the French position in Louisiana, via a change of sides or a declaration of neutrality, this was not the case. If anything, it pushed these nations closer to the French. More importantly, such an accomplishment on the English side could lead to a potential disaster. When the plan to win over the Choctaw and Yazoo was first broached in 1708, Nairne pointed out this simple problem. "Wee believe Tho a friendship should be Contracted with the said Indians it will not be Lasting unless it Can be done with the consent of the Creek." This was still true, as the Chickasaw and Creek would never accept a Choctaw-English arrangement which deprived these tribes of their standing and a source of slaves. Nor could the English colony risk unleashing the wrath of either of these nations upon the colony, as would soon be demonstrated by the Yamassee War in 1715. Thus, for all practical purposes, the expeditions against the French allies were never anything more than excuses for slave raids hiding under the banner of queen and country.[13]

For Spanish Florida the news of peace was welcomed but too late. There was little left of what had once been a thriving mission system. Perhaps five hundred now dwelled near Castle San Marcos, the rest had either been killed, captured, or scattered, leaving much of northern Florida deserted. The Carolinians would point to how Spanish power in the region was destroyed, but there was never much there. Florida was for missions and to keep others from using the ports along the coast. The concern for fulfilling these tasks, and more importantly the costs, led to a mere 355 troops assigned to guard St. Augustine and the nearby missions. Take into account illness and desertion, and the numbers available were actually far less. While the Franciscans' endeavors proved successful, problems appeared when it became clear that the growth of the mission system had outrun the governor's ability to defend it. With a growing threat from the English and their allies to the north, pleas for more men and arms echoed throughout most of this period of the Spanish colony but were seldom answered. Although there were barriers of trust involved, measures were finally adopted to allow the missions to defend themselves, but even here a lack of resources meant these efforts were never carried to completion. Thus, when the English and their Creek and Yamassee allies pushed on this house of cards, it collapsed, and with it, Spanish Florida.

CHAPTER TWENTY-THREE

# The Old Invasion Plan

THE IDEA OF AN ATTACK ON QUEBEC was hardly new. By late 1708 it had been suggested numerous times by several governors and prominent citizens. In each case more pressing matters in Europe or abroad meant that it was not seriously considered. Now as letters poured into London detailing the devastation the conflict had wrought on the fishing trade, the loss of settlements along the fertile Maine frontier, the disruption and destruction in Massachusetts and New Hampshire, as well as the constant harassment from a den of French privateers at Fort Royal, it began to paint a picture that could not be ignored.

Enter at this point an unlikely figure, one Samuel Vetch. Vetch, who had been a merchant before the war, had served as one of Dudley's envoys to Quebec during the peace talks between the colonies. During his stay in Quebec Vetch had become friendly with many French merchants and officers. This, along with attempts to politically attack Dudley had led to charges that Vetch had been involved in illegal trade with the enemy. While perhaps true, Vetch was exonerated of all charges. Even so, the incident placed a shadow on both Dudley and Vetch's reputations. Now as talk circulated of attacking Quebec, Vetch came forward with a plan.

When the details of the plan were laid before all, it soon became clear what Vetch had been after with his familiarity with the French. During his travels he had come to the conclusion that an attack on Quebec was not only plausible but practical if supported financially and militarily by the English government. Vetch had closely observed the fortifications of the French colonial capital, its troop strengths, and the populace that could be called upon to aid in its defense. He claimed this number could not exceed five thousand men, but this was clearly an overestimate as these five thousand men were scattered over different towns and posts in Canada. Were the queen to dispatch six men-of-war, two bomb ketches, two battalions of regular troops, and a train of artillery, these forces when combined with a thousand colonial troops and a fleet of colonial transports at Boston, could be in position to sail against the French stronghold in May 1709. To further divide the limited French resources and improve the chances of success against Quebec, a second element was added to the plan. This separate attack called for a land campaign against Montreal by 1,500 men from New York, New Jersey, Pennsylvania, and Connecticut. Together with whatever Iroquois volunteers that could be convinced to join at Albany, they would proceed toward Montreal via the familiar Wood Creek-Lake Champlain waterways, launching their campaign as soon as news reached them that the fleet had arrived at Boston.

What was in essence the old invasion plan of 1690 quickly won support in the Massachusetts Assembly, which empowered Vetch with an address to the queen regarding the project. Vetch's ardent belief in the plan was as important as his timing in the matter. The Whig ministry, pressed by their political rivals on the static state of the war, seized on the plan and granted his requests. A British squadron carrying five regular regiments was promised. Massachusetts, New Hampshire, and Rhode Island were to furnish additional ships and twelve hundred troops toward the effort. The rendezvous of the two forces was scheduled to take place at Boston in May of 1709. From here the entire force would sail for Quebec a few weeks later.[1]

Armed with royal instructions, Vetch set off for America along with a volunteer, Colonel Francis Nicholson, the former lieutenant governor of Virginia. Because of bad weather the pair did not reach Boston until late April of 1709. No time, however, was wasted upon their arrival. The duo made a whirlwind tour of the northern colonies, displaying their orders and calling upon the various governments to raise their contingents. When they reached New York, the news caused an instant change in the colony's neutral policies. Here was what was asked for from the beginning, a combined attack on Canada. New York moved into motion, raising her quota of eight hundred men and sending Peter Schuyler to enlist Iroquois aid in the venture. Connecticut followed suit, as did New Jersey, albeit much slower, but Pennsylvania was of another mind. The Quaker-dominated colony wanted nothing to do with the conflict, although after some negotiations it finally agreed to provide a sum of £3,000 in lieu of a manpower contribution.[2]

Next came the question of a commander. The ministry had directed newly arrived Governor John Lovelace of New York to appoint a commander for the Montreal expedition, but he had died before the letters and royal warrants had reached him. His replacement, Lt. Governor Ingoldsby, along with several of the participating governors, nominated Colonel Nicholson to command the venture. There were a few objecting voices, but in general the choice was a wise compromise. Nicholson was not seeking the position, but as with the selection of Winthrop twenty years before, colonial jealousies had damaged the selection process to such an extent that Nicholson felt that had he not accepted "there would have been insuperable difficulties."[3]

Nicholson reached Albany in late May, where the New York militia and the four regular independent companies were already encamped. Here he held a council of war with his officers. There were two possible routes before the army. Both required plying the Hudson and facing its various obstacles up to a point called the Great Carrying Place, about forty miles north of Albany. Here a series of rapids and impressive waterfalls made further navigation impossible as the river began a great westward arch away from Lake George and Wood Creek. From the Great Carrying Place, however, there lay two possible paths. The first, almost due north, led to the head of Lake George some thirteen miles away, while the second, a northeastern route, led to the waters of Wood Creek sixteen miles away. In either case a road would have to be hacked out of the intervening forest, but the Lake George route, although slightly closer, had a catch; Lake George narrows at its northern end and spills into Lake Champlain through a series of spectacular waterfalls. The army would have to disembark near this point and carry its boats and supplies around the obstacle to a rocky peninsula on Lake Champlain called Ticonderoga before continuing its journey down Lake Champlain. Wood Creek, on the other hand, presented no such difficulties. Although narrow enough in most parts to be blocked by fallen trees, the creek emptied directly into the upper parts of Lake Champlain near a marshy expanse known as South Bay. Just as Winthrop had twenty years before, Nicholson dismissed the Lake George route. The idea of disembarking the army at the outlet of Lake George in the possible presence of an awaiting enemy was, in his mind, an invitation to disaster.

With the route established, Nicholson moved forward to secure his supply line. By late June a series of palisade forts and wooden storehouses had

A portion of a c.1710 map showing the Hudson River from Albany to Woodcreek. Note the falls marked on the map with solid lines. (*Boston Public Library*)

been completed, leading upriver from Fort Albany to the newly built Fort Schuyler at the head of Wood Creek. By now the New Jersey and Connecticut troops had joined his forces, as well as six hundred Iroquois and Mohegan warriors enticed by Peter Schuyler to join the expedition. Subject to no authority but their own, the natives came and left as they pleased. Many were simply curious and stayed only long enough to satisfy their curiosity, while others were bored and hung about the camps in an attempt to entertain themselves. Almost all were half-hearted about the entire affair, which, at best, placed Iroquois neutrality and their position between the two colonial powers in question.[4]

Nicholson's army, which excluding his native allies numbered some fifteen hundred men, now settled into the backbreaking work of maintaining its supply lines until word of the fleet came from Boston. Supplies were loaded into canoes at Albany and sailed ten miles upriver to Van Skaiks Island near the lower confluence of the Mohawk River. Here the water became so shallow that the canoes had to be brought ashore and carried overland to a storehouse built at Half Moon, a peninsula formed by the junction of the Mohawk and Hudson Rivers. The supplies were then loaded onto wagons and carried twelve miles north to Stillwater where the army had built a palisade fort called Fort Ingoldsby. Here the supplies were placed back into boats and taken eighteen miles upriver to a point called the First Carrying Place. A set of shallow rapids at this location often forced the crews to drag their canoes along through armpit-high water to reach the staging point on shore. The canoes were then unloaded and their contents carried seven hundred yards around the intervening rapids. They were then loaded into another set of canoes and transported four miles to the Second Carrying Place. Once again, the crews emptied their vessels and dragged their contents eight hundred yards around the shallow rapids. Here the supplies were loaded into a final set of canoes and sent sixteen miles upriver to the Great Carrying Place, where the army had built a second palisade fort called Fort Nicholson. From here wagon teams carried the supplies to a set of storehouses halfway up the recently cleared trail to Wood Creek. Teams of wagons sent from Fort Schuyler were dispatched to these storehouses to cover the remaining eight miles.

It was a daunting task that required the daily effort of over a third of the army just to maintain. The sheer strain on the few serviceable teams, combined with a summer drought, killed horses faster than they could be replaced. Not that it mattered, given that the existing wagons were rendered unserviceable by the stump-strewn paths they plied. By early August the army was forced to drag most of its supplies overland on sleds pulled by hand or, in many cases, on the very backs of its soldiers. The dry summer also made it difficult on the canoe crews. The reduced river levels forced them to pull their canoes through the water in places where they wouldn't normally have had to. Even so, the army was fortunate. Had it been a wet summer it would have been worse. The trails would have turned into a quagmire of mud, and the more perishable provisions would have been completely lost to the moisture, as the troops learned during the few rain showers that did come. As it was, over a quarter of the bread hauled to Fort Schuyler was lost on the trip due to its exposure to water, not to mention the losses due to theft and graft, which one New Jersey officer estimated to be as high as 50 percent.

The impractical supply situation was further compounded by the nature of the troops themselves. With the possible exception of the regiments from Albany and Ulster, none of the soldiers were familiar with the tasks before

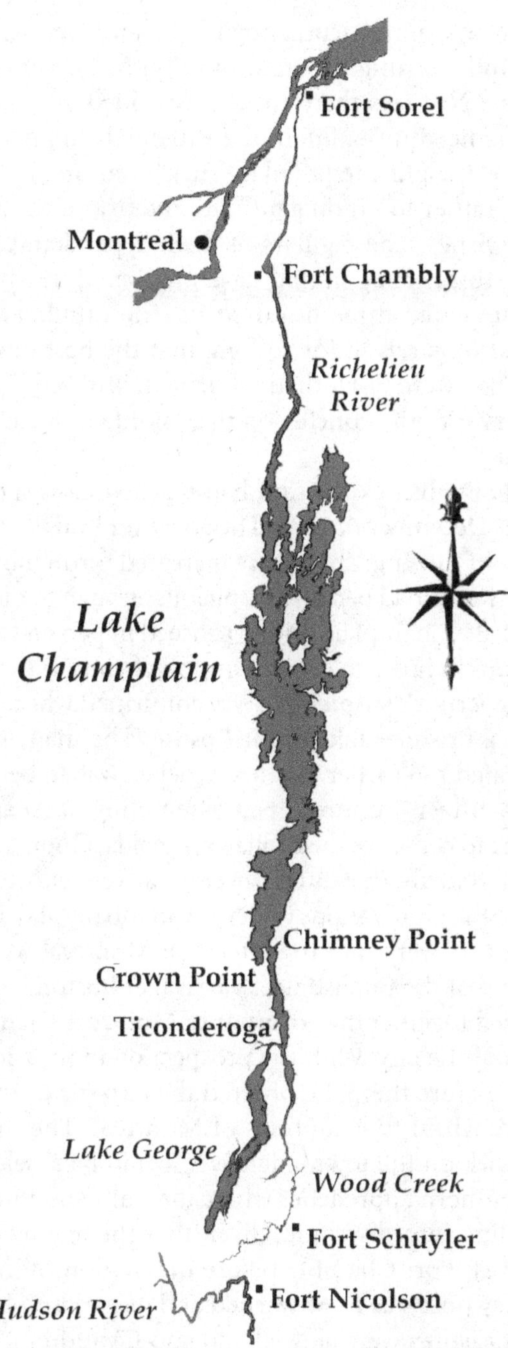


The Champlain Valley.

them. The men from Connecticut, Long Island, and New Jersey were indifferently armed and thoroughly unfamiliar with the woodland arts and woodland warfare. Nor was there time to provide basic training in these subjects, given the need to maintain the extended supply lines. They also lacked the military discipline required for such a venture. Their officers were characterized as "rather too indulgent" and the troops as "too indifferent" to their officers' wishes. The regulars of the independent companies were considered even worse. They should have numbered nearly four hundred but scarcely approached three hundred in true numbers. They had remained neglected in garrison for so long that the best of them had long since deserted. They were ill-clothed, ill-armed, ill-disciplined, and ill-led, leading one observer to the conclusion that "not two thirds of them are fit for the expedition."[5]

Rumors of the English expedition had reached Governor Vaudreuil in Quebec as early as December of 1708. The governor initially dismissed these, but signs and talk of the English venture increased throughout the spring of the next year. In May he had become suspicious enough to dispatch scouting parties out onto Lake Champlain and to proceed in person to Montreal with five hundred troops in order to oversee improvements to the city's defenses. In late June the governor's suspicions were confirmed when an Abenaki war party brought in a prisoner taken near Boston. The man, an ensign in the militia, corroborated the earlier rumors. Quebec was to be attacked by sea and Montreal by fifteen hundred men assembling at Albany. Also, Peter Schuyler had gone to convince the Mohawk, Oneida, Onondaga, and Cayuga to join the effort. Shortly thereafter, several natives reported to Vaudreuil that they had seen the preparations underway in Albany and along the northern Hudson. Reports were that the attack on Montreal would proceed as soon as news came of the English fleet's arrival at Boston.[6]

Vaudreuil called together the governor of Montreal, Claude de Ramezay, and the captains of the city. With the prospect of an invasion and another Iroquois conflict before them, he ordered the citizens of the outlying settlements to retire within the confines of Montreal. The militia would be called out and work on the town's defenses would be accelerated, particularly along the southern approaches where the walls and fortifications were known to be falling into disrepair. Given that the enemy would have no choice but to invest Fort Chambly before moving on Montreal, the commander of this key post was to be warned and its garrison bolstered. While such defensive measures were all well and good, Vaudreuil knew that they failed to address the real problem. If the English should launch simultaneous attacks on Quebec and Montreal, he did not have enough men nor supplies, particularly in terms of powder, to defend both and still maintain the other posts against Iroquois incursions. What he really needed was to deal with the English attacks one at a time. Fortunately, with a large number of troops already at hand in Montreal, and the English fleet still en route to Boston, he was in a position to do just that.

Ramezay was given three battalions of militia and one hundred colonial marines for the task. Added to this were a number of Abenaki, who had proven their mettle time and again in the ongoing conflict with New England. The entire force, amounting to some 1,650 men, was to rendezvous by mid-July at Fort Chambly, where its supplies and provisions had already been stockpiled. Vaudreuil's orders to Ramezay were explicit. He was to launch a surprise attack on the English camp at Wood Creek, limit himself to destroying the enemy's boats and supplies, and then withdraw back down the lake before they could organize any response. As many of the troops might still be needed for the defense of Quebec, a major engagement was to be avoided at all costs.[7]

Satisfied with his arrangements, Ramezay departed Fort Chambly in late July. The flotilla of canoes and bateaux pushed south to Sable Point, where they encountered a pair of French Indians returning from a raid. The men informed Ramezay that they had skirted an enemy force the night before near Point à la Chevelure (Crown Point). Unclear on the numbers involved or their disposition, Ramezay, without consulting his senior officers, sent a reconnaissance party forward under the command of his nephew, an inexperienced officer by the name of Pierre La Pérade. Pérade was to scout the suspected enemy position near Point à la Chevelure and then rendezvous with the main force the next evening at the mouth of Otter Creek.

Late the next day the army took to their boats and set sail, arriving at Otter Creek shortly after sunset. Pérade, however, was nowhere to be found. A few hours after midnight the young officer and his detachment paddled into Porter Bay where the army had made camp. Still drenched in perspiration, he reported that after failing to find any signs of the enemy at Point à la Chevelure, he had pushed farther up the lake to investigate a column of smoke. Convinced that he had found the enemy camp, he arranged his men in an ambush about a mile below their camp. In doing so, however, several of his Indians had themselves fallen into an ambush. After losing one of their numbers in extricating themselves from the trap, the entire detachment reformed and returned to join the main army.

It was unwelcome news for Ramezay, aggravated by the fact he was still unclear on the enemy's strength given that Pérade had been ambushed before being able to ascertain their numbers. The element of surprise now seemed lost. His initial plan to land at Point à la Chevelure was cast aside, and it was agreed at a council of war that the army would land a few miles below the point the next morning.[8]

At dawn on the morning of August 1, 1709, the army put ashore in a sandy cove along the north side of what is today Chimney Point. The Abenaki contingent landed a short distance away, farther up the peninsula. The canoes were pulled ashore, and after briefly forming their ranks, the army was ordered into the tree line. The Abenaki, having landed somewhat farther away and in advance of the main body, mistook the breaking brush and heavy footfalls of the French troops for those of the enemy. The forest rang with war whoops and a few shots were fired before they realized their mistake. However, it was too late. The militia panicked before the abortive attack, and a mad rush for the boats ensued.

Officers called in vain for the troops to hold their positions, while the Abenaki watched in disbelief as the French "scattered like partridges" at the imagined onslaught. "In truth," one witness wrote, "it was amazing that only one shot fired in the woods was enough to send us back into out boats in the greatest of confusion." Originally at the head of his men, Ramezay now found himself alone and, within a few moments, lost in the tangle of trees and brush. At the boats, chaos reigned. Some of the militia reached their canoes, and a few even fled down the lake. Officers drew their swords and threatened those who would follow. Hoarse shouts went out to form ranks, and jittery nerves threatened to launch a volley into the tree line. Throughout all of this Ramezay was nowhere to be found. "But somehow we rallied and put ourselves in order," the same witness recorded, "even though every tree seems to hold an enemy behind it."[9]

At length some measure of control took hold, and an embarrassed Ramezay was found, just in time to receive a report from a scout named Deruisseau that nine hundred of the enemy were approaching through the woods and that seven canoes had been seen rounding the point to the army's right. The troops were ordered back into the woods as the first of the canoes came into sight. Some of the men who were still on the beach exchanged volleys with the English as they dashed for cover. Soon all seven canoes could be clearly seen, and shots began issuing forth from the tree line, raising spouts of water around the enemy. The English, part of a hundred-man detachment ordered by Major Johannes Schuyler to occupy Point à la Chevelure a few days before, fired back as best they could, but given the clear imbalance in the volume of fire, they soon began to veer away.

Unable to control themselves any longer, a pair of Abenaki dashed for their canoe and made straight for the enemy. Following their example, sev-

Claude de Ramezay, left. While Ramezay's expedition up Lake Champlain could not be called a failure, he and his forces conduct during landing operations at what would later become known as Point Fear, did little to convince one that it was a success. (*National Archives of Canada*) Samuel Vetch, right. While Vetch's plan to invade Canada in 1709 would end in failure it was not from lack of effort on his part or the colonial governments involved. (*New York Public Library*)

eral Canadians pushed off in pursuit a few moments later. Soon a dozen canoes joined the chase. The English canoes, either damaged or unable to shake their pursuers, grounded themselves at Point à la Chevelure, and their occupants fled into the woods as fast as their legs would carry them. A group of Abenaki and Canadians followed but, having found nothing but a few packs, gave up the search a short time later. Scouting parties were sent out, and the troops reformed themselves to receive the expected attack from nine hundred of the enemy, but one never materialized.[10]

With the woods pronounced clear of enemy troops, the army moved to Point à la Chevelure and pitched camp. The skirmish had produced only a handful of casualties on either side, but it had raised serious questions with Ramezay as to the continuation of the campaign. A pair of Dutchmen, survivors from that morning's engagement, were brought into the camp later that evening, having mistaken a French scouting party for an English one. They reported that there were twelve hundred troops entrenched at Fort Schuyler and that five hundred Iroquois were expected to join them any day.

A council of war was held the next morning to determine the army's next step. The meeting quickly split into two opposing sides. Several officers were for pushing on. The enemy scouts were scattered, terrified, and many were on the wrong side of the lake. If the army marched immediately it could be in a position to launch an attack on the English works about Fort Schuyler by nightfall, long before these enemy scouts could return to give any warning. Ramezay and the other officers were for abandoning the venture. The element of surprise had been lost, and the English, known to be entrenched, were almost as numerous as the French. There was also the possibility that the arriving Iroquois would attack the army's boats while they were engaged before the English fort, cutting off their only line of retreat. An attack at this point, it was argued, would risk losing a major portion of the army, especially when one considered the conduct of the troops during the recent engagement. The opposing officers tried in vain to convince the French commander otherwise, but in the end, he saw the risks as too great. Later that day he released his native contingents, and the following morning the troops took to their boats and returned to Fort Chambly.[11]

In retrospect, Ramezay's decision proved to be a wise one. Contrary to the belief of some of his officers, by two o'clock that afternoon several of the English scouts had made their way south and sounded the alarm. Given that Fort Schuyler was incomplete, the garrison of one thousand colonials and two hundred Iroquois set about fortifying the encampment with an abatis of fallen trees. The work was completed fairly quickly, and the troops anxiously waited for the French advance. Two days later three hundred and fifty Mohawk reinforced the detachment, lifting the spirits of the defenders and making any possibility of a French attack unlikely.[12]

With the French threat removed, Nicholson's men resumed their daily activities. There was still no word from Boston, and as August slipped into September, the grumbling among the troops increased. Fog, rain, and autumn temperatures made the task of moving supplies a nightmare. Desertion was on the rise, and the supply system was beginning to break down under the strain, creating temporary shortages. The men had been equipped for a summer expedition, and as such, many were ill-prepared for the autumn weather. The cramped conditions, backbreaking work, and lack of adequate clothing opened the door to sickness, which quickly took hold, especially among the troops stationed at Fort Schuyler. "The New England men," Captain John Harrison wrote to a friend in New Jersey, "die like rotten sheep and come from the camp everyday such by ten or eleven a day in horse litters." Harrison concluded his letter with a foretelling comment. "This part of the world is the coldest and worst that I ever saw in all my life; but if it was ten times worse I will not leave it without the general's leave, but I do believe in fourteen or fifteen days you will find enough that wish this."[13]

In Boston frustration reigned as well. Twelve hundred men had been raised from Rhode Island, New Hampshire, and Massachusetts. By late May they were encamped under arms at Boston. To carry this contingent twenty-two transports had been assembled and loaded with six months of provisions. Here they waited in anticipation of the British fleet. In mid-August Dudley wrote London informing them that the entire force was ready to sail in ten hours once the fleet arrived. The latter he was daily expecting, noting that if it did not arrive soon the expedition could find itself before Quebec in the clutches of fall, which was far more severe along the banks of the St. Lawrence than in New England.

For Dudley and the northern colonies there was an additional problem that came with the delay. With a large number of men involved in the Boston and Lake Champlain portions of the campaign, it left far fewer to guard the townships along the frontier. News of small raids on Exeter, Northampton, Brookfield, Wells, and a host of other hamlets reached the forces at Boston who sat idle. For many this was home. Reports of a large attack on Deerfield brought some comfort. This time the village was prepared and repelled the invaders with the loss of only one man. Even so, many a soldier encamped in Boston wondered, if they were not going to attack Quebec, when would they be released to defend their homes?

Lookouts at Castle William and along the coast spent long days scouring the horizon in vain, their hopes occasionally lifted only to find it was a false alarm. In Boston the troops drilled and waited beside the transports that rode quietly in the harbor. By early October the situation was reaching a crisis. Whatever enthusiasm there had been for the project had disappeared with the falling leaves. The costs incurred in keeping the troops under arms and the transports under contract were staggering. Just as importantly, these troops were needed on the frontier or back on their farms. By now it was clear that there would be no expedition against Quebec, but there was still hope that if the fleet arrived in time the effort could be diverted against Port Royal.

To the west failing morale, sickness, and the deteriorating supply lines were destroying the Montreal expedition's military capabilities. There were also rumors that Governor Vaudreuil had assembled a large force at Fort Chambly, perhaps with the thought of launching another, more powerful attack against Nicolson's forces. The news was enough to cause Governor Saltonstall of Connecticut to write his colleagues that "unless some speedy care be taken . . . the fort with all the stores will be in danger of falling into enemy hands." Some efforts were made by Nicholson to quell the temper of his troops, but it was a patch that wouldn't last unless something was done quickly.

In mid-October Dudley summoned Nicholson to Boston. The frigate HMS *Enterprise* had entered Boston Harbor with news that the invasion had been called off. Pressing military matters in Europe had diverted the English fleet to Portugal. The letter did not give any other directives. Some wished to press on to Port Royal with the forces on hand, but Dudley had seen the results of such expeditions. For the governor it was clear. Without the support of British forces there would be no attack on Port Royal.[14]

As Captain Harrison had predicted, once the news reached Nicholson's troops it seems to have triggered a general exodus. In a confused homeward flight, Forts Schuyler, Nicholson, and Ingoldsby were burnt, along with all the boats and supplies stockpiled at these locations. In the course of a few days the army ceased to exist, and the long summer's work was reduced to ashes. The actual details of what transpired are unclear, and strangely, there is little mention of it in the records of the day. Nicholson was not present at the time, lending belief that one of his junior officers, such as Peter Schuyler, ordered the retreat. Whatever the case, the whole incident seems to have been embarrassing enough that all involved decided that the less said on the matter the better.[15]

CHAPTER TWENTY-FOUR

# The Fall of Port Royal

The year 1709 HAD PROVEN DIFFICULT for Governor Vaudreuil and New France. While rumors of an English invasion abounded a more troubling development was occurring. Abraham Schuyler had begun making inroads with the Iroquois, particularly the Mohawk. When Schuyler appeared among the Onondaga with his message, he encountered Jesuit Father Lamberville. The two men had a long discussion in which Schuyler admitted to presenting the war hatchet to the Iroquois, claiming he was ordered to do so. He then expressed his concerns for the father's safety, as it appeared many Iroquois wanted to accept his gift. Schuyler suggested that Lamberville should go to Quebec to inform the governor of what had transpired. The veiled threat was not lost on the Jesuit, who soon departed. A few days later Schuyler spoke with Father Pierre Mareuil, who had stayed behind. He made it clear that, given the current environment, Mareuil was not safe and that he should return to Albany with Schuyler and his delegation. Mareuil agreed, and within a few days all French influence over the Onondaga had been removed. Not long after Lamberville's and Mareuil's residences, as well as a small chapel, were burned down, likely by some of Schuyler's operatives.

The news when combined with information coming from a number of prisoners, "demonstrates to us," Vaudreuil wrote of the moment, "that we were on the eve of a most sanguinary war in this country, and the more to be apprehended as it appeared that the Iroquois were declaring against us." With a new war with the Five Nations imminent Vaudreuil met with Ramezay and the leading officials of Montreal. It was agreed to call in the outer settlements and move all the grain and cattle into the town. Given that Fort Frontenac was isolated and not strong enough to withstand a siege, the governor ordered the post to be abandoned. The order had yet to be issued when Joncaire and Father d'Heu arrived at Montreal with a delegation of forty Seneca. Joncaire convinced Vaudreuil that abandoning Frontenac was not necessary, and after a council with the Seneca, the governor agreed. The largest and westernmost of the Five Nations was not interested in Schuyler's proposals and would remain neutral. Much of this Vaudreuil attributed to the influence of Joncaire "whom they call their Son, on account of having taken him prisoner in an action in which he gallantly performed his duty. They spared his life and adopted him into their Tribe as their Son. He is much beloved." With Joncaire among the Seneca, Schuyler's influence meant nothing. However, this did not mean that the rest of the Five Nations would remain neutral.[1]

Reports of English plans against Canada slowly began to appear before the governor, who responded by setting the populace into motion improving the defenses of Montreal and Quebec. After spending the summer of 1709 suffering from a series of false alarms, with the return of Ramezay's detachment from Lake Champlain in mid-August matters became clearer. While nothing had materialized against either Montreal or Quebec it seemed that at least the Mohawk and perhaps the Onondaga had joined Nicholson's expedition on Lake Champlain. For the moment there was little to do but wait. The governor was short on powder and basic arms and could muster perhaps 1,600 men at Montreal and Three Rivers and another 3,300 at Quebec. With this, and whatever manpower he could draw upon from the west (should it arrive in time), he was to defend against a simultaneous attack on the two principal towns of New France. If English accounts were to be believed, Vaudreuil informed the minister of the marine, "The lowest estimate was, that I should be attacked at Quebec by six thousand men and at Montreal by two thousand. It was even pretended that among the number of these 6000 men against Quebec, there were to be five regiments of Regulars; the remainder were raked up in Scotland and promised, as a bounty, free plunder and fine lands already cleared in this province."[2]

On September 10 Joncaire arrived in Quebec escorting an Iroquois envoy named Arousent. Arousent had just recently been at Nicholson's camp. He confirmed that the English were encamped at Wood Creek and that they had received no news about the fleet arriving at Boston. The Onondaga,

Cayuga, Oneida, and Mohawk had all declared for the English and many had pledged to join Nicholson. The orator then apologized to Vaudreuil saying that they had not been able to "resist the powerful solicitations of Peter Schuyler." More importantly, Arousent warned the governor that Schuyler had planned to build a fort at the headwaters of Lake George and another at Crown Point, a two-day voyage by water from Fort Chambly. The posts were to be garrisoned through the winter and used as a launching pad for any future expeditions.

The news was both good and bad. The bad news was that the English were looking to fortify Crown Point. Under no circumstances could the governor let the English establish themselves on Lake Champlain, a few days' voyage from Chambly and Montreal. Under the prevailing circumstances this would have proved a major problem, but the good news was that the English fleet had not arrived. Vaudreuil realized that even if they did, at this point it was too late in the season for an attack on Quebec. This meant that he could shift some of his manpower to Fort Chambly and wait there for any advance by Nicholson.

By late September Vaudreuil had gathered together over two thousand men at Fort Chambly. Here he obtained a better understanding of the Iroquois defection to the English cause when the Mohawk sent Arousent with a message to the mission Iroquois. "It was with great regret they had consented to Peter Schuyler's message," Arousent informed the French allies, "the hatchet which had been placed in their hands did not afford them any pleasure, but that it was impossible for them to refuse it, not daring to do so, considering the large military force that was at Orange and that was arriving there every day." They urged their kin to put down their arms and abandon the French cause, otherwise they could expect no quarter. The mission chieftains declined the offer and laughed at the threat, pointing to the French army gathered around Montreal and Chambly. They then advised the Mohawk that they would be better served reflecting on the fact "that the English had abandoned them in the last war, and would do the same thing again in this, as soon as there would be peace in Europe."[3]

The English threat evaporated not long after when Nicholson's troops precipitously destroyed their posts on the upper Hudson and retreated to Albany. Strangely, the peace with the Five Nations remained intact. There was still the unsettling matter of the Iroquois volunteers that had served with Nicholson, but as these individuals had not technically done anything Vaudreuil was willing to let the matter pass, hoping that the English failure would prove persuasion enough to discourage any future volunteers. When Father Mareuil returned to Canada, he explained that while the Mohawk and Onondaga had declared for the English, they had made it clear to the Jesuit that "the English would derive no great benefit from their alliance."[4]

While Vaudreuil was not interested in pressing the issue with the Five Nations by going on the offensive, it was clear that the peace with New York had been ruptured along the Lake Champlain corridor. This in turn meant that the foremost post along this route, Fort Chambly, needed to be strengthened. To deal with this the governor ordered Josue Boisberthelot de Beaucours to construct a regular stone fortification over the site of the current wooden one. The fort was only to be capable of withstanding light artillery fire, primarily because it was considered unlikely that the English could haul heavy cannon over Lake Champlain. Beaucours laid out the new Fort Chambly in a square with three-story-tall bastions at each of its corners. Thirty-foot high curtain walls constructed of limestone and masonry linked the bastions together making the entire structure approximately 170 feet to a side. A fortified entrance was placed on the west wall facing the Chambly Basin. The bastions and the wall along the side facing the Richelieu River were pierced for cannon, and firing ports were set into the four-foot-thick walls. Long buildings were built against the east, south, and west walls, which served as storehouses, workshops, and barracks. Powder magazines and covered wells within the lower parts of the bastions completed the works. When the stone structure was finally finished a few years later Vaudreuil informed the minister of the marine that Fort Chambly was "now beyond insult."[5]

Elsewhere the governor continued his work on Quebec and Montreal, not convinced that the English wouldn't return the following year. He reported that the defensive works at Quebec, while well thought out, proceeded too slowly, and he pleaded to Paris for powder, arms, trade goods, and men, pointing out that the twenty-eight companies of marines under his command now only averaged thirty men a company instead of fifty. To compound matters, rumors began arriving that there was unrest between the Sac and Ottawa that threatened to break out into a war. In all, it had proven a trying year, but when an Onondaga delegation arrived after the first snows seeking peace, Vaudreuil held out hope that 1710 would be a better.[6]

For Dudley, Vetch, Nicholson, and everyone else involved in the campaign of 1709, it had been a calamity. Sickness had claimed far more than French muskets, and nothing beyond the construction and destruction of several forts on the New York frontier had been accomplished. All involved looked to dismiss the year as if it had never happened. Massachusetts was hard pressed to pay and supply the forces on hand with the annual costs for defending the frontier and seaboard being close to £30,000. The failed expedition had doubled this sum, but the colony had cheerfully paid this, Dudley informed the Board of Trade, "in hopes, Her Majesty, if the war continues, will be pleased to revive that expedition in the Spring."[7]

The Massachusetts Assembly asked Nicholson to travel to London and make the case for resuming the expedition next spring. Peter Schuyler also traveled to London accompanied by several Iroquois sachems. They too looked to plead the case for renewing the campaign in the spring of 1710. These endeavors appeared fruitful when Secretary of State Sunderland agreed to resuscitate the campaign. This time, however, at Nicholson's urging, he included an attack on Port Royal before a descent on Quebec. He sent Nicholson back to Boston in May with orders to raise the colonial contingent, while a British fleet and five regiments of regulars under General Richard Shannon would be assembled and dispatched to Boston in a few months. If all went well this British force would combine with its colonial counterpart, advance on Port Royal, and after its capture set sail for Quebec. The secretary, however, wisely realized that Shannon's troops might not arrive in time and gave Nicholson a sizable detachment, which when combined with the colonial efforts in Boston would still be able to seize Port Royal.

Nicholson dropped anchor in Boston Harbor on July 15. He immediately called together the governors of New England and New York and read them his orders. Few had faith that a British fleet would appear, but at the very least it seemed that Port Royal was to be dealt with. To ensure this part of the plan Nicholson brought with him a regiment of Royal Marines, the fifty-gun warships HMS *Dragon* and HMS *Falmouth*, the thirty-six-gun frigate HMS *Feversham*, the thirty-two-gun frigate HMS *Lowestoft*, and perhaps more importantly, the bomb ship *Starr*. This force alone was enough to take Fort Royal, but to ensure success, it was to be augmented by a thousand colonial troops provided for by New York and the New England colonies via a quota Sunderland had laid down.

It was a tall order to muster so many troops so late in the year, but Governor Dudley was able to report in early September that nine hundred men had been assembled at Boston, enticed in part by the advancement of a month's pay and an agreement that they could keep their government-issued arms after the campaign was over. Transports, and particularly provisions and siege guns, took longer than expected. The provisions were eventually had at inflated prices, while the two Royal Engineers in the expedition, Captain Alexander Forbes and Captain Redknap, who was serving as a volunteer, built field carriages for the expedition's siege train of ten heavy guns taken from Castle William and Fort William and Mary.

A change in English government brought a new secretary of state, William Legge, the Earl of Dartmouth. The delays and inevitable confusion such a transfer of power brings meant that Dartmouth did not consider the British component of the Quebec campaign until July. At this point it was a question of whether or not the fleet could reach Quebec and seize the city before the St. Lawrence began to ice over. After consulting with someone familiar on the subject, who demonstrated his lack of expertise by informing the new secretary of state that operations before Quebec were possible up through November, Dartmouth ordered the five regiments to Portsmouth and directed the navy to provide the transports and warships for the expedition.[8]

These forces had yet to be assembled when in late August Dartmouth realized that the delay was likely fatal to the campaign. Still hoping to salvage some victory from the effort he wrote the colonial governments expressing his regrets that plans to dispatch this force had been laid aside due to contrary winds and other important services. Plans for an expedition next year were being considered, but in the interim the attack on Port Royal should proceed with the forces on hand in Boston.

The message would not arrive in time, but it did not matter. By late September it was agreed that even if the British fleet did arrive it was too late to attack Quebec. As such, Nicholson and the colonial governors decided to move forward with the attack on Port Royal. The troops were embarked as well as any last-minute supplies, to include fifty barrels of powder for the siege train, and on September 29 the fleet of half a dozen warships and thirty transports raised sail. Six days later the flotilla dropped anchor in Port Royal Basin, having already suffered their most significant loss in the campaign when the small schooner *Caesar* ran aground near the entrance to the Basin and was dashed against the rocks by wind and wave with the loss of twenty-six men.[9]

For Governor Subercase the flotilla was an ominous sight. He had perhaps three hundred men at his disposal, assuming that at least some of the local militia would respond to his call in such a one-sided affair. His fort was a crumbling mess, covered with patches and makeshift sandbag solutions. He had not been properly supplied in several years and was short on almost every element needed to defend the stronghold. The commandant had continually requested men and supplies, but at the same time he had sent back seventy men that Vaudreuil had sent a few months before, likely because of an inability to feed these reinforcements.

Whatever the case, it was perhaps for the best. The next morning English detachments came ashore on both sides of the river. On the south shore

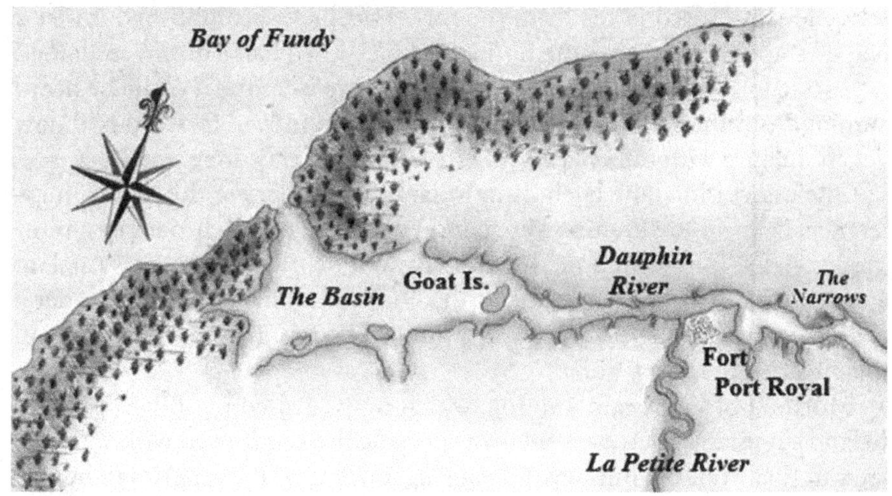


Port Royal, Nova Scotia, and the surrounding area.

Colonel Robert Reading and Captain Redknap came ashore below the fort with two hundred marines, while on the north shore Vetch and Captain Forbes landed with a company of grenadiers. With both sites secured Nicholson gave the order for the main army to land. Colonel Tailor's and Colonel Walton's provincial regiments were sent to the north shore while the rest of the army led by Nicholson landed on the south shore a few hours before sunset. After marshaling together their forces, both detachments advanced to the beat of the drum.

Even if he had wanted to Subercase didn't dare oppose the landing, fearing that many of his men would desert at the first opportunity. Instead he trained the fort's guns on the advancing columns. The cannonballs tore through the foliage and one passed quite near Colonel Reading at the head of his regiment but did little else. At dusk both Vetch's and Nicholson's detachments halted for the night. The former was almost directly across the river from the fort, while the latter had taken a position on the east bank of the Petite River.[10]

Subercase had sent out several patrols that skirmished with Nicholson's men, but when dawn came the English formed their ranks and advanced to within a mile of the fort. The stronghold's guns barked in defiance and scattered musket fire came from the nearby houses, but it did little to dissuade the enemy who encamped for the evening. Nicholson sent an advance guard forward with orders to push in the enemy pickets and entrench themselves four hundred paces from the fort. This they accomplished under a hail of grapeshot and small arms fire which claimed half a dozen casualties.

As Nicholson's men dug in, the hollow thump of mortars could be heard coming from the river. The bomb ship *Starr* had moved forward and now began dueling with Subercase's guns. No damage was done on either side, but the effort did allow Nicholson to land his artillery without any interference. Later in the evening Vetch and Forbes led a detachment of a hundred men to Spur Point directly across from the fort. The plan was to plant a dozen small Coehorn mortars at this location to bring the fort under a constant fire, but the distance was found to be too great and the ground unsuited for the guns.

Morning brought rain and fog, which only covered the English efforts to land supplies. Subercase kept up a sporadic fire and dueled with the *Starr* later in that evening, but beyond causing a handful of casualties there was nothing he could do to prevent the enemy from raising batteries for the siege guns they had brought ashore. This task was hampered by rainy weather for several days, but by October 12 Forbes and Redknap had set up three batteries of guns only a few hundred yards from the fort's walls. In keeping with tradition, a chorus of trumpets and drums filled the air for a few minutes before the command to fire echoed from each of the batteries. Cannonballs struck the stronghold's walls, sending up clouds of dirt and masonry, while mortar rounds burst overhead and within its confines.[11]

Nicholson halted the barrage after a few volleys and under a flag of truce sent Colonel Tailor with a surrender summons. The militia within the fort had already petitioned Subercase to surrender, and with nothing to be gained by continuing the one-sided affair, he agreed to seek terms. Nicholson granted the garrison full honors of war and transport back to France as a salute to their gallant defense. As for the local citizens, if they took an oath of allegiance to Queen Anne they were free to keep their land and possessions, otherwise they had to depart within a year. Subercase accepted the generous terms and the capitulation was signed a few days later.[12]

For the English and especially Dudley, it was the victory that had eluded them for years. As it turned out fears about the strength of the French stronghold proved unfounded. Excluding the wreck of the *Caesar*, Nicholson's casualties had been light with some thirty killed or wounded. Port Royal was quickly renamed Annapolis Royal and heralds sent out to spread the good news. Dudley perhaps summarized the victory best. Port Royal, he informed the queen, which had "been these seven years the great pest and trouble of all Navigation and Trade of your Majesty's provinces on the coast of North America" was no more.[13]

On the French side, there was criticism regarding Subercase's release of the reinforcements sent to him by Vaudreuil, but given the circumstances the governor admitted that it would not have changed the outcome. "I am fully convinced, My Lord," Vaudreuil wrote the minister of the marine, "that, whatever resistance he could make, having only the garrison with him, he would be overpowered by superior force. This is a justice that I feel obliged to render him; but nevertheless, I cannot help complaining of the little attention he has paid to the reiterated notices I sent him that he was to be besieged." Indeed, the warnings were crucial, but outnumbered ten to one in a fort that was falling down around him, short of food and powder, and surrounded by a garrison that might desert on a moment's notice, perhaps what is more surprising is that Subercase was able to secure any surrender terms at all.[14]

CHAPTER TWENTY-FIVE

# Walker's Expedition

Soon after the captured French garrison of Port Royal was marched out of the fort's main gates a detachment of 450 marines and colonial volunteers took their place. The Union flag was raised and Vetch was named governor of the town. Stores, arms, and provisions were transferred into the stronghold before the fleet departed for Boston a few days later with the details of their conquest.

Also departing was Major John Livingston and St. Castin. Livingston was carrying a letter to Vaudreuil informing him of Subercase's surrender and the treatment of the garrison. The letter also contained a warning from Nicholson and Vetch. If the governor continued to attack the New England frontier, "inhumanly murthering a great many poor inocent people, and children," there would be reprisals against the French inhabitants of Acadia, which were now at the mercy of the English. "But as we abhor the barbarietys of your savage war," the English leaders informed the French governor, "we hope you will give us no occasion to coppy after you in this respects."[1]

Livingston, Castin, and a handful of Micmac guides were carried to Penobscot Bay. Here they acquired canoes and ascended the Penobscot River. The first day of the journey a canoe accidentally capsized in the frigid waters. One of the guides drowned and Livingston lost his musket and all of his supplies. It was a bad omen that would cause some to mutter, for good reason as it turned out. It was a grueling trip in the late fall weather.

Rapids, ice jams, and obstacles forced them to carry their canoes for miles in the growing blanket of snow. They broke what ice they could and eventually abandoned their leaking vessels and set out on snowshoes. The party then encountered a chain of lakes. Most were only partially frozen at this point, forcing the detachment to march around the obstructions, but they agreed to brave one by advancing on the thin ice on their stomachs, a long pole clutched in their hands as they inched forward. Later, out of food and exhausted, the detachment discovered that they had walked in a circle. After a series of draining marches, the end appeared near until a wigwam was suddenly discovered and refuge found. It was also discovered they were near the St. Lawrence, and within a few days' time Livingston would find himself before Governor Vaudreuil.

Vaudreuil was measured in his response to Nicholson's and Vetch's demands. When Livingston pressed for the release of Reverend Williams's daughter, the governor informed him that it was not in his power to secure her. The same was true of all the English held by the Indians; they were his allies, and as such, he held no power over them in these matters. He could inquire and that was all. In regard to abandoning the *petite guerre*, the governor said little because he had no intentions of complying. Instead, he commissioned St. Castin as a lieutenant in the marines and sent him back to Acadia. St. Castin had a good deal of influence over the Wabanaki of the region, and the governor planned on using this. The new lieutenant was ordered to rally the Wabanaki and the French settlers of the region and conduct a guerrilla campaign against the English, who in reality only controlled everything within a cannon shot of their fort.

With the matter addressed Vaudreuil turned to greater concerns. A war with the Iroquois, or at least the four eastern nations, would be devastating to the colony, particularly given its weakened state. Had the issue been clearer Vaudreuil might have struck first, but while the four Iroquois nations had claimed to side with the English there had yet to be a clash of arms with the French. Even so, the situation was grave enough that Vaudreuil thought it wise to call upon the support of the high-country nations. With the Seneca firmly entrenched in neutrality, these reinforcements would not only increase his strength but would also place the pro-English Iroquois in the undesirable position of starting a wider war with New France's allies—one that they had previously lost and one that would likely not include the powerful Seneca this time. Voyageurs were sent west with the call, and Vaudreuil sent emissaries to the eastern Iroquois in the spring explaining that they had nothing to fear from the high-country nations coming down to Montreal, so long as they abided by the Treaty of Montreal. "But at the same time," the governor warned the Iroquois, "they had everything to fear from these Nations and my just vengeance, if, contrary to the neutrality we had agreed on, they should take up the hatchet against us in favor of the English."[2]

With the fall of Port Royal Nicholson was anxious to return to England and press for a campaign against Quebec. The general carried with him letters from the New England governments and several prominent citizens all speaking to the same matter. All thanked the queen for her support in the taking of Port Royal, and all pleaded for a strike against Quebec and Montreal in the spring. As one representative from Massachusetts put the matter, "no settled repose is to be expected till Canada (the American Carthage) is subdued." The New England colonies were ready to support such a measure even though the war had already worn heavily upon them. Requests were made of Her Majesty to place a quota on the colonies as far south as Virginia and to enact the previous plan of 1709.

This time, the words were spoken in a more receptive environment. The old plan was revived and the French colony at Placentia was added as well. In early April 1711 Rear Admiral Hovenden Walker was tasked with commanding the naval portion of the expedition, while Brigadier General John "Jack" Hill would command the land forces. The troops assembled at Plymouth, England, in late April, and by May 3 the fleet of eleven warships and forty-one transports was ready. Colonel Richard King, who had been appointed chief engineer and quartermaster general for the expedition, had overseen loading of the munition vessels and the artillery train which consisted of twelve twenty-four-pounders, eight twelve-pounders, four eight-inch mortars, and four petards. Hill's six regular regiments boarded shortly thereafter and the next morning the force set sail. The weather scattered a number of vessels, but by late June the bulk of the flotilla had dropped anchor at Boston.

The New England and New York governments were completely unprepared for Walker's arrival, having only received news of the expedition when Nicholson arrived at Boston with supplies for the Lake Champlain component of the expedition a few weeks before. The miscommunication led to confusion and numerous delays. "For as this Fleet did not come two years ago and last year as they were assur'd they would," King wrote of the problem, "they did not expect it or believe it was arriv'd here." While the colonies scrambled to assemble their men and naval forces, the sea-weary Redcoats encamped on Noddle's Island, where "the ground was dry, the water good, and the air sweet and refreshing."[3]

One of the first issues to be resolved was the departure of a pair of transports for New York. These vessels, which carried the supplies, munitions,

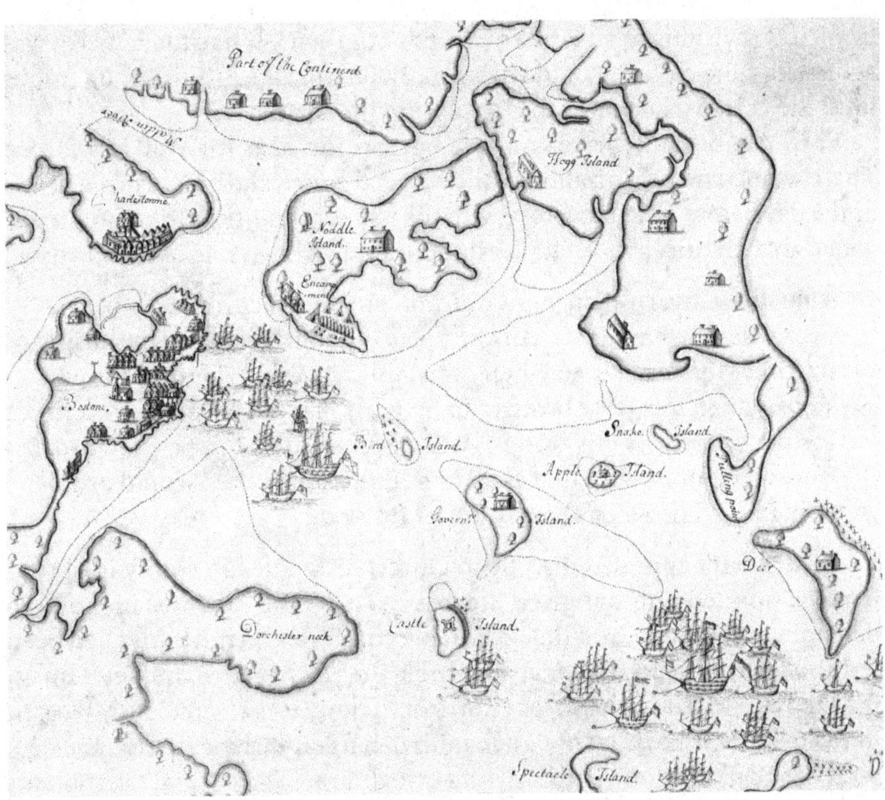


Boston Harbor, 1711. The map shows the passages into the harbor, the newly errected Fort William on Castle Island, and the British troop encampment on Noddle's Island. (*Boston Public Library*)

and clothing for Nicholson's Lake Champlain expedition, had arrived ahead of the fleet under the protection of a pair of warships, but for some reason Nicholson, who arrived with them, had not ordered the craft to proceed to New York City. Nicholson was currently in New London laying out the details of the Lake Champlain expedition with a number of colonial governors, so Walker instructed the HMS *Chester* to convoy these transports to New York, but they were so ill-prepared for the voyage that it would be almost a week before they were ready to set sail.[4]

Just as pressing were provisions for the troops encamped at Noddle's Island and the promised three months' worth of provisions for the upcoming expedition. Scrambling after the fleet's arrival, the Massachusetts government promised to "make the utmost dispatch in raising the troops and providing the other necessarys they were to furnish and oblige the country to bring in provisions of all kinds to refresh our men." To facilitate this, it was agreed that the colony would advance £3,000 to subsist the arriving troops until the colonial assembly met to take up the matter.

Each day became more frustrating than the next for Walker's forces. There seemed no organization to the colonial effort, and each day the delays of the day before rolled together with the issues of moment to create an impenetrable logistical knot. "It plainly appeared," King wrote of the situation,

> That the Government here did not put in execution any of the promisses they made us. For the bread we contracted for, to subsist our men during our stay here, was not deliver'd. The fresh provisions, which was to be brought in, in great plenty, was not sufficient for the quarter of our troops. And all other things to be provided, were brought us with that sloth and indifference, there could be no fixing any time when they would be finish'd.[5]

General Hill appealed directly to Governor Dudley to rectify the problem. He pointed out that given the loss of trade, the expenses incurred in defending the colony, and the deplorable condition their frontier had been reduced to after years of French and Indian raids that one "could not imagine they would defeat this great effort her Majesty was so graciously pleased to make in their favor by not giving provisions and whatever else was necessary for carrying on vigorously the expedition." The general's comments appeared to have worked as Dudley contracted a pair of local merchants, William and Francis Clarke, to work with Massachusetts commissary Belcher on supplying the needs of the fleet. Two other officials were assigned to see to the needs of the encampment at Noddle's Island.[6]

While there now appeared some order to the New England efforts it literally came at a price. The contractors informed Admiral Walker that they could provide the needed supplies, but they refused to honor the normal exchange rate from British pounds to colonial species. Both Walker and Hill complained about the practice and the matter was addressed when the Massachusetts Assembly met on July 5 and set the exchange rate at 140 percent, which was noted as "10 to 15 percent less than it usually is at, but our necessities oblig'd both our General and Admiral to accept this rate."[7]

On July 17 good news arrived from New York. The two stores ships from Boston had arrived. Governor Robert Hunter reported that the troops raised for General Nicholson's expedition had been assembled and that the small boats and other provisions needed were being forwarded to Albany. If all went well Nicholson's force would be ready by the end of the month. The news accelerated the preparations among the fleet and land forces. Most of July was spent loading provisions and preparing the fleet to sail. Materials to build firing platforms for the guns were stowed on the vessels assigned to the ordnance train, as were several siege engines King had built. There was a brief delay when one of the transports that carried three hundred men from Kirk's regiment was found to be in such poor condition that it could not make the voyage, but the matter was quickly rectified by chartering two smaller vessels from local merchants.

While progress was being made as far as material preparations another problem had emerged: desertion. Within the span of a month some 250 English sailors and soldiers had disappeared into the colonial landscape. "I had almost forgot to mention one grievance we met with here, which is insupportable especially on such an occasion as this," King informed London. "'Tis the encouragement given here by the people to deserters, and the severe Acts of Parliament against land or sea forces making any reprizal; I mean to recruit and compleat their respective compliments. This hardship falls very heavy on the Naval Force, as its more frequently here." Walker and Hill complained to the governor and the assembly that the populace was complicit in this behavior and that measures needed to be enacted to halt the trend.[8]

For their part the assembly and the governor had previously enacted laws addressing "Enticing, Harboring, Concealing, or Conveying away of Deserters," which was punishable by a fine of £25 and six months imprisonment for each instance, but seeing that this ordinance was having little effect, they passed an additional resolution that called for "a more Speedy Prosecution of Offenders" in mid-July, which now included a reward system. A few days later on July 16, Governor Dudley took a much firmer stance on the matter and called out the militia of eighteen towns to monitor the roads and "examine all strangers and travelers," in hopes of deterring those aiding in the desertions. While Walker and Hill approved of the effort, by now such actions made little difference and the matter was eventually handled by ordering all the seamen and troops back onto the transports on July 20.[9]

A few days later Walker was surprised by visitors. A delegation of three Iroquois sachems had arrived. The chieftains marveled at the assembled flotilla, now well over sixty strong, and admitted that they were surprised to see it "for this fleet did not come two years ago or last year as they were assured it would." Having toured the ships and seeing the huge number of men they held, the sachems informed Walker and Hill that they were now convinced of their ally's commitment to pursue the war against the French. Knowing this they would wholeheartedly join the cause and rendezvous with Nicholson's men at Albany, but they warned the admiral to hurry or "the fine season would be over before we could finish our expedition."[10]

Walker was not concerned. Although the delays had caused him to postpone the attack on Placentia, it was agreed that this isolated post could be dealt with at a later time. At the moment it was still July, and the fleet was ready to sail. This would easily put him before Quebec by this time next month. Once before the city Walker and Hill would turn the operation over to King. The Royal Engineer, drawing upon his experiences in Flanders under Marlborough, had already sketched out plans to forward provisions, erect magazines, and secure the path of the army's march. He had also seen to the distribution of landing craft among the fleet and the proportion of men to each craft and arranged a set of signals to be used during landing operations. The plan was to invest Quebec the same day the landings were made, the latter likely in the same location as Phipps had chosen given the limited number of options. To facilitate this, King was to land in advance of the army with fifty men in order to determine the best approach over the St. Charles River toward the fortress. The main body would then advance along these lines and invest the town under the cover fire of Walker's impressive array of warships.

Unlike Port Royal it would not be easy. Several eyewitness reports confirmed that the defenses of Quebec were "very strong, and the avenues leading to it from the River choak'd with woods, rocks, and precipices." To deal with these potential obstacles King procured a team of thirty horses and ordered a crane and a number of siege engines built "to surmount any difficulties of that nature we shall meet with." The engineer did not believe that taking the French stronghold would be easy, given its natural advantages, but he was convinced that with resolve and a systematic approach that they could be overcome.[11]

The colonial troops embarked aboard their vessels the next day. The senior British officers marveled at the disorder and haphazard manner in which this was accomplished. Some of the colonial ships did not even have crews, while others lacked simple necessities such as sailing equipment and beds for the troops they would be carrying. It was a logistical nightmare that would take a week to sort out. King groaned at the latest delay. "All has been done with indolence and indifference," he penned in his journal.

> It being evident to anybody that has seen this country, that they could fit out and man twice the number of vessels they were to furnish for this Expedition in much less time than they have had to do it in. Therefore I can't imagine what their designs could be by all

> these delays if they were not to delay us here, till the advanc'd season of the year will probably defeat us. And what almost confirms me in this opinion is, that it's certain that those who ride and proffit by their present dissorderly Governmt. now see how reasonable it is to change: that the conquest of Canada will naturally lead the Queen into it: and shew her how absolutely necessary it is to put all this Northern Continent of America under one form of Government for the real good of the present Coloneys.[12]

Seven sloops loaded with supplies arrived from New York a few days later, which gave the fleet the three months of provisions Admiral Walker had requested. By July 29 the New England vessels had been manned and early the next morning over seventy Royal Navy and colonial vessels carrying some 6,500 troops and 4,500 sailors put out to sea under a brisk southwestern wind.[13]

Nicholson was once again chosen to lead the Montreal element of the plan. The expedition was a near duplicate of the first. New York, New Jersey, Connecticut, and Pennsylvania were called upon to supply men, money, and materials toward the effort. And as before, Pennsylvania balked at the idea. The remaining colonies, however, raised their contingents, and by late August some fifteen hundred troops were encamped in and about Albany.[14] Added to this were some eight hundred Iroquois who had pledged their support to the cause.

On August 27 Nicholson ordered his colonial troops forward. The next day he followed with the Iroquois contingent and a handful of Mohegan volunteers. Detachments began rebuilding the storehouses and forts between Albany and Wood Creek, while others revived the old supply lines. The same supply issues existed, but this time things went smoother, no doubt aided by the previous experience. At Wood Creek a new fort was erected. Named in honor of the queen, Fort Anne was a simple palisade fort with bastions at the four corners and a number of small buildings clustered within its interior. By mid-September Nicholson had amassed several hundred boats here, along with the bulk of his forces, his artillery, and enough supplies to move forward. The encampments about the fort began to take on a hurried excitement. Supplies were moved down to the boats, ammunition and provisions allotted to the troops, and orders drawn for the passage of the army onto the lake. Given that the fleet was known to have left Boston a few weeks earlier, for all involved it seemed that the moment was finally at hand.[15]

On August 14 Walker's fleet was a few miles from the Island of Anticosti near the mouth of the St. Lawrence River. Progress had gone so well that talk began to circulate about an attack on Placentia in the event that Quebec fell quickly. This seemed even more likely after the HMS *Chester* rejoined Walker's fleet with a small prize in tow. King spoke at length with the master of this captured vessel who was from Placentia. While the captain's information regarding the French colony was of use, it was the fact that he had navigated the St. Lawrence to Quebec forty times that caught the engineer's attention. The expedition had not been able to obtain enough seasoned pilots before they left, leaving King to inform Walker and Hill that the Frenchman was likely the best pilot they had on hand and that something should be done to elicit his services. The two men agreed and Walker offered the French captain five hundred pistols "if he would carry us up to Quebec." When he saw some hesitation in the Frenchman's face, he sweetened the deal, informing the mariner that he "would find a way to make up all his losses." The admiral then ordered a hundred pistols be delivered to the French captain immediately. The offer had the desired effect and the Frenchman remained with Walker aboard the HMS *Edgar* for the rest of the expedition.[16]

Governor Vaudreuil traveled to Montreal in the summer of 1711. Here he was delighted to meet five hundred men of the high-country nations who had come down to honor his request. Onondaga and Seneca representatives soon arrived as well. The former warned Vaudreuil that there was an English army forming at Albany and that an English fleet had sailed from Boston for Quebec. The governor thanked the representative for the information, which agreed with reports coming from other English prisoners regarding the size and strength of Walker's force. He informed the representatives that he did not wish war with the four eastern Iroquois nations, but he would not shrink from it should they attack. To make the point, the next day he held a war banquet for over eight hundred high-country and mission Indians in front of the Iroquois delegates. Soon the war song was being sung as the mission Indians and Nipissings struck at the war pole. The high-country nations showed some reluctance until a score of Huron from Detroit set up a cry and joined the fray. The ice broke and a swirling mass of freshly painted bronze warriors danced about the pole, soon joined by a large number of Canadians, bush runners, and officers of the marine. Vaudreuil glanced at the Iroquois but said nothing. He did not have to: the message was clear.

The Iroquois delegation departed shortly thereafter and so too did the governor. The reports of the English efforts had forced him to raise the alarm. He called out the militia and ordered work accelerated on the fortifications of Quebec and Montreal. As the first of these was the one most

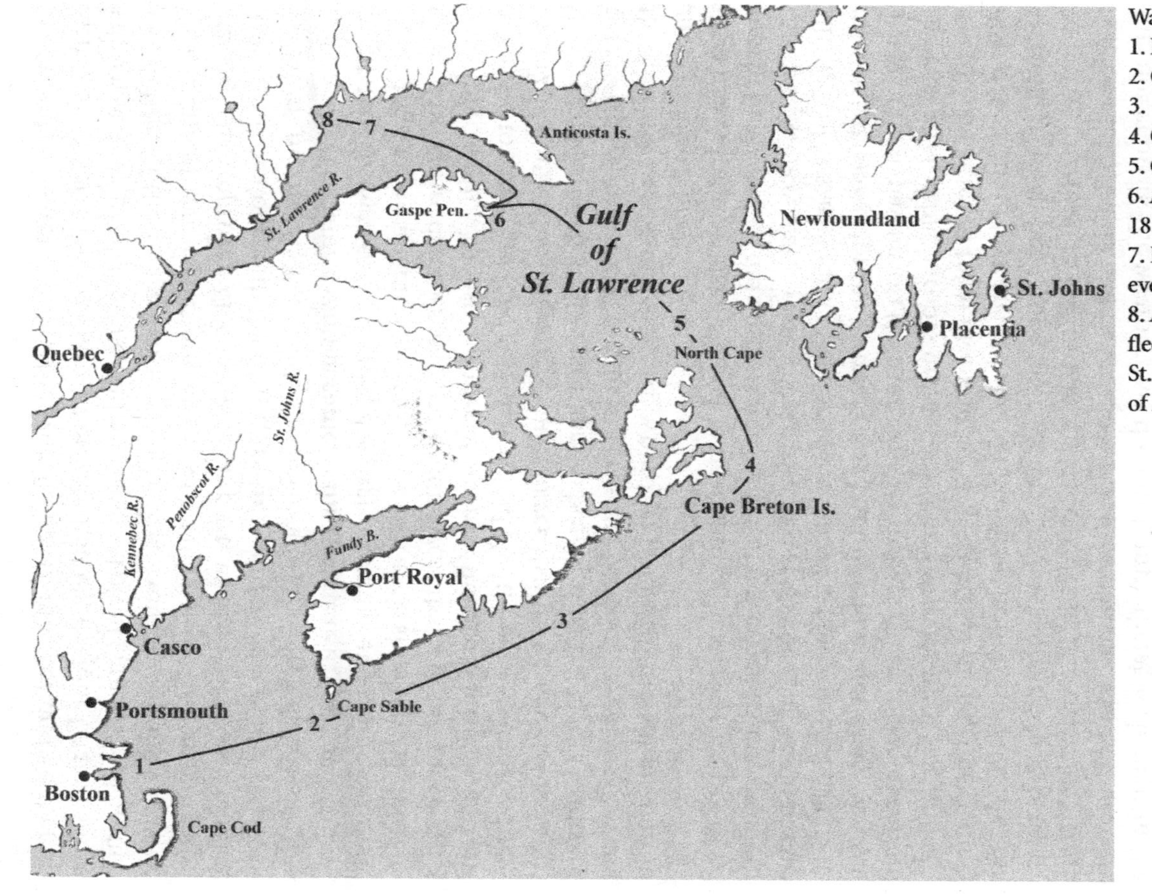


Walker's Expedition, 1711.
1. Fleet departs Boston, July 30.
2. Cape Sable, August 3.
3. Off Nova Scotia, August 8.
4. Off Cape Breton, August 10.
5. Off North Cape, August 12.
6. Anchored at Gaspee, August 18 to 20.
7. Fleet halts at dusk on the evening of August 23.
8. A gale wrecks elements of the fleet on the north shore of the St. Lawrence River on the night of August 23-24.

threatened the governor returned with Ramezay and six hundred men in early September. News had already arrived that eighty-four English ships, a dozen or so ships-of-the-line, had been spotted off of Gaspe. Word of such a large fleet in the St. Lawrence set off a near panic among the citizenry. Vaudreuil sent war parties out along both banks of the St. Lawrence and manned the improved defenses at Beauport, where Phipps had landed, while families along with their livestock were sent to hide in the woods. In the meantime, the 3,500 defenders toiled away at the city's defenses.

It now just became a waiting game. If the reports reaching Vaudreuil regarding the strength of the English fleet were accurate, and many were quite close, it was a dire situation for the colony. Just a few ships-of-the-line outgunned his entire defenses, and indications were that a dozen such vessels were approaching. English numbers, five or six thousand regulars, and another two to three thousand colonials, would give the enemy almost a three-to-one advantage in manpower—manpower that they could use to invest the city and bring their heavy artillery to bear against the town's landward defenses. Surrounded and caught in a crossfire between the enemy fleet and their army's siege guns, the town would be pounded into submission in short order.

While Admiral Walker seemed to have found the experienced pilot he sought in Boston, he did not necessarily like what the man had to say about the St. Lawrence. Major vessels never wintered at Quebec but would hazard all forms of obstacles rather than being ice bound for the winter, the Frenchman stated, and as for the form of these hazards and obstacles, he was well aware of them having lost two vessels in his voyages. Steep rocky shores and the lack of suitable harbors or bays for long stretches were two impediments. The latter of these meant that a ship had to sit in the river channel overnight. This in turn created another problems he informed the admiral, given that, "It has been impossible for any Person, by their strictest Observations, hitherto to know the Currents and Tides in the River, the Stream being violently rapid and fierce, as well as uncertain, in most Places." Were this not enough, the weather was the most unpredictable element in the trek. Storms and heavy fog were so frequent that they "might well be esteemed continual." Combined with the tricky currents and lack of shelter, the French captain reported that "he had several times expencnc'd upon his lying by (which he was very often constrained to do in dark Nights and foggy Weather) That when they might expect themselves on the North, they should find they were driven on the South Shoar, and so on the contrary."[17]

The fleet anchored in the Bay of Gaspe on August 18 to wait out bad weather and contrary winds. None of the pilots dared enter the river under such conditions. On the twentieth the signal was given to return to sea, but little progress was made. This changed when the wind shifted on the twenty-second and the fleet made an impressive thirty-four miles up the St. Lawrence. The twenty-third proved even more productive as rain and a fresh gale from the east pushed the task force another forty-five miles. By nightfall, however, matters had taken a turn for the worse. Bands of fog, rain, and heavy winds battered the fleet and it was "so excessively dark," one witness recalled "that we could not see from one end to the other of our vessel." Onboard the HMS *Edgar* Walker and his pilots were debating what to do. The poor conditions had made it difficult to fix the fleet's position on the river and it was too dark to see either shore. All agreed that it was clearly too dangerous to proceed, so at eight o'clock Walker signaled the fleet to turn their bows south, and under just mizzen and main topsail lay across the river perpendicular to the wind. The thought was that at worst the fleet would drift slightly to the southwest, but for the most part the wind and the current would nullify each other and keep the fleet in the main channel.[18]

A few hours later on board the HMS *Windsor*, the ship's bells had just finished ringing out five times when a lookout cried out, land to starboard! Fooled by the distance the warship's captain raised every inch of sail the vessel had, but it was only delaying the inevitable. The rising winds were pushing the vessel toward the north shore. With rocks and breakers to either side of the vessel the captain ordered the anchor thrown out in seven fathoms of water near Isle aux Oeuf (Egg Island). Even with this the ship appeared doomed. "Till the minute we came to an anchor it rained very hard and blew a perfect storm directly on shore, when all of a sudden it fell quite calm," King recalled. "If it had continu'd with the great violence it did before we came to an anchor; our anchors could not have held and we should have all been lost. For the wind and the vast seas which ran would have broke our ship in a moment in ten thousand pieces against the rocks."[19]

Onboard the *Edgar*, Walker had been roused out of his sleep and came up on deck in his gown and slippers. He found the deck crew in great confusion claiming they had seen land to starboard. "I called out as loud as I could to quiet the Men," the admiral recalled. Assuring them "that I saw no Land to Leeward, the Moon just then breaking out, and the Fog clearing up and when the Pilot came, he told me it was the North Shoar, being what we least expected." Hearing this Walker ordered every square inch of sail to be raised and the vessel stood out into the main channel.[20]

The *Windsor* held its position until the wind shifted later that morning. It was a frightful scene as the warship inched its way back out into the river.

"All the night we heard nothing but ships firing and showing lights as in the utmost distress," King recalled. "So that we could not but conclude that the greatest part of our Fleet was lost; and indeed there were not 10 ships in the whole that were not in danger of being cast away." Massachusetts commissary Sampson Sheaf, aboard a New England vessel not far away agreed, later testifying that he could "hear the shrieks of the sinking, drowning, departing souls" throughout the night.[21]

By morning the devastation had become clear. What the French could not have hoped to accomplish in a month, the St. Lawrence had accomplished in a few hours. In all eight vessels had been dashed against the rocky north shore, seven of them troop transports. The smaller vessels in the fleet spent the next few days pulling exhausted men off the north shore and combing the nearby waters for any other survivors. Their efforts saved 499 men, but the loss was staggering: over 700 soldiers from 26 different infantry companies and perhaps another 150 sailors.

A council of war was called on August 25 to discuss the expedition's next move. While Walker still had his warships and over five thousand troops at his disposal, as well as a fine train of artillery, there was little doubt as to the outcome. The pilots were questioned one at a time, and to a man they said they did not think they could take the fleet to Quebec. Even the captain of the captured French sloop pointed out that given the season "it would be very difficult and he could not answer for it." The event had shattered the expedition's spirit, and soon it was "unanimously agreed that it was not practicable to go up the River with this Fleet so late in the season without Pilates (Pilots)."[22]

It meant the end for the 1711 campaign against Quebec. For a time, there was talk of deploying the fleet against Placentia, but a shortage of provisions and the anticipated stiff resistance by the French, who would be able to call upon several thousand men of the seasonal fishing fleet still in port, led to this plan being abandoned as well. With little else to be done Walker sent news to Boston and New York to recall Nicholson's army and set sail for England. As the fleet made its way home King pondered on what the failure of the expedition meant for the colonies. "I can't express the greatness of my concern for the disappointment," he wrote Secretary St. John,

> Nor the uneasiness it gives me to think what a loss it will prove to our poor American Coloneys, how much it will contribute to depopulate their frontiers: to diminish their trade and discourage all people by the constant wars they must now be oblig'd to maintain, from settling among them or improving the lands. And what is still

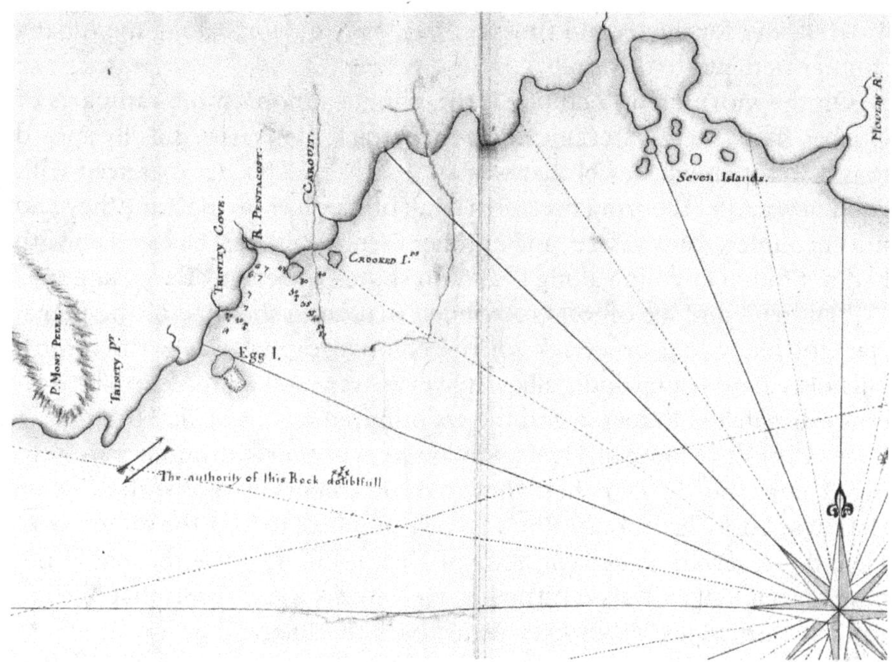


A portion of a map of the St. Lawrence River showing the location of Egg Island and the nearby northern shore. (*Library of Congress*)

> a more melancholy reflextion, that they dare hardly expect any relief for the future, when they see this great effort England made to succour them thus ruffled and defeated.[23]

With his preparations near complete, Nicholson received an express from the governor of New York. He could hardly believe his eyes as the words confronted him. The English fleet had wrecked along the banks of the St. Lawrence in bad weather. Seven transports and nearly seven hundred men had been lost in the calamity. The admiral and his council had elected to abandon the attack on Quebec. Nicholson was advised to abandon his expedition as well. It was too much for the able officer. Enraged, he tore the express in two, but not satisfied with this he turned to his wig. His wig, however, proved too durable, so in frustration he flung it to the ground and stamped on it, all the while shouting a string of insults toward his naval counterparts. Nicholson's officers passed around the torn message as the general's fury finally abated into disgust. A council of war was held, but all knew its outcome. With the French now free to shift their entire strength toward Montreal, there was only one thing left to do. A general retreat was ordered, and for the second time in three years the forts along the Albany frontier were put to the torch.[24]

On the morning of October 7, the signal cannon on the ramparts of Quebec flared to life, freezing all in their tracks, but news quickly spread that it was a French vessel that was approaching. The *Heros* arrived with good news. After scouring the north bank of the river up to Gaspe they had not encountered any vessels, and another French ship they had spoken with had not found anything along the south shore. The enemy fleet was gone.

Vaudreuil and his officers concluded that given the time of the year it was not likely that an attack on the colonial capital was forthcoming. Nicholson and his Iroquois allies, however, were still a problem. The governor dispatched Ramezay and the six hundred troops he had brought to Quebec back to Montreal. He then followed in person with another six hundred troops shortly thereafter. These reinforcements merged with those on station at Fort Chambly, swelling French numbers to over three thousand. Here the governor waited for news of Nicholson. As it was, he would not have to wait long. Scouts returned in a few weeks with reports that Nicholson had burned his forts and retreated back to Albany.

Vaudreuil and his men celebrated and then breathed a collective sigh of relief. While they had been prepared to meet the enemy, the prospects did not look good, but as it had with the obstruction of Phipps in 1690 it appeared that the St. Lawrence had protected those along its banks. The minister of the marine Pontchartrain perhaps summed up the feeling best, "It is an interposition of Providence and a visible mark of its protection, for which the entire Colony ought to return God thanks."[25]

CHAPTER TWENTY-SIX

# The Last Days

In Placentia, Governor Costebelle had been alarmed by the news that Walker's fleet might target the colony, especially after their reported wreck in the St. Lawrence River. The war in Newfoundland had ground to a halt after the French abandoned St. John's in the spring of 1709. A few raiders still practiced their trade but in numbers too few and efforts too infrequent to make any difference. The English colonies were rebuilt, as were the fortifications which were manned with new troops and supported by an increased Royal Navy presence. The result was an explosion in the English fishing industry as the number of vessels visiting the colony steadily increased, and, of particular note, the number of colonist's vessels engaged in the trade nearly doubled within two years.

While the English colonies on the Avalon Peninsula flourished, Placentia languished. Weakened by privateers intercepting its supplies, desertion, and a deteriorating naval position, the outpost was in no position to risk any of its garrison on another grand adventure. Although there had been whispers regarding English plans to besiege Placentia, they had proven nothing more than speculation until word of Walker's force arrived. The reports sent Costebelle and the garrison into motion. Fortunately, the fishing fleet was still at port swelling the governor's ranks to a few thousand men. In addition, a pair of privateers and a small force of men were present. Costebelle had hoped to use these vessels to launch a surprise attack on Annapolis Royal, as Port Royal was now called, but this was now quickly laid aside. In the past such numbers would have deterred an attack on the French colony, but this time it might not matter. Even though they possessed over a dozen ships-of-the-line, it was unlikely the English would sail into the narrow confines of Placentia Harbor and conduct a point-blank duel with the fort and its supporting batteries. What was of more concern was that Walker's fleet was reputed to be carrying five thousand regular troops and artillery to besiege Quebec. If these troops and their guns were landed above or below the harbor and marched on the town, the outcome was nearly certain. Fortunately for Costebelle and his garrison, after a few tense weeks word finally arrived that Walker had returned to England, which left the colony free to resume a low-profile pattern for the remainder of the war.[1]

In Nova Scotia the conflict would settle to a simmer but not until after a number of sharp clashes. Although Nicholson had appointed Vetch governor of Annapolis Royal and the surrounding territory, in reality this only encompassed the length of a good cannon shot from the fort. The countryside was still teaming with Wabanaki and French settlers anxious to cast out the English invaders. Vaudreuil was of a like mind and determined to support them. He directed St. Castin, his lieutenant in Acadia, to do everything in his power "to keep the Indians of these districts in our interests and urge them to continue the war against the English." To assist in this the governor dispatched a pair of missionaries to incite the local Wabanaki and funneled what men and supplies he could spare into the region.

Castin and his second-in-command Charles-Henry de la Grois, the Marquis Dalogny, set their forces to work and skirmishes became common. "Wee have been much alarm'd all winter with designs of the Indians and French from Canada making an attempt on us," Vetch wrote London on June 14, 1711. The probing enemy was only part of the problem, as the onset of illness and desertion proved far more damaging with over a quarter of his garrison falling prey to one or the other. Just as trying were supply problems and the ruinous condition of the fort. Nicholson had left Captain Forbes at Annapolis Royal and tasked him with repairing the dilapidated stronghold. After surveying the structure Forbes marveled at the extent of the task before him. The ramparts, exposed to too many winters, were falling down and a new barracks needed to be constructed for the four hundred colonial troops that now made up the fort's garrison. Fortunately for the Royal Engineer he possessed both guns and manpower. The former he mounted on newly constructed firing platforms while the latter he put to work dealing with the fort's most glaring defects. "The Governor hath given orders for cutting 4000 sparrs to renew the pallisadoes of the covered way," Forbes reported to the Ordnance Board. "Which we are under an absolute necessity to do with all possible dispatch, lest the Indians and French here by the influence and assistance of their friends in Canada, should make any attempt upon us." The condition of the fort and the sheer amount of work to be done appeared overwhelming, but Vetch had faith in Forbes's abilities, informing the English court that, "as he is extreamly capable so he is indefatigably diligent."[2]

With the coming of spring Forbes turned to the more involved undertaking of rebuilding the fort's ramparts. Huge amounts of wood were needed for this and a dozen smaller tasks, but by mid-June the existing supply could not keep up with demand. The nearest stand of suitable trees was close to two miles away up the Riviere du Dauphin (Annapolis River). Here at the edge of the forest, trees were cut and floated down river to the fort. The local inhabitants did a great deal of this work, occasionally supplemented by a few of the fort's garrison, but a rash of threats from small French and Indian war parties in the area had all but halted the effort. To entice the inhabitants to return to work Vetch had sent Forbes and Major William Elliot along with sixty of the garrison to cover the work parties.

The detachment left in two large flat-bottom boats and a canoe which carried Forbes, Elliot, and several others. The vessels had almost reached the logging camp when they were ambushed by a large French and Indian war party hidden along the banks of the river. Forbes and the other occupants of the canoe were killed in the opening volleys. The English troops in the larger vessels landed in response to the fire, but the French and Indians, far better concealed and larger in number, kept them pinned down on the beach. With over a half of the detachment killed, wounded, or captured the order was given to withdraw, but it was too late. With the ring closing there was no choice but to surrender, and the entire detachment, with one exception, was taken captive.

After striking this unexpected blow against the enemy, Jesuit Father Antoine Gaulin gathered together over two hundred men and blockaded the English fort. With the stronghold invested, Gaulin wrote to Vaudreuil for men and then set sail for Placentia in search of powder and arms. Such thoughts, however, were short lived. Vetch had written Boston concerning his plight, and when the report reached Walker, the admiral dispatched the forty-gun HMS *Sapphire* and a large contingent of New England troops to relieve the garrison. With the influx of men and supplies into Annapolis Royal, and news that the supply vessel from Placentia had been captured, any thoughts of besieging the fort soon vanished and the French and Indian forces faded back into the countryside where they would remain for the rest of the conflict.[3]

Few were as relieved by Walker's failed attempt as the denizens of Quebec, but while the colonial capitol still remained in French hands, it like Newfoundland, was being weakened by its interdicted supply lines to France. Everything was in short supply: powder, arms, basic commodities, and trade goods for the allied nations. Taken together it created a dark mood among the French and their allies, many of whom had not responded to the alarm raised by the English fleet. "All these threats having made some impression on the minds of the Indians," Vaudreuil informed the minister of the marine, "and even on certain of the French who were apprehensive that the Indians would abandon us."[4]

While Vaudreuil was able to secure his allies and offset the apprehension generated by the English attack, a greater threat loomed with the actions of the Five Nations. The Onondaga, Cayuga, Oneida, and Mohawk had officially sided with the English. Fortunately, they had not done anything at this point that would break the peace treaty. As the summer of 1712 took hold it appeared that Peter Schuyler and his associates would change this. Even though Vaudreuil had threatened to unleash the French-allied tribes upon the Four Nations, some one thousand English, Iroquois, and English-allied nations gathered together at an Onondaga village to listen to Schuyler and his urgings to fall upon the French frontier.

Not counted among these were the Seneca. A number of Onondaga sachems pleaded with a Seneca delegation bound for Montreal to abandon their efforts, but the Seneca were not interested. They warned their Iroquois brothers that although the English wished it, there was nothing to be gained by warring with the French. Had they already forgotten how poorly the last war with the French and their allies had gone? The Seneca had not, as most of the attacks had fallen on them. No, they would go to Montreal and pledge their neutrality. While a few chieftains of the other Iroquois nations were for joining the English in taking up the hatchet against the French, most were of the mind of the Seneca and instead listened and nodded at Schuyler's and his associate's words without any real intentions of becoming involved.[5]

For New France this neutral stance was fortuitous, as there was fear that the Iroquois might become involved in a revolt in the west. Schuyler, and those in the Four Nations that supported his anti-French position, had influenced the Fox (Meskwaki) Nation in what is today Wisconsin. Early on the Fox had attempted to act as French middlemen between the Ottawa to the north and the Sioux to the west. Not only did this fail, but they found the French influencing a number of their traditional enemies. With a deteriorating trade position, the Fox leadership listened intently to the urgings of Schuyler and his Iroquois allies. At last there was an agreement between the Fox, Mascouten, and Kickapoo to destroy Fort Pontchartrain at Detroit and expel the French. The Fox would then reestablish the post with English help and assume the sought-after role of middleman.

To implement this plan, a pair of Fox chieftains erected a palisade village next to Fort Pontchartrain in the spring of 1712. The fort's forty-six-year-old commandant, Jacques-Charles Renaud Dubuisson, initially welcomed the new denizens of Detroit, but he complained when they set up their structure only fifty paces from Fort Pontchartrain. The Fox ignored the objections and there was little the French commander could do. The fort's garrison was only thirty men, and the nearby Ottawa and Huron villages, who Dubuisson could turn to for support, were of little help given that most of the able-bodied men had yet to return from their winter hunts. The Fox completed their village and then began to intimidate the garrison, which quickly reached the point that Dubuisson barred the natives from the fort.

At this stage all that was required for the Fox chieftains, Lamina and Pemoussa, to execute their plan was the arrival of their allies. Instead, news arrived in early May that an Ottawa and Potawatomi force under the Ottawa war chief Saguinaw had fallen upon a pair Mascouten villages and killed or carried away at least 150 of the tribe. The news infuriated the Fox who became so aggressive that they set fire to an Ottawa home near the fort's gate.

At this point a trusted pro-French Fox by the name of Joseph informed Dubuisson of the plan to attack and burn down the French fort. Acting on the news the commandant tore down any of the out structures that could be used for cover or used to set the fort on fire, as many were located close to the stronghold's walls. He then sent an urgent plea to his Huron, Ottawa, and Potawatomi allies, as well as another express to the Chippewa and Mississaugas of Lake Superior. On May13 one of Dubuisson officers returned from the Miami country. He had no news of the relief force or its march, which "gave me much trouble," the French commander noted, as "I did not know on what saint to call." A few hours later a breathless Huron messenger entered the fort with news that a six-hundred-man Potawatomi, Ottawa, and Huron war party was a short distance away and "would soon arrive to aid me, and to beat those miserable nations, who had troubled all the country."[6]

The next day the native column, which consisted of troops from over a half a dozen nations, marched into Fort Pontchartrain. A band of forty Mascouten issued forth from the Fox stronghold to challenge the arrivals and demonstrate their defiance but quickly returned under a hail of musket balls. After a council of war, where the chieftains pledged their men to the defense of the fort, Dubuisson distributed what powder and arms he had in the fort, and with a war cry that trembled the ground, the siege of the Fox village began. For almost three weeks the French and their allies fired on the Fox a mere pistol shot away, while a four-hundred-man detachment surrounded the village to prevent any reinforcements or supplies from reaching it. Dubuisson had a pair of twenty-foot scaffolds erected, which allowed his troops to fire down into the Fox village. The effort was so successful that no one could reach the well in the center of the compound, and many "were obliged to dig holes four or five feet deep in the ground, and shelter themselves there." Even so, the Fox were determined to resist and erected a scaffold of their own, which caused the French commander enough problems that he used the fort's two cannon to bring the structure down.

Days of musket balls, flaming arrows, and the occasional blast of grapeshot were finally interrupted by several peace councils, but each time an arrangement could not be arrived at and the fighting resumed. It was clear that the Fox could not hold out much longer, and on the ninetieth evening of the siege the tribe took advantage of a rainy night to abandon their palisades. While they were able to escape, it only delayed the inevitable. A pursuit was organized and they were found a few miles away on a small peninsula that jutted into Lake St. Clair. The Fox's position and fortified encampment brought forth a second siege. This one, however, did not last long. While the Fox had shown remarkable courage and tenacity, after four days they could no longer go on and surrendered unconditionally. The women and children were spared but most of the rest were put to the knife or made slaves, and many of the latter would not live long enough to spend any significant time in servitude. It was done. French control over Detroit, and the strength of its alliances had been confirmed at the cost of over a thousand Fox and Mascouten killed, captured, or reduced to slavery. "In this manner came to an end, sir," Dubuisson wrote Vaudreuil, "these two wicked nations, who so badly afflicted and troubled all the country."[7]

New France would not be alone with Indian troubles. In North Carolina the lord proprietors had established a colony in Pamlico Sound and another near modern-day Newbern, made up primarily of Huguenots and Swiss immigrants. The land grants overlapped territory claimed by the Tuscarora nation. A simmering feud resulted until September 22, 1711, when, having seen enough, 1,200 Tuscarora broke into several groups and fell upon the unsuspecting settlements. The surprise was near complete. The hamlets on Roanoke Island were destroyed and some 130 denizens killed or carried off. The settlements at Newbern, which lost sixty of their number, suffered a similar fate and were soon reduced to ashes. Not content with this, the raiders broke into smaller parties and attacked isolated homesteads through the region before finally declaring themselves satisfied after a three-day-long frenzy.[8]

The governor of North Carolina appealed to Charles Town for help, and the South Carolina legislature responded by raising a detachment of two hundred natives, mostly Yamassee, and a few dozen settlers. Under the command of Colonel John Barnwell the detachment marched north in December 1711, and after a series of skirmishes, they had trapped a larger number of Tuscarora in a wooden fort along Contentnea Creek by the first week of April 1712. With his forces depleted by sickness, his supplies nearly exhausted, and the Tuscarora holding a number of colonists as hostage in the fort, Barnwell sought a diplomatic solution. A treaty was agreed upon, which left the fort and the colonial captives in Barnwell's hands in exchange for the freedom of the Tuscarora defenders.

It hardly solved the matter. Both sides almost immediately broke the treaty, and within a few months North Carolina was again appealing to Charles Town for aid. This time the South Carolina assembly sent Colonel James Moore. When he arrived in North Carolina Moore found the supplies promised by the government had not arrived. This forced Moore's men to live off the land, which created a situation with the local colonists such that "some of the people here have been seemingly more ready to ryse upe against them than march out against the enemy." Delayed by bad weather until mid-March Moore recruited a number of North Carolina volunteers giving him close to a hundred colonists and nine hundred Indians when he finally moved forward and found the Tuscarora at a wooden fort called Nooherooka on Contentnca Creek.

The colonel surrounded the fort and began trenching operations. By March 20 a tunnel had been dug under one of the fort's walls and a mine prepared. Around ten o'clock that morning Moore ordered the mine to be exploded and told the trumpeter to sound the charge. The powder for the mine being wet, it did little damage, leaving the colonel to take the fort by storm. His men gave a "huzzah" and leapt forward converging on several points along the structure's perimeter. The Tuscarora fired from the fort's flankers and took a heavy toll on the attackers but could not stop them from breaching the walls at several points. Once in the fort it proved a gruesome hand-to-hand encounter, with the Tuscarora refusing to yield until the next morning. Close to 270 Tuscarora were killed in the assault and another 800 taken captive. Although the victory had ended the conflict, the cost had been high, with Moore suffering close to 150 casualties. Given that North

Fort William and Mary, the site of the 1713 Anglo-Wabanaki Peace Treaty. (*Boston Public Library*)

Carolina was unable to prosecute a conflict against this tribe, a general peace was negotiated, which, to the relief of many, meant that Moore and his men would return to South Carolina.[9]

For New England it appeared that the war would not end. While the French still showed little interest in attacking the New York frontier because of the fragile state of Franco-Iroquois relations, this was not true of the New England frontier. "This will be a bitter pill for New England," one English officer wrote of Walker's failure. "The French will now employ their Indians with redoubled rage and malice, to distress and destroy our exposed frontiers." In fact, a greater threat emerged first: fire. On the evening of October 2, 1711, a small fire started in the business district of Boston, and before a concerted response could be organized, several buildings had become engulfed. The flames spread throughout the night, and by the time they were

extinguished the next morning most of the business district was smoldering ruins.

Winter was quiet, but the predicted raids returned with improving weather. Exeter, Wells, Oyster River, and a host of Maine and New Hampshire towns east of the Merrimac River were attacked throughout the spring and summer of 1712. For all their violence and mayhem, the French and Indian war parties were a fraction of their former incarnations. There were no large-scale attacks as in years past but instead a stream of shallow cuts—hit and run raids and ambuscades conducted by a handful of raiders that targeted isolated homesteads, travelers, and the outskirts of towns. Dudley dispatched patrols to intercept the raiders, and occasionally muskets flashed in the frontier forests when these forays encountered their opponents, but far more often they returned empty handed. It was costly and tiring to a colony that had been at war for almost ten years, but the size of the raiding parties, their targets, and their reluctance to press home attacks made it clear to New England that the enemy was tiring as well.[10]

In late October a letter arrived in Boston from the secretary of state, the Earl of Dartmouth. Dudley was overjoyed by the news and read the letter twice just to make sure. A general truce had been declared by the French and English governments. Peace negotiations in Europe had been proceeding since January and had recently accelerated, bringing forth a six-month cease-fire. To the north Vaudreuil would receive a similar letter from the king and one from Dudley as well, announcing the good news. While the actual period of the cease-fire only extended to December 1712 neither side was interested in violating the truce, and as such hostilities ground to a halt.

There was rejoicing and relief on all sides as the long conflict appeared to be coming to an end, but for Dudley and a good portion of New England, there still remained another issue to contend with: the Wabanaki. The governor suspected that negotiations with the confederacy might prove easier than imagined. "These Indians are weary of the war, having lost some hundreds of their number, and are not now left above 3 or 400 men." The answer in the governor's mind was to erect English settlements nearby to govern them, provide them with trade goods, and ensure their commitment to a lasting peace. Ultimately, however, unless French influence over the Wabanaki was removed, which meant removing the Catholic priests who resided among them, there would be no way to ensure a lasting peace. "In the mean time," Dudley informed London, "I shall bring them to as good a quiet as I can."[11]

The Wabanaki had been inquiring into peace talks as well. The truce between the French and the English had left them in a difficult position. It was clear once again, regardless of their promises, that the French could not supply or support the Wabanaki in their conflict against the English. The confederacy's losses had been sizable, and with a logistical dilemma before them, many had migrated to the St. Francois mission near Montreal. Those that remained puzzled over a truce between the foreign kings that failed to mention the Wabanaki. It was enough for the sagamores of the confederacy to agree to a meet with Governor Dudley at Portsmouth in July 1713.

With Fort William and Mary in the background Dudley dictated the terms of the resulting treaty. The agreement called for the Wabanaki to confess that they had broken the treaties of 1693, 1699, 1702, and 1703 and cast themselves upon the mercy of Queen Anne for all "past rebellions, hostilities, and violations." The Wabanaki were to proclaim themselves British subjects and cease all acts of hostility toward the subjects of the queen. They were to be subject to British law, have their trade regulated, and agree to "never entertaine any treasonable conspiracy with any other nation," against English subjects. English settlers would return to their homes along the coast of Maine without molestation, and the lands east of the Kennebec River, as stated in the earlier treaties, were to remain theirs. The Wabanaki sagamores agreed to the terms, which fulfilled their biggest demand that English settlements be confined to the west of the Kennebec River, and for both sides the fighting finally came to an end.[12]

Less than a month later a circular letter to all the colonial governors arrived announcing peace in Europe. His armies exhausted and his coffers empty, King Louis XIV was forced to not only make a number of concessions in Europe that ended his bid for power over the continent but a number of significant concessions in North America as well. First, Placentia, the small and seemingly unconquerable French colony in Newfoundland, would become British. In fact, the entire island was ceded to Great Britain, although the French still retained the rights to fish along specific parts of the coast. Port Royal or Annapolis Royal, would officially become British, as would all of Acadia as defined by its murky "ancient boundaries." Hudson Bay would be restored to the British crown and the French would attend to the losses accumulated by the Hudson Bay Company a sum calculated to be close to £200,000. Lastly, the Five Nations were proclaimed to be British subjects, although one wonders if there were any brave enough to travel west and personally announce this news to the Seneca. To the south, Britain obtained commercial concessions from the Spanish West Indies, mostly centered about the slave trade, and while Florida remained in Spanish hands, it would clearly never be the same.[13]

The American colonies were elated by the news. New France's maritime holdings were greatly restricted by removing its principal ports both above (Placentia) and below (Port Royal) the Gulf of St. Lawrence. This not only created trade opportunities but greatly reduced the threat of enemy privateers to the New England fishing industries. Iroquois land was now technically English land, which greatly expanded the Crown's holdings into the interior of the continent, and the acquisition of Acadia now offered opportunity for New England settlers, although the ill-defined limits of the colony would bring on yet more problems. While little changed in the south with Spanish Florida and French Louisiana remaining intact, as far as the English were concerned, the first was no longer an issue and the second would be dealt with in time.

For New France the Five Nations now being British subjects no longer made a difference. The Seneca were pro-French and the other Four Nations would now be bound by English law, ending any rogue actions against the French colony and thereby removing a mechanism by which the British could undermine New France without becoming directly involved. Hudson Bay meant little at this stage. A singular attempt by the French to seize the English forts on James Bay in 1709 was quickly thwarted, leaving the French commander and a score of his men dead before the walls of Fort Albany. The remaining French outpost on the Nelson River was so weak and devoid of trade goods that it was actually far more threatened by its native neighbors than the English.

The loss of Port Royal and Placentia, however, had serious consequences. The maritime door into Canada via the St. Lawrence River had now been narrowed. Queen Anne's War had pointed to how crucial this lifeline to France had become, and now with nearby ports to house squadrons of enemy privateers the Gulf of St. Lawrence would become the noose by which the colony would be strangled in the next conflict. Of all matters, this was of prime importance. Enough so that only a short time after the Treaty of Utrecht was signed the sound of hammer, pick, and saw could be heard coming from Cape Breton Island, and soon the outlines of one of the greatest fortresses ever built in North America began to take shape.

For the moment, however, peace was the order of the day and would remain so for over a generation. Committees organized by the Crowns to demarcate the colonial boundaries and address outstanding issues met with some success, and while it was not always peaceful, it was peaceful enough that both the English colonies and New France would flourish. Even in the south the animosities and rivalry between the Spanish and the English would take on a more subdued tone—that is until one day a British captain named Jenkins lost an ear.

# *Epilogue*

## *A Quarter-Century of Conflict*

With the conclusion of Queen Anne's War, a quarter of a century of conflict had come to an end in North America. After a brief period of peace, the sequel to King William's War proceeded much differently than the first act, in part because the conflict was no longer confined primarily to the northeast. Intrigues that threatened the peace in the west and war in the south had expanded the second French and Indian War to include Spanish Florida and the new French colony of Louisiana.

While the French could be said to have won King William's War, they may be said to have been lucky to have survived Queen Anne's War. What is perhaps notable about this twenty-five-year conflict between New France and New England is that it begins with a combined attack on Quebec and Montreal in 1690, at the start of King William's War, and for all practical purposes, ends with another attack on Quebec and Montreal in 1711. In the latter case, Quebec appeared doomed. Given the weakened state of Canada and the disparity of arms and men, even Vaudreuil pondered his chances of success. This was not an invasion force of amateur colonials as under Phipps; this was the Royal Navy carrying half a dozen regiments of the line and a siege train under the command of a man who had served under the Duke of Marlborough in Flanders. For many it appeared that only a disaster befalling the enemy fleet could save the colony. On a dark August night this is exactly what occurred when a number of Walker's troopships went aground on the north shore of the St. Lawrence River.

While the admiral still possessed sufficient forces to reduce Quebec, expeditions that suffer such setbacks seldom rally to push on, and this one was no exception. Walker withdrew, and Quebec was spared.

For New York and New England, it was a difficult blow, primarily because it was the best way to bring the frontier wars to an end. They could not possibly defend their borders from determined French and Indian raiders, no matter what was being projected onto the public. As the Iroquois had suggested long before, "cut the head off the snake and the rest will die." In fact, it was the English colonies' inability to enact this simple approach that disgusted the Five Nations, and it was not until several sachems of the Five nations saw Walker's fleet that they became convinced that their allies had finally become serious again. It was indeed the solution, and while attempts to implement the 1690 plan during King George's War (1744-1748) also met with failure, this plan would ultimately work in 1759 when General James Wolfe attacked Quebec while General Jeffery Amherst advanced against French holdings in the Champlain Valley.

By failing to execute the obvious solution the English colonies had turned the conflict over to New France and their policy of *petite guerre*. Frontenac, Callières, and Vaudreuil all used this war of raiding and terror to effectively separate the English colonies from one another by playing on their immediate fears of security. It was a resourceful, cost-effective way to control the initiative and scope of the war, but it came with its own seeds of destruction. It bred generational hatred across the New England and New York frontier that clung to an answer that had been known from the first days: the conquest of Canada. And even here, the French would suffer from their war policy. The pursuit of *petite guerre*, while militarily effective, could never defeat the English colonies and came at the cost of losing the ability to negotiate a settlement that might have saved a portion of New France. Thus, when Frontenac attacked the English frontier in 1690, he rejected this negotiated solution, and when governors that succeeded him pursued the same approach, the die was cast for New France.

In the French Maritimes the war had started well but ended in disaster. Port Royal, which was threatened by Church and had held against two sizable but ill-coordinated New England expeditions in 1706, finally fell in 1710. It is remarkable that such a poorly maintained and defended structure should have inspired such awe from the English, but it would not be the only fort in North America with such an undeserved reputation. Colonial raids into Acadia, combined with naval power that choked off supplies, threatened the French colony but still left the French and their Wabanaki allies in control of the countryside when the conflict ended. Just as much of a loss, perhaps even more, was the surrender of the colony of Placentia under the terms of the peace treaty. The unconquerable little French colony, the major port in Newfoundland for French fishing fleets that fed tens of thousands in France, and the staging point from which with a handful of frontiersmen, soldiers, and Wabanaki had wrought massive economic damage on the English fishing industry, completely disproportional to their number on multiple occasions, was turned over in a brief ceremony. It had simply proven too much of a menace and the English demanded its surrender.

In the west the French managed to prevent English intrigues from undermining the peace with the Iroquois. While there were several instances that shook the French alliances and the treaty, it was in part a sincere desire on the part of the Five Nations to abide by the Treaty of Montreal that prevented an open war with the Five Nations. Even in regard to the latter days of Queen Anne's War, when large numbers of Iroquois volunteers appeared with Nicholson's expeditions in 1709 and 1711, the Five Nations had not officially sided with the English. When pressed to decide the following year, all but the Seneca agreed to side with the English, but more importantly, after doing so the remaining four nations did little that would jeopardize their neutrality.

It was a wise approach, one that the Wabanaki had briefly considered at the start of the war and perhaps one they wished they had followed. In fact, one of the true losers in Queen Anne's War was the Wabanaki. In some sense their plight is very reminiscent of the Iroquois in King William's War. They had been assured French support but were left for the most part to carry the war to the enemy themselves, all while promised supplies either never materialized or were seized by English privateers before they could reach their destination. Because of this many were transplanted to the St. Francois mission, but for those left behind the war had eroded their numbers, resources, and will. Abandoned by the French under the official treaty, they were forced to seek a separate peace with the English and accept Dudley's terms.

Queen Anne's War in the south was strangely familiar and yet carried a different tone at the same time. Here the final count was clear and in part has already been discussed. Spanish Florida would never be the same, but the fledgling French colony of Louisiana not only managed to survive under the leadership of Bienville but had also managed to check English westward expansion. Both events were remarkable, for different reasons, but the English efforts in the south require some comment. The settlement of Charles Town, its growth, booming industry in the Indian slave trade, and expansion policies are much different than encountered in the northern theater, and perhaps are best explained by remembering that the colony was a company. Much like the Hudson Bay Company, the East Indies Company, the French Company of the North, and a dozen other state-sanctioned private ventures, profit was the first motive. In fact, when one looks at the actions of some of the beforementioned companies there is a similarity in behavior and attitude. Much like the fur trade to the north, the Indian slave trade provided for instant riches and rewards for those willing to undertake it, and like the fur trade there was never a lack of native partners looking to improve their own status and standing, as pointed to by the Westro, Savannah, Creek, Yamassee, Chickasaw, and several others. The umbrella of Queen Anne's War simply offered opportunity to conduct these operations on a large scale, while expanding the colony's influence throughout the southern tribes. While this approach was successful, it faced a fundamental problem. It was divisive. It had begun with the Westro and Savannah, who were abandoned for the more numerous and powerful Creek and Yamassee. The Chickasaw were entertained and provided arms, but there was fear at some point that abandoning the Creek and Yamassee for another native nation that was politically or geographically expedient might one day cause major problems. As it would turn out some of these issues would come to a brutal forefront a few years later during the Yamassee War (1715-1717) which ravaged the colony.

For the moment, however, South Carolina was one of the major winners in the colonial conflict. It had repelled an attack against Charles Town and struck back with such a vengeance that it collapsed Spanish Florida and threatened French Louisiana. Carolina traders had pushed hundreds of miles into the southern interior making contacts and expanding the colony's influence. The money from the slave trade was financing the colony, which was turning into an agricultural powerhouse and one of the busier ports along the Atlantic seaboard.

While many of the base issues still remained both in the North and South between the French and the English, another issue was simmering between the English colonists and the government of England. Left to their own devices for many years, and for much of the quarter of a century of conflict in question, they viewed the king and England with a skeptical eye and clung to the liberties granted in their colonial charters. This independent attitude immediately caught Colonel Richard King's attention when he arrived in Boston in the summer of 1711. Toward the end of his stay in the New England town King wrote a letter to the secretary of state for the Northern Department, Henry St. John, with his observations. "I can't express the uneasiness we have all been in for our long stay in Boston," he informed the Secretary,

> You could not imagine what difficulties we met with through Nicholson's neglect in not sending his two transports with a man of war to New York to convoy our provisions from thence; through the misfortune that the Coloneys were not inform'd of our coming two months sooner; and through the interestedness, ill nature and sowerness of these People; whose Government doctrine, and manners; whose hypocrisy and canting are insupportable. . . . 'Tis easy to determine the respect and obedience H.M. may reasonably expect from them for the future, and how absolutely necessary it is, and with what great truth one may affirm, that till all their Charters are resum'd by the Crown, or taken away by an Act of Parliament; till they are all settled under one Government with an entire liberty of conscience; and an invitation to all nations to settle here, they will grow every day more stiff and disobedient, more burthensome than advantageous to Great Britain.[1]

While these seeds of independence might be viewed as the beginning of an American identity, if so, it was one that still had to suffer through the painful lessons of division for years to come in order to understand the power of unity and its relationship to liberty.

# *Notes*

ABBREVIATIONS

*DCB* (*Dictionary of Canadian Biography*)
*NY Col. Doc.* (O'Callaghan, *Documents Relative to the Colonial History of the State of New York*)
*DHSNY* (O'Callaghan, *Documentary History of the State of New York*)
*RAPQ* (*Rapport de l'Archiviste de la Province de Quebec*)
NAC (National Archives of Canada, Ottawa)
*NEHGR* (*New England Historical and Genealogical Register*)
*NYHSC* (*New York Historical Society Collections*)
*MHSC* (*Massachusetts Historical Society Collections*)
*JR* (*Jesuit Relations and Allied Documents*)
*Cal. A&WI* (*Calendar American & West Indies Papers*)
*RAPQ* (*Rapport de L'Archiviste de la Quebec*)
*FHQ (Florida Historical Quarterly)*

CHAPTER 1: A SERVANT OF THE CROWN

1. *NY Col. Doc.*, IV, 74-75.
2. *Cal. A&WI*, XIV, 506, 534, 541; XV, 313, 318-319, 358-359, 380-384, 399; *N.H. Prov. Papers*, II, 305-312; *NY Col. Doc.* IV, 259-261.
3. *Cal. A&WI*, XV, 591-592, XVI, 83-84; *NY Col. Doc.*, IV, 277, 284-292, 302-303.
4. *Cal. Tres. Papers*, 1697-1702, xi (Rapin, III – see cal.).
5. Janvier, "The Sea-Robbers of New York," *Harper's Monthly Magazine*, Nov. 1894, 813-815; *Life of Bellomont*, 20-25.
6. McDonald, "'A Man of Courage and Activity': Thomas Tew, Anglo-American Piracy, and the Manhattan to Madagascar Trade Network, 1690-1720," 1-9; *Cal. A &WI*, XIV, 503-506; *NY Col. Doc.*, IV, 221-224; Janvier, 813-827.
7. *Cal. A&WI*, XVI, 121-122.
8. Ibid., XVI, 165, 203-204, 224-229.

9. *Journal NY Council*, I, 119.
10. *NY Col. Doc.*, IV, 302-310. In his outrage over Fletcher's clear corruption Bellomont also accused him of a number of other improprieties including negligence in the colony's military affairs. While there is no question as to Fletcher's corruption as it concerns pirates and the illegal trade, in the same vein there is no good evidence to point to his incompetence when it came to military matters.
11. The muster rolls of the four independent companies taken in September 1698: Bellomont's Company - Officers/NCO: 6, Rank and file: 59; Captain Nanfan's Company – Officers/NCO: 6, Rank and file: 48; Major Ingoldsby's Company - Officers/NCO: 5, Rank and file: 50; Captain Weem's Company- Officers/NCO: 5, Rank and file: 66. These numbers put the four companies at 61 percent of their full compliment. (*Cal. A&WI*, XVI, 450.)
12. *The Dictionary of National Biography*, XVII, 184-185; *NY Col. Doc.*, IV, 244, 256; *English Army Lists and Commission Registers, 1661-1714*, III, 234; Porter, *The History of the Corps of Royal Engineers*, I, 56, 61, 136.
13. *NY Col. Doc.*, IV, 440-441.
14. *Cal. A&WI*, XVI, 223; *NY Col. Doc.*, IV, 328-330. Romer was perhaps understating the state of the fortifications. Bellomont, who personally viewed the works at Albany and Schenectady in June, wrote the Board of Trade that, "The Forts of Albany and Schenectady are so weak and ridiculous, that they look like pounds to impound cattle in, than Forts." (*NY Col Doc*, IV, 608).
15. *NY Col. Doc*, IV, 329-330, 440-441. Romer estimated the cost of the proposed works along the New York frontier, as:

at Albany a Fort, £4,000
at Schenectady a Fort, £4,000
at Rudgio a Fort, £6,000
at Sheractoge (Saratoga) a redoubt, £1,000
at Canestigogione a redoubt, £1,000
at the Half-moon a redoubt, £1,000

The actual location of Rudgio is unclear, and the only clue comes from Bellomont who states that, "Rudgio is suppos'd our northernmost between the Province of New York and Canada, as Ste. Croix is our most Eastern boundary next to N. Scotia, which is the reason Col. Romer thought those two forts would require more strength and cost than the rest." (*Cal. State Papers*, XVIII, 691).
16. *Cal. A&WI*, XVI, 499-500.
17. Ibid., 377-378, 499-500; *NY Col. Doc.*, IV, 362-367; Wraxall, 28-30.
18. *NY Col. Doc.*, IX, 692-695.
19. Colonel Nicholas Bayard outlined such a case in a letter to Bellomont. (*NY Col. Doc.*, IV, 353.)
20. *Cal. A&WI*, XVI, 377-378, 499-500; *NY Col. Doc.*, IV, 362-366.

### CHAPTER 2: PIRATES AND PRIVATEERS

1. *Cal. A&WI*, XVII, 214.
2. Ibid., 291.
3. Ibid.; *Mass. Acts and Resolves*, VII, 680-681. Bellomont and Romer visited the fort together in mid-June. Unfortunately, the occasion was marred by an accident when a

cannon that Romer requested be fired burst, killing one gunner and severely wounding another. (Ibid., 618)
4. *Doc. Hist. Maine*, X, 45-46. Romer would later say of Fort William and Mary's location that, "No place I have seen in my Travails being naturally better scituated & more suitable for defence." (Ibid., IX, 158.)
5. *Cal. A&WI*, XVII, 412; *Doc. Hist. Maine*, X, 46-52.
6. *Cal. A&WI*, XVII, 412-413.
7. Ibid., XVII, 412-413, 486-490.
8. *NY Col. Doc.*, IV, 513, 530-531; *Cal. A&WI*, XVI, 581-582, XVII, 403; Chalmer, I, 289-291.
9. *Cal. A&WI*, XVII, 431.
10. *NY Col., Doc*, IV, 551-552; *Cal. A&WI*, XVII, 382, 390, 402-404. The captain of the *Maryland Merchant*, which was set free after its cargo was seized, reported that the pirate captain claimed to be none other than Captain Kidd but that his crew called him John James. (Ibid., 390.) Bellomont was not alone in his request for Royal Navy vessels. The governor of Barbados, Ralph Grey, pointed out that he had only one "heavy, crazy vessel, miscalled a cruiser" with which to suppress "any pirates that infest these seas." (*Cal. A&WI*, XVII, 37.)
11. *Life of Bellomont*, 25-28; *NY Col. Doc.*, IV, 762-765.
12. Janvier, "The Sea-Robbers of New York," 819-821; *Cal. A&WI*, XVII, 366-379; Clowes, II, 498-499; Dolin, *Black Flags, Blue Waters*, 104-106.
13. *Cal. A&WI*, XVII, 370-372.
14. Janvier, "The Sea-Robbers of New York," 820-823; *Cal. A&WI*, XVII, 366-370; *Life of Bellomont*, 47-48.
15. *Cal. A&WI*, XVII, 369, 413-414.
16. Howell, *State Trials*, XIV, 123-234; *Cal A &WI*, XVII, 369-378. Written by a relative of Bellomont's the 1701 pamphlet entitled *A Full Account of the Proceedings in Relation to Captain Kidd*, presents the story from the governor's side.
17. *Life of Bellomont*, 48-53; *Cal. A. &WI*, XIX, 107.

## CHAPTER 3: THE GREAT PEACE OF MONTREAL

1. Havard, *The Great Peace of Montreal*, 62-66; *NY Col. Doc.*, IV, 337-338, 420.
2. Charlevoix, V, 48; *NY Col. Doc.*, IV, 240.
3. Havard, *The Great Peace of Montreal*, 66-69.
4. *NY Col. Doc.*, IV, 407-409.
5. Ibid., 487, 492-497; Wraxell, *An Abridgement of the Indian Affairs*, 31-32; Charlevoix, V, 94-95.
6. *NY Col. Doc.*, IV, 564-573; Havard, *The Great Peace of Montreal*, 77-78, 90; Charlevoix, V, 99-100.
7. *NY Col. Doc.*, IV, 597, 606-612.
8. Charlevoix, V, 100-103; Goldstein, *French-Iroquois Relations*, 192-193; *NY Col. Doc*, IX, 708-713;
9. Charlevoix, V, 103-106; *NY Col. Doc.*, IX, 711-712; Havard, *The Great Peace of Montreal*, 95-97.
10. *NY Col. Doc.*, IX, 716.
11. Ibid.

12. Eccles, *Frontenac*, 328-330; *NY Col. Doc.*, 711-712, 715-720. English reports of the conference can be found in *NY Col. Doc.*, IV, 798-807.
13. Charlevoix, V, 135-141; Havard, *The Great Peace of Montreal*, 100-104; Callières to Ministre, Oct 4, 1701, MG1-C11A, vol 19, fol. 114-122v. Several skirmishes occurred between the Iroquois and New France's western allies during this time, but in most cases, this was the result of news of the provisional treaty having not yet reached the tribes in question.
14. Charlevoix, V, 140-154; *NY Col. Doc.*, IX, 722-725; Callières to Ministre, Aug 6, and Oct 4, 1701, MG1-C11A, vol 19, fol. 112-113v, 114-122V.

CHAPTER 4: THE TREATY OF CASCO

1. *Cal. A &WI*, XIX, 107-109, 119-120, 153-154, 158-159, 186-202.
2. *NY Col. Doc.*, IV, 850-874.
3. Ibid., 871; *Cal. A &WI*, XX, 175-176. "If we lose the Five Nations," Colonel Robert Quary warned London, "there will be nothing to hinder our enemies from ranging over the main and bringing ruin and destruction on which Government they please." (*Cal. A &WI*, XX, 176.) Of course, the French would have never allowed their allies to trade with the Five Nations, nor would the Iroquois have allowed the French allies to freely pass through Five Nations lands and trade directly with the English.
4. *Journal NY Council*, I, 156; *NY Col. Doc.*, IV, 880-882, 920; Wraxell, *An Abridgement of the Indian Affairs*, 38-42.
5. *NY Col. Doc.*, IV, 871.
6. *Cal. A &WI*, XIX, 24-25; *N.H. Prov. Papers*, II, 339-342.
7. *Mass. Acts and Resolves*, VIII, 294-296; *Cal. A &WI*, XIX, 105-106. One colonial official wrote the Board of Trade that, "Mr. Stoughton, is a person learned and conversant in books, but wholly unacquainted with military discipline, so that great country lyes exposed to the incursions of their merciless enemies, the French and Indians." (Ibid., 105.)
8. *N.H. Prov. Papers*, II, 299-300; *Cal. A&WI*, XX, 119-123; *Doc. Hist. Maine*, X, 87-95.
9. *Cal. A&WI*, XIX, 576-577.
10. *NY Col. Doc.*, IV, 883-884, 912, 955, 967-971.
11. Ibid., 977-990.
12. *Mass. Acts and Resolves*, VII, 311, 388, 693-695, 702; Kimball, *Dudley*, 76-82; *Cal. A&WI*, XXI, 436.
13. Lecky, I, 27-33; Lanctot, II, 150-151. The war started on July 9, 1701, but it would not be until May 1702 that England entered the conflict.
14. *Cal. A&WI*, XX, 501-505; Kimball, *Dudley*, 106-108.
15. Penhallow, 2-4; Drake, 149-151; *Cal. A&WI*, XXI, 34-35, 187-189, 267, 601-603; *Histoire Des Abenaki*, 316-317; "Sewell Diary," *MHSC*, ser. 5, VI, 85-87.
16. *Doc. Hist. Maine*, IX, 145-146; *Mass. Acts and Resolves*, VIII, 286-287; Penhallow, 4. Penhallow claimed that the original Wabanaki plan was "to make the English the Victims of that Day. But Providence so order'd it, as to place their chief Counsellours and Sachems in the Tent where ours were seated, by which means they could not destroy one without endangering the other!" (Ibid.)

CHAPTER 5: THE PATH TO WAR

1. *NY Col. Doc.*, IX, 736-738; Charlevoix, V, 154-156; Horton, "Paul Le Moyne de Mari-

court," DCB, II. Brandao estimates about 1,400 Iroquois casualties caused by the French during King William's War. However, much of the conflict was conducted by New France's allies against the Five Nations.
2. Eccles, *Canada Under Louis XIV*, 244-246; *NY Col. Doc.*, IX, 736-738; Lanctot, II, 146-147.
3. Eccles, *Canada Under Louis XIV*, 246-249; *Histoire Des Abenaki*, 315.
4. Charlevoix, V, 156; *NY Col. Doc.*, IX, 736-738; *Coll. Man. N.F.*, II, 402-403.
5. Clowes, II, 501; *Cal. A&WI*, XXI, 721-722; Anspach, *Newfoundland*, 120-121.
6. *NY Col. Doc.*, IX, 739.
7. *Coll. Man. N.F.*, II, 405; *RPAQ 1921-1922*, 226-232; Lanctot, II, 151.
8. "Rigaud de Vaudreuil, Phillippe de," DCB, II.
9. *NY Col. Doc.*, IX, 742-745.
10. *Coll. Man. N.F.*, II, 405-406. While an extreme solution the governor made clear that "the safety, the very existence of the French population was a supreme reason which silenced all the others." (*Histoire Des Abenaki*, 317.)
11. Drake, 153-154; *Coll. Man. N.F.*, II, 405-406; *Cal. A &WI,* XIX, 640. Also, at this time the younger St. Castin, who was a Penobscot chieftain, had his home ransacked by English privateers, which, given St. Castin's status, was viewed as an insult to all in the confederacy. (Drake, 154; Williamson, *Hist. Maine*, II, 41-42.)
12. Bourne, *History of Wells*, 245-256; Williamson, *Hist. Maine*, II, 42; Sylvester, *Indian Wars of New England*, III, 25-33.
13. Penhallow, 5-6; Drake, 158-159; *Cal. A&WI*, XXI, 646-647, 689, 920; Williamson, *Hist. Maine*, II, 42-43; *Doc. Hist. Maine*, IX, 178-179.
14. Drake, 159-161; Williamson, *Hist. Maine*, II, 43-44; *Cal. A&WI*, XXI, 689-690.
15. Tapley, *The Province Galley*, 5-6; Penhallow, 6-8; *Doc. Hist. Maine*, IX, 143-144, 150-152; *Cal. A&WI*, XXI, 689-690.
16. *Coll. Man. N.F.*, II, 405-406; *NY Col. Doc.*, IX, 756, 762; Charlevoix, V, 160-161.

CHAPTER 6: THE FRONTIER IN FLAMES

1. *Cal. A&WI*, XXI, 689-692; "Winthrop Papers, *MHSC*, Series 6, III, 139-140, 149-154.
2. *NY Col. Doc.*, IV, 1069-1072.
3. *Cal. A&WI*, XXI, 690-691; *Doc. Hist. Maine*, IX, 151-154.
4. Drake, 163-165; *Mass. Acts and Resolves*, VIII, 400. Wyatt would be promoted to lieutenant the following spring.
5. *Mass. Acts and Resolves*, VIII, 44-45, 48, 66-67, 311, 319; Williamson, *Hist. Maine*, II, 44; Penhallow, 10; Drake, 166-167.
6. Drake, 168-170; Williamson, *Hist. Maine*, II, 44-45; Penhallow, 10-11; "Sewell Diary," 95.
7. *NY Col. Doc.*, IV, 1099-1100; Sheldon, *Deerfield*, 292-294; *Mass. Acts and Resolves*, VIII, 350-351; Hutchinson, *Hist. Mass.*, II, 136-137; *RPAQ 1938-39*, 43-44, 54-55; Charlevoix, V, 156, 161.
8. Hutchinson, *Hist. Mass.*, II, 137-138; *NY Col. Doc.*, IV, 1099-1100; "Winthrop Papers," 176-177, 182-183, 244-246; Williams, *Redeemed Captive*, 9-11; Sheldon, *Deerfield*, 292-297.
9. Drake, 175-180; Sheldon, *Deerfield*, 303-303, 310-312; Penhallow, 11-13.
10. Sheldon, *Deerfield*, 302-303, 312-313.

11. Drake, 180-181; Sheldon, *Deerfield*, 309-310.
12. Williams, *Redeemed Captive*, 12-13; "Winthrop Papers," 176-177; Sheldon, *Deerfield*, 297-303.
13. "Winthrop Papers," 180-181; Williams, *Redeemed Captive*, 13-15; Sheldon, *Deerfield*, 304-309; *NY Col. Doc.*, IX, 762; *Cal. A&WI*, XXII, 140.
14. Williams, *Redeemed Captive*, 13-35; Sheldon, *Deerfield*, 315-317.
15. *NY Col. Doc.*, IX, 748-749.

## CHAPTER 7: CHURCH'S EXPEDITION

1. "Benjamin Church," DCB, II.
2. Dudley, *Life*, 110-111; Church, *Journal*, 158-163; Penhallow, 16-17.
3. Church, *Journal*, 163-166; *Mass. Acts and Resolves*, VIII, 328-330.
4. Church, *Journal*, 166-169. The names of the transports and their masters can be found in *Mass. Acts and Resolves*, VIII, 338-339.
5. *Cal. A&WI*, XXII, 213-214, 274; *N.H. Prov. Papers*, II, 434-435; *Documents Relating to Towns in New Hampshire*, XII, 679-680.
6. Trumbull, *History of Northampton*, 491-493.
7. Ibid., 493-496; *NY Col. Doc.*, IX, 762; *Cal. A&WI*, XXII, 213; *Mass. Acts and Resolves*, VIII, 401; "Winthrop Papers," 200-201, 205-206.
8. Church, *Journal*, 169-172; "Winthrop Papers," 551-555.
9. Hutchinson, *Hist. Mass.*, II, 143-144; Church, *Journal*, 173-174; Penhallow, 16-17.
10. Church, *Journal*, 175-180.
11. Ibid., 181-189; *Mass. Acts and Resolves*, VIII, 314; *Coll. Man. N.F.*, II, 416-420; *Boston News-Letter*, Aug. 7, 1704; Saint-Père, *Une colonie féodale*, I, 320-322.
12. Hutchinson, *Hist. Mass.*, II, 145-146; *Mass. Acts and Resolves*, VIII, 332; Church, Journal 188-189; *Coll. Man. N.F.*, II, 416-425; Charlevoix, V, 170-172.
13. *Cal. A&WI*, XXII, 213-214.
14. *NY Col. Doc.*, IX, 763-764.
15. Nourse, *Rec. of Lancaster*, 146-148; Penhallow, 23-25; *Boston News-Letter*, Aug 7, 1704; Pike, *Journal*, 26-27.
16. *Coll. Man. N.F.*, II, 418, 424-425; *NY Col. Doc.*, IX, 758-759, 765; Charlevoix, V, 167.

## CHAPTER 8: THE AVALON PENINSULA

1. *Cal. A&WI*, XX, 112, 520-522, 635, 721-727, XIX, 20; Prowse, *Newfoundland*, 251.
2. *Cal. A&WI*, XX, 56, 76, 78, 117-118, 750-751, XIX, 71-72, 507.
3. "Daniel d'Auger de Subercase," DCB, II.
4. Burchett, *Transactions at Sea*, 631-634; *Cal. A&WI*, XX, 721-722, 738-739; Prowse, *Newfoumdland*, 239.
5. Clowes, II, 502-503; Burchett, *Transactions at Sea*, 600-601, 604-605; *Cal. A&WI*, XXI, 534-536. "The night before the Admiral sailed," the governor complained to London, "most of the men of warr's boats and crews went ashoare at Port Royall and Kingstown, and under pretence of searching for sailers that had deserted, carried off several of the inhabitants of the Point and Kingstown." (Ibid.)
6. *Rep Can Archive 1899*, sup. 26.
7. Charlevoix, V, 161-162.
8. *Cal. A&WI*, XXI, 667-668, 717-718, 871; Anspach, *Newfoundland*, 121-123; Burchett,

*Transactions at Sea*, 605-607. Graydon stated that while at Jamaica he found his fleet short 1,800 seamen and 800 soldiers. (Ibid., XXI, 718.)
9. Clowes, II, 502-504. Clowes speaks of the incident and outcome in the following manner: "That Graydon was rough, overbearing and truculent, rests on better evidence. That he was an incompetent officer seems certain; and that he thoroughly deserved his fate is altogether very probable." (Ibid., 504.)

CHAPTER 9: THE SIEGE OF ST. JOHN'S

1. *Cal. A&WI*, XXII, 1-2.
2. *Boston News-Letter*, Dec 4, 1704. *Cal. A&WI*, XXII, 269-270, 290, 333, 347-348. Llyod was exonerated of the charges laid against him and would return to St. John's.
3. Charlevoix, V, 161, 169-170; Penhollow, 26-27; Catalogne, 61-62; *Cal. A&WI*, XXII, 326; *Boston News-Letter*, Oct. 9, 1704. *RPAQ, 1922-1923*, 348, *1938-1939*, 24-25.
4. "Costebelle Journal," *Mag. Amer. Hist.*, I, no. 1, 107-109; Catalogne, 61-62, 64-65; Charlevoix, V, 172-173.
5. Catalogne, 65-66; Penhallow, 30.
6. *Cal. A&WI*, XXII, 501, 539-540, 570, XXIII, 11; *Boston News-Letter*, May 14, 1705.
7. Prowse, *Newfoundland*, 242-244; Catalogne, 66-68; *Cal. A&WI*, XXII, 539-541.
8. Catalogne, 67-69; *Cal. A&WI*, XXII, 539-540, 549, 570, XXIII, 11; "Costebelle Journal," 109-111.
9. "Montigny Journal," *RPAQ, 1922-1923*, 293-296; *Cal. A&WI*, XXIII, 83; Catalogne, 69-70; *Boston News-Letter*, May 14, 1705.
10. "Montigny Journal," *RPAQ, 1922-1923*, 296-298; Charlevoix, V, 174.
11. Prowse, *Newfoundland*, 242-243; *Cal. A&WI*, XXII, 538-543, 549-550, XXIII, 10-11; Penhallow, 30-31.

CHAPTER 10: THE FRAGILE PEACE IN THE WEST

1. *NY Col. Doc.*, IX, 750-751.
2. Charlevoix, V, 159-160; *NY Col., Doc.*, IX, 747-748.
3. Sheldon, *Early Michigan*, 198-199; *RPAQ, 1938-1939*, 59-60; *NY Col., Doc.*, IX, 759-764; Charlevoix, V, 163-164, 168-169.
4. *NY Col. Doc.*, IX, 766-768.
5. Ibid., 767-769; *RAPQ, 1938-1939*, 91-94.
6. *Cal. A&WI*, XXI, 672-673; *NY Col. Doc.*, IV, 1120-1121.
7. Ibid., 1121-1123, 1128.
8. *Cal A&WI*, XXI, 672-673, 879-880, XXII, 78, 685; *RPAQ, 1938-1939*, 57; *NY Col Doc*, IX, 775; *MP Hist. Coll.*, XXXIII, 242.
9. *Windsor Border Region*, xli-xlii, 13-24; Zoltvany, "Antoine Laumet de la Mothe Cadillac," DCB, II; *MP Hist. Coll.*, XXXIII, 96-101,131-151, 158, 182-187.
10. Charlevoix, V, 183-185; Kingsford, *Canada*, 432-433; *MP Hist. Coll.*, XXXIII, 288-289; Sheldon, *Early History of Michigan*, 196-197. Along with Toni's absence when Madame Cadillac departed for Montreal to join her husband, the Ottawa became suspicious given that Cadillac had informed them that, "Although I am going away, have no fear so long as my wife remains here; but if you see her go down, then you will have reason to fear." (*MP Hist. Coll.*, XXXIII, 432.)
11. Sheldon, *Early History of Michigan*, 206-217; Charlevoix, V, 185-186; *MP Hist. Coll.*,

XXXIII, 262-270, 272-276, 432-436.
12. *Mich. Hist. Coll.*, XXXIII, 285-286.
13. Ibid.
14. Sheldon, *Early History of Michigan*, 226-229; Charlevoix, V, 187-188; *Mich. Hist. Coll.*, XXXIII, 272-284, 288-296.
15. Sheldon, *Early History of Michigan*, 229; *Mich. Hist. Coll.*, XXXIII, 272-284.
16. Sheldon, *Early History of Michigan*, 232-243.
17. Ibid., 243-244.
18. Charlevoix, V, 188-190; *NY Col. Doc.*, IX, 779-781; 804-805, 808-811; *Mich. Hist. Coll.*, XXXIII, 319-334. Vaudreuil wrote the minister of the marine, "I cannot, My Lord, consent to give over to destruction a Nation that has been faithful to us in the last war, and has, in this affair at Detroit, perhaps more bad luck than bad disposition." (*NY Col. Doc.*, IX, 780.)
19. Sheldon, *Early History of Michigan*, 271-273; *NY Col. Doc.*, IX, 814-815. While Vaudreuil wanted to quietly resolve the matter, so as not to jeopardize the Franco-Ottawa alliance, he was critical of Cadillac's promise to the Miami that he would put Le Pesant to death, which, when it did not occur, only caused future problems. (*Mich. Hist. Coll.*, XXXIII, 402-405.)

### CHAPTER 11: AN UNEASY TRUCE

1. *Mass. Acts and Resolves*, VIII, 497-498.
2. Dudley, *Life*, 113; *Mass. Acts and Resolves*, VIII, 496-500; Kingsford, *Canada*, 425-426.
3. *Coll. Man. N.F.*, II, 432-433; *Mass. Acts and Resolves*, VIII, 480, 501; Charlevoix, V, 175-176. Baptiste had been a well-known French privateer during King William's War. He seems to have been involved in enforcing French fishing rights off the coast of Acadia and likely took a few English fishing vessels that were violating this exclusion zone. He was captured before Queen Anne's War, tried as a pirate, and sentenced to hang, when the prisoner exchange negotiations halted this sentence. (Maisonnat, dit Baptiste, Pierre, DCB, II.)
4. *Mass. Acts and Resolves*, VIII, 480-481, 512-513. It is not known if Vaudreuil had secretly empowered Courtemanche to prolong the negotiations by agreeing to such an arrangement.
5. *NY Col. Doc.*, IX, 770-772.
6. *Mass. Acts and Resolves*, VIII, 544-546; Kimball, *Dudley*, 113-116.
7. *NY Col. Doc.*, IX, 775-776; Sheldon, *Deerfield*, 332-333; *Mass. Acts and Resolves*, VIII, 613; *Boston News-Letter*, June 3, 24, Aug 5, 1706.
8. *Coll. Man. N.F.*, II, 452-456; *Mass. Acts and Resolves*, VIII, 544-546; Drake, 210-215; Penhallow, 29-30, 33, 37. While Louis agreed to the terms of the treaty Vaudreuil proposed to Dudley, orders would reach Dudley in the fall of 1706 directing him not to proceed any farther with Vaudreuil's proposed treaty. (*NY Col. Doc.*, IX, 779; *Cal. A&WI*, XXIII, 187.)
9. Penhallow, 32, 34-39.
10. Drake, 218-219; *Boston News-Letter*, July 15, 1706.

### CHAPTER 12: FORT CAROLINE

1. French, *Hist. Coll.*, I, 177-178, II, 159-160, 163; Gorman, "Ribault's Colonies," *FHQ*, XLIV, No. 1-2, 51-53; *Hist. Coll. S.C.*, I, xxxi-xxxii.
2. French, *Hist. Coll.*, I, 196-198, 208-216, II, 167-175, 186-189.
3. Lowery, *Spanish Settlements*, 53-58; Charlevoix, I, 148-149, 152-153; French, *Hist. Coll.*, I, 238-239;
4. Charlevoix, I, 165-170; French, *Hist. Coll.*, I, 269-277; Lowery, *Spanish Settlements*, 80-83; *Hist. Coll. S.C.*, I, xlix-liv.
5. Charlevoix, I, 175-176; Lowery, *Spanish Settlements*, 85-87.
6. French, *Hist. Coll.*, I, 316-322; Charlevoix, I, 177-179; Gorman, "Ribault's Colonies," *FHQ*, XLIV, No. 1-2, 55-56; *Hist. Coll. S.C.*, I, liv-lv.

### CHAPTER 13: HUGUENOTS AND CONQUISTADORS

1. Lowery, *Spanish Settlements*, 102-108, 134-145; Steele, *Warpaths*, 26-27. Don Frances de Alava, the Spanish ambassador to France, warned Philip that the French Florida settlements were a serious problem given the "pirates of Normandy and Brittany were so ravenous in their greed for the Indian fleets." (Lowery, *Spanish Settlements*, 103.)
2. French, *Hist. Coll.*, II, 191-210; Charlevoix, I, 182-188.
3. Fairbanks, *Spaniards in Florida*, 15-17; French, *Hist. Coll.*, II, 209-214; *Hist. Coll. S.C.*, I, liv-lvii.
4. Lowery, *Spanish Settlements*, 164-165; Charlevoix, I, 192-193.
5. French, *Hist. Coll.*, II, 216-224; Charlevoix, I, 194-195; Fairbanks, *St. Augustine*, 13-23.
6. Lowery, *Spanish Settlements*, 168-171; French, *Hist. Coll.*, II, 224-228; Fairbanks, *Spaniards in Florida*, 17-20; Charlevoix, I, 196-200; Manucy, "Pedro Menendez," *FHQ*, XLIV, No. 1-2, 76.
7. French, *Hist. Coll.*, II, 228-231; Lowery, *Spanish Settlements*, 172-178; Charlevoix, I, 201-207; Fairbanks, *Spaniards in Florida*, 20-22. One Spanish witness noted that "A great Lutheran cosmographer and magician was found among the dead." (French, *Hist. Coll.*, II, 228.)
8. French, *Hist. Coll.*, II, 216-222, 231-234; Charlevoix, I, 207-221; Dewhurst, *History of St. Augustine*, 46-51; Fairbanks, *Spaniards in Florida*, 23-30; Gorman, "Ribault's Colonies," *FHQ*, XLIV, No. 1-2, 58-59. If one thought that Spain's most Christian king would have objected to Menendez's methods, they would be mistaken. It was a much different age as seen in the king's response to the general's actions; "We believe you have done this with full justification and prudence, and hold ourselves well served thereby." (Manucy, "Pedro Menendez," *FHQ*, XLIV, No. 1-2, 70.)
9. Charlevoix, I, 223-225; Lowery, *Spanish Settlements*, 324-326; French, *Hist. Coll.*, II, 265-270.
10. Charlevoix, I, 225-228; French, *Hist. Coll.*, I, 347-349, II, 270-276; Dewhurst, *History of St. Augustine*, 57-61.
11. French, *Hist. Coll.*, I, 349-352, II, 277-281; Lowery, *Spanish Settlements*, 327-329.
12. Charlevoix, I, 230-235; *Hist. Coll. S.C.*, I, lxiv-lxvii; French, *Hist. Coll.*, I, 352-362, II, 281-289; Lowery, *Spanish Settlements*, 328-335, 454-457. The king could not officially approve of Gourgues's actions, nor would he condemn him, as his action quickly resonated with many French citizens who viewed it as a restoration of French honor. (Lowery, *Spanish Settlements*, 335-336.)

CHAPTER 14: MISSIONARIES AND SOLDIERS

1. Covington, "Drake Destroys St. Augustine, 1586," *FHQ*, XLIV, No. 1-2, 81-93; Fairbanks, *Spaniards in Florida*, 65-67; Dewhurst, *History of St. Augustine*, 66-73; Reynolds, *Old St. Augustine*, 53-61.
2. Sweet, *Spanish Missions of Florida*,18-25; Parker, "St. Augustine in the Seventeenth Century," *FHQ*, XCII, No. 3, 555-557; Swanton, *Early History of the Creek*, 80-85; Engelhardt, *Missionary Work of the Franciscans*, 66-68; Weber, *Spanish Frontier*, 72-73; Fairbanks, *Spaniards in Florida*, 67-68.
3. Swanton, *Early History of the Creek*, 85-88, 109-111, 119-120; Weber, *Spanish Frontier*, 87-89; Sweet, *Spanish Missions of Florida*, 24-29; Steele, *Warpaths*, 30-32; Parker, "St. Augustine in the Seventeenth Century," *FHQ*, XCII, No. 3, 557-560; Johnson, "The Yamassee Revolt of 1597," *Georgia Historical Quarterly*, VII, no. 1, 43-53.
4. Worth, *The Timucua Rebellion of 1656*, 192-213, 253-271, 278-279; Erhmann, "The Timucua Indians," *FHQ*, XVIII, No. 3, 168-190. As one Franciscan friar would later comment on the governor's demand that the Timucua report to St. Augustine, "it is a very different matter to give orders to a Spaniard, who knows what it is to obey, than [to give them] to one who does not know how to accept such orders." (Worth, *The Timucua Rebellion of 1656*, 213.)
5. Fairbanks, *Spaniards in Florida*, 71-72; Weber, *Spanish Frontier*, 100-101; Swanton, *Early History of the Creek*, 337-339; Sweet, *Spanish Missions of Florida*, 48-49.
6. Reigelsperger, "Spanish Florida in the 1668 Seales Raid," *FHQ*, XCII, No. 4, 580-590; Arana, *History Castillo de San Marcos*, 3-6; *Cal. A&WI*, VII, 90, 93.
7. *Cal. A&WI*, XI, 642-643, 685, 718; Arana, *History Castillo de San Marcos*, 31-32.
8. Matter, *Missions in the Defense of Spanish Florida*, *FHQ*, LIV, No. 1, 22-32; Crane, *The Southern Frontier*, 24-30; Boyd, Florida Spanish Missions in 1675, *FHQ*, XXVII, No. 2, 181-188.
9. Weber, *Spanish Frontier*, 90, 126; Arana, *History Castillo de San Marcos*, 19-23, 26-28.
10. Arana, *History Castillo de San Marcos*, 26-36; Deagan, *Excavations at the Castillo de San Marcos*, 3-5.
11. Arnade, *The Siege of St. Augustine in 1702*, 9-11; Subhash, Janotti, "Impact response of Coquina," *Dynamic Behavior of Materials*, I, 1-4. The authors of this paper demonstrate that the porous structure of Conquina gave it deformational properties that not only absorbed the impact of a cannonball but allowed this energy to dissipate through the porous network thereby minimizing any cracking in the fort's walls. (Ibid.)

CHAPTER 15: CAROLINA

1. *Hist. Coll. S.C.*, I, 61-63; *Cal. A&WI*, VII, 19, 32-36, 70-71, 86-87; McCrady, *South Carolina*, 56, 120-129, 170-171; Rivers, *Hist. Sketch of S.C.*, 129-130, 382. Charles II's grant to the lord proprietors can be found in *Hist. Coll. S.C.*, II, 37-57.
2. *Hist. Coll. S.C.*, II, 62-79.
3. McCrady, *South Carolina*, 94-105, 302; *Cal. A&WI*, VII, 32, 57; *Hist. Coll. S.C.*, II, 83.
4. Sally, *Narratives of Early South Carolina*, 132-134; Rivers, *Hist. Sketch of S.C.*, 129, 131-133, 353, 358; *Cal. A&WI*, VII, 89-92, X, 496. On several occasions in the early 1670s the lord proprietors established laws that said, "Noe Indian upon any occasion or pretence whatsoever shall be made a Slave, or without his owne consent carryed out of Carolina." (Rivers, *Hist. Sketch of S.C.*, 358.)

5. *Cal. A&WI*, X, 60-61, XI,11-12; Rivers, *Hist. Sketch of S.C.*, 388-389.
6. *Cal. A&WI*, XI, 16-18, 508-510.
7. Crane, *The Southern Frontier*, 24-26; Swanton, *Early History of the Creek*, 90-93.
8. *Cal. A&WI*, XII, 12-13; Gallay, *Indian Slave Trade*, 74-77; McCrady, *South Carolina*, 195-196.
9. *Cal. A&WI*, XII, 10-14, 39-40, 178-179; McCrady, *South Carolina*, 204-211.
10. Swanton, *Early History of the Creek*, 299-304; Crane, *The Southern Frontier*, 30-31; Rivers, *Hist. Sketch of S.C.*, 142-144; Gallay, *Indian Slave Trade*, 80-83.
11. *Cal. A&WI*, XII, 336-337, 451-452; McCrady, *South Carolina*, 216-220; Rivers, *Hist. Sketch of S.C.*, 144-145.

## CHAPTER 16: LOUISIANA AND THE BROTHERS LE MOYNE

1. French, *Hist. Coll.*, I, 1-20; Charlevoix, V, 117-118.
2. Cruzat, "New Orleans Under Bienville," *Louisiana Hist. Quarterly*, I, no 3, 58-64; French, *Hist. Coll.*, I, 21-23, II, 48-58; Dunn, *Spanish-French Rivalry*, 185-191.
3. French, *Hist. Coll.*, I, 23-25.
4. Charlevoix, V, 120-123; French, *Hist. Coll.*, II, 66-72; Swanton, *Tribes of the Lower Mississippi*, 274-277.
5. French, *Hist. Coll.*, I, 26-31, 36-42, II, 109-112.
6. *Cal. A&WI*, XVIII, 69-71; Crane, *The Southern Frontier*, 56-57; La Harpe, *L'Etablissement des Francais a la Louisiana*, 18-21. Also called Capt. Bond in English sources.
7. Crane, *The Southern Frontier*, 48-55.
8. *Cal. A&WI*, XIV, 512, XVI, 391-393; Coxe, *Carolana*, 1-2.
9. Crane, *The Southern Frontier*, 57-59; *Cal. A&WI*, XVII, 578-580, XVIII, 22-23.
10. Charlevoix, V, 123-125; French, *Hist. Coll.*, I, 51-60.
11. Dunn, *Spanish-French Rivalry*, 197-202.
12. Dunn, *Spanish-French Rivalry*, 204-205; La Harpe, *L'Etablissement des Francais a la Louisiana*, 30-31; Margry, IV, 539-542; Charlevoix, V, 127-128.
13. French, *Hist. Coll.*, I, 60-61, 75-76; Gallay, *Indian Slave Trade*, 122-124; Margry, IV, 426-430, 501-502.
14. Gallay, *Indian Slave Trade* 128-131; La Harpe, *L'Etablissement des Francais a la Louisiana*, 35-36; Crane, *The Southern Frontier*, 67-69.
15. Margry, IV, 494-495, 507, 543-550; La Harpe, *L'Etablissement des Francais a la Louisiana*, 36-38, 71.
16. Reed, *Masters of the Wilderness*, 123-127.
17. Margry, IV, 516-521; Gallay, *Indian Slave Trade*, 131-132; Crane, *The Southern Frontier*, 69-70.
18. Margry, IV, 518, 530-531.

## CHAPTER 17: MOORE'S FOLLY

1. Margry, IV, 546-549, 550-552, 594-605. Iberville pointed out that one of Pensacola's weaknesses was its lack of settlers, which was not surprising given that there was almost no trade and the area was nothing but sand and pine forests. (Margry, IV, 547.)
2. Crane, *The Southern Frontier*, 69-73; Margry, IV, 579-580, 594-595.
3. Boyd, *Here They Once Stood*, 36-38; *Hist. Coll. S.C.*, II, 351; Swanton, *Early History of the Creek*, 120-121.
4. Salley, *Journals S.C. Assembly, 1702*, 47; *Cal. A&WI*, XX, 208.

5. Salley, *Journals S.C. Assembly, 1702*, 63-65; McCrady, *South Carolina*, 377-379.
6. Rivers, *Hist. Sketch of S.C.*,196-199; Sally, *Journals S.C. Assembly, 1702*, 84-92; McCrady, *South Carolina*, 378-382; Sally, *Narratives of Early South Carolina*, 271-272.
7. *Cal. A&WI*, XX, 745-746, XXI, 13-14; Wright, *Anglo-Spanish Rivalry*, 61-63.
8. *Cal. A&WI*, XX, 745-746; Rivers, *Hist. Sketch of S.C.*,199-201.
9. Boyd, "The Siege of St. Augustine," *Florida Hist. Qtr.*, XXVI, no 4, 345-349; Arnade, *The Siege of St. Augustine, 1702*, 22-28, 39-47; *Cal. A&WI*, XX, 28-29, 182-183.
10. Arnade, *The Siege of St. Augustine, 1702*, 54-59; Boyd, "The Siege of St. Augustine," *Florida Hist. Qtr.*, XXVI, no 4, 349-352; Arana, *History Castillo de San Marcos*, 38-39.
11. *Cal. A&WI*, XXI, 183, XXI, 218; Arnade, "The English Invasion of Spanish Florida," *Florida Hist. Qtr.*, XLI, no 1, 32-34; Crane, *The Southern Frontier*, 75-77; Wright, *Anglo-Spanish Rivalry*, 61-63.

CHAPTER 18: THE APALACHEE AND THE SIEGE OF CHARLES TOWN

1. Gallay, *Indian Slave Trade* 133-140; French, *Hist. Coll.*, I, 80-83.
2. Salley, *Journals S.C. Assembly, 1703*, 105-106; Arnade, "The English Invasion of Spanish Florida," *Florida Hist. Qtr.*, XLI, no 1, 34-35; McCrady, *South Carolina*, 390-392.
3. Rivers, *Hist. Sketch of S.C.*, 208-209; "Moore Letter," *Hist. Coll. S.C.*, II, 574-575; Crane, *The Southern Frontier*, 77-80.
4. *Cal. A&WI*, XXII, 145; "Moore Letter," *Hist. Coll. S.C.*, II, 575-576; McCrady, *South Carolina*, 393-394; Swanton, *Early History of the Creek*, 122-124; Sweet, *Spanish Missions of Florida*, 55-56. Moore was thanked by the lord proprietors and "wiped off the ignominy of his failure at St. Augustine, and increased his means by the sale or bondage of Indian captives." (McCrady, *South Carolina*, 393-394.) Based on a March 30, 1704, letter from Governor Zuniga, Shea, in *The Catholic Church in Colonial Days*, pointed to a different side of Moore when he noted that "Many of the prisoners were at once tied to stakes, tortured and burned to death. Father (Angel) Miranda appealed in vain to Governor Moore to prevent such horrible cruelties on prisoners before his very eyes; but to no purpose." (Ibid., I, 461-463.)
5. Arnade, "The English Invasion of Spanish Florida," *Florida Hist. Qtr.*, XLI, no 1, 35-37; Gallay, *Indian Slave Trade* 145-149; Sweet, *Spanish Missions of Florida*, 56-57; French, *Hist. Coll.*, I, 96, III, 31-32.
6. La Harpe, *L'Etablissement des Francais a la Louisiana*, 89-91; Cushman, *Hist. Choctaw, Chickasaw, and Natchez*, 76-77.
7. Guerin, *Hist. Maritime France*, IV, 476-477; Crouse, *Soldier of New France*, 249-251.
8. *Cal. A&WI*, XXIII, 72-78; Guerin, *Hist. Maritime France*, IV, 161; *Boston News-Letter*, April 15, May 6, 1706.
9. *Cal. A&WI*, XXIII, 142-147; *Boston News-Letter*, May 13, May 20, 1706; Guerin, *Hist. Maritime France*, IV, 161-162.
10. La Harpe, *L'Etablissement des Francais a la Louisiana*, 99-100; French, *Hist. Coll.*, III, 35; Guerin, *Hist. Maritime France*, IV, 162; *Boston News-Letter*, June 3, June 10, 1706; *Cal. A&WI*, XXIII, 246-247; *Mass. Acts and Resolves*, VIII, 568, 699.
11. *Cal. A&WI*, XXIII, 248-249; *Boston News-Letter*, Oct 14, 1706. Lefebvre is referred to as Le Feboure in most English accounts.
12. McCrady, *South Carolina*, 397-399; *Cal. A&WI*, XXIII, 249-250; *Boston News-Letter*, Oct 14, 1706; Rivers, *Hist. Sketch of S.C.*, 210-212.

13. *Boston News-Letter,* Oct 14, 1706; *Cal. A&WI,* XXIII, 250-252.
14. Rivers, *Hist. Sketch of S.C.,* 212-214; *Cal. A&WI,* XXIII, 251-254, 290; *Boston News-Letter,* Oct 14, 1706.

CHAPTER 19: THE PORT ROYAL EXPEDITIONS

1. *Cal. A&WI,* XXII, 130, 228, 462.
2. *Winthrop Papers,* MHSC 6th series, III, 547-549.
3. Ibid., 549.
4. Ibid., 549-550. There is no doubt that Romer's letter came across as shrill, although when reading it one gets a sense that some of this may have been the result of his poor English.
5. Porter, Whitworth, *History of the Corps of Royal Engineers,* I, 137, 139; *English Army Lists and Commission Registers,* 1661-1714, V, (1702-1707), 120, 123; *Cal. A&WI,* XXII, 447, 586. It should be pointed out that at this time engineers held a warrant from the Ordinance Department, but this did not translate into an actual army rank.
6. *New Hampshire Provincial Papers,* II, 463; *Documentary History of the State of Maine,* IX, 218; *Mass Acts and Resolves,* VIII, (1703-1707), 522-523, 532. In his report to the Massachusetts legislature Redknap lists the cost of building a new seventy-by-seventy-foot fort at Winter Harbor as £1854, and estimated that it would take ninety-seven men four months to complete the task. When the Massachusetts Assembly saw the projected costs, the venture was put on hold. (Ibid.)
7. *New York Colonial Documents,* IV, 1185; *Boston News-Letter,* May 27, Aug 5, Oct 7, 1706; *Mass Acts and Resolves,* VIII (1703-1707), 551-552, 585-586; *Cal. A&WI,* XXIII, 246-247.
8. *Mass Acts and Resolves,* VIII (1703-1707), 568; *Cal. A&WI,* XXIII, 234, 247.
9. *Cal. A&WI,* XXIII, 29-32.
10. *Mass Acts and Resolves,* VIII (1703-1707), 684, 694; *Cal. A&WI,* XXIII, 678-679; Drenth & Riley, *First Col. Soldiers* II/1, 80-85.
11. Calnek, W.A., *History of the County of Annapolis,* 55; *Mass Acts and Resolves,* VIII (1703-1707), 715; *Calendar American & West Indies Papers,* Vol. 23 (1706-1708), 438-439, 560, 587-588; "Barnard Journal," MHSC, 3rd series, V, 189-191.
12. *History of the County of Annapolis,* 4-55; *Cal. A&WI,* XXIII, 777-778; *Coll. Man. N.F.,* II, 464-465, 467-468; "Barnard Journal," 191-192; René Baudry, "Auger de Subercase, Daniel D," in DCB, II.
13. "Winthrop Papers," MHSC, 6th series, III, 390-392; *Cal. A&WI,* XXIII, 677-678, 777-778; *Mass Acts and Resolves,* 1703-1707, 725.
14. Ibid., *History of the County of Annapolis,* 56; *Cal. A&WI,* XXIII, 677-678, 777-778. "Barnard Journal," 192-193.
15. "Winthrop Papers," MHSC, 6th series, III, 391; *Mass Acts and Resolves,* (1703-1707), 725; *Cal. A&WI,* XXIII, 777-780; *Coll. Man. N.F.,* II, 466-467, 468-469.
16. Calnek, W.A., *History of the County of Annapolis,* 56-57; *Mass Acts and Resolves,* (1703-1707), 725; Penhallow, 42-43. In regard to Redknap's accusation that the colonial force lacked the military discipline and skill to conduct a siege, Governor Dudley had earlier expressed concerns about just such a matter. "I am sensible," he informed the Massachusetts Assembly not long after the expedition departed for Port Royal, "her Majesties Subjects of these Provinces have not seen such regular Service as the Wars of

Europe or the present expedition may demand but I am well assured of their Courage." (Kimball, Everett, *Public Life of Joseph Dudley*, 121.)
17. *Coll. Man. N.F.*, II, 466, 469.
18. "Winthrop Papers," MHSC, 6th series, III, 388. *Mass Acts and Resolves*, 1703-1707, 723-727; Drake, 233.
19. *Cal. A&WI*, XXIII, 678-679.
20. Ibid.
21. Kimball, *Life of Dudley*, 121-122; Donahue, *Mass. Soldiers in Queen Anne's War*, xi-xii; *Cal. A&WI*, XXIII, 587-588; *Doc. Hist. Maine*, IX, 238-239.
22. *Mass Acts and Resolves*, 1703-1707, 728-731; *Doc. Hist. Maine*, IX, 235-238.
23. *Doc. Hist. Maine*, IX, 244-245; *Mass Acts and Resolves*, 1703-1707, 735-737; *N.H. Prov. Papers*, II, 506.
24. *Coll. Man. N.F.*, II, 470, 477-478; *Mass Acts and Resolves*, 1703-1707, 743-744; Hutchinson, *Hist. Mass.*, II, 167-171.
25. Charlevoix, V, 196-200; *Mass Acts and Resolves*, 1703-1707, 745-746; *Coll. Man. N.F.*, II, 478-481; "Barnard Journal," 193-196; Drake, 234-236.
26. *Coll. Man. N.F.*, II, 483; *Cal. A&WI*, XXIII, 560.

CHAPTER 20: THE DESTRUCTION OF HAVERHILL

1. *NY Col. Doc.*, IX, 814-815. While understandable issues, the French court was not pleased with the governor's conduct in this area. "After all that had been written directing you to cause the English of Boston to be harrassed either by parties of Frenchmen or Indians," the minister of the marine wrote Vaudreuil in June 1708, "his Majesty expected to receive news of some expedition against them, and is not satisfied with the inactivity in which you remain with such numerous forces as you have. Since the people of that government were thereby enabled to attack Acadia. He positively desires you to send frequent parties against them, and even to seize the first opportunity that will offer, to go yourself to attack them in their posts provided you be sure of success. Observe only that it be effected at the least possible expense, and transmit to me a report of what you will do." (*NY Col. Doc.*, IX, 813.)
2. *NY Col. Doc.*, IX, 816-818; *Cal. A&WI*, XXIV, 70-72. Cornbury informed the Board of Trade that if they sent more merchandise that he could not only secure the Five Nations to English interests, but he could also "debauch a great many of the French Indians from them." (*NY Col. Doc.*, V, 65-66.)
3. *NY Col. Doc.*, IX, 817; Drake, 238-240.
4. *RPAQ 1939-1940*, 429-431; Charlevoix, V, 203-205. A list of French officers on the expedition can be found in *Michigan Pioneer Hits. Coll.*, XXXIII, 387.
5. Drake, 244-245; *History of Haverhill*, 119-122.
6. *History of Haverhill*, 123-125; *RPAQ 1939-1940*, 431-432; *Cal. A&WI*, XXIV, 240-241.
7. Charlevoix, V, 205-207; 03-205; *RPAQ 1939-1940*, 432-433, 457-458; *History of Haverhill*, 125-126; Hutchinson, *Hist. Mass.*, II, 173-174; *Cal. A&WI*, XXIV, 240-241. An account of one of the prisoners taken can be found in Joshua Coffin's *A Sketch of the History of Newbury*, 331-334.
8. *History of Haverhill*, 126-129.
9. *NY Col. Doc.*, IX, 133-135; Munro, 49, 83-84, 90-91.

10. Clowes, II, 360-361. In mid-July 1708, Intendant Raudot wrote the French court with a proposition to settle Cape Breton Island near the entrance to the Gulf of St. Lawrence, in part, to act as "an advance sentinel to protect the French marine in time of war." (*Report Canadian Archives for 1900*, 227.)

CHAPTER 21: SOLDIERS, SAILORS, AND FISHERMEN

1. *Cal. A&WI*, XXIII, 262-264. Lloyd estimated the losses incurred by the colony at £188,000 and while the total catch for 1705 was actually larger than that for 1703 (the records for 1704 were lost when the vessel carrying them was taken by the French), the inhabitants' portion of this catch was down by over a third, 48,000 quintals vs. 67,000 quintals. The following year, 1706, would see a catch of over 106,000 quintals with the inhabitants' share of this over 72,000 quintals. (*Cal. A&WI*, XXI, 870, XXIII, 7, 298; Prowse, *Newfoundland*, 246, 251.)
2. Charnock, *Biographia Navalis*, III, 147; Prowse, *Newfoundland*, 246-248. Note date in Prowse should be 25 July 1707.
3. *Cal. A&WI*, XXIII, 542-544, 562-563; Charnock, *Biographia Navalis*, III, 147-149; Anspach, *Newfoundland*, 142-149.
4. *Cal. A&WI*, XXIII, 328, 357, 373-374, 416, 544, 686-687, 708, 739-740.
5. Thorpe, George Vane, DCB, II; Abbey, *Report on Portland Manuscripts*, VIII, 346; *Cal. A&WI*, XXIV, 115-118, 146-147, 168.
6. Charlevoix, V, 212-213; "Durand La Garenne au Ministre, Feb. 21, 1709," MG-C11C, fol. 256-263; Pothier, "Joseph de St. Ovide," DCB, II; Richard, *Report Can. Archives*, 1889 (sup.), 393-394,
7. *Cal. A&WI*, XXV, 71-73, 296-297; Charlevoix, V, 213.
8. *Cal. A&WI*, XXIV, 216-218, 543-550, XXV, 297-299; "Durand La Garenne au Ministre, Feb. 21, 1709," MG-C11C; fol. 256-263; "St. Ovide au Ministre, Jan. 20, 1709, MG-C11C, fol. 276-283. Vane, after speaking with a number of French officers, came to the conclusion that the French were given information from someone within the garrison, but he was never able to identify the source. (*Cal. A&WI*, XXV, 297-298.)
9. "St. Ovide au Ministre, Jul 1, 1709," MG-C11C, fol. 294-299; Durand La Garenne au Ministre, Feb. 21, 1709," MG-C11C; fol. 256-263; Richard, *Report Can. Archives*, 1889 (sup.), 431-432; Pothier, "Joseph de St. Ovide," DCB, II; Charlevoix, V, 213-215.

CHAPTER 22: WAR AND PROFIT

1. Crane, *The Southern Frontier*, 80-81; Grady, *Anglo-Spanish Rivalry*, 226-227.
2. Swanton, *Early History of the Creek*, 339-341; Grady, *Anglo-Spanish Rivalry*, 226-227; Gallay, *Indian Slave Trade*, 148, 294-296; *Cal. A&WI*, XXIV, 422. Gallay estimates that between the Apalachee, Timucua, and the other tribes farther down the Florida peninsula that the number of native enslaved was at a minimum from fifteen thousand to twenty thousand. (Gallay, *Indian Slave Trade*, 148, 296.)
3. Faye, "Spanish Fortifications of Pensacola," *FHQ*, XX, No. 2, 152-156; Griffen, "Spanish Pensacola," *FHQ*, XXXVII, No. 3-4, 243-246, 251-252; *Cal. A&WI*, XXIV, 422.
4. Griffen, "Spanish Pensacola," *FHQ*, XXXVII, No. 3-4, 252-253.
5. Salley, *Journals S.C. Assembly, Oct. 1707-Feb. 1708*, 4, 13, 23-25, 27, 33-34; Gallay, *Indian Slave Trade*, 128-129; King, *Bienville*, 156; *Cal. A&WI*, XXIV, 433-435; Crane, *The Southern Frontier*, 87-91, 94-95.

6. *Cal. A&WI*, XXIV, 421; *Le Jau Chronicle*, 39; Malone, *Dictionary American Biography*, XIII, 379.
7. *Cal. A&WI*, XXIV, 421-424.
8. Gallay, *Indian Slave Trade*, 219-222; *Cal. A&WI*, XXIV, 433-435; Crane, *The Southern Frontier*, 93-95.
9. La Harpe, *L'Etablissement des Francais a la Louisiana,* 88-104; French, *Hist. Coll.*, I, 97-98; Swanton, *Tribes of the Lower Mississippi*, 30-31, 300, 337-338; King, *Bienville*, 140-144, 160-161.
10. Gayarre, *Hist. Louisiana*, I, 87; King, *Bienville*, 152-155.
11. King, *Bienville*, 166-170; French, *Hist. Coll.*, I, 99; La Harpe, *L'Etablissement des Francais a la Louisiana*, 105-106.
12. King, *Bienville*, 174-176; Gayarre, *Hist. Louisiana*, I, 99-100.
13. Gallay, *Indian Slave Trade*, 288-292; *Cal. A&WI*, XXVI, 295-296; Crane, *The Southern Frontier*, 94-97; La Harpe, *L'Etablissement des Francais a la Louisiana*, 108; Salley, *Journals S.C. Assembly, Oct. 1707-Feb. 1708*, 50.

CHAPTER 23: THE OLD INVASION PLAN

1. Vetch, Samuel, 1668-1732, *DCB*, II; *Cal. A&WI*, XXIV, 41-51, 57-58, 147-150, 283-286.
2. *Cal. A&WI*, XXIV, 398-40; Also see proclamations issued by Nicholson & Vetch in Boston and New York (May 9 and 26, 1709), and Lt. Governor Ingoldsby (June 30); Also see New York's "An Act to Detach Four Hundred and Eighty Seven Men," (June 7) and New Jersey's "Acts Passed. . ." (June 30). (*Early American Imprints*, 1st series, 39493, 39483, 39484, 1415, 1412.)
3. *Cal. A&WI*, XXIV, 399-406, 419-420; *NY Col. Doc.*, V, 81. Vetch claimed that Nicholson initially "showed a great deal of adversion," toward the idea of commanding the Albany expedition but later relented when pressed by the various governors to do so.
4. *Cal. A&WI*, XXIV, 419-420, 437-439. McCully, "Catastrophe in the Wilderness: New Light on the Canada Expedition of 1709," *WMQ*, #11, July 1954, 441-456.
5. "Catastrophe in the Wilderness. . .," 441-456; Captain John Harrison Letters, in William Whitehead's *Contributions to the Early History of Perth Amboy*, 86-88.
6. *NY Col. Doc.*, IX, 828-830, 835-836. Schuyler's efforts proved successful. In a July 1709 meeting at Albany the Five Nations vowed to break the current peace treaty with New France and promised Lt. Governor Ingoldsby that 105 Oneida, 100 Cayouge, 150 Mohawk, and 88 Onondaga would join the expedition. To this should be added another 60 Connecticut River Indians who also pledged their support. Only the Seneca, not wishing to resume the conflict with Canada's western allies, refused to aid the effort. (Wraxell, *An Abridgement of the Indian Affairs. . .*, 69.)
7. Memiore pour M. de Ramezay, July 14, 1709, and Council of War Point-a-la-Chevelure, Aug 2, 1709, MG1-C11A, vol 30, fol. 112-114v, 131-132; Ramezay, Claude de, 1659-1724, *DCB*, II; *NY Col. Doc.*, IX, 830. Ramezay claims his forces consisted of 1,200 French and 450 Indians. (ibid.)
8. Catalogne's Journal, *Collection de Manuscrits . . . Nouvelle France*, I, 615-617; *NY Col. Doc.*, IX, 830.
9. *Collection de Manuscrits . . . Nouvelle France*, I, 617-618.
10. Ibid.; "Catastrophe in the Wilderness . . .," 453-454.

11. *Collection de Manuscrits . . . Nouvelle France*, I, 617-618; Council of War Point-a-la-Chevelure, Aug 2, 1709, Paroles des Sauvages du parti commandé par Monsieur de Ramezay, Aug 2, 1709, and Ramezey to Ministre, Nov 4, 1709, MG1-C11A, vol. 30, fol. 131-132, 128-130, 346-351v; *NY Col. Doc.*, IX 830-831, 837-839. Not surprisingly, casualty reports from the skirmish varied, but in general it seems both sides lost half a dozen or so killed and wounded. One unofficial English report stated English losses at five English Indians, two Dutchmen, and four French Indians killed. (Josiah Rossetter to Rowland Cotton, September 12, 1709, *MHS*, Miscellaneous Manuscripts, VII.) The Dutchmen claimed as casualties were no doubt the two captured by Ramezay the evening after the skirmish.
12. *NY Col. Doc.*, IX, 838-839.
13. Whitehead, *Contributions to the Early History of Perth Amboy*, 87-89; "Catastrophe in the Wilderness. . .," 441-456.
14. *NY Col. Doc.*, IX, 842-843; "Catastrophe in the Wilderness. . .," 441-456; *Cal. A&WI*, XXIV, 488-496.
15. *NY Col. Doc.*, IX, 843.

CHAPTER 24: THE FALL OF PORT ROYAL

1. *NY Col. Doc.*, IX, 747, 828-830.
2. *NY Col. Doc.*, IX, 831-833; Charlevoix, V, 215-216. Vaudreuil noted that the defensive preparation were made "so much the more difficult as those who ought to assist me in encouraging the people to make every sacrifice to defend themselves, were the first to insinuate to them, notwithstanding all the news I was receiving, that it was impossible the enemy would invade this country." (Ibid., 832.)
3. *NY Col. Doc.*, IX, 833-835; Richard, *Report Can. Archives*, 1889 (sup.), 46, 220, 222-223. It was further added "that if Peter Schuyler caused the Mohawks too much regret, they would always be very much welcomed by us." (*NY Col. Doc.*, IX, 834.)
4. Charlevoix, V, 220-221.
5. Beaudet, *Archaeology at Fort Chambly*, 11-12, 41-42, 51-52; *NY Col. Doc.*, IX, 841, 846, 851.
6. Charlevoix, V, 222-223; *NY Col. Doc.*, IX, 840-842.
7. *Cal. A&WI*, XXV, 25, 29-30; Kimball, *Dudley*, 125-126.
8. "Nicholson's Journal," *Coll. N.S.Hist. Soc.*, I, 59-65; *Cal. A&WI*, XXV, 12-13, 25, 84, 103-104, 126-129, 134-136; Donahue, *Mass. Troops in Queen Anne's War*, xvii-xviii; *Conn. Troops in Queen Anne's War*, 4-6, 13-14.
9. *Cal. A&WI*, XXV, 183-184; "Nicholson's Journal," 64-66; Clowes, II, 526-527. A complete list and the organization of Nicholson's forces can be found in Drenth & Riley, *The First Colonial Soldiers*, II/1, 89-96.
10. *Coll. Man. N.F.*, II, 528-529; "Nicholson's Journal," 64-67; Wilson, "An Acadian Governor," *The International Review*, 486-487; Drake, 259-260.
11. "Nicholson's Journal," 67-79; Trumbull, *Hist. Conn.*, I, 462.
12. "Nicholson's Journal," 79-89; *Coll. Man. N.F.*, II, 529-530
13. "Nicholson's Journal," 79-89; *Coll. Man. N.F.*, II, 529-530; *Conn. Troops in Queen Anne's War*, 17-21; *Cal. A&WI*, XXV, 220-221, 226-227, 229-233.
14. *NY Col. Doc.*, IX, 853-854.

CHAPTER 25: WALKER'S EXPEDITION

1. *Cal. A&WI*, XXV, 230-231.
2. *NY Col. Doc.*, IX, 853-854.
3. Hovenden Walker, *A Journal or Full Account of the Late Expedition to Canada* (London: D. Browne, 1720), 164-179 (hereafter *Walker's Journal*); "King's Journal I," *Cal. A&WI*, XXVI, 42, 47. King's guns were to be serviced by 102 men drawn from the artillery and engineering ranks. (Cleaveland, 73-174.) The warships in Walker's fleet were the *Edgar* (70), *Swiftsure* (70), *Torbay* (80), *Monmouth* (70), *Sunderland* (60), *Kingston* (60), *Montague* (60), *Devonshire* (80), *Diamond* (40), *Humber* (80), *Dunkirk* (60), *Experiment* (40), and the bomb vessels *Basilisk* and *Granada*. He would later be joined by the *Leopard* (50), *Windsor* (60), *Chester* (50), and *Sapphire* (40). (*Walker's Journal*, 188-191, 200; William L. Clowes, *The Royal Navy: A History from the Earliest Times to the Present*, vol. II (London: Sampson Low, Marston & Co., 1898), 526-527.)
4. "Proceedings of the Congress held in New London," *NY Col. Doc.*, V, 257-261; *Walker's Journal*, 68-70; "King's Journal I," *Cal. A&WI*, XXVI, 43.
5. Ibid., 44.
6. "Proclamation by Governor Dudley, July 2, 1711," *Cal. A&WI*, XXVI, 36; *Walker's Journal*, 81-83.
7. "Brigadier General Hill to Lord Dartmouth, July 31, 1711," *Cal. A&WI*, XXVI, 55-56; "General Hill's Journal," ibid., 59; "King's Journal I," ibid., 45. Thomas Hutchinson, *The History of Massachusetts Bay*, vol. I (Salem: Thomas C. Cushing, 1795), 191-192. When Walker heard that the exchange rate would be set by the Massachusetts Assembly he wrote, "By all I could perceive it was likely to be very disadvantageous to the Queen's Interest." (*Walker's Journal*, 82-83.)
8. *Walker's Journal*, 92-93; "King to St. John, July 25, 1711," *Cal. A&WI*, XXVI, 40, 47.
9. "Proclamation by Governor Dudley, July 13, 1711," *Cal. A&WI*, XXVI, 35-37;. Ellis Ames and Abner Goodell (eds.), *Acts and Resolves of the Province of Massachusetts Bay*, vol. I (Boston: Wright & Potter, 1869), 686; Nathaniel Bouton, *Documents and Records Relating to the Province of New Hampshire*, vol. II (Manchester: John B. Clarke, 1868), 625-626. The next day Walker issued a general pardon for any seaman, soldier, or marine that would return to service. ("Hill's Journal," *Cal. A&WI*, XXVI, 35-36.)
10. "King's Journal I," *Cal. A&WI*, XXVI, 47. Walker and King were aware of the Five Nations current peace treaty with the French and urged the delegates to consider claiming British sovereignty, which would, of course, have had the effect of redefining the borders in North America. (*Walker's Journal*, 104-105,109.)
11. Ibid. "So if storms, contrary winds, and the difficult navigation of the River (St. Lawrence) don't defeat us," King wrote the British minister, "I believe it's certain nothing else can." (*Cal. A&WI*, XXVI, 39-40.)
12. "King's Journal I," *Cal. A&WI*, XXVI, 48.
13. *NY Col. Doc.*, V, 262-265, 277-278; *Cal. A&WI*, XXVI, 39-50, 55-66, 100-104. *Boston News-Letter* Sept. 3, 1711.
14. Colonel Richard Ingoldby's regiment of independent companies and militia 600, Colonel Peter Schuyler's regiment 550, and Colonel Joseph Whiting's Connecticut regiment 360. Adding in the allied Indians puts Nicholson's strength at around 2,300 men. (*Cal. A&WI*, XXVI, 100-104.)

15. *Cal. A&WI*, XXVI, 39-50, 55-66, 100-104; *Boston News-Letter*, September 3, 1711; *The Journal of Rev. John Buckingham's during the Campaign of 1711*, ———.
16. "King's Journal I." *Cal. A&WI*, XXVI, 49-50; "King to St. John, Aug. 14, 1711," ibid., 70-71; *Walker's Journal*, 90, 117-118. Walker had recruited a number of pilots at Boston, but many admitted that they had little experience on the St. Lawrence. Almost to a man, however, they agreed that the eighty-gun HMS *Humber* and the eighty-gun HMS *Devonshire* were too large to guarantee their safe passage up the river. As a result, Walker would order these vessels to cruise the entrance to the river for a few weeks before returning home. (*Walker's Journal*, 275-279; "King's Journal I," *Cal. A&WI*, XXVI, 45.)
17. Ibid., 119-120. Colonel Samuel Vetch, who had presented the original invasion plan to the British court in 1709, and was part of the expedition, claimed that Walker had been duped by his unreliable French pilot. Walker actually had several pilots aboard the *Edgar*, one of whom was a Frenchman he had recruited at Plymouth. Walker agreed that this man was questionable, but it is difficult to call the French captain of the captured sloop unreliable when his comments proved prophetic.
18. *Walker's Journal*, 123-124; "King's Journal II," *Cal. A&WI*, XXVI, 92.
19. "Hill to Hunter, July 25, 1711," *NY Col. Doc.*, V, 276-277; "King's Journal II," *Cal. A&WI*, XXVI, 92-93.
20. *Walker's Journal*, 124-125.
21. "King's Journal II," *Cal. A&WI*, XXVI, 93; "Commissary Sampson Sheaf's Letter," in Hutchinson,198.
22. "King's Journal II," *Cal. A&WI*, XXVI, 93-94, 96; *Walker's Journal*,124-126, 128, 275-279. "Hill to Hunter, July 25, 1711," *NY Col. Doc.*, V, 276-277. The vessels lost were the *Colchester* (530 tons), *Nathaniel and Elizabeth* (297), *Samuel and Anne* (225), *Marlborough* (218), *Chatham* (150), *Isabella* (326), *Smyrna Merchant* (364), and the New England provision ship *Content* (120). (*Walker's Journal*, 128, "King's Journal II," *Cal. A&WI*, XXVI, 96.)
23. "King to St. John, Sept. 11, 1711." *Cal. A&WI*, XXVI, 91-92. The expedition's bad luck continued upon reaching England. On October 15, a few days after arriving at Spithead, Walker's flagship HMS *Edgar* blew up at dock as the result of a magazine accident. Walker and the ship's captain were ashore at the time. Initially the matter was not investigated, but several years later it was taken up and as a result Walker was removed from the flag officer list. (Clowes, 528-529.)
24. *Cal. A&WI*, XXVI, 88-90, 100-104; *NY Col. Doc.*, V, 262-265, 277-278; Kalm, *Travels*, II, 135.
25. *NY Col. Doc.*, IX, 862.

CHAPTER 26: THE LAST DAYS

1. Richard, *Report Can. Archives*, 1889 (sup.), 461, 464-465.
2. *Coll. Man. N.F.*, II, 531-532, 534-536; *Cal. A&WI*, XXV, 343-344, 549-550. Even with his losses Vetch reported the garrison of Annapolis Royal at 449 on June 1, 1711. (*Cal. A&WI*, XXV, 551.)
3. *Cal. A&WI*, XXV, 343-345, 552-554, XXVI, 41-42, 58; Wilson, "An Acadian Governor," 494-497; Murdoch, *Hist. Nova Scotia*, I, 322-326; Calnek, *History of Annapolis*, 63-65; Bannon, "Antoine Gaulin: An Apostle of Early Acadia," *Can. Catholic Hist. Assoc. Report*, XIX, 55-56.

4. *NY Col. Doc.*, IX, 861.
5. *NY Col. Doc.*, IX. 863-865.
6. "Dubuisson Report," *Hist. Wisconsin*, II, 315-319; *NY Col. Doc.*, IX, 863-864; Charlevoix, V, 256-258.
7. "Dubuisson Report," *Hist. Wisconsin*, II, 319-332; Charlevoix, V, 256-265. Dubuisson had a few of the garrison wounded, and his allies had sixty killed or wounded, many during the first siege. As it would turn out, this would prove to be but the first of several Franco-Fox conflicts.
8. Hawks, *N.C, Hist.*, II, 530-531. As for the actual cause of the incident, Col. John Barnwell, who would lead an expedition against the Tuscarora, wrote, "I examined several of the prisoners who provoked the Enemy to committ these Murders, and all agree in one story that the beginning of the Quarrel arose about an Indian that the White men had punished for a small fault committed in his drink, that at the same time 12 Senecas came & made peace with them, and told them that the Whites had imposed upon them and that when the whites had used them so, they knocked them on the head, they advised them that they were fools to slave & hunt to furnish themselves with the white people's food, it was but killing of them & become possessed of their substance, that they did not fear the want of ammunition for that, they would come twice a year & furnish them with it." Barnwell, "The Tuscarora Expedition." (*S.C. Hist. & Gen.* Mag., IX, 35.)
9. *S.C. Hist. & Gen.* Mag., IX, 28-54, X, 33-48; *Cal. A&WI*, XXVII, 139-140, 189; *Journals S.C. Assembly, Oct. 1711-Nov. 1711*, 346-349. Governor Edward Hyde of Virginia spoke to Barnwell's peace treaty with the Tuscarora. "Then as for the pretended peace that Col B (Barnwell) said he had made with them, that there is nothing in it, Barnwell himself saying it was a sham business to put them off until he was better prepared for them, neither hath he ever yet given accounts to us what it was, & then if there was a peace Col. B himself hath broken it by killing & taking several of the Indians since, who being along with Tusqueroras in Hancock Fort, were equally concerned in the peace with them." (*Journals S.C. Assembly, June 1712*, 899-900.)
10. Drake, 284-289; Hutchinson, II, 181-182; Penhallow, 71-74.
11. *Cal. A&WI*, XXVII, 79-80, 82, 102-104; Richard, *Report Can. Archives*, 1889 (sup.), 465.
12. *Cal. A&WI*, XXVII, 229-231.
13. Almon, *A Collection of Treaties*, I, 136-141, 171-176.

EPILOGUE: A QUARTER-CENTURY OF CONFLICT

1. "King to St. John, July 25, 1711." *Cal. A&WI*, XXVI, 39-40.

# *Bibliography*


Manuscript Sources

Canada. National Archives. (Ottawa)
Manuscript Division
MG1: Fonds des Colonies
Sèrie C11A, Canada et Dépendances (Lettres des Gouverneurs, Intendants, officers et autres)
Sèrie F3 Collection Moreau de Saint-Méry

Published Sources

Abbey, Welbeck. *Report on the Manuscripts of his Grace the Duke of Portland*, VIII. London: His Majesty's Stationary Office, 1907.

Almon, John (ed.). *A Collection of all the treaties of peace, alliance, and commerce between Great Britain and other powers: from the revolution in 1688 to the present time. . .* 2 vols. London: J. Almon, 1772.

Ames, Ellis (ed.). *The Acts and Resolves of the Province of Massachusetts Bay*. Vol. VII (1692-1702), VIII (1703-1707). Boston: Wright & Potter, 1892, 1895.

Anon. *A Full Account of the Proceedings in Relation to Captain Kidd*. London: Booksellers of London and Westminster, 1701.

Anon. *A Letter to a Noble Lord Concerning the Late Expedition to Canada*. London: A. Baldwin, 1712.

Anspach, Lewis. *A History of the Island of Newfoundland*. London: J. Allman, 1819.

Arana, Luis. *History Castillo de San Marcos*. St. Augustine: Historic Print and Map Co., 2005.

Arnade, Charles. "The English Invasion of Spanish Florida," *FHQ*, XLI, no. 1, 29-37.

——. *The Siege of St. Augustine in 1702*. Gainesville: University of Florida Press, 1959.

Bannon, Richard. "Antoine Gaulin: An Apostle of Early Acadia," *Canadian Catholic Historical Association Report*, XIX, 49-59.

Barnard, John. "Autobiography of Rev. John Barnard," *Collections of the Massachusetts Historical Society*, 3rd series, V. Boston: Mass. Historical Society, 1836, 177-243.

Barnwell, John. "The Tuscarora Expedition," *South Carolina Historical and Genealogical Magazine*, IX, no. 1, 28-54.

Barnwell, Joseph. "The Second Tuscarora Expedition," *South Carolina Historical and Genealogical Magazine*, X, no. 1, 33-48.

Baudry, René. "Daniel d'Auger de Subercase," DCB, II (1701-1740).

Beaudot, Pierre and Cloutier, Céline. *Archaeology at Fort Chambly*. Ottawa: Canadian Parks Service, 1989.

*Boston News-Letter*

Bourne, Edward. *The History of Wells and Kennebunk*. Portland: B. Thurston & Co., 1875.

Bouton, Nathaniel. *Documents and Records Relating to the Province of New Hampshire, Vol. II: 1686-1722*. Manchester: John B. Clarke State Printer, 1868.

Boyd, Mark. "Enumeration of Florida Spanish Missions in 1675," *FHQ*, XXVII, no. 2, 181-188.

——. "The Siege of St. Augustine in 1702," *FHQ*, XXVI, no. 4, 345-352.

Boyd, Mark, Smith, Hale, and Griffin, John. *Here They Once Stood; The Tragic End of the Apalachee Missions*. Gainesville: The University of Florida Press, 1951.

Brandão, José António. *"Your Fire Shall Fire No More." Iroquois Policy towards New France and Its Native Allies to 1701*. Lincoln: University of Nebraska Press, 1997.

Brodhead, John Romeyn. *History of the State of New York*. 2 vols. New York: Harper & Brothers, 1853, 1871.

Brymner, Douglas (ed.). *Supplement Report on Canadian Archives 1889*. Ottawa: E. Dawson Printer, 1901.

——. *Report on Canadian Archives 1895*. Ottawa: E. Dawson Printer, 1896.

Buckingham, Thomas. *Roll and Journal of Connecticut Service in Queen Anne's War*. New Haven: Tuttle, Morehouse, and Taylor, 1916.

Burchett, Josiah. *A Complete History of the Most Remarkable Transactions at Sea*. London: J. Walthoe, 1720.

Calnek, W.A. *History of the Country of Annapolis.* Toronto: William Briggs, 1897.

Catalogne, Gedeon de. *Relation sur le Canada, 1682-1712.* Quebec: Middleton & Dawson, 1871.

Chalmers, George (ed.). *A Collection of treaties between Great Britain and other powers.* 2 vols. London: J. Stockdale, 1790.

Charlevoix, Pierre-François-Xavier de. *History and General Description of New France.* 6 vols. Paris: 1744. (Trans. and ed.) John Gilmary Shea. New York: Francis P. Harper, 1900.

Charnock, John. *Biographia Navalis.* 4 vols. London: R. Faulder, 1795.

Carroll, B.R. *Historical Collections of South Carolina.* 2 vols. New York: Harper & Brothers, 1836.

Church, Thomas. *The History of King Philip's War.* Boston: Solomon Southwick, 1716.

Clowes, William. *The Royal Navy: A History from the Earliest Times to the Present.* 6 vols. London: Sampson, Low, Marston, and Co., 1897-1902.

*Collection de manuscrits contenant letters, mémoires, et autres documents historiques relatifs à la Nouvelle-France, recueillis aux Archives de la Province de Québec, ou copies à l'étranger.* 4 vols. Québec, 1883-1885.

*Collections of the Michigan Pioneer and Historical Society,* XXXIII. Lansing: Robert Smith Printing, 1904.

"Costebelle's Journal," *Magazine of American History,* I, no.1, 107-112.

Covington, James. "Drake Destroys St. Augustine, 1586," *FHQ,* XLIV, no. 1-2, 81-93.

Coxe, Daniel. *A Description of the English Province of Carolana.* London: B. Crowse (1722). 1840.

Crane, Verner. *The Southern Frontier, 1670-1732.* New York: W.W. Norton & Co. (1928). 1981.

Crouse, Nellis. *Lemoyne d'Iberville: Soldier of New France.* Ithaca: Cornell University Press, 1954.

Cruzat, Heloise. "New Orleans Under Bienville," *Louisiana Historical Quarterly,* I, no. 3, 54-86.

Cushman, H.B. *History of the Choctaw, Chickasaw, and Natchez Indians.* Greenville: Headlight Printing House, 1899.

Dalton, Charles. *English Army Lists and Commission Registers.* 6 vols. (1661-1714). London: Eyre & Spottiswoode, 1892-1904.

Deagan, Kathleen. *Excavations at the Castillo de San Marcos.* Tallahassee: Florida State University, 1980.

Dewhurst, William. *The History of St. Augustine, Florida.* New York: G. P. Putnam's Sons, 1881.

*Documentary History of the State of Maine*. 24 vols. Portland: Bailey and Noyes, 1869-1916.

Donahue, Mary. *Massachusetts Officers and Soldiers 1702-1722: Queen Anne's War to Drummer's War*. Boston: Society of Colonial Wars, 1980.

Drake, Samuel. *The Border Wars of New England*. New York: Charles Scribner's Sons, 1897.

Drenth, Wienand, and Jonathon Riley. *The First Colonial Soldiers*. 2 vols. Eindhoven: Drenth Publishing, 2014-2015.

Dunn, William. *Spanish and French Rivalry in the Gulf Region of the United States, 1678-1702*, PhD thesis, University of Texas, 1917.

Eccles, W.J. *Canada Under Louis XIV, 1663-1701*. Toronto: McCelland and Stewart Ltd., 1964.

—-. *Frontenac: The Courtier Governor*. Toronto: 1959. Lincoln: University of Nebraska Press, 2003.

Engelhardt, Zephyrin. *Missionary Work of the Franciscans: Florida*. Tampa: State of Florida, 1930.

Erhmann,W.W. "The Timucua Indians," *FHQ*, XVIII, no. 3, 168-190.

"Extracts from Journals of the Common House of Assembly of South Carolina for Oct. 1711-Nov. 1711," *The Colonial Records of North Carolina*, I. Raleigh: P.M. Hale State Printer, 1886, 820-825.

"Extracts from Journals of the Common House of Assembly of South Carolina for 1712," *The Colonial Records of North Carolina*, I. Raleigh: P.M. Hale State Printer, 1886, 897-901.

Fairbanks, George. *The History and Antiquities of the City of St. Augustine, Florida*. New York: Charles Norton, 1858.

—-. *The Spaniards in Florida*. Jacksonville: Columbus Drew, 1868.

Faye, Stanley. "Spanish Fortifications of Pensacola, 1698-1763," *FHQ*, XX, no. 2, 151-168.

French, B.F. *Historical Collections of Louisiana and Florida*. I, II. New York: Sabin & Sons, 1869 and Albert Mason, 1875.

Gallay, Alan. *The Indian Slave Trade*. New Haven: Yale University Press, 2002.

Gayarre, Charles. *History of Louisiana*, I. New York: Redfield, 1854.

Goldstein, Robert A. *French-Iroquois Diplomatic and Military Relations, 1609-1701*. The Hague: Mouton & Co., 1969.

Gorman, Adele. "Jean Ribault's Colonies in Florida," *FHQ*, XLIV, no. 1-2, 51-66.

Grady, Timothy. *Anglo-Spanish Rivalry and the Development of the Colonial Southeast,1670-1720*. PhD thesis, College of William and Mary, 2006.

Griffen, William. "Spanish Pensacola, 1700-1763," *FHQ*, XXXVII, no. 3-4, 242-262.

Guerin, Leon. *Histoire Maritime de France*. 6 vols. Paris: Boulanger et Legrand, 1851-1856.

Hammond, Isaac. *Documents Relating to Towns in New Hampshire*, XII. Concord: Parsons B. Cogswell, 1883.

Havard, Gilles. *The Great Peace of Montreal of 1701*. (Trans. Phyllis Aronoff). Montreal: McGill-Queen's University Press, 2001.

Hawks, Francis. *History of North Carolina*, II. Fayetteville: E.J. Hale and Son, 1858.

Horton, Donald. "Paul Le Moyne de Maricourt," DCB, II (1701-1740).

Howell, T.B. *A Complete Collection of State Trials*, vol. XIV. London: T.C. Hansard, 1816.

Hutchinson, Thomas. *The History of the Province of Massachusetts Bay*. 3 vols. London: M. Richardson, 1765-1828.

Janvier, Thomas. "The Sea-Robbers of New York," *Harper's Monthly Magazine*, Nov. 1894, 813-827.

Jau, Dr. Francis Le. *The Carolina Chronicles of Dr. Francis Le Jau, 1706-1717*. Los Angeles: University of California Press, 1956.

Johnson, J. G. "The Yamassee Revolt of 1597 and the Destruction of the Georgia Missions," *Georgia Historical Quarterly*, VII, no. 1, 44-53.

*Journal of the Legislative Council of the Colony of New York, Begun the 3rd day of April 1691 and ended the 27th of September, 1743*. Albany: Weed, Parsons & Co., 1861.

Kalm, Peter. *Travels into North America*. Trans. John Reinold Forster. 3 vols. London: T. Lowndes, 1771.

Kimball, Everett. *The Public Life of Joseph Dudley*. London: Longmans, Green & Co., 1911.

King, Grace. *Jean Baptiste Le Moyne, Sieur de Bienville*. New York: Dodd, Mead, and Co., 1893.

Kingsford, William. The History *of Canada*, 10 vols. London: Trubner & Co., 1888-1898.

Knight, Sarah Kemble. *The Journals of Mdm. Knight and Rev. Mr. Buckingham . . . written in 1704 & 1711*. New York: Wilder & Campbell, 1825.

Lajeunesse, Ernest. *The Windsor Border Region*. Toronto: University of Toronto, 1960.

Lanctot, Gustave. *A History of Canada, 1600-1763*. 3 vols. Trans. Josephine Hambleton and Margaret Cameron. Cambridge: Harvard University Press, 1963-65.

La Harpe, Benard. *Journal Historique de L'Etablissement des Francais a la Louisiana*. Paris: A.L. Boimare, 1831.

La Potherie, Bacqueville de, Claude-Charles. *Historie de l'Amérique Septentrionale.* 4 vols. Paris: Nion & Didot, 1722.

Lecky, William Edward Hartpole. *A History of England in the Eighteenth Century.* 8 vols. New York: D. Appleton and Co., 1878-1917.

Lowery, Woodbury. *Spanish Settlements: Florida 1562-1574*. New York: G. P. Putnam's Sons, 1911.

Manucy, Albert. "The Man who was Pedro Menendez," *FHQ*, XLIV, no. 1-2, 67-80.

Margry, Pierre. *Decouvertes et Etablissements des Francais*. IV. Paris: Maisonneuve, 1881.

Matter, Robert. "Missions in the Defense of Spanish Florida, 1566-1710," *FHQ*, LIV, no. 1, 18-38.

Maurault, L'Abbe J.A. *Histoire des Abenaki*. Sorel, Quebec: Gazette de Sorel, 1866.

McCrady, Edward. *The History of South Carolina under the Proprietary Government, 1670-1719*. New York: Macmillan Co., 1897.

McCully, Bruce T. "Catastrophe in the Wilderness: New Light on the Canada Expedition of 1709," *William and Mary Quarterly*, series 3, no. 11 (1954), 441-456.

McDonald, Kevin. "'A Man of Courage and Activity': Thomas Tew, Anglo-American Piracy, and the Manhattan to Madagascar Trade Network, 1690-1720," UC Santa Barbara, 2005.

Mirick, B.L. *The History of Haverhill, Massachusetts*. Haverhill: A.W. Thayer, 1832.

Munro, William. Documents Relating to the Seigniorial in Canada. Toronto: Champlain Society, 1908, 49, 83-84.

Murdoch, Beamish. *History of Nova Scotia*. 3 vol. Halifax: J. Barnes, 1865-1867.

"Nicholson's Journal of the Capture of Annapolis in 1710," *Collections of the Nova Scotia Historical Society*, I. Halifax: Morning Herald, 1879, 59-104.

Nourse, Henry. *The Early Records of Lancaster, Massachusetts, 1643-1725*. Lancaster: W.J. Coulter, 1884.

O'Callaghan, E.B. (ed.). *Documents Relative to the Colonial History of the State of New York*. 15 vols. Albany: Weed, Parsons & Co., 1856-1877.

—-. *Documentary History of New York*. 4 vols. Albany: Weed, Parsons & Co., 1849-1851.

Parker, Susan. "St. Augustine in the Seventeenth Century: Capital of La Florida," *FHQ*, XCII, no. 3, 554-576.

Peckham, Howard. "Benjamin Church," DCB, II (1701-1740).

Penhallow, Samuel. *The History of the Wars of New England with the Eastern Indians*. Boston: T. Fleet (1726), 1924.

Peyster, Frederic. *Life and Administration of Richard, Earl of Bellomont*. New York: New York Historical Society, 1879.

Porter, Whitworth. *The History of the Corps of Royal Engineers*. vol. 1. London: Longmans, Green, & Co., 1889.

Pothier, Bernard. "Monbeton de Brouillan, *dit* St. Ovide, Joseph de." DCB, III (1741-1770).

Prowse, D.W. *A History of Newfoundland*. London: Macmillan, 1895.

Quint, A.H. *The Journal of the Rev. John Pike of Dover, New Hampshire*. Cambridge: John Wilson and Son, 1876.

Rameau, M. *Une Colonie Féodale en Amerique*, I. Paris: Didier, 1877.

*Rapport de L'Archiviste de la Quebec pour 1921-1922*. Quebec: Redempti Paradis, 1922.

*Rapport de L'Archiviste de la Quebec pour 1922-1923*. Quebec: Redempti Paradis, 1923.

*Rapport de L'Archiviste de la Quebec pour 1938-1939*. Quebec: Redempti Paradis, 1939.

*Rapport de L'Archiviste de la Quebec pour 1939-1940*. Quebec: Redempti Paradis, 1940.

Redington, Joseph. *Calendar of Treasury Papers, 1697-1702*. London: Longman & Co., 1871.

Reed, Charles. *The First Great Canadian: The Story of Pierre Le Moyne, Sieur D'Iberville*. Chicago: A.C. McClurg & Co., 1910.

——. *Masters of the Wilderness*. Chicago: University of Chicago Press, 1914.

Reigelsperger, Diana. "Pirate, Priest, and Slave: Spanish Florida in the 1668 Seales Raid," *FHQ*, XCII, no. 4, 577-590.

Reynolds, Charles. *Old St. Augustine*. St. Augustine: E.H. Reynolds, 1885.

Rivers, William. *A Sketch of the History of South Carolina*. Charleston: McCarter & Co., 1856.

Sainsbury, W. Noel et al. (eds.). *Calendar of State Papers, Colonial Series, American and West Indies, Preserved in Her Majesty's Public Records Office*. 45 vols. London: His Majesty's Stationery Office, 1860-1864.

Salley, Alexander S. *Journals of the Common House of Assembly of South Carolina for 1702*. Columbus: The State Company, 1932.

Salley, Alexander S. *Narratives Early South Carolina, 1650-1708*. New York: Charles Scribner's Sons, 1911.

——. *Journals of the Common House of Assembly of South Carolina for 1703*. Columbus: The State Company, 1934.

——. *Journals of the Common House of Assembly of South Carolina for Oct. 1707-Feb. 1708*. Columbus: The State Company, 1941.

"Sewell Diary," *Collections of the Massachusetts Historical Society*, 5th series, VI. Boston: Mass. Historical Society, 1895.

Shea, John. *The History of the Catholic Church in the United States*, I. Akron: D.H. McBride, 1886.

Sheldon, E.M. *The Early History of Michigan*. New York: A.S. Barnes and Co., 1874.

Sheldon, George. *A History of Deerfield, Massachusetts*. 2 vols. Greenfield, Mass.: E.A. Hall & Co., 1895-1896.

Smith, William. *History of Wisconsin*, II. Madison: Beriah Brown, 1854.

Steele, Ian K. *Warpaths*. New York: Oxford University Press, 1994.

Subhash, Janotti, "Impact response of Coquina," *Dynamic Behavior of Materials: Proceedings of the Society for Experimental Mechanics 2015*, I, 1-4.

Swanton, John. *Early History of the Creek Indians and their Neighbors*. Washington: Government Printing Office, 1922.

——. *Indian Tribes of the of the Lower Mississippi Valley*. Washington: Government Printing Office, 1911.

Sweet, Zelia. *Spanish Missions of Florida*. Tampa: State of Florida, 1938.

Sylvester, Herbert. *Indian Wars of New England*. Vol III. Boston: W.B. Clarke Co., 1910.

Tapley, Harriet. *The Province Galley of Massachusetts Bay, 1694-1716*. Salem: Essex Institute, 1922.

Thorpe, F.J. "George Vane," DCB, II (1701-1740).

Thwaites, R.G. (ed.). *The Jesuit Relations and Allied Documents*. 73 vols. Cleveland: The Burrow Bros. Co., 1896-1901.

Trumbull, Benjamin. *A Complete History of Connecticut*, I. Hartford: Hudson & Goodwin, 1797.

Trumbull, James Russell. *The History of Northampton, Massachusetts*. 2 vols. Northampton: Press of Gazette Printing Co., 1898.

Walker, Hovenden. *A Full Account of the Late Expedition to Canada*. London: G. Strahan, 1720.

Waller, G.M. "Vetch, Samuel," *DCB*, II (1701-1740).

Weber, David. The *Spanish Frontier in North America*. New Haven: Yale University Press, 1992.

Whitehead, William A. *Contributions to the Early History of Perth Amboy*. New York: D. Appleton & Co., 1856.

Williams, John. *The Redeemed Captive*. Springfield, Mass: H.R. Huntting Co., 1908.

Williamson, William D. *The History of the State of Maine*. 2 vols. Dallowell, Maine: Glazier, Masters and Co., 1832.

Wilson, James. "An Acadian Governor," *The International Review*, XI (1881), 462-502.

"Winthrop Correspondence: Winthrop Papers, Part IV," *Collections of the Massachusetts Historical Society*. 5th Series, VIII. Boston: Mass. Historical Society, 1882.

"Winthrop Papers: Part V," *Collections of the Massachusetts Historical Society*, 6th series, III. Boston: Mass. Historical Society, 1889.

Worth, John. *The Timucua Missions of Spanish Florida and the Rebellion of 1656*. University of Florida: PhD thesis, 1992.

Wraxell, Peter. *An Abridgement of the Indian Affairs*. Cambridge: Harvard University Press, 1915.

Wright, J. Leitch Jr. *Anglo-Spanish Rivalry in North America*. Athens: University of Georgia Press, 1971.

Zoltvany, Yves. "Rigaud de Vaudreuil, Phillippe de," *DCB*, II (1701-1740).

——. "Antoine Laumet de la Mothe Cadillac," *DCB*, II (1701-1740).

——. "Ramezay, Claude de, 1659–1724," *DCB*, II (1701-1740).

# *Acknowledgments*

First and foremost, thank you Lord. Second, as with all my works, none of this would have occurred without the support of my beautiful wife Pam, or our children. Nor could this have occurred without the resources of several excellent institutions, many of which had helped with my previous works; The Massachusetts Historical Society, the University of Arizona Library, the Bailey-Howe Library at the University of Vermont, and Dartmouth's Baker Library were all of great assistance in this endeavor. I would also like to thank John Buxton for the extraordinary work used for the book cover. It is technically the Battle of Lovell's Pond in the 4th Anglo-Wabanaki War (1722-1725), or Drummer's War as it was commonly called, but it so closely represented the numerous actions fought along the New England frontier a generation before that it seemed a perfect fit. My thanks to my colleagues and friends for their words of encouragement, and of course, a nod goes out to Folgers and a host of generic substitutes.

Lastly, I would also like to thank those who risked life and limb to fight the forest fires that occurred in southern Arizona in 2020. As I watched the month-long blaze through the window in front of my desk, I could not help but see the character of many of those I was writing about reflected in the courage and fortitude of these unsung men and women, who, like so many others, step into the gap for another. My many thanks for your efforts and the reminder that many of the traits that made us such a great nation still exist today.

# Index

Westholme Titles of Related Interest

*Apocalypse 1692: Empire, Slavery, and the Great Port Royal Earthquake* by Ben Hughes

*By Wind and Iron: Naval Campaigns in the Champlain Valley, 1665–1815* by Michael G. Laramie

*In the Shadow of Salem: The Andover Witch Hunt of 1692* by Richard Hite

*The Involuntary American: A Scottish Prisoner's Journey to the New World* by Carol Gardner

*King William's War: The First Contest for North America, 1689–1697* by Michael G. Laramie

*Settling the Frontier: Urban Development in America's Borderlands, 1600–1830* by Joseph P. Alessi

*We Could Perceive No Sign of Them: Failed Colonies in North America, 1526–1689* by David MacDonald and Raine Waters

*When I Die, I Shall Return to My Own Land: The New York City Slave Revolt of 1712* by Ben Hughes